STUDIES IN LIFELONG EDUCATION

FOUNDATIONS OF
LIFELONG EDUCATION

With contributions by

A. J. CROPLEY, University of Saskatchewan, at Regina

C. DE'ATH, Waterloo University, Ontario

H. JANNE, International Council of Educational Development, New York

P. M. KIRPAL, Institute of Cultural Relations and Development Studies, New Delhi.

B. SUCHODOLSKI, UNESCO Institute for Education, Hamburg

A. VINOKUR, University of Paris X-Nanterre

A67

FOUNDATIONS OF
LIFELONG EDUCATION

Edited by

R. H. DAVE

International Institute for Educational Planning, Paris.

Published for the

UNESCO INSTITUTE FOR EDUCATION

by

PERGAMON PRESS

OXFORD · NEW YORK · TORONTO · SYDNEY · PARIS · FRANKFURT

067512

U.K.   Pergamon Press Ltd., Headington Hill Hall, Oxford
                        OX3 0BW, England

U.S.A.   Pergamon Press Inc., Maxwell House, Fairview Park,
                        Elmsford, New York 10523, U.S.A.

CANADA   Pergamon of Canada Ltd., P.O. Box 9600, Don Mills
                        M3C 2T9, Ontario, Canada

AUSTRALIA   Pergamon Press (Aust.) Pty. Ltd., 19a Boundary Street,
                        Rushcutters Bay, N.S.W. 2011, Australia

FRANCE   Pergamon Press SARL, 24 rue des Ecoles, 75240 Paris,
                        Cedex 05, France

WEST GERMANY   Pergamon Press GmbH, 6242 Kronberg-Taunus,
                        Pferdstrasse 1, Frankfurt-am-Main, West Germany

First edition 1976

Library of Congress Cataloging in Publication Data

Main entry under title:

Foundations of lifelong education.

(Studies in lifelong education ; 1)
Includes bibliographical references.
1. Adult education--Addresses, essays, lectures.
I. Dave, R. H. II. Cropley, A. J. III. Series.
LC5215.F66   374   76-25153
ISBN 0-08-021192-5
ISBN 0-08-021191-7 pbk.

*In order to make this volume available as economically and rapidly as possible the author's typescript
has been reproduced in its original form. This method unfortunately has its typographical limitations
but it is hoped that they in no way distract the reader.*

Printed in Great Britain by A. Wheaton & Co. Exeter

NOTES ON CONTRIBUTORS

CROPLEY,   Arthur John (Australia). Studied at universities of Adelaide and Alberta, and is now Professor of Psychology at the University of Saskatchewan at Regina. He has taught in Australia, England and Canada and among his publications are: *Creativity and Intelligence; Creativity; Creativity, Intelligence and Achievement* and *Lifelong education: a panacea for all educational ills?*

DAVE,   Ravindra H. (India). Studied at universities of Bombay, Gujerat and Chicago. In 1976 joined the International Institute for Educational Planning (Paris), after completing four years as Technical Director at the UNESCO Institute for Education, Hamburg. His previous experience included the post of Dean of Educational Development, National Council of Educational Research and Training, New Delhi; he directed the first Asian Curriculum Research Project. His publications include *Lifelong Education and School Curriculum; Reflections on Lifelong Education and the school,* and *Studies in Educational Evaluation and Assessment.*

De'ATH,   Colin (New Zealand). Studied at universities of Auckland and Pittsburgh and is now Assistant Professor in the faculty of Environmental Studies, Department of Man-Environment at Waterloo University, Ontario. Is also consultant to the Ministry of State for Urban Affairs, Ottawa. Before migrating to Canada he had worked as researcher, consultant and administrator in Papua and New Guinea and other countries. He is a Fellow of the American Anthropological Association and of the American Association for the Advancement of Science. His publications include: *Black Education in the U.S. and its Relevance to International and Development Education* and *Urban Anthropologists and Urban Planning in Canada.*

JANNE,   Henri (Belgium). Studied at Brussels University. He directed a number of government economic and social services, retiring from the post of Director General of Economic Co-ordination in 1949. Became Director of the Institute of Sociology at the University of Brussels. In 1961 he became a member of the Senate, and from 1963 to 1965 was Minister of National Education and Culture. Formerly a President of *l'Académie Royale des Sciences, des Lettres et des Beaux-Arts;* he was also corresponding member of *l'Institut de France* (Académie des Sciences Morales et Politiques) and is a member of the Governing Board of the International Council of Educational Development (New York). His publications include *Technique, Developpement économique et Technocracie; Le Système Sociale, Essai de Théorie Générale* and *Le Temps du Changement.*

PREM KIRPAL   (India). Studied at universities of Punjab and Oxford. He is the founder and president of the Institute of Cultural Relations and Development Studies, New Delhi, and has been Director, National Council of Educational Research and Training, New Delhi; Chairman of the Executive Board and Director of the Department of Cultural Activities, UNESCO, Paris. He had previously been Professor of History and Political Science at Punjab University, Lahore. His publications include: *Education—Twenty-five Years of Independence* and *Higher Education in India: Priorities and Problems.*

Notes on Contributors

SUCHODOLSKI, Bogdan (Poland). Studied at universities of Cracow, Warsaw, Berlin and Paris. In 1938 he was Professor at Lwow University, but during the nazi occupation of Poland became one of the principal organizers of the Underground University of Warsaw. In 1946 he became Professor of Education at Warsaw University and held this post for 22 years. He was also Director of the Institute of Pedagogical Sciences from 1958 to 1968, Head of the Laboratory of History of Science and Technology in the Polish Academy of Science, and from 1969 member of the Academy's Presidium. From 1969 to 1973 he was President of the International Association for the Advancement of Educational Research and from 1968 to 1971 Vice-President of the Académie Internationale de l'Histoire des Sciences. He took part in the first meeting of UNESCO which was held in London in 1945, and is the Vice-Chairman of the Governing Board of UNESCO Institute for Education, Hamburg. Among his published works, many of which have been translated into other languages, the following may be mentioned: *Education for the Future. Foundations of the Marxist Theory of Education. Origins of the Modern Philosophy of Man. Development of the Modern Philosophy of Man. Human World and Education. Foundations of Socialist Education. Three Pedagogies. Labyrinths of the Present Time. Who is a Man? Theorie der sozialistischen Bildung.*

VINOKUR, Annie (France). Studied at the universities of Algiers, Paris and Nancy, and is now Professor of Political Economy at the University of Paris X-Nanterre. She also directs the *Groupe de Recherche sur l'Economie de l'Education* at the University of Nancy. Her publications include *Economie de l'Education.*

CONTENTS

1   067512

6	Contents

FOREWORD

In March 1972 the decision was taken that the Unesco Institute for Education should focus its international cooperative research programme on "the content of education in the perspective of lifelong learning". One of its first tasks was to attempt to gain a systematic understanding of what was meant by the rather general term "Lifelong Education".

It soon became evident that behind the seeming clarity of this idea, there was more than a reaction against a historically conditioned interpretation of the educational goals, content of learning, forms and organization of services and educational achievements, which have characterized the educational scene during the last few decades.

Often referred to as a "master concept" and a "guiding principle", Lifelong Education appeared to be a reinterpretation of education, integrating the partial insights and experiences gradually gained through the solution of specific educational problems into an overall conception. Education is viewed as a continuing process guided by the over-riding goal of improving the quality of life. It takes place in many different complementary forms, of a sequential as well as of a parallel nature. The individual is always at the hub of this process. All other components of the educational action should combine to develop his capacity for self-learning.

Most of the above statements about the concept of Lifelong Education might not appear new and the above description of its major characteristics does seem to coincide with ideas which, in some cases, can be traced right back to the oldest educational literature. New, however, is the attempt to use this concept as a norm for educational practice at national level and for the whole range of age groups and educational services.

One of the striking facts about the idea of Lifelong Education is that it has not been the inspiration of a single individual, country or international institution. Countries and institutions have collectively formed channels of diffusion into which have poured the ideas of theoreticians and practitioners from many areas of knowledge, regions of activities and countries in different stages of development.

The fair amount of literature which already exists on Lifelong Education has permitted the identification of a sizeable number of its characteristics and this has proved useful for promoting theoretical discussion as well as for the process of practical implementation. The systematic process of analysis and synthesis leading towards the integration of all the aspects covered by the idea of Lifelong Education will have to be further pursued, however, before a consistent and comprehensive theory may be achieved. Due to the comprehensiveness of the idea of Lifelong Education, this systematic process cannot be undertaken exclusively by educational sciences, for there is a need to include areas not normally receiving the weight due to them. The present study is only a step towards this goal.

I would like to express my gratitude to those scholars who have participated in this project and who have generously contributed their knowledge to achieve the high standard of this study. In this task cooperation was quite essential, and this they readily gave, thereby greatly increasing the value of each individual's scholarly contribution.

I would also like to express my deep appreciation of Dr. R. H. Dave's achievement in conceiving, conducting and bringing this difficult project to so satisfactory a conclusion.

M. Dino Carelli
Director
Unesco Institute for Education

INTRODUCTION

"Err and err and err again, but less and less and less". These witty
words by Piet Hein, when applied to education and particularly to educational decision-making, sum up the purpose of the foundations study reported in this volume.

It is evident from recent developments in the field of education, especially at the international level, that a wider and deeper meaning of education is being rediscovered with a view to revamping the whole field and
thus making it more functional and effective. The new meaning is symbolized
by the term lifelong education, which includes formal, non-formal and informal patterns of learning throughout the life-cycle of an individual for
the conscious and continuous enhancement of the quality of life, his own
and that of his society. It has been repeatedly stressed by educators and
others during the first half-decade of the seventies, and even earlier,
that the concept of lifelong education should be adopted as a major guiding
principle for reviewing and reconstructing educational systems everywhere in
the world. In fact, this has already started happening in several countries
in different regions. Application of this "master concept" to the planning
and programming of all forms and sectors of education obviously involves an
extensive process of decision-making. The key question in this context is:
How can these decisions be made as valid as possible? No doubt, there is a
risk of committing errors in making complex decisions. But how can we minimize these errors, and make them "less and less and less"? This is indeed
a big challenge confronting educators, social reformers and policy makers.

One promising step towards meeting this challenge is to acquire an
increasing degree of clarity and depth in our understanding of the idea of
lifelong education and its multiple implications with the help of a number
of relevant disciplines of knowledge. In other words, we must construct the
foundations of lifelong education if a clearer understanding and effective

implementation of this concept is to be ensured. This volume reports the findings of an initial exercise in this direction.

The eight chapters in the book fall into two broad groups. Chapters 2 to 7, constituting one group, present the foundations content by disciplines. The other group consists of the first and the last chapters, which contain methodological discussion as well as intra- and interdisciplinary content analysis and synthesis.

One of the main tasks of this inquiry was to examine a number of basic issues concerning lifelong education with the help of the accumulated knowledge in relevant social sciences and other fields. Why should education be treated as a lifelong process? When it is so treated, what are the new roles and responsibilities that the field of education should assume? How are the functions of lifelong education related to historical and contemporary developments in society? What are the goals, contents and processes of learning appropriate to the aspirations of lifelong education? How far is lifelong education, in its new perspective, feasible and practicable in different socio-economic and ideological conditions? What are the likely obstacles in realizing the ideals of this "master concept"? What precautions and preconditions should be taken into account in planning and programming education systems aligned to the concept of lifelong education? These and other such fundamental issues were raised in a variety of ways to an interdisciplinary and international team in order to seek solutions and clarifications for further operational action. Chapters 2 to 7 present the findings of the discipline experts on the basis of their individual as well as collective work, and highlight the perspectives of lifelong education in the context of their respective fields.

Chapter 1 is chiefly devoted to the methodological considerations. Matters such as the nature of the foundations content, general steps that may be followed for constructing discipline-based foundations, and the ways of incorporating several elements of *interdisciplinarity* into the study are discussed in this chapter. In addition, it includes information about the background and genesis of the study and the overall procedures followed for conducting it.

The methodological considerations are extended further in Chapter 8.

However, the bulk of this chapter is devoted to a number of illustrations of general perspectives and guidelines derived from a systematic analysis and synthesis of the content presented in chapters 2 to 7. Each individual discipline makes its own contribution towards the building of broad-based foundations. At the same time, it is essential to ascertain the joint contribution of all foundations, viewed together around important aspects of lifelong education such as the scope, practicability, goals, content, processes, structures, etc. Multiple examples of these have been worked out, and a number of illustrative ideas that are important for educational decision-making are highlighted in this last chapter.

Different readers may be interested in different materials contained in this volume. Those interested in one or more foundations by disciplines may choose to skip much of the first chapter. The summary specially provided at the end of this chapter should prove useful to them. These readers may also profit from the relevant portions of section 3 of the last chapter, which they may wish to see either *before* or *after* going through a particular discipline-based chapter. Readers who are more interested in the methodological issues and interdisciplinary aspects may concentrate on Chapter 1 and section 4 of the last chapter.

Any work based on a number of disciplines poses some difficulty in reading to the educator - whether he is an educational planner, curriculum developer, teacher, teacher educator or researcher. Among the disciplines selected for this study, those with which educators are perhaps least familiar are anthropology and ecology. Hence a glossary of selected terms has been given by the author at the end of Chapter 6.

The task of initiating a systematic exercise for constructing the foundations of lifelong education is by no means an easy one. It calls for concerted work not only on the foundations content based on a number of different disciplines but also on methodology. In carrying out this work, I have received invaluable help, constructive comments and active co-operation from all members of the interdisciplinary study team. For all this, I am extremely grateful to Arthur Cropley (Psychology, Australia - presently in Canada), Colin De'Ath (Anthropology and Ecology, Canada), Henri Janne (Sociology, Belgium), P. N. Kirpal (History, India), Bogdan Suchodolski (Philosophy, Poland), Annie Vinokur (Economics, France), M. D. Carelli (Lifelong Education, Unesco Institute,

Hamburg), E. Gelpi (Lifelong Education, UNESCO), and Paul Lengrand (Lifelong Education, France). My special thanks are due to Arthur Cropley who, besides working on the psychological foundations, extended valuable help in discussing and drafting the last chapter on illustrative content analysis and synthesis. I am also thankful to the staff of the Unesco Institute, and in particular to Ursula Giere, Johanna Kesavan, Louise Miller, Kenneth Robinson, Peter Sachsenmeier, Elke Schlinck-Lazarraga, and Nalini Stiemerling for providing great help and co-operation in editing and producing the book.

It is hoped that this collective work will make a humble contribution towards the furtherance of understanding and implementation of lifelong education.

R. H. Dave

C H A P T E R   1

FOUNDATIONS OF LIFELONG EDUCATION:
SOME METHODOLOGICAL ASPECTS

R. H.   D a v e

1. Educational Challenges and Lifelong Education

The idea of lifelong education has gained international significance in recent years. Although this idea is as old as human history, the new significance and wider acceptance that it has lately attained is based on the assumption that it holds promise of meeting the new educational challenges of the present and also those of the foreseeable future. Its appeal seems to lie largely in the fact that it has a potential to respond to the new challenges without ignoring the valuable educational policies and practices developed so far. This is because it acts as an organizing and unifying principle for different developments concerning all stages, forms and patterns of education.

The contemporary period of history is characterized by rapid and unprecedented change in practically all aspects of life. What A. N. Whitehead observed in the early thirties about the time-span of change and its impact on education has become more relevant in the seventies, and trends in many fields clearly suggest that his farsighted statement will apply even more as we move towards the year 2000 and beyond. Whitehead said:

> ... in the past the time-span of important change was considerably longer than that of a single human life. Thus mankind was trained to adapt itself to fixed conditions.
>
> To-day this time-span is considerably shorter than that of human life, and accordingly our training must prepare individuals to face a novelty of conditions. [1]

The exponential growth of knowledge in science and spectacular advances in technology have given rise to rapid and far-reaching changes in practically all domains of human life. Developments in other fields of knowledge, accompanied by marked shifts in the demographic and related characteristics of society, have also contributed significantly to the current spate of change. What is unique in the present spiral of change is that many of the developments have taken global proportions, transcending the national and regional boundaries more rapidly than ever before. Spectacular innovations in transport, communications, agriculture, textiles, medicine, manufacturing industries, and other fields are diffused rapidly all over the world. While it is true that the rate of absorption of any particular innovation varies with country and culture, and also that the nature of its impact differs in different societies, the pace of diffusion of many new ideas, materials and techniques is indeed very fast, and the spread is rapidly becoming global. These ideas, materials and techniques are not confined to science and technology alone but include developments and changes in political, cultural, social and economic fields as well. In fact, the far-reaching socio-economic developments accompanied by a special emphasis on the principles of democratization have contributed a great deal to the present phenomenon of change.

All these changes have created new educational challenges and have questioned the relevance and efficacy of most prevalent systems of education that grew in response to a more stable and less complex mode of personal, social and professional life. The increasing speed of obsolescence of knowledge and skills calls for the consideration of new educational goals and strategies that will be capable of educating every individual, not only about the known but also for the unknown. As Paul Lengrand asserts, "the notion that a man can accomplish his life-span with a given set of intellectual and technical luggage is fast disappearing".[2]

The staggering developments occurring in quick succession in communications, agriculture, industry and similar fields, followed by the equally staggering impact of these developments on social, economic, political and cultural life, generate a persistent demand for continuing the process of renewal of knowledge, skills and values throughout life.[3]

Apart from the problems emerging from the phenomenon of rapid and revolutionary change in extra-educational domains, the situation within the field of education itself has given rise to new challenges. At least three important factors need to be briefly mentioned here:

(1) For the first time in history, education has been universally
and officially accepted as a human right.[4] The new value attached
to education has resulted in an unprecedented expansion of educational facilities. While a few countries like Germany and Japan
made the initial level of education free and compulsory in the
nineteenth century, most others created and expanded educational
facilities for the masses during the current century. This movement gained greater momentum every decade and was stepped up
further in the fifties and the sixties, particularly in those
countries that achieved independence during this period. Educational facilities are still expanding in all countries; some
are continuing to focus on the primary level whereas others, the
more developed ones, are concentrating on the secondary and higher levels to meet the mounting pressure from the lower rungs of
the educational ladder.

(2) Despite this unprecedented quantitative expansion and the consequent spurt in educational expenditure which, in budgetary terms,
ranks a close second in world expenditure of public funds, coming
just after military budgets,[5] the results achieved so far can
scarcely be considered satisfactory. As Unesco's International
Commission on the Development of Education observed, although the
number of children attending school has increased considerably
since 1960, the number of those who are still denied basic education has also increased. "More go to school than ever - and more
than ever stay outside" says a Unesco leaflet published during the
World Population Year 1974. At the level of higher education, many
advanced nations are finding it difficult to meet the rising educational aspirations of their populations and have not been able to
provide entry for all who are eligible and willing to study. This
factor is further complicated by educated unemployment and under-
employment. On the other hand, less advanced countries do not have
enough facilities to train required manpower, and there too educated unemployment in certain sectors as well as the mismatch between edcuation and employment are not infrequent. At the adult education stage the picture is equally grim. It is true that in per-

centage terms illiteracy among the world's adult population
has decreased from 44.3% in 1950 to 34.2% in 1970, but in absolute figures, the number of illiterates has increased during this period from 700 million to 783 million, and the number
is likely to reach 820 million in 1980.[6] Of course the situation differs from region to region, and from country to country
within a region; however, the global scene points to the hard
fact that educators and others concerned are fighting a losing
battle.

(3) These grave and massive problems have recently been further
aggravated by a number of serious questions raised by educators,
economists, politicians and others regarding the quality, adequacy and relevance of the present system of education. Its
effectiveness is being seriously doubted in both developed and
less developed countries. The problems of quality and relevance
have become yet more critical in the case of those developing
countries where a foreign system of education was transplanted
and has not taken root. Criticisms have been levelled against
the present system because it isolates the school from the home
and community, and thus has an alienating influence on the learner. The system is inflexible, too formal, and often found to be
dysfunctional when viewed in the context of community needs or
new developments. These and similar issues pose new intra-educational challenges besides those mentioned earlier.

As a positive response to these problems, the concept of lifelong education has been suggested as a possible solution by many educational thinkers, researchers and international organizations. In fact the very first recommendation
of the International Commission on the Development of Education states:

We propose lifelong education as the master concept for educational policies in the years to come for both developed and
developing countries.[7]

Elucidating the recommendation further, the Commission asserts the universal applicability of this "master concept" to meet the educational challenges
of our time:

The various applications of this idea will of course differ greatly.
We may even say ... that it could be applied in as many different

ways as there are countries in the world ... But we remain convinced that the question of lifelong education, the decisions to
take and the paths to follow in order to achieve it are the crucial issues of our time, in all countries of the world, even in
those which have yet to become fully aware of this idea.[3]

Other organizations, such as the Council of Europe and OECD, have also
emphasized the importance of this concept to meet new educational challenges.
The Council of Europe has carried out several surveys and has produced a good
deal of literature on this subject with special reference to its member states.
Similarly, the OECD has developed the idea of recurrent education, which it
views as a strategy for lifelong education. Also, in the literature of the past
few years many educational thinkers and scholars, including Adiseshiah, Coombs,
Filipovic, Houle, Husén, Janne, Jessup, Lengrand, Shimbori and Suchodolski,[9-18]
to name only a few, have highlighted the need and significance of the concept
of lifelong education for reforming the policies and programmes of education.
(See sec. 8.1 of this chapter for further delineation of the concept).

In view of the great importance attached to this concept for future development, it is necessary to carry out appropriate research and developmental
programmes. The research work should cover both conceptual and operational
areas so that the implementation of the idea may be facilitated. The programmes
recently undertaken by the Unesco Institute for Education are in response to
this urgent need. They include a variety of research, developmental and diffusion activities to unfold and apply the master concept of lifelong education.

2. Genesis of the Present Study

Many factors prompted us to take up a study on the development of the
foundations of lifelong education. Some of the crucial ones that provided the
background and genesis are mentioned below:

(1) From our exploratory study on lifelong education, which
    included an extensive survey of existing literature on the
    subject, it was revealed that although a good deal of lit-
    erature on the concept has recently been produced and the sig-
    nificance of the idea for educational regeneration repeatedly
    mentioned, little systematic work has so far been reported on
    the psychological, sociological, anthropological and other

aspects of the concept. On the other hand, the literature
stresses the urgency of applying the idea to different levels
and forms of education in order to meet present problems and
new educational challenges. It is obvious that the implementation task cannot be undertaken with a reasonable degree of
validity and confidence without clarifying the new and multi-
faceted perspectives of the concept and without developing at
least a working theoretical base for taking operational decisions.

(2) Although an extensive amount of theoretical literature on
education exists, it cannot be used adequately without reorganization and major reformulation because it is not generally based on the assumption that education is a lifelong
process. Much of the existing material on the foundations of
education is based on a rather narrow conception of education
that is confined to primary and secondary schooling. Even when
it goes beyond these stages and includes pre-school, tertiary
and adult levels, it limits itself to highly formal and institutionalized learning. The need has now arisen to comprehend the new scope and wider role of education. This situation necessitates the initiation of a process of constructing
the foundations of lifelong education and developing a suitable methodology for this purpose.

(3) In addition to the fact that the foundations of education are
often focussed on the formal school stage, they are traditionally derived from psychology and philosophy, although the latter
has recently received less attention. The significance of systematically constructed sociological foundations has only lately been
realized. Despite the recent broadening of perspectives, several
other disciplines such as anthropology, ecology, and physiology
are not taken into account adequately and directly. For a comprehensive concept like lifelong education, which seeks to include all stages, forms and patterns of enlightenment throughout
the life-span, a broad theoretical base constructed with the help
of available knowledge in a number of relevant disciplines, be-

sides the traditional ones, is very desirable.

(4) Furthermore, the existing literature on the foundations of education points to the fact that in many cases they are based on individual and isolated disciplines (e.g., psychological foundations, sociological foundations). Even when more than one discipline is tapped in a particular work, the different discipline experts generally work in isolation from one another without having an opportunity to follow an interdisciplinary approach and without using common working tools, such as an inventory of the nature of content or a statement of operational steps. An interdisciplinary approach is no doubt difficult, and appropriate methodologies are not readily available. Nevertheless, a comprehensive and unifying concept like lifelong education demands that multidisciplinary and, if possible, interdisciplinary approaches should be thought out and at least a beginning made in this direction.

(5) Much of the available literature on the foundations of education suffers from yet another limitation. Very often this material is developed primarily for the consumption of teachers under training. This is not surprising because the courses on the foundations of education have become a part of the curriculum of colleges of education during the last few decades. As a result, the content of this material is often syllabus-based, its presentation textbook-like, and so on. By contrast, the present need for constructing the foundations of lifelong education stems from the requirements of a much wider audience. The target population includes educational policy makers and planners, administrators and curriculum framers, researchers, teacher educators and practising teachers, and educators in the fields of workers' education, cultural education and mass media, besides teachers under training. To fulfil this need, several analytical and experimental studies are required, some of which may attempt to answer immediate questions while others, including the longitudinal ones, may run side by side with implementation programmes.

(6) The research and diffusion activities carried out so far by the
UIE in the field of lifelong education have revealed signs of
readiness on the part of many countries to work out the operational aspects of lifelong education and move towards the phase
of implementation.[19] As pointed out earlier, UNESCO has already
provided a lead in disseminating the concept to its member
states. The Council of Europe and OECD have also examined the
concept in various meetings, surveys and publications on lifelong learning and recurrent education. Several socialist countries, including Hungary, Poland and Romania, have accepted
lifelong education as one of the principles for reforming
their educational systems. In Latin America, Cuba and Peru
have already initiated the process of implementation, while
other countries such as Argentina and Venezuela have displayed
their interest in the idea through study and research. The
Canadian provinces of Alberta and Ontario have produced special
Commission Reports for the future development of education,
both documents accepting lifelong education as a major guiding principle. Similar activities have been undertaken by
several universities and other educational agencies in the
United States. In the African region, Tanzania has recently
developed innovative programmes for community learning on the
lines of lifelong education. Other countries, like Ivory Coast
and Zambia, have also been examining the idea for practical implementation. Among the Arab countries, Algeria has likewise initiated educational innovations to realize the aspirations of
lifelong learning. In the Asian region, Japan is engaged in examining the concept critically and has already brought out study
reports and other literature on the subject. Through a presiden-
tial decree and other guideline documents, Indonesia has accepted lifelong education as a master concept in re-organizing and
reforming its education system. In Pakistan the newly established People's Open University has explicitly adopted the idea of
lifelong education as its chief conceptual base. Other countries,

067512

like the Republic of Korea, India and Malaysia, have also
shown great interest and have initiated several activities
in this field. Similar signs are visible in Australia and
New Zealand. It is evident from this brief overview that
many countries in all parts of the world are in a state of
readiness to take concrete action towards the realization of
the aspirations of lifelong education. In such a situation
one of the most urgent tasks is to unfold the multiple perspectives of lifelong education and formulate basic guidelines for facilitating the process of making valid operational
decisions. The task of developing some illustrative material
and exploring methodological procedures, once initiated at an
international level, can then be taken up at national and sub-
national levels in order to formulate more specific basic
guidelines.

These then are some of the major factors and forces that prompted the
present study. Besides highlighting the need for and significance of the study,
they have indirectly provided criteria for defining its objectives and scope,
and have also indicated the audience to which it should be directed.

3. Objectives and Scope of the Study

One of the main purposes of this project was to initiate a systematic
inquiry directed towards the development of the interdisciplinary foundations of
lifelong education. Another purpose was to gain experience in the methodological
aspects of such a conceptual study. The genesis of this study shows that these
tasks are of fundamental importance for the operationalization of the concept of
lifelong education and for undertaking further research and developmental activities to this effect.

In considering the question of implementation, it becomes necessary at the
outset to view this concept in a broad perspective and understand its basis in
psychological, sociological, ecological and other domains of life. Therefore this
study was designed to make an attempt at unfolding the multiple perspectives of
lifelong education with the help of several pertinent disciplines. Furthermore,

it is common knowledge that for the purposes of implementing a comprehensive
idea like lifelong education, a large number of operational decisions need to
be taken in the areas of policy and planning, organization and structures,
objectives and curriculum content, instruction and evaluation, and so on. It
was obviously not intended under the present project to formulate detailed
specifications of any of these aspects of education. The intention was to
begin the process of developing guidelines which might provide a theoretical
base for reasonably valid and internally consistent operational action. In
addition, such a theoretical base may help identify the internal consistency
as well as contradictions and conflicts existing in a given system of education when examined in the framework of lifelong education.

Due to its comprehensive nature, lifelong education influences all intra-
educational elements such as structures, curriculum, organization, teacher
preparation and the like. Simultaneously, this concept bears on a variety of
extra-educational elements including personal, societal, historical, cultural
and philosophical configurations of individuals and societies in local, national
and global settings. To build a bridge between a variety of intra-educational
components on the one hand and a large number of extra-educational elements on
the other is indeed a formidable task. Yet it is extremely important as one of
the initial steps in any overall strategy designed to realize the aspirations
of lifelong education. This study was, therefore, aimed at making a small beginning towards the fulfilment of this need, with due recognition of the difficulties involved, by means of identifying a number of aspects and concepts of
several disciplines that characterize the multiple configurations just mentioned,
and interconnecting them with various elements of lifelong education so as to
start a process of constructing broad-based foundations.

In order to ensure that the foundations are broad-based and comprehensive
in scope, it was considered necessary to include a larger number of disciplines
than usual. Accordingly, the following seven disciplines were included:

Anthropology	Philosophy
Ecology	Psychology
Economics	Sociology
History	

Anthropology and ecology were combined as they are closely connected.
Originally it had been planned to include biology, or more specifically, human

physiology as well, but this could not be done due to practical difficulties. However, the foundations based on psychology, anthropology and ecology have taken into account several of the physiological aspects, either directly or otherwise. Similarly, cultural, political and technological aspects have been covered directly or indirectly by sociology, history and other selected disciplines. It is, however, recognized that more direct work in several additional disciplines or fields of study would be necessary for a more elaborate inquiry.

3.1 About interdisciplinarity

The selection of a number of disciplines obviously makes this study multidisciplinary in scope. The indirect coverage of some aspects of other fields such as physiology, technology, and culture expands the multidisciplinary scope further. But it was intended to make this project as interdisciplinary as possible by allowing different disciplines to interact and throw light on goals, content, perspectives and other aspects of lifelong education.

There are of course many difficulties involved in any interdisciplinary study, and consequently methods of inquiry that allow such an approach are not readily available. However, the clarification on interdisciplinarity offered by the OECD Centre for Educational Research and Innovation,[20] especially in the context of the problems of teaching and research in universities, is indeed very useful. According to CERI's report, *multidisciplinarity* involves juxtaposition of various disciplines, sometimes with no apparent connection between them, e.g., music, mathematics and history. *Pluridisciplinarity* involves juxtaposition of disciplines assumed to be more or less related to one another, for example, mathematics and physics. In the case of *interdisciplinarity*, there should be an interaction among two or more disciplines. This may range from the simple communication of ideas to the mutual integration of organizing concepts, methodology, procedures, etc. This also presupposes the organization of research in a fairly large field. An interdisciplinary group consists of persons trained in different fields of knowledge (disciplines) with different concepts, methods, data and terms, and is engaged in a common problem with continuous inter-communication among the participants from the different disciplines.[21] Following this line of thought, some efforts were made in this project to move from the multi- to the interdisciplinary level. In the context of the above definition, several elements of interdisciplinarity were built into the study by

- setting up an *interdisciplinary study team* consisting of representatives of different disciplines;

- organizing the inquiry on the *broad field* of lifelong education;

- undertaking *a common effort* of developing multiple perspectives of lifelong education and evolving guiding principles for practical application;

- establishing fairly continuous *inter-communication* by means of circulating a common project design, prepared by the members from time to time as well as by holding intermittent meetings for the exchange of ideas, approaches and content; and

- carrying out an illustrative *cross-disciplinary* content analysis and synthesis of the discipline-based documents.

These steps by no means exhaust all possibilities in this direction. They only indicate the efforts, however limited, made to introduce several elements of interdisciplinarity into the present study.

It may, however, be noted that interdisciplinarity ought to be functional and not be pursued as a ritual. The intradisciplinary perspectives and guidelines are also important in their own right for the purpose of taking various practical decisions concerning lifelong education, and hence they should not be neglected. In view of this, it was decided to present the individual discipline-based foundations in the report along with a few illustrations of interdisciplinary analysis. Also, the intradisciplinary content analysis on an illustrative basis was considered important over and above the development of a few examples leading to bridging or fusing the findings of discipline-based foundations. Furthermore, it was felt that the real interconnection among discipline-based foundations should emerge at the actual application stage. Consequently, the content of the foundations as such should respect both the autonomy of individual disciplines and ways of connecting related ideas across disciplines, thus adopting a functional approach to the question of interdisciplinarity.

3.2 International character of the study

The scope of this study was also determined by the international character of the programmes of the Unesco Institute for Education. This project was one of the several activities undertaken by the UIE in the area of lifelong education

which aim at contributing to the effort now being made on an international
level towards the elucidation of this concept. Hence the present study, as a
first exercise in this conceptual area, was not focussed on the needs of one
particular country or culture, but was designed as an international project.
Although in its international character it has limitations as well as advantages, it was considered appropriate because one of the intentions of the
study was to identify some conceptual guidelines and perspectives. Without
being exhaustive these could be used as examples and, at the same time, could
be tried out as working procedures which might assist national-level agencies
in undertaking similar tasks in their own countries. On account of the international character of this inquiry, the experts in various disciplines who co-
operated in the study were not asked to follow a particular philosophical
approach, nor were other such conditions imposed. On the contrary, accepting
this situation as a delimiting factor for the study as a whole, and following
a pluralistic approach, they were asked to decide for themselves (i) their own
ideological approach, (ii) whether to adopt a macro- or micro-level approach in
their work, and (iii) whether they would keep in view only industrialized
countries, or less industrialized countries, or both.

Furthermore, while the multi-dimensional and fundamental nature of the
inquiry could have justified a project spread over many years, this study, being
a first attempt, was designed on a modest scale. This was also necessary in order
to obtain first results without much delay, in view of the urgency of the need
for establishing a working base. Once this is done, further research of a more
elaborate nature can be carried out concurrently with operational programmes.

4. About Methodological Aspects

Various approaches can be adopted for developing the interdisciplinary
foundations of lifelong education. Each approach has its own basic assumptions
and resource implications. For example, a team of experts representing different
disciplines and familiar with the field of lifelong education can be set up and
located at one place for a year or more. If possible, more than one expert for
each discipline should be involved so that various schools of thought within the
disciplines are represented. Moreover, the experts may not only utilize existing

knowledge in their disciplines but also conduct empirical studies and surveys
as considered necessary.

While the various possible approaches may have special merits, they also
pose difficulties in terms of financial resources, availability of personnel to
work together at one place over an extended period of time, and so forth. It was,
therefore, necessary to be pragmatic and evolve an approach which was expeditious,
well within our resources, and would unite scholars from the relevant disciplines
in a study team without dislodging them from their permanent work place.

In view of various determining factors and alternative possibilities such
as those just mentioned, the following approach was adopted for the present study:

   i. Establishment of an interdisciplinary study team.

  ii. Development of working tools such as a general project
      design, a statement of conceptual features of lifelong
      education, a statement indicating operational steps for
      developing the foundations, an inventory of content
      categories, etc.

 iii. Establishment of intercommunication through meetings and
      work sessions for all or some members of the team as
      necessary and feasible. Circulation and joint discussion
      of draft documents prepared by individual members of the
      study team.

  iv. Intradisciplinary content analysis on an illustrative
      basis.

   v. Interdisciplinary synthesis on an illustrative basis.

  vi. Preparation of the final document containing both discipline-
      based foundations and the illustrative content analysis and
      synthesis.

Further information about these steps is provided in subsequent sections to
clarify several methodological aspects including the composition of the study
team, working procedure, nature of the content, operational steps and disciplinary
aspects and concepts found relevant for constructing the foundations of lifelong
education.

5. Composition of the Study Team

Formation of a study team was one of the several steps taken to ensure some degree of interdisciplinarity as stated earlier. The team consisted of ten members in all; six representing disciplines and four others well versed in the theoretical and practical aspects of lifelong education. The discipline experts were: A. J. Cropley (Psychology), Colin De'Ath (Anthropology and Ecology), Henri Janne (Sociology), P. N. Kirpal (History), Bogdan Suchodolski (Philosophy) and Annie Vinokur (Economics). The other four members were: M. D. Carelli, R. H. Dave, E. Gelpi and P. Lengrand.

The discipline experts were either already knowledgeable in the field of lifelong education or were given the opportunity to familiarize themselves with the concept through literature study and discussion. It may be noted that there was one expert for each discipline except in the case of the closely interlinked fields of anthropology and ecology which were represented by one person.

6. Working Procedure

At the outset the team was supplied with the general project design, outcomes of the exploratory study on lifelong education published in two monographs and some other literature on the subject. The experts were then requested to formulate preliminary ideas about the foundations based on their own disciplines and prepare draft papers for a meeting. These drafts were circulated in advance so that team members could first examine them in the context of their own respective disciplines and thus begin the process of generating complementary and interlinked ideas, and second, could offer comments on content as well as on methodology. After each meeting the draft papers were revised. Each discipline-based foundations document thus underwent at least three revisions.

In all six meetings, lasting from 2 to 5 days, were held between September 1973 and March 1975. The three comprehensive meetings treated all the disciplines at initial, intermediary and final stages of work. A substantial portion of time in each meeting was devoted to examining discipline-based content, identifying the points of similarity and differences among different foundations, and suggesting modifications in draft papers in the light of the group discussion.

The complete team could not be present at all meetings for various reasons. However, within the relatively short span of time devoted to the project, procedures like (i) advance circulation of draft materials to all, (ii) distribution

of several basic working tools in the form of a variety of statements, (iii)
extended work sessions at UIE for some of the experts, and (iv) frequent
meetings and dialogues with one or more members of the team offered multiple
opportunities for exchanging ideas and inter-linking work in different disciplines
around a common nucleus provided by the concept of lifelong education.

From the methodological standpoint three important elements were closely
considered during the course of the study and also during various meetings:

i. Nature of the content of the foundations of lifelong education

ii. General operational steps for constructing the foundations

iii. Intra and interdisciplinary content analysis and synthesis
for the identification of guiding principles and perspectives

A few statements used as working tools in the study were prepared in respect of these methodological elements and supplied to the team members for
conducting their discipline-based studies in an interdisciplinary context. More
details about the first two elements are given below in sections 7 and 8, and
the third one is elaborated in the last chapter.

7. Nature of the Content

One important methodological issue pertained to the *nature of the content*
of these foundations. What sort of content should form the foundations of lifelong education? What sort of content should be deliberately excluded? How would
this content be different from the generally available material on the foundations
of education?

As mentioned earlier, it was felt that these foundations should not be in
the form of minute specifications of objectives, curricula or educational plans.
Their content should also be distinguished from the material about specific
methods of instruction or structural and organizational details.[22] What the
foundations content should provide was *guidelines* for identifying and developing
specific goals, content, methods, evaluation procedures, educational structures
and so forth. It should also unfold the *perspectives* of lifelong education in
order to obtain the insight necessary for formulating educational policies, plans,
structures, etc. The theoretical and empirical knowledge available in different
disciplines should in some measure validate and amplify the different character-

istics of the concept by elucidating their scope, supporting factors and limiting conditions. The content matter of the foundations of lifelong education
should thus establish a multi-dimensional theoretical base for decision making.

Moreover, this content should take into account the entire life-span
including the various educative agencies operating in the life-space of an
individual, rather than follow a narrow conception of education as formal
schooling during childhood and youth. Thus, although schooling was not to be
neglected, the field should embrace the vertical time dimension from birth to
death, and the horizontal space dimension including education in the home,
school, community, places of work, culture and recreation, religious institutions,
and through mass media and other structures and situations of formal, non-formal
and informal learning.

It may be mentioned here that in the present study, the entire arena could
not be treated in sufficient depth and detail on account of several limiting
factors. However, since a fair number of disciplines have been included, it has
in fact been possible to cover quite a good area within the vertical and horizontal dimensions of the total life-cycle.

Given this definition of the content, the discipline experts were requested to provide perspectives and guidelines from the standpoint of their respertive
disciplines by drawing upon the relevant knowledge at their command from their
particular fields. To facilitate this process, a statement of content categories
shown in Chart 1.1 was prepared as a general working tool and given to the
discipline experts. The chart proved helpful in co-ordinating work among the
different disciplines and in working out subsequently the criteria for content
analysis.

CHART 1.1

NATURE OF THE CONTENT
of the Foundations of Lifelong Education

CONTENT CATEGORIES

1. Guidelines for policies, plans and goals (explicit or implicit, general or curricular)

2. Guidelines for content, methods and learning processes, structures, organization, etc.

3. Overall need for and justification of lifelong education

4. Clarification and elaboration of specific terms and sub-concepts of lifelong education

5. Elucidation and refinement of assumptions underlying the concept

6. Supporting factors providing a kind of validation of specific elements of the concept based on empirical findings or logical deduction

7. Limiting conditions (indicating limitations of the idea)

8. Precautions and pre-conditions

NOTE: (i) All these categories are not applicable to all disciplines. Different disciplines will stress particular categories. In fact, every discipline has one *unique* contribution to make in the process of theory building and validation. At the same time, there will be many guidelines and perspectives that will have the support from two or more disciplines.

(ii) These categories are not exhaustive, nor do they indicate sequence of presentation of contents. But they help in conceptualizing the nature and breadth of the content. The list serves as a tool for certain methodological steps involved in the study.

8. General Operational Steps

Having identified the nature of the foundations content, the next methodological issue to be considered is the formulation of a general procedure for developing the content.

Obviously, one of the important steps in the process should be to familiarize oneself with the concept of lifelong education. This concept should then be allowed to interact with various aspects and concepts of the discipline concerned so that several guiding principles and perspectives begin to emerge. The steps involved in this process are not necessarily sequential or uni-directional, but call for an interface between the concept of lifelong education and relevant aspects of the discipline. Such an encounter includes many processes like analysis and synthesis; identification of relevant aspects and concepts of the discipline and interpreting them to generate a number of ideas and arguments in the form of guidelines and perspectives; and finally, acceptance, modification or rejection of these ideas and arguments by professional judgment, discussion and available research evidence. As a result of such a cognitive confrontation, reflection and group discussion, a set of findings are arrived at which are then to be organized and presented in a suitable context.

This indeed is a very complex and multi-pronged procedure, and cannot be adequately organized into a set of steps. However, an enumeration of the general operational steps involved could be made to serve as a practical tool which indicates a broad line of action particularly for team work and offers a basis for the clarification and concretization of this process. Such a statement worked out at the initial stage of the study is presented in Chart 1.2.

CHART 1.2

GENERAL OPERATIONAL STEPS

for Developing the Foundations of Lifelong Education

1. *Analysis of the concept of lifelong education* in terms of its meaning, functions, qualities, characteristics, etc.

2. *Identification of important aspects and concepts from the discipline*
   that are relevant to different features and characteristics of lifelong education.

3. *Interpretation of these aspects and concepts of the discipline to
   formulate guiding principles for lifelong education* in the form of
   supporting factors, limiting conditions, goals, processes, precautions, preconditions, relationships, possibilities, prediction
   of likely consequences, etc.

4. *Organization of the findings in a suitable sequence* for the purpose
   of sharing with others.

As a first step, the concept of lifelong education was examined in a
variety of ways by team members both individually and collectively. This process continued throughout the period of the study. Some key elements of the
concept are briefly discussed in the following sub-section (8.1). The remaining
sub-sections are devoted to the elaboration of the other three operational steps
given in this chart.

8.1 The concept of lifelong education

Lifelong education is a process of accomplishing personal, social and
professional development throughout the life-span of individuals in order to enhance the quality of life of both individuals and their collectives. It is a
comprehensive and unifying idea which includes formal, non-formal and informal
learning for acquiring and enhancing enlightenment so as to attain the fullest
possible development in different stages and domains of life. It is connected
with both individual growth and social progress. That is why ideas such as
"learning to be" and "a learning society" or "an educative society" are associated with this concept.

From the standpoint of the individual, Lengrand describes lifelong education as representing "an effort to reconcile and harmonize different stages
of training in such a manner that the individual is no longer in conflict with
himself. By laying stress on the unity, the all-roundness and the continuity
of development of the personality, it leads to the formulation of curricula
and instruments of education that create permanent communications between the
needs and lessons of professional life, of cultural expression, of general development and of the various situations for and through which every individual
completes and fulfils himself".[23] Similarly, when viewing this idea from the
societal angle, Jessup observes that lifelong learning "is an ideal that comes
out in countless ways. It is a temper, a quality of society, that evinces itself in attitudes, in relationships, and in social organization."[24]

When the principle of lifelong education is universalized and applied on
a mass scale to different societies, it is likely to take different operational
modalities under different socio-economic, political and cultural conditions.
The operational modality given to lifelong education depends on a number of
intra- and extra-educational variables characterizing various countries, cultures and even their individual members. Such a flexible and open approach is
an important element of lifelong education because this concept is fundamentally
based on the assumption that continuing enlightenment can be acquired by individuals and societies through different paths, and that these alternative
courses will enable all of them to move forward towards the attainment of a higher and better quality of life.

It is often difficult to conceptualize lifelong education in its entirety
on account of its comprehensiveness and multiple modalities. Consequently, different scholars have highlighted different facets of the same idea, as is evident
from the existing literature.

Because of this situation, the Unesco Institute carried out an exploratory
study through literature survey and interviews and arrived at a set of some
twenty concept-characteristics of lifelong education that describe its meaning,
functions, goals, relationships and other qualities. For example, lifelong education seeks to view education in its totality. It covers formal, non-formal and
informal patterns of education, and attempts to integrate and articulate all
structures and stages of education along the vertical (temporal) and horizontal
(spatial) dimensions. It is also characterized by flexibility in time, place, con-

tent and techniques of learning and hence calls for self-directed learning,
sharing of one's enlightenment with others, and adopting varied learning styles
and strategies. Further, the three major prerequisites considered as important
for realizing the goals of lifelong education are: learning opportunity, motivation and educability. The goals include the fulfilment of adaptive and creative
functions of the individuals leading to the continuous improvement of the quality
of personal and collective life.

A list of concept characteristics (Appendix 1) developed through a systematic study was given to the members of the team as a working tool, along with
other relevant outcomes and additional reading materials. Based on the list of
concept characteristics, a number of key words and phrases connected with them
and some of their major implications were also listed and supplied. This general
checklist, given in Appendix 2, served as a supporting working tool for taking
the first operational step for developing the foundations content. Furthermore,
the conceptual features of lifelong education were discussed by the study team
in different meetings in order to ensure a good degree of common understanding
and communicability about this multi-dimensional idea.

8.2 Identification of relevant aspects and concepts of selected disciplines

This is an important step in moving towards the construction of the foundations because it is at this level that multiple interactions between the concepts of disciplines and elements of lifelong education take place as described
in the beginning of this section.

In the present case, this interactive process was allowed to occur under
each discipline throughout the period of study in an interdisciplinary context.
As individual papers ran through successive drafts, clarity in respect of applicability and relevance of different aspects and concepts gradually emerged.
Several additions and alterations were carried out in this respect during successive phases of work. At the final stage, the major aspects and concepts actually
applied in developing the foundations were isolated. Lists of aspects and concepts actually applied in varying degrees by each discipline to the concept of
lifelong education were prepared by examining the discipline-based documents and
were finalized with the help of the authors concerned. These are presented in
Table 1.1.

TABLE 1.1

RELEVANT ASPECTS AND CONCEPTS OF THE SELECTED DISCIPLINES

Discipline	Relevant Aspects and Concepts
1. Philosophy	1.1 Dimensions of human personality
	1.2 Purpose and worth of life of man
	1.3 Relationship between the individual and society, and of these with lifelong education
	1.4 Quality of individual and collective life and the dynamic development of personality
	1.5 Life of the masses in their everyday existence
	1.6 Lifelong education and social reconstruction
	1.7 Values in life and value of life
	1.8 Community experiences
	1.9 Civilization of means and civilization of ends
	1.10 Production-centred, consumption-centred and education-centred societies
	1.11 Basic processes of alienation influencing the individual
	1.11.1 Social alienation
	1.11.2 Cultural alienation
	1.11.3 The world of things and the world of values
	1.12 Efficiency and freedom
	1.13 Tragedy and human liberty
	1.14 Pragmatic and humanistic culture
2. History	2.1 An interactive balance between the spirit of man, society and technology in all civilizations known to history

Discipline	Relevant Aspects and Concepts
	2.2 The concept of evolutionary humanism; man's emerging role in the shaping of his own destiny
	2.3 Emergence of a global civilization
	2.4 Historic processes of the liberation of the mind of man and of the fabric of social organization
	2.5 Theory of development
	2.6 The communication revolution as a product of history
	2.7 The idea of lifelong education in history; its relevance to transition to new systems, especial in the living traditional cultures of developing countries
	2.8 Broadened horizons of history and new ways of synthesizing knowledge of the past into significant patterns relating to the nature of man and his society
	2.9 History as a mode of thought and unifying princi of knowledge and awareness
	2.10 Relevance of history to the search for the meani of life, the conduct of human affairs, planning human growth, enriching learning motivations and promoting cultural learning
	2.11 Concepts of peace, universality, development, quality of life and new humanism
	2.12 Integration of education and culture
	2.13 Renewal of values
	2.14 History as personal experience
3. Sociology	3.1 Interpersonal relations
	3.2 Typical structures and social groups
	3.3 Personality as a product of social life

Discipline	Relevant Aspects and Concepts
	3.4 Division of labour
	3.5 Industrial relations
	3.6 Social mobility
	3.7 Time-budgeting
	3.8 Roles and status (especially familial)
	3.9 General mechanisms for the maintenance of social relations
	3.10 Social change
	3.11 Urban phenomena and education - (environment, ecology, space)
	3.12 Micro and macro-sociological levels
	3.13 Class-communication and education
	3.14 Leisure and cultural aspects of education (cultural lags)
	3.15 Sociology of education
	3.16 Global society and systemic approach - functional and dialectical
4. Psychology	4.1 Intrapsychic development
	4.2 Interpersonal relationships and social roles
	4.3 Cognitive Development
	4.4 Development of skills
	4.5 Development of motivation and affect
	4.6 The concept of knowledge
	4.7 Change, novelty and uncertainty influencing motivation
	4.8 Educational equality

Discipline	Relevant Aspects and Concepts
	4.9 Continuousness of growth
	4.10 Competence of infants and adults
	4.11 Co-ordination of psychological domains - interaction of motivation, emotion and cognition
	4.12 Change as a psychological threat
	4.13 Intellectual functioning at all stages of life
	4.14 Vertical and horizontal integration concerning different aspects of growth
	4.15 "Process" learning and "Content" learning
	4.16 Developmental plasticity - importance of early experience - plasticity in later life
5-6 Anthropology and Ecology	5-6.1 Acculturation, enculturation and socialization
	5-6.2 The existential self - global ecosystem
	5-6.3 Survival environments
	5-6.4 Built environments
	5-6.5 Growth and life cycles
	5-6.6 Global fate groups
	5-6.7 Dependency relationships
	5-6.8 Life support systems
	5-6.9 Man-environment evolutionary patterns
	5-6.10 Preliterate, intermediate and modern societies
	5-6.11 Bio-techno-systems
	5-6.12 Man-machine interface
	5-6.13 Life cycles and growth phases

Discipline	Relevant Aspects and Concepts

5-6.14 Collective evolution

5-6.15 Rhythms of humans, human collectives, and that of the natural environment of which man is an integral part

5-6.16 Kinesics, proxemics, ethology and zoosemiotics, iconics, trophallaxis as aspects of communication

5-6.17 Micro-futures

5-6.18 Ethnogenesis

7. Economics

7.1 Investment in human capital (micro and macro-level)

7.2 Productivity - production function - "human resources"

7.3 "Filter" theories

7.4 Labour market (competitive, segmented)

7.5 On-the-job learning

7.6 Qualification and personal distribution of income

7.7 Working force - (exchange value and use value of)

7.8 Mode of production

7.9 Material base and superstructure of social formations

7.10 Cycle of capital

7.11 Mobility

7.12 Reproduction of the labour force

This table has several methodological purposes and uses, two of which are stated below as examples:

8.2.1 *Evidence of comprehensive coverage*

For the development of well-rounded foundations of lifelong education, it is essential to ensure a comprehensive coverage of relevant concepts from different disciplines for the purpose of deriving a variety of well-balanced guiding principles.

Table 1.1 shows the extent of comprehensiveness of the present study. It is evident that a number of important aspects and concepts of different disciplines have been tapped to develop perspectives of lifelong education and to derive guiding principles. Some of the aspects like dimensions of human personality, process of alienation influencing the individual, emergence of a global society, theory of development, inter-personal relations, social mobility, concept of knowledge, change as a psychic threat, socialization, man-environment evolutionary patterns, labour market, and mode of production are indicative of comprehensiveness and variety in coverage.

It is also interesting to note from Table 1.1 that one and the same theme has been examined under different disciplines, thus providing an interdisciplinary perspective. For example, the question of *human personality* treated under the philosophical foundations is also examined as *spirit of man* under history, as *intrapsychic development* under the psychological perspective, and as *personality as the product of social life* under the sociological foundations. Similarly, the phenomenon of *change* has been viewed as a factor influencing social relations, personal adjustment, level of motivation, value systems, survival environments, mode of production and so forth by the representatives of different disciplines. These themes indicate another dimension of comprehensiveness.

For a more rigorous examination of comprehensiveness a set of criteria can be established and further analysis of Table 1.1 carried out. These criteria should be cross-disciplinary and established on a logical basis. For example, one of the ways of arriving at cross-disciplinary criteria is to draw them from the definition of lifelong education. As stated in the previous section, lifelong education aims at personal, social and vocational development. These three domains of development can therefore be utilized for working out categories of content analysis, such as (i) Personal, (ii) Interface between Personal and Social, (iii) Social, (iv) Interface between Social and Vocational, etc. Even further sub-classification of each domain can be made. The "Personal" domain of development, for instance, can be classified as (i) Physical, (ii) Mental, (iii) Emotional, and (iv) Transcendental. In this manner, a number of cross-disciplinary criteria can be

generated and content analysis of the aspects and concepts of disciplines
carried out to ascertain the extent of their comprehensiveness. The findings
can also be quantified to develop an index of comprehensiveness by taking the
factors of frequency and significance into account. This is beyond the scope of
the present study. However, there is a need for conducting empirical work in
this area for evolving a methodology for more systematic construction of the
foundations of education.

8.2.2 _An inventory for future use_
        In a sense, Table 1.1 emerges as a useful concomitant outcome of the
present study from the methodological standpoint because it can now serve as a
working instrument for other similar studies. It provides a preliminary checklist or inventory to make such studies more systematic and also relatively more
objective. In any initial study of the present kind, it is necessary to follow
a more intuitive approach. However, it should now be possible to carry out
foundation studies in a more rational and yet more comprehensive manner without
totally neglecting the intuitive aspect.
        Such a working tool may also facilitate collective work by teams of ex-
perts in individual disciplines or groups of disciplines since it provides a concrete and common starting point. Needless to say, the present inventory should be
modified and augmented as more experience is gained in the systematic development
of the foundations of lifelong education.

8.3 Derivation of perspectives and guidelines
        The third important step in constructing the foundations is to interpret
relevant aspects and concepts of different disciplines and formulate guiding
principles and perspectives of lifelong education. This step is closely linked
with the second one and is an integral part of the complex process of analysis,
synthesis, reflection and evaluation as described before. Its importance lies in
the fact that it represents a progression from the stage of an abstract process to
that of concrete outcomes in the form of the foundations content.
        The outcomes so derived should be in line with the nature of the content as
discussed in the previous section and pointed out in Chart 1.1. The present study
has yielded a large number of outcomes in the form of perspectives and guidelines.
        For example, from the philosophical foundations emerge a number of guide-

lines for *goals* such as the following:

(1) *Constantly exceeding the boundaries of*
    one's own achievement – A lifelong pursuit

   i) According to the concept of lifelong education, man can
find his vocation and his happiness only by constantly
exceeding the boundaries of what he has already achieved ... Lifelong education closely corresponds to the
process of multiplying the dimensions of human existence.
(pp. 64/65 and 74).

  ii) The more our actions and aims tend to exceed our horizon
and achievements, the more does our existence deserve
the epithet "human". (p. 87).

Similarly, the anthropological and ecological foundations point to a
number of *precautions* and *preconditions* to be kept in view while *planning* any
programme of lifelong education. Several points such as the following emerged
when the nature and process of communication in the context of lifelong education were examined from the anthropological aspect:

(2) *Communication modes and survival pathology*

   i) Too much reliance on any *one* human communication channel,
e.g. the auditory-oral, may be unsatisfactory for purposes of social control and species survival. Put slightly
differently, social control or organizational strategies
which emphasize only one mode of communication may have an
in-built survival pathology. (p. 270).

(3) *Urbanization and problems of affective development*

   i) In extensive modern metropolitan cities, where business,
industry and commerce are predominant, small communities
cannot usually exist, and it is in this milieu that social relations have a short time scale. (p. 268).

  ii) This means that individuals must always learn to communicate
with new people and about new things, and respond to the
imperatives of new technologies. Such experiences may encourage cognitive learning but are scarcely conducive to
the development of in-depth affective (emotional) relationships. (ibid.)

 iii) Such a deficit is rather unfortunate, for it is this latter
kind of interaction which engenders the most meaningful
kinds of human communication. Serial human relationships and
extended relationships with centralized technological systems
are *not* conducive to the development of meaningful, affective
social communication patterns. (ibid.)

iv) It is indeed ironic that global technologies and resource flow systems make people more dependent on
distant others for survival. To the extent that they
are caught up in this syndrome (growth of large systems
and superficial human communication), they are unable
to establish small-scale affective communication systems which are so vitally important to the growth and
development of particular individuals. (p. 268).

These statements point to the critical importance of providing sufficient variety and diversity in communication channels through *plans* and *programmes* of lifelong learning (formal, non-formal and informal) for the healthy
development of a community. They also hint at the need for devoting special
attention to the objective of affective development in urbanized communities
if the quality of individual and collective life is to be sustained.

Likewise, when tackling the issues concerning the challenge of change
and the role of lifelong education, useful *perspectives* of the concept and
guidelines for curricular decisions have been developed under the psychologic
foundations such as the following:

(4) *Motivating properties of change and uncertainty*

i) Change brings threats to psychological life. At the same
time, it is a key element in growth and development. For
the effects of change to be psychologically beneficial,
they must be experienced to an extent, and at a speed
which is tolerable to the people concerned. (p. 192).

ii) An important factor in the development of a society
whose members can profit from change is the extent to
which its citizens are prepared for change. (ibid.)

iii) ... the presence of change and uncertainty may motivate
them to seek adaptive adjustments. To a considerable extent, the *motivating properties of uncertainty* are modified by prior experience with it. Thus, it is argued ...
that an educational system which provides children with
opportunities to experience uncertainty and to make adaptive adjustments to it will be necessary if students
are to be prepared to live full and satisfying lives.
(pp. 195/196).

These illustrations indicate some of the kinds of outcomes derived under
this particular operational step. Many more examples covering different content
categories are presented in the last chapter.

8.4 Organization and presentation of the findings

The last operational step is obviously the organization and presentation of findings in a suitable sequence for the purpose of sharing them with others. There are, of course, various ways of doing this. In this study the findings have been presented in two ways: (i) as documented by different experts, and (ii) as illustrations of content analysis and synthesis.

The first mode of presentation was considered important for the purpose of maintaining the context of individual findings and the arguments associated with them. The perspectives and guidelines worked out by different experts on the basis of arguments drawn from their own and allied disciplines have the elements of sequence and continuity. These elements have therefore been preserved by presenting individual documents as different chapters.

For operational purposes, however, it is necessary to identify and isolate specific perspectives and guidelines in order to facilitate their application. It is also necessary to examine several findings across different disciplines so as to arrive at interdisciplinary guidelines. To meet these needs, the second mode of organization and presentation was considered appropriate, as may be seen in the last chapter. However, as this pattern of presentation cannot be made exhaustive without risking enormous duplication, it has been deliberately confined to certain illustrations.

9. Summary

This chapter deals with several methodological aspects concerning the development of the foundations of lifelong education. Simultaneously, it presents an account of the procedure adopted for the study and delineates its background, objectives, scope, etc. Some of the major points are summarized below:

1) The new perspective of lifelong education has emerged as a positive response to both intra-educational problems and extra-educational changes.

2) One of the essential steps for the effective implementation of this concept is to construct foundations leading to broad perspectives and guidelines that are helpful in decision making.

3) The foundations should not be based on a rather narrow conception of education confined to primary and secondary
schooling, as is often the case. On the contrary, education
should be viewed as a lifelong process encompassing the horizontal and vertical dimensions of the total life-span. For
this purpose a suitable methodology needs to be evolved.

4) In order to ensure a comprehensive coverage of the life-span
of an individual on the one hand and various societal facets
and settings on the other, the foundations of lifelong education should be based on a larger number of relevant disciplines than only the two or three that are usually applied to
education. The disciplines included in the present study are:
Anthropology, Ecology, Economics, History, Philosophy,
Psychology and Sociology. In addition, cultural, physiological and other aspects have been indirectly covered to a certain extent.

5) Several elements of interdisciplinarity were built into the
study without neglecting the autonomy of individual disciplines
and the unique contribution that each one can make. By setting
up an interdisciplinary study team, establishing co-ordination
and inter-communication among its members, and by other
similar steps, an attempt was made to move from the multi- to
the interdisciplinary level of inquiry.

6) The nature of the foundations content was one element among
the methodological considerations. This was clarified by working out content categories such as supporting factors, limiting conditions, precautions and pre-conditions, elucidation of
underlying assumptions, and guidelines for formulating policies,
plans, goals, curriculum, etc. These categories were later
used to provide criteria for content analysis.

7) Yet another issue of methodological interest pertains to the
identification of operational steps for developing the foundations content. The steps involved in this process are not
necessarily sequential or uni-directional but involve a cognitive confrontation and interaction between the concept of
lifelong education and relevant aspects and concepts of the
discipline concerned. However, the general operational steps
appear to include (i) the analysis of the concept of lifelong
education, (ii) identification of relevant aspects and concepts
from the discipline concerned as well as allied areas of knowledge, (iii) derivation of perspectives and guidelines based on
several complex processes, and (iv) organization of the findings in a suitable sequence.

8) The relevant aspects and concepts that were actually applied in
varying degrees to the concept of lifelong education are presented in Table 1.1. This table indicates the extent of comprehensiveness and can be used as an inventory for future studies
of a similar nature.

9) Several working tools in the form of checklists and de-
scriptive statements used during the study are presented
in this chapter. They were prepared for clarifying the
concept of lifelong education, for co-ordinating the work
among the discipline experts and for similar purposes.

NOTES

1. Whitehead, Alfred North. *Adventures of Ideas*. Cambridge, Mass.: The
University Press, 1947. p. 118.

2. Lengrand, Paul. *An Introduction to Lifelong Education*. Paris: UNESCO,
1970. p. 44.

3. Dave, R. H. *Lifelong Education and School Curriculum*. Hamburg: Unesco
Institute for Education, 1973. p. 12. (uie monographs 1.)

4. United Nations. *Universal Declaration of Human Rights*, (1948). New
York: UN Office of Public Information, 1964. Article 26.

5. Faure, Edgar; Herrera, Felipe; Kaddoura, Abdul-Razzak; Lopes, Henri;
Petrovski, Arthur V.; Rahnema, Mayid, & Ward, Frederick Champion.
Learning to Be: The World of Education Today and Tomorrow. Paris:
UNESCO; London: Harrap, 1972. p. 12.

6. Ibid., pp. 35 - 39.

7. Ibid., p. 182.

8. Ibid.

9. Adiseshiah, Malcolm S. *It is Time to Begin. The Human Role in Development:
Some Further Reflections for the Seventies*. Paris: UNESCO, 1972. 182 pp.

10. Coombs, Philip H. *The World Educational Crisis*. New York: Oxford University
Press, 1968. 241 pp.

11. Filipovic, Dragomir. "Permanent Education and Reform of the Educational
System in Yugoslavia". *Convergence* 1 (1968), No. 4. pp. 42 - 46.

12. Houle, Cyril O. "Continued Professional Education in the USA". In Jessup,
F. W. (Ed.) *Lifelong Learning: A Symposium on Continuing Education*.
Oxford: Pergamon Press, 1969. pp. 53 - 69.

13. Husén, Torsten. "Lifelong Learning in the "Educative Society'". *Convergence* 1 (1968), No. 4, pp. 12 - 21.

14. Janne, Henri. *L'Education permanente, Facteur de Mutation du Système d'Enseignement actuel.* Strasbourg: Conseil de l'Europe, 1969. (Etudes sur l'Education permanente 6.) 1, 34 pp.

15. Jessup, F. W. "The Idea of Lifelong Learning". In *Lifelong Learning: A Symposium on Continuing Education.* See Note 12. pp. 14 - 31.

16. Lengrand, Paul. *An Introduction to Lifelong Education.* See Note 2. 99 pp.

17. Shimbori, Michiya. "Lifelong Integrated Education. A Japanese View". In *Lifelong Education.* New Delhi: Asian Institute of Educational Planning and Administration, 1970. pp. 52 - 79.

18. Suchodolski, Bogdan. *Lifelong Education: Problems, Tasks, Conditions.* Contribution to the Interdisciplinary Symposium on Lifelong Education, from 26 September to 2 October 1972, in Paris. Paris: UNESCO, 1972. 10 pp.

19. For example, see *Recurrent Education: A Strategy for Lifelong Learning.* Paris: OECD, Centre for Educational Research and Innovation, 1973. 91 pp. - *Report on Permanent Education in Europe.* Contribution to the International Education Year. Strasbourg: Council of Europe, 1970. 45 pp. (Document No. 2817.)

Some other examples of national level publications are:

Alberta Commission on Educational Planning. *A Future of Choices. A Choice of Futures.* Report of the Commission on Educational Planning. Chairman: Walter H. Worth. Edmonton, Alberta: The Cabinet Committee on Education, 1972. 325 pp.

The Learning Society. Report of the Commission on Post-secondary Education in Ontario. Toronto: Ministry of Government Services, 1972. VII, 266 pp.

Romero Brest, Gilda L. de; Pain, Abraham, & Bursilowsky, Silvia. *Lifelong Education: An Alternative Strategy for Educational Planning.* Buenos Aires: Centro de Investigaciones en Ciencias de la Educación, 1972. 97, 3, 7 pp.

Skander, O. *Strategies for Directing Existing Educational Systems towards Lifelong Education: What the Algerian Experience has to Contribute.* Contribution to the Interdisciplinary Symposium on Lifelong Education. See Note 18. 19 pp. and annex. (ED-72/CONF. 1/5.)

A Survey of the Demands for Lifelong Education. Interim report. Tokyo: Research and Statistics Division, Ministry of Education, 1972. 48 pp.

Towards a Learning Society: A Plan for Education, Science and Technology 1972 - 1984. Madras: State Planning Commission Ezhilagam, 1972. 90 pp. (Plan Document No. 1.)

Zaki, W. M. *The People's Open University - The Concept, Programme, Structure and Physical Facilities.*. Islamabad: People's Open University, 1975. 73 pp.

Lifelong Education. Conditions, Needs, Resources. Canberra: Australian Association of Adult Education, 1974. Vol. 2. 99 pp.

Report of Committe on Lifelong Education. Wellington: New Zealand National Commission for UNESCO, 1972. 112 pp.

In some cases educational laws and other official documents provide similar references (e.g. Peru). A number of additional references are available in the bibliography of *Lifelong Education and the School* (uie monographs 2)

20. Centre for Educational Research and Innovation. *Interdisciplinarity; Problems of Teaching and Research in Universities.* Paris: OECD, 1972. p. 321.

21. Ibid. pp. 25 - 26.

22. Butts, R. Freeman. "Foundations of Education". In Rivlin, Harry N. (Ed.). *Encyclopedia of Modern Education.* New York: Philosophical LIbrary of New York City, 1943. pp. 314 - 315.

23. Lengrand, P. *An Introduction to Lifelong Education.* See Note 2. p. 54.

24. Jessup, F. W. "The Idea of Lifelong Learning". See Note 15. p. 31.

APPENDIX I

CONCEPT CHARACTERISTICS OF LIFELONG EDUCATION*

1. The three basic terms upon which the *meaning* of the concept is based are *life*, *lifelong* and *education*. The meaning attached to these terms and the interpretation given to them largely determine the scope and meaning of lifelong education. *(Meaning* and *Operational Modality)*

2. Education does not terminate at the end of formal schooling but is a *lifelong process*. Lifelong education covers the entire life-span of an individual.

3. Lifelong education is not confined to adult education but it encompasses and unifies all stages of education - pre-primary, primary, secondary and so forth. Thus it seeks to view *education* in its *totality*.

4. Lifelong education includes *formal, non-formal and informal patterns of education*.

5. The *home* plays the first, most subtle and crucial role in initiating the process of lifelong learning. This process continues throughout the entire life-span of an individual through *family learning*.

6. The *community* also plays an important role in the system of lifelong education right from the time the child begins to interact with it. It continues its educative function both in professional and general areas throughout life.

7. *Institutions of education* such as schools, universities and training centres are important, but only as one of the agencies for lifelong education. They no longer enjoy the monopoly of educating the people and can no longer exist in isolation from other educative agencies in their society.

8. Lifelong education seeks continuity and articulation along its vertical or longitudinal dimension. *(Vertical Articulation)*

9. Lifelong education also seeks integration at its horizontal and depth dimensions at every stage in life. *(Horizontal Integration)*

10. Contrary to the elitist form of education, lifelong education is *universal* in character. It represents *democratization of education*.

11. Lifelong education is characterized by its *flexibility* and *diversity* in *content*, *learning tools* and *techniques*, and *time* of learning.
12. Lifelong education is a *dynamic approach* to education wich allows adaptation of materials and media of learning as and when new developments take place.
13. Lifelong education allows *alternative patterns* and forms of acquiring education.
14. Lifelong education has two broad components: *general* and *professional*. These components are not completely different from each other but are *inter-related* and *interactive* in nature.
15. The *adaptive* and *innovative functions* of the individual and society are fulfilled through lifelong education.
16. Lifelong education carries out a *corrective function*: to take care of the shortcomings of the existing system of education.
17. The ultimate goal of lifelong education is to maintain and improve the *quality of life*.
18. There are three major *prerequisites* for lifelong education, namely *opportunity*, *motivation* and *educability*.
19. Lifelong education is an *organizing principle* for all education.
20. At the *operational level*, lifelong education provides a *total* system of *all* education.

 Source: R. H. Dave. *Lifelong Education and School Curriculum*. Hamburg: Unesco Institute for Education, 1973. pp. 14 - 25. (uie monographs 1).

APPENDIX II

SOME CHARACTERISTICS AND FEATURES OF LIFELONG EDUCATION
- A CHECKLIST -

      Given below is a checklist of key words and phrases that are connected
with different features and characteristics of lifelong education. They are
not mutually exclusive. Duplication is tolerated for the purpose of including
certain terms having partly similar meaning and which have come into currency
in the pertinent literature. The checklist provides a rough and ready analysis
of the concept of lifelong education for quick review.
1. Coverage of practically the entire life-span.
2. Education viewed in its totality (e.g., pre-basic, basic, post-basic,
   recurrent, concurrent). Encompassing and unifying all stages and forms
   of education.
3. Inclusion of formal, non-formal and informal patterns of learning (e.g.,
   family learning and mass media, etc., besides schools and training
   centres).
4. *Horizontal integration*
   4.1 - Home
        - Neighbourhood
        - Local community
        - Larger society (national and international)
        - World of work
        - Mass media
        - Recreational, cultural, religious and other such agencies
   4.2 - Between subjects of study
   4.3 - Between different aspects of development such as physical,
          moral, intellectual, etc. during a particular stage of life
5. *Vertical articulation*
   5.1 - Between different stages of learning (pre-school, school,
          post-school (and recurrent)
   5.2 - Between different levels and subjects within a particular stage.

5.3 - Between the roles assumed by the individual at different
      stages of life

5.4 - Between different aspects of development over time, such
      as physical, moral, intellectual, etc.

6. Universal in character. Democratization of education.

7. Allows the creation of alternative arrangements of structures for
   acquiring education.

8. General and professional fields of education are inter-related
   and interactive.

9. Emphasis on self-directed learning.

10. Emphasis on self-learning, inter-learning, self-evaluation,
    participatory evaluation of the individual's performance,
    co-operative evaluation of group work, etc.

11. Individualization of learning and evaluation.

12. Inter-generational learning, family learning, community
    learning.

13. Exposure to broad areas of knowledge.

14. Inter-disciplinarity, unity of knowledge. Emphasis on quality
    of knowledge besides quantity.

15. Flexibility and diversity in content, learning tools and techniques,
    time and place of learning.

16. Dynamic approach - assimilation of new developments in knowledge and
    in means and media of communication from time to time.

17. Enhancement of educability (learning to learn, to share experiences
    with others, to evaluate, and to improve).

18. Enhancement of motivation for learning.

19. Creating learning opportunities. Utilizing these opportunities.
    Creating a learning climate. (Three major prerequisites:
    opportunity, motivation and educability).

20. Adaptive and innovative functions. Emphasis on creativity
    and innovativeness.

21. Facilitates smooth change of life roles at different periods in
    the life-span.

22. Understanding and renewal of one's own value system.

23. Maintenance and improvement of the quality of individual and collective life through personal, social and professional growth. Emphasis on the quality and efficiency of life, besides longevity.
24. Development of a learning society; an enlightened and enlightening society. Also learning to be and learning to become.
25. Unifying and organizing principle for all education.

C H A P T E R   2

LIFELONG EDUCATION -
SOME PHILOSOPHICAL ASPECTS

Bogdan   S u c h o d o l s k i

I

Is there any sense in philosophical reflections on the subject of lifelong education? Is it not enough that educationally-oriented politicians and
economists, and of course educationalists themselves, are engaged in these
problems? Is it not enough that psychologists and sociologists also deal with
this matter? Can philosophers really make any useful contribution in this
specialized field, which has its own competent aspects and responsible administrators? There are several answers to these questions. A possible answer -
and a commonly accepted one - is that problems of educational policy are after
all technical problems, and that their solution requires appropriate knowledge
in order to take effective and adequate measures. It is, however, possible to
take the view that every question connected with education is also a question
of human life and its quality, and consequently a philosophical question.

From this point of view philosophical reflections on lifelong education
become absolutely necessary. Our subject will necessarily arouse the philosopher's interest to a greater extent than any other problem connected with
education because it affects everyone, and during the whole course of his
life. An influence of this kind is closely connected with the question: Which
values in life are to be considered as most essential?

In this paper we pursue two objectives. First we want to uncover - on
the basis of an account of the origin of lifelong education and an analysis
of its present situation - a deeper and perhaps in a more general sense a

more human issue which is often neglected by educationalists who are interested
in the theoretical or practical aspects of the subject, and thus limit their
view to strategies of action and to methods or organization. Our second aim is
to identify - and perhaps even to suggest ways of realizing - a certain reorien-
tation of life which is a basic requirement for lifelong education.

1. Origin of Lifelong Education

To begin with, we want to state briefly - though this really ought to be
discussed in greater detail - that the concept of lifelong education is by no
means a new one. Even though we shall not deal with the distant past - we will
not cover references to lifelong education found in the cultures of ancient
China, India, Greece, in the early Christian culture, in Humanism, and in the
Neo-Humanism developing in the beginning of the 19th century - we still have
to consider the fact that the doctrine of lifelong education was already formulated in the first quarter of this century in the famous memorandum connected with the report of the Adult Education Committee in the United Kingdom.[1] In
this report an authoritative body of specialists in the field of adult education stressed the fact that "Adult education is not a luxury for a limited,
exclusive group of specially selected individuals, but an integral part of
social life. For this very reason adult education must be made available for
all as well as be made permanent".

The necessity for lifelong education has become apparent to everyone
concerned with adult education. This basic idea was made popular by A. B.
Yeaxlee's famous book.[2]

The main foundation for the view that continuing education is an absolute essential for life today is the fact that in modern times the democratization of everyday life as well as cultural life tends to proceed so rapidly and in so many directions that we cannot expect the traditional "elite-
conscious" school system to prepare individuals for the resulting changes.

At the end of the 18th and in the first half of the 19th century, the
oppressed classes in America and Great Britain made efforts to break the
barriers which excluded them from any but the most elementary education
and from participation in cultural life. In this connection the experiences

of the 19th century English institutions of adult education which were linked
with the labour movement are particularly instructive. Similar tendencies appeared under different socio-economic conditions - this time in connection
with the peasant movement - in Denmark, which has since become the mother of
people's universities.

Because of these developments the idea of lifelong education has become
associated with compensation for deficiencies of childhood and adolescence.
Adult education was considered as a process which could be initiated and completed at any time in life, as a constant effort towards the breaking down of
the class barriers of the school system, by means of which an "elite-con-
scious" society tried to exclude the lower classes. As the school system had
distributed the benefits of education in an unjust and unfair way, it became
the task of adult education to make up for these deficiencies and injustices.
The greater the discrepancy became between the tendencies towards democracy
and equalization on the one hand and the elite-stabilizing school system in
all highly developed countries on the other, the greater the stress that
was laid on adult education. There are many possibilities of compensating
for the deficiencies of childhood and adolescent education. They range from
courses for those who have not been given the opportunity of attending
school and who are not even able to read and to write, to courses in lieu
of academic studies for those who are denied access to university because
the official entrance qualification is jealously guarded by the establishment. Consequently, adult education becomes increasingly important.

Engaged in activities in this field, educationalists have made many
valuable observations. One of these is that the process of educating adults
is entirely different from the educational process of children and adolescents. It has become more and more obvious that adults - primarily because
of their greater experience of life - can learn certain things better than
children and adolescents. Psychologists have stated that the mind not only
retains its creative capacity and power of comprehension in adulthood, but
that in certain fields there is a further development of these qualities
which is impossible at an earlier age. Sociologists have shown through in-
vestigations of primitive societies that only adults are capable of that
kind of learning which deeply changes the way of life. The history of philosophical and religious trends can be interpreted as a chronicle of inner

changes which have caused modifications of attitudes to life and changes in the
traditional way of living.

Thus interpreted in a new way, adult education has ceased to be a merely
"compensating" type without any special tasks of its own. The great need for
adult education could no longer be explained by the fact that many people had
to make up for educational deficiencies of childhood and adolescence. Now, the
need for adult education is accounted for by the fact that in many relevant
fields the kinds of learning skill required demand a certain maturity which is
found only in adults. Thus the field of adult education manifests the value of
an education which permeates the whole course of life.

II

Another source on which the investigation of lifelong education can draw
is the experience gained in connection with a special process of education
which is nowadays initiated by scientific progress on the one hand and by
changes in the evaluation of vocational qualifications caused by scientific
progress on the other. It has become obvious that the vocational training
which a person receives during his adolescence will soon be out of date if it
is not "brushed up", completed, and sometimes even modified.

In the past, interest in adult education was a characteristic feature of
underdeveloped countries, whereas today it is the highly developed countries
that promote it on a large scale.

This is to guarantee adequate fulfilment of all professional tasks which
require a permanent revision of professional training. Nowadays the process of
acquiring further professional qualification gains increasing importance and
its forms vary more and more. Besides changing the context to take account of
the latest scientific advances, new institutions and methods are developing by
means of which active participation of students in the process of technical
and scientific advancement is encouraged. Looked at from this point of view,
adult education gains new qualities. It shows the interaction between education and the development of the personality in the whole course of life.

Nowadays a new aspect of education - as far as it concerns professional
qualification - has become relevant. Fluctuations in the demand for qualified

specialists on the labour market become a positive factor as well as a negative one. There is no demand for some qualifications, whereas the demand for others increases. Many people are forced to change their profession, others want to do so. In these circumstances, there is free scope for all aspirations to a higher social status. In many countries aspirations of this kind have become the most important motive for changes in the field of educational activities. These activities help people either to advance to a higher position within their own profession or to get new qualifications because they aspire to a new position in a different profession. Both cases represent an educational process of requalification. This is a *new aspect of an education* which is accomplished by people at different phases of their lives.

                                    III

        The third source of a modern programme of lifelong education is a fundamental change in the way of living of the masses which can be noticed in our days. This development is the result of many separate factors: the rise in the standard of living, the increase of leisure time, changes in the political situation, new possibilities of communication connected with several new forms of tourism, mass media which allow the people to participate in cultural life - all these factors have accelerated an evolution which could be defined as a change from a society centred upon production to a society centred upon consumption. In our times the great European middle-class traditions were based on Calvinistic and Puritan ethics as well as on the ascetic thrift of the pioneers of capitalism. These traditions, which made man a servant of production, have been shaken if not abolished. The ideal of happiness, on the other hand, is gaining more and more influence. Happiness, in this connection, could be defined as the full exploitation of all elements of modern life. The "consumption-oriented" way of life encourages the acquisition of material goods and a superficial attitude to cultural life.
        One can, with good reason, point out the superficiality of this way of life. One can take the view - which is shared by many people - that man as a "consumer" is as much a slave of material things as he was during all the years spent as a servant of production. One can also assume an attitude of

contempt and indignation towards this "cultural consumption", if one considers it as a degradation of cultural life.

It is, however, not to be denied that this "consumption-oriented" way of life is a release from the dull and restricted existence subject to the pressure of everyday duties which prevented a genuinely human existence. Listening to the radio, watching television, visiting museums and monuments of art on journeys arranged by travel agencies - all these things may not be regarded as parts of a particularly valuable way of life, but even so they do form an integral part in the lifelong process of widening mental horizons, in the process of stimulating the mind and the imagination. This is a process of education which may not be very profound, but it is a process which has great importance and far-reaching social consequences. Thus lifelong education is now considered as that share in the culture of a highly developed society which everyone has a right to claim.

It is a well-known fact that many organized efforts have been made in order to render this process of participation more profound and, above all, to avoid the limitations and dangers of a commercialized cultural life. These attempts have added a new dimension to the whole set of problems connected with lifelong education. This new dimension is a special feature of our contemporary civilization, a civilization characterized by the dominating influence of mass media and leisure.

What matters is the question of how to prepare people for a new way of life, how to make them resistant to superficial treatment of cultural values. A preparation of this kind requires a critical examination of the whole traditional system of education. Thus the notion of lifelong education gains new meaning. Even though it is - as pointed out above - based on experience gained through teaching adults, it has now become a definition for a whole educational system covering the entire course of life from cradle to grave. It is no longer exclusively linked with adult education - although it concerns this period of life, too. It is associated with the idea of continuity and entirety. At the same time, we notice a shift of emphasis in the traditional system of education. Hence one may draw the conclusion that education has to exceed the bounds of school lessons, examinations, and certificates, that it is a more extensive, more complex process - and at the same time a freer and more spontaneous one. However, it is closely connected with the experience of life and with changes in the social and occupational situation. In this sense "parallel" education becomes more and more important. It results from non-scholastic factors of increasing complexity.

IV

However - and this is what matters for philosophical reflections - there are certain motives and aspirations in the process of modern education which ought to be dealt with in greater detail. The higher and more homogeneous the standards of living in a society become, the greater is the participation in secondary and university education, and the more people take part in cultural life - or at least are given the opportunity of doing so. In the same proportion the traditional connection between educational level and social status no longer holds. Once education has become available to all, it will no longer be a factor in the formation of an elite and in the stabilization of its position. While retaining its value as a means of preparation for social and vocational tasks, education acquires a value of its own. It is no longer desirable as a means of advancement in society, or because of the financial benefits it brings, but as a means of developing a need for and interest in cultural values, because it corresponds to the orientation of human liking and propensities, and because it makes life more colourful and more worthwhile. Thus education helps to intensify our awareness of the values of life and so creates one form of human happiness. One cannot generalize from these phenomena, but in many countries they have already become a new reality. They are the early signs of a fundamental revaluation of the social role of education and of a change in the motives people have for learning.

The view of education as a value in itself and not merely as a means of gaining higher social status or material advantages is of great interest for a concept of lifelong education. We see increasing evidence of the view that education must not be limited to the field of vocational improvement, but should aim at a more general human development. A modern concept of an "education-centred society" must consider chiefly the following aspects: What matters is not only the fact that modern civilization requires continuing vocational training, but the fact that modern civilization has to lay the founda-

tions for life values and create the motivation for their full realization -
and this is possible only through education.

The concept of an "education-centred society" promises to show the way
out of the hopeless situation resulting from the "producing society" and the
"consuming society". Keeping the restraints and obligations imposed on society by production and consumption within rational boundaries, this new concept manifests the profound values of the human existence, thanks to an intensification of all human abilities and energies that further the development of the whole personality.

The realization of the individual's potential in production or consumption, as well as in activities exceeding these fields, as, for example, in
social or creative activities, becomes the foundation of lifelong education.
This interpretation of education implies completely new tasks and content.
The limitations and the one-sidedness of traditional educational ideas become
manifest. All this leads us to the conclusion that the essence of education
itself has to be understood in a new way. In this context the following statement made by Paul Lengrand [3] seems very much to the point:

> Education is not an addendum to life imposed from outside. It is no more
> an asset to be gained than is culture. To use the language of philoso-
> phers, it lies not in the field of 'having' but in that of 'being'.
>   The being in a state of 'becoming' at each different stage and in
> varying circumstances is the true subject-matter of education.

Thus the doctrine of lifelong education becomes a source of critical revision of the fundamental concepts of education; it becomes a decisive factor
in the formation of a contemporary educational concept which interprets education as a process of development in human life closely connected with the humanistic values. This interpretation of education joins on to the most valuable pedagogic traditions from Socrates to Comenius and Dewey. It integrates
the best pedagogic experiments and the most successful attempts to solve educational problems which have been made in several countries.

The view of lifelong education as a process covering all periods of
life is a more complex one than was previously imagined, since it includes various kinds of experience as the relationship becomes closer between education
on the one hand and the individual as well as the society on the other. At the
same time the process of education is rendered freer and more spontaneous. According to this conception, man can find his vocation and his happiness only

by constantly exceeding the boundaries of what he has already achieved. New
horizons of cognition and new spheres of activity are made the source as well
as the consequence of lifelong education, which in its varied forms is recurrent proof of man's loyalty to the ideals of humanity. In this interpretation
lifelong education is an expression and at the same time the motivating factor of an inward youthfulness, which - in connection with flexibility and
open-mindedness - is a distinctive feature of contemporary civilization. The
ideals of producing and consuming which have formed the contemporary mode of
everyday life are counterbalanced by ideals which are modern in the sense
pointed out above, and which are manifested in an "education-centred society"
based on the idea that the continuous development of man forms an integral
part of his existence. This development is a continuous process of going beyond existing reality, the process of self-realisation in creating a new reality. Various interpretations of this aim are connected with philosophical
conceptions of life in different cultures.

2. The Present Situation of Lifelong Education and Future Strategies

V

The origins of lifelong education as seen by us lead directly to a weak
point in contemporary approaches to it. Nowadays lifelong education has become
a reality to a certain degree, and a precisely identified guiding principle
for educational policy. In several countries the postulates of lifelong education have been realized, in varying measure, in different fields. Various attempts are made to differentiate the plans, but all highly developed countries
- irrespective of their economic systems - share similar tendencies as well as
similar difficulties. Actually, all the plans can be explained by the same industrial, technical, and scientific developments.

Before we turn our attention to the variations that arise between countries due to the differences in their economic and value systems, we have to
deal with the foundations of lifelong education and with those educational
problems which all countries have in common. If the process of education is

not to be confined to childhood and adolescence, if it is to include the whole
of life in combination with professional activity, some very important decisions must be taken. It is not only a matter of increasing provision for adult
education, but also of a complete reorganization of the educational system.

If the educational process is to include all stages of life, its whole
character will be fundamentally changed. Also the objectives of each stage
will change. The educational process will no longer be associated with school
and book-learning, and with merely intellectual faculties. It will be closely
related to the totality of life experiences and human activities, to maturity
of feelings, power of imagination and strength of mind, to the curiosity which
accompanies the search for answers to all questions, and to the feeling of
responsibility for words and actions in social contacts. Art as a factor in
education will be given equal status to scholarship, as will social, professional and leisure activities.

Books will no longer be the only instrument of education because the
theatre, radio, television, the cinema and other types of technological development will gain importance as media of education. We had all these instruments in mind when stating that there is a complex and abundant "parallel
education" present today. In this field activity and initiative will find
free scope. The system of lifelong education requires a rationally motivated
integration of educational activities for all periods of life. An integration
of the educational processes in family life, elementary and secondary schools,
vocational and adult education would help to counter the overemphasis laid on
the education of children and adolescents. The experience drawn from all walks
of life would render the educational process more authentic. Treating education as an all-embracing process would make it possible to lay more emphasis
on the development of the artistic and expressive capacities, on the motivation and liking for further learning, on the ability to verify and perfect
one's knowledge. A different kind of integration would be a combination of
educational institutions with other agencies, e.g. with cultural institutions,
professional and social surroundings, and with the reality of art.

The consequence of the fact that education is influenced by many non-
scholastic factors will be a revival and a reformation of educational institutions. The realization of both these types of integration will represent an
achievement of the great objectives of our epoch in the field of general and

universal education.

VI

The extension of education over the whole span of life has even more
important consequences:

It is a well-known fact that technical and scientific progress has become one of the main reasons for the reform of the traditional educational
system, because it requires a continuous updating of vocational qualifications. Through the measures taken in this field new perspectives of the relationship between occupation and education have become manifest. Contrary to
previous belief that vocational activities could not be combined with further
studies, it became obvious that a combination of this kind was not only
possible but necessary. It is only a matter of adequate organization of both
occupation and education. Of course, this will require changes in industrial
law and in organization; it will also require changes in the forms and methods of education. In the efforts towards the realization of lifelong education it has become clear that vocational activities will benefit from being
accompanied by scientific reflection and scientific criticism. This interrelationship will be the foundation for reforms because theory can be verified
immediately by practical experience.

The question arises of how to combine education and occupation in the
sense pointed out above within the system of secondary education. There can
be no doubt that any model of secondary education which limits its objectives exclusively to the age of adolescence is anachronistic and should be
discarded. All societies need a system of secondary education that is available at all stages of life. It is hard to understand why the institutions of
secondary and higher education should "produce" people with a high standard
of education if for the rest of their lives the updating of their qualifications is subject to all sorts of accidental influences, regardless of its
importance as the central factor in scientific and technological progress.
The concept of a secondary education accessible to people at any phase in life
necessitates fundamental changes in the character and organization of all its
institutions. But there are other questions which, being more crucial, deserve

a more detailed discussion.

At which time in life is it advisable to start the coordination of education and occupation, which is a characteristic and decisive factor in modern life? Is it necessary to lay some theoretical foundations in the form of studies independent of practical work before qualifying for a vocation which is on a relatively high level right from the beginning, or is it also possible to find other formulae that would allow practical and educational work to be combined at a considerably earlier age? In this case the process of "parallel education" accompanying practical work would be an integral part of vocational advancement.

The practical consequence would be that after the completion of a general secondary education including elements of scientific and technological specialization, every adolescent would start working in the profession of his particular specialization. This would require a reorganization of professional work to make further education really feasible in the profession chosen, and would accelerate the process of coordinating practical and educational work which will be the foundation of modern life. According to this concept the aims of adult education would relate closely with the objectives of education in the previous period of life, i.e. in adolescence. Education would turn its attention to different categories of professions and to all periods of life. It may, of course, seem doubtful whether it would be advisable in all types of professional specialization to start professional work with comparatively low qualifications and gain promotion only with practical experience. Objections can also be raised as to the orientation of studies in basically theoretical subjects whose interrelationship with practical experience is not so clear. But there can be no doubt that this kind of system would eliminate many of the difficulties connected with an early selection for higher studies. Education would no longer maintain an elite if everyone were offered practically the same opportunities of using his vocational abilities and advancing in the profession chosen.

Whereas any system with limited access to higher studies has to rely on doubtful and uncertain prognoses, the new system would be based on reality, represented by the adolescents' achievements in both professional and academic work. Their future prospects would result from this evaluation which would naturally be controlled by rational criteria.

Whether we take a radical position or not, whether we want to prepare adolescents for their vocation and to perfect the education of those already engaged in practical work or whether we want more theoretical studies along with practical work, in either case we are confronted with a completely new vision of future society: all members of this new society will be engaged in professional work as well as in a process of lifelong education.

VII

These far-reaching changes inherent in the system of lifelong education, which imply a reform not only of the school system but also of out-of-school factors, have not been fully realized anywhere, not even in the modern idea of schools without walls. There are not even plans ready for implementation.

It becomes obvious that the slogans used to draw attention to the problems of lifelong education are accompanied by only a few limited, over-anxious attempts to realize some of its aspects. Vocational qualifications are acquired by means of several training courses of short duration. These attempts can in no respect be regarded as a full realization of the programme of lifelong education. The difficulties arising in the realization of this programme are of a different nature in different countries. In some countries the economic system focuses human attention on material values, it lays the foundations of rivalry and aggression and encourages exaggerated consumption, it makes man a slave of ambition and status symbols. Such an economic system cannot guarantee the full realization of the idea of lifelong education. In socialist countries the conditions for the realization of lifelong education are much more favourable, since the economic system protects its citizens from this deformation of the ideals of life. The social structure of these countries does not encourage a materialistic outlook because there is no opportunity for activities directed towards material success. These restraints enable the people in socialist countries to concentrate on more essential values of life, on cultural and social activities. Some financial and organizational efforts have been made in order to guarantee the extension of education throughout life. But even so, its realization does not automatically result from a social system which offers possibilities for only one particular principle of life. Even in socialist countries educationalists attempting full realization of lifelong education are faced with an increasing number of obstacles. These difficulties are very similar to those arising in capitalist countries.

VIII

The obstacles to the realization of lifelong education are of various kinds, two of which deserve a more detailed analysis. Firstly, it is the prevalent opinion that professional work must be subjected to constant controls of its efficiency. Whether this efficiency is measured in terms of individual success or of public revenue - in either case it is considered as the only valid criterion for the evaluation of professional work. The view that human work can be treated as a means of realizing each individual's faculties - and this is, after all, the basic idea of lifelong education - is considered as visionary and utopian. Obviously, scholastic education and further professional qualification can only be judged by their efficiency; but the general programme of lifelong education is not to be evaluated within these dimensions.

We can only hope that in future man will no longer be treated as a factor of production or service but as an individual developing according to the principles of lifelong education, in the same way as the place of work - at least in socialist countries - is coming to be considered a field of social as well as professional activity. This hope is nourished by the increase of economic democracy and self-government.

The second obstacle to the realization of lifelong education is the division of society into classes, stabilized by the school system. There have been many attempts to put an end to the function of the school system as a factor of social selection, but they meet with persistent opposition regardless of the economic system.

Moreover, scientific and technological progress and the increasing participation of the people in cultural life require a more flexible system of education accessible to all. Contemporary educational policy, however, maintains the educational monopoly of the school. In these circumstances the discrepancy between the educational needs of modern society and the limited and obsolete nature of school education becomes more and more obvious. The increasing discontent prevailing among young people provides a realistic illustration of this discrepancy.

The difficulties in the realization of the process of lifelong education
are so considerable that we have to discuss them in greater detail.

3. The Problem of Overcoming Alienation by Means of Lifelong Education

IX

Obviously the prospects of speedy realization of lifelong education depend mainly on educational policies. International educational institutions,
in the first place UNESCO, have made considerable efforts to explain the concept of lifelong education and dissiminate information about it, and they are
preparing various directives and suggestions. It is also clear that much will
depend on the ability of those who will put the programme into practice in
everyday life. Preparation of the necessary materials and technical aids will
also be of great importance. Well-devised plans and well-prepared specialists
as well as good equipment are necessary if lifelong education is to be realized and if it is to be available to all. But there are still other factors
we cannot ignore. School organization depends largely upon the governing
authority concerned with educational administration and supervision of
teachers' work. The realization of the whole programme of lifelong education
depends to an even larger extent on the factors determining the basic conditions and the principles of human existence, although the connection between
these aspects and education is more indirect. Lifelong education is only to
a certain extent a matter of organization implemented by teachers and educators. It is deeply rooted in the social circumstances which determine the
motives of human action and thereby influence the evaluation of different
principles and different objectives in human life. If we accept the ideas of
lifelong education, we should also accept one particular mode of life. We
have to accept the principle that education, interpreted in a broad sense
as the intensification of human development, should be regarded as the most
essential value in life. According to this principle, the influence of education will dominate the organization of everyday life, and we can only
accept this principle if we believe that the social circumstances in which

we find ourselves provide a possibility for the full realization and development of all human faculties. If man finds himself in surroundings that are hostile or alien to him, education cannot be the dominating factor in life. In philosophical terms, one might say that the indispensable condition for the realization of the programme of lifelong education is to overcome alienation. Lifelong education can only become a reality in surroundings that are neither hostile nor indifferent. Are we really at the beginning of this epoch?

It is difficult to give a very optimistic answer to this question. An analysis of the social and economic situation shows that there are many conditions favourable to lifelong education. The material foundations of our contemporary life offer people the freedom to choose their form of everyday life. Thus, people's occupation becomes a field for the realization of their personal abilities, and the possibilities of taking part in the developments of social life encourage reflection and initiative. The most important task consists in the social promotion and personal development of everybody, at every level. However, our contemporary civilization tends to destroy the demand for education. Only outstanding, creative people feel the need for lifelong education; it is not needed as an element within a mechanism. As the environment seems more and more hostile and alien to us and makes us feel like slaves, the aspirations lifelong education would help to fulfil wither away.

In this connection there are three important aspects of social cirumstances which have to be organized in a particular way if motivation for lifelong education is to be permanent and general. It is not its institutional organization that makes lifelong education difficult to realize; the main problem is to generate and sustain motivation among all people. Motivation is the foundation and at the same time the consequence of lifelong education.

X

The first aspect of reality is social life. Reality gives people particular limited possibilities. If man feels the social situation to be hostile and alien to him, if he feels its slave, then the motivation for lifelong education will be atrophied, even if it may live on for some time in the form of protest or in an effort to escape from reality. This would mean - in Marxist terminology - that in "hostile" or "alien" surroundings man cannot exist as a true representative of his species. Only the overcoming of alienation shows us the way to a "human" form of life and, consequently, arouses our interest in the world and in education. Of course, contemporary civilization in its organizational and institutional form is felt to be a huge mechanism which can destroy man. But it is also evident that the modern centres of production can eliminate one important source of alienation. The democratic achievements of socialist countries and the democratic development in the system of planning and administration have laid the foundation of a way of life which makes everyone understand its individual relevance, so that people do not feel like a tiny cog within a wheel. Under these circumstances the chances of the motivation leading to lifelong education are steadily increasing. The possibility of participating in social life and acquiring responsibility helps to create this motivation.

XI

A second aspect of contemporary reality relates to the material things surrounding us. We are seldom aware of the fact that the surroundings created by modern civilization are represented by material things which appeal to us in different ways.

This aspect of contemporary civilization has recently attracted the attention of sociologists and psychologists. Nowadays our surroundings are not formed or influenced by opinions and spiritual values. More and more we are surrounded by material things which are either desirable or indifferent, useful or amassed without any purpose, corresponding to our needs or "hostile" to them. These things may be of genuine or artificial value. They are connected with several aspects of civilization: with fashion, prestige or rivalry, temptation, desires and boredom. In surroundings dominated by these factors our way of life represents a modern form of alienation. We have to put an end to two great myths existing in consumption-centred societies: the myth of a "civilization where everything is obtainable by pressing buttons", and the myth of "consumer goods as indicators of human-qualities".

If our modern technical and scientific progress developed into a civilization where any benefits considered worthwhile could be secured by mechanical but useful and efficient manipulation, there would be no further need for any education - not even lifelong education. If people's only desire were for consumer goods that can - indeed must - be bought in order to show them off in public to gain prestige, education would become superfluous; it would be sufficient to possess things. Material value would be the connecting link between consumption and production; it would beset man on all sides. It would be the instrument as well as the central point of human existence - and would give free scope to ambition and covetousness. Education may be a means to develop the right attitude towards material goods.

Quite often the quantity of goods possessed by a person is taken as a criterion for the evaluation of his personal qualities; it also manifests social rank and prestige. Human life is ruined by the excessive value attached to material goods at the expense of human spiritual evaluation. A principle of life based not on material values, but on education - which implies acceptance of spiritual values - will find no support unless we free ourselves from the fetishism of material values.

Human life must become a field of creativity and human contacts which enrich the human mind. This is also the implication of Hegel's statement that man can "double" his existence. Lifelong education closely corresponds to this process of multiplying the dimensions of human existence. A "one-dimensional" man needs hardly any education, since the guiding principles of his life are governed solely by the criteria of efficiency, and his prospects for the future are limited by utility and power.

It will not be easy to overcome these difficulties. It requires not only a socio-economic system where the possession of things is no longer an indication of the "position" a person has reached; it also requires a different kind of education in order that people understand how "things" are made. The world of science and technology is a hostile and alien world so long as we do not understand its structure. Once we have accepted science and technology as achievements of the human mind, they become an objective reality it has created and not a means of mental enslavement. So one can take the view, even if it may sound paradoxical, that one indispensable condition for the realization of a continuous and generally available education is education itself. Changes in the motivations and needs for education can be compared to an avalanche. An avalanche carrying with it all the snow in its path grows bigger and more powerful and can carry more and more snow, ice, stones, and trees in proportion to its increasing weight. In the same way the needs for education, once aroused and satisfied, produce more and deeper needs of the same type.

XII

The third aspect of reality relevant to lifelong education is culture. At first sight there seem to be no difficulties. But there is a phenomenon that might be defined as "cultural alienation" - a notion which in the European philosophical tradition was used chiefly in Humboldt's reflections on cultural alienation and methods which could help to overcome it and developed in Hegel's philosophy as a concept of negativity. In other words: Culture can be a serious obstacle as well as a valuable aid to an intensification of the process of lifelong education. The first difficulty is connected with the postulate that on the one hand culture should be within everybody's grasp, while on the other hand it should be "difficult" in order to arouse our curiosity and a desire to master the difficulties. This complex interrelationship between "near" and "far" is a central aspect of an education based on cultural values. They must be placed within the boundaries of human faculties, they must correspond to an individual's needs and not exceed his horizon of understanding, but at the same time they must be on a level high enough to present a challenge. However, if science is too difficult to grasp, it becomes an indifferent, hostile reality, and if, on the other hand, it can be understood without any effort, it will be too weak to cause any profound change. Art must directly express the inner experience of the artist. If it was merely a static reproduction instead of a dynamic creation, it would not be powerful enough to arouse an inner need for development. Man can fulfil himself not by copying and reproducing himself but by changing and developing. In modern civilization this dialectical tension has become weak. On one side, there are works of art that seem utterly incomprehensible even to fairly well-educated people; they are snobbish, pretentious and esoteric, and can be appreciated only by a specialized elite,

which - in isolation from society - uses a language of its own. On the other
side, there is "cultural consumption". It also has far-reaching effects, as
it is organized by the profit-seeking "amusement-industry" which entertains
the masses with comic strips or thrilling but primitive, trivial books and
mechanical means of distraction.

Of course, neither extreme can be a positive factor in a culture-ori-
ented programme of lifelong education, neither can be the centre of an "educative society". Culture which is too "difficult" or too "alien" will produce only trivial emotions, vulgar diversions of an antisocial, aggressive
character and sexual titillations.

Any cultural policy attempting to end the dialectical contradiction
between man and works of art, which is an obstacle to the development of
lifelong education, must face this difficulty. It may be easier to work
against the destructive nature of the "cultural industry" than to reori-
entate creative artistic work. In socialist systems cultural activity is
not directed towards the dangerous ends which are exploited in capitalist
countries. But even in a socialist system it is difficult to effect these
changes.

However, great emphasis must be placed on creative artistic work. It
should be intelligible to all social classes; it should express ideas and
feelings in a form that corresponds to the language and experience of all
social classes. Legal restrictions, pressure, or censorship cannot further
this development. What we need are valuable, comprehensive, and at the
same time directly intelligible creations in all fields of cultural life,
from the sciences to the fine arts. Actually, nobody knows which conditions, which motives and which kinds of appeal are necessary to arouse and
encourage cultural interest among the masses. Demands for cultural values
from small groups are, therefore, helpful and important. These demands express a basic need for change in the whole sphere of social movements that
cause man to orientate his life according to the ideas of lifelong education,
and thus enrich it. This is a fundamental pre-condition of happiness.

XIII

These reflections show that the problems connected with the realization of lifelong education considerably exceed the range of thought of education-oriented politicians, who treat education as a matter of producing qualified workers and specialists. It also exceeds the horizon of educationalists in general. In a certain sense lifelong education represents the entirety of learning and teaching. Though part of its role is to update vocational qualifications and promote vocational advancement and success, lifelong education can and must obviously be organized as a whole.

The first task will be to design lifelong education as a continuum for the various stages of life and increasing maturity. The second task will be to define the procedures, methods and media of the educational process. But lifelong education has another dimension which is much more profound than the requirements of vocational updating, advancement and success. This dimension can be defined as the "human" one, because it concerns the question whether one considers certain values and principles of life as absolute and therefore as providing the criteria for the selection of the motives of human action which shape everyday life. For these very reasons lifelong education depends on all factors characterizing the *condition humaine*. And though these factors may lie outside the educationist's sphere of action, they are of great importance, for the structure of social reality and the processes taking place in the social surroundings can either encourage the demand for lifelong education or hinder and even destroy it.

The world of material things produced by man can become a labyrinth which completely entangles him, but it can also be instrumental in making him free and enriching his mind. Culture can help to develop the personality, to make it dynamic and flexible, but it can also cause cynicism and indifference. Only by overcoming all these alienations can we pave the way for lifelong education, which in a deeper sense represents an entire philosophical system centred upon man and his creative development.

One might ask whether our discussion of the social foundations and the prospects of the concept of lifelong education and its requirements does not under-estimate the organizational efforts already made in this field, whether it does not underrate the educational strategy used to inspire

teachers. We have intended nothing of the kind. Our aim is to show that lifelong education is deeply rooted in human life, and that the need for lifelong
education increases in some circumstances, whereas others destroy it. That is
why we have to deal with factors beyond the sphere of pedagogic influence, so
that the educationalist's point of view may be heard in the discussion about
the reforms of cultural and social life. This discussion is of vital importance to contemporary civilization, since it opens the way for its further
development and lays the foundations for a happy and dignified life for every
individual.

XIV

The foregoing reflections show to what extent the realization of the programme of lifelong education depends on overcoming three basic types of alienation found in modern life. They also make it obvious that the realization of
lifelong education finally depends on the outcome of the great social struggle
about a reform of our contemporary civilization, and on the resulting changes
in its basic social requirements and in its future. This explains why some social classes are more interested than others in the issue of this struggle.
These are the classes which take part in it because they feel its immediate
urgency and are able to understand its objectives. Obviously, this will apply
to different classes in different countries, and, consequently, the action
programmes are different in different countries.

In some countries our statement applies to the intellectuals whose visions of future society contrast with the short-sighted calculations of the
planners who merely reproduce the unsatisfactory contemporary situation. It
is beyond any doubt that in many countries there are social classes distinguished by their courage and their power of constructive thinking, whose
visions create completely new prospects of the education-centred society of
the future. Gramsći, among others, expressed the same point of view.

In other countries, our statement applies to the working classes. The
traditional needs of these classes - so characteristic of the labour movement
of the 19th century - have culminated in the demand for a social system which
will treat human work as a form of social interaction and expression of

creativity, and see it as representing the cultural values of human existence. Sometimes these initiatives come from the young who criticize the
impersonal and rigid organizational structures and the gradual destruction
of humanistic values. Their protests, now more vigorous than ever before,
point to the need for a way of life which allows increased individual experience and social interaction.

It is difficult to find common ground between the demands of these
social groups. However, all these phenomena lead us to conclude that the
future of our civilization depends on rational and responsible actions, and
that the problems cannot be solved mechanically. This outlook necessitates
not only a rational control of development; it also requires a type of education which enables people to exercise this control and to acquire complex
personal experience which will enrich their lives.

For these very reasons the initiatives of certain groups are of great
importance for the realization of lifelong education. These groups try -
in their own limited surroundings - to create a new model of life. Within
the boundaries of their limited possibilities they attempt to find new
models for human existence. The initiatives of these courageous and pio-
neering groups create oases in the desert of our civilization which has
damaged our environment and reduced the significance of meaningful human
relationships. These initiatives form the first steps towards more far-
reaching actions. If the experience of these groups is synthesized and disseminated, it will be possible to show the real essence and value of lifelong education.

4. The Prospects for Man in a Society Centred upon Production and Consumption

XV

The thesis that the development of lifelong education depends on the
character of the respective civilization and on the degree to which the
various types of alienation have been overcome must be supplemented. Though

lifelong education is deeply rooted in social reality, its immediate foundation is the human individual. In some cases his life takes its directive
from many different motivations and different aspirations towards various objectives. In other cases he selects certain values as significant for his own
life. This leads us to a thorny question: Does modern man want to be educated
during the whole course of his life? Does he want to learn in the particular
way we have in mind? In order to answer this question we must turn to history.
Our modern civilization has been formed in the atmosphere of Calvinist and
Puritan ideology. This ideology stressed the necessity of renouncing luxury,
and promised that the reward for carrying out one's mission would be worldly
success which was not, however, to be used for selfish or hedonistic purposes. People should concentrate all their strength on the "thing". They
lived in total devotion to the materialistic values they had created, and to
the institutions and things they had to administer and service: banks, firms,
factories, ships. It was their duty to economize and to invest, to increase
the fortune inherited from their ancestors and pass it on to their sons. In
later capitalist societies this mentality became even more extreme, as the
economic system by its very structure and organization acted as a constraint
both on those who wanted to exercise initiative and make money and on those
who merely wanted to safeguard what they already possessed. People were ad-
monished to strive for higher ranks and honours, to devote their energy to
selected activities, such as science, technology, arts, civil service, vocational activities. But these appeals only represented the idealistic superstructure built on those facts of economic history. Human life was of an
introverted character, it was a kind of "service", never "pleasure". This
mentality, sometimes ascetic, sometimes heroic, but in most cases simply
obedient and devoted, became the decisive factor in the development of
bourgeois society, which helped to "build up" the capitalist system. It was
also somewhat hypocritical: forbidden pleasures were enjoyed surreptitiously.

     This style of life came to be generally accepted by different social
classes and by individuals. It even disarmed revolutionary tendencies. Its
strategy was based on the temptation held out by the prospect of advancement
on the basis of "work and thrift". For a long time the naive delusion per-
sisted that self-sacrifice was a value in itself (the possibility that it
might also be profitable for the owner of the factory and the owner of the

means of production was not considered). This was also the central point in the controversy about the nature of morality which Joseph Conrad treated in his novels, in particular about the question whether the seaman's loyalty to his ship is not just a service to the shipowner. However, it must be admitted that this mentality gave a certain meaning and value to human life, because it gave it a clear direction and explained why it was necessary to live in that particular way.

XVI

This whole ideology belongs to the past. The triumph of capitalism has resulted in a new constellation which is dominated by the ideal of consumption. It encourages material exploitation of success and privileges. Material profit is regarded as a means of securing the advantages and comforts of life. Life is taken as a variety of pleasurable needs alternating with their satisfaction. This hedonistic mentality is also deeply rooted in social history, but it gained intensity in the middle of our century and has spread to all social groups, whereas in the past it was limited to a small elite. The main slogans of contemporary capitalist societies emphasize the possibilities of broadening the basis of their prosperity within a "society of abundance", a "society of full employment", or a "welfare society".

But unforeseen complications have emerged. The orientation of life towards consumption has resulted in extremely anti-cultural and anti-social stances, which are at the same time anti-individual. The classic attitude of the consumer society: "Welfare - what more does man need?" rapidly leads to a degree of satisfaction beyond which lie boredom and satiated indifference towards all those activities of life that require a certain effort. The consequence of this orientation can only be a succession of titillations caused by motives such as rivalry and envy, enslavement to fashion and propaganda, snobbism and curiosity. Stimulants like alcohol and drugs extend the area of consumption, which soon seems limited and grey if restricted to "normal" limits.

The ideology of consumption has proved valuable as a programme of common welfare by freeing people from need and fear and allowing everyone to lead a "human" life. But, while raising their material living standards, it leaves

them alone in a "spiritual desert", it does not point to any values which
would make life worth living, nor does it encourage human contacts and cooperation. This ideology does not help in organizing human existence; it
even makes life very complicated by striking man with the blindness of ego-
tism engendered by consumption, so that he loses his orientation in the
search for a meaning in life. The youth protest movements must be given
credit for unmasking the ideology of a consumption-oriented society by revealing the resulting hopelessness, the empty promises it holds out. Recently
certain objective factors, such as inflation, umemployment etc., have also
exposed the shortcomings of the ideology of consumption.

Similar developments have helped to explode the myth that welfare is
the only basic requirement for human happiness and the sole purpose of life.
The consequence has been the formulation of a programme which aims at freeing
man not only from the fetters of production, but also from those of consumption. This latter principle - contrary to all its slogans - limits man's prospects in life and disorientates him in his social development. The new programme which is to overcome these limitations and disadvantages emphasizes
the value of a way of life which is free from the constraints pointed out
above, and also from the limitations imposed by the methods of planning and
projecting. This type of life is concentrated upon the intensification of
individual and social experience in order to enable man to use his powers of
imagination and expression.

It is, however, most improbable that this new principle of life will put
an end to the old forms of action and behaviour and so result in the abolition
of the institutional and structural limitations which are deeply rooted in society. It is unlikely that this new concept of life, as manifested in protest
movements and in attempts to escape from the limitations of reality, will guide
most people in their efforts to release themselves from the fetters imposed on
them by the ideology of consumption. Perhaps this is not even intended by those
who take part in the protest movement, since the act of protest attracts more
attention than constructive proposals.

XVII

The need to find a way out of the labyrinth of the production and consumption society is one of the justifications for advocating a "learning society", in which the whole existence of man would be centred upon education.
But a society of this kind is an ideal that can only be realized if lifelong
education is available to all. Consequently it cannot be taken for granted that
the learning society would ensure general realization of lifelong education;
the "learning society" depends on lifelong education, and not vice versa. The
crucial question therefore arises: To what degree will motivation for lifelong education influence people today? Can we assume that this motivation will
really help to solve the crisis of the "producing and consuming society"?

There is room for doubts whether the educational orientation of life
does in fact possess the power one would like to ascribe to it. An educational
orientation is after all a kind of egoism - a sublimated egoism, it is true,
useful for society and supplying life values for the individual. But the educational principle encompasses neither social contact and interaction nor responsible commitment to tasks. Of course, motivation for education contrasts
strongly with the ideology of consumption and with "mass culture", but still it
does not include the objectives of devoted commitment to man's higher social objectives, and it is alien to the spirit of heroism and tragic responsibility.

The concept of a learning society based on the view that every individual should be enabled to organize his life according to his interests limits
man to the bounds set by his desire for individual isolation. Even though in the
concept of a learning society these interests are sublimated, even though the
degree of individual isolation would vary with each person's choice of cultural
values, this concept still implies the limitation of man to the confines of his
own individual existence.

However, these restrictions may be dangerous and - in certain respects -
a cause of unhappiness. The development of modern civilization has destroyed the
traditional bonds which used to hold people together. Industrialization and the
concomitant process of urbanization have demolished the structures of "neighbour-
ly solidarity", led to the disintegration of traditional family ties and social
links, and produced the restlessness and superficiality characteristic of mass
civilization. As a result of all these developments our existence has become

solitary and isolated.

At first this type of existence was regarded as promising and desirable because it released people from the obligations imposed by the traditional social bonds. But gradually it revealed its true character. Its consequences were boredom, hopelessness, and disintegration. Mental disorder of various kinds stemming from the dissociation and isolation of the individual described above has become prevalent.

This confirms our assumption that man's chief purpose in life is to exceed the limits set by the necessity of taking care of his own material and spiritual needs. He can overcome these limits in two ways: first, by renewing, extending and deepening his contacts with other people, and secondly, by a profound commitment to social tasks.

XVIII

Seen from this point of view, the question of social contacts and social interaction is the central problem of modern life and hence of education. For this reason it is our aim to lay the foundations for kindness towards others and willingness to cooperate in early childhood. Family and pre-school education must foster the child's natural desire to express himself and to meet with response, because these feelings and desires are characteristic of man at any phase in life. It is also necessary to transform the school system, which encourages competition and negative selection. And we must further the development of a community spirit in the child and offer him wider possibilities of gaining experience in more fields of human activity in all later periods of life

But all these efforts can only provide the necessary preconditions and motivation. The direction of individual development depends on the individual himself, on the ability and intelligence he shows in solving the critical problems of his own life. At any phase of life this is equally possible and equally important in order to create, and satisfy, a lasting desire for social contacts.

The sphere of social contacts and social interactions expands and changes during the course of life. First it is represented by the family and a limited circle of close friends, then it is extended to the field of social and occupational contacts, to the family one founds when one marries and settles down, and to the people with whom one makes friends.

In the light of this experience we can hardly agree with the view that the whole area of human relationships is only a traditional relic unnecessary to modern man. Of course the development of contemporary civilization - industrialization, urbanization and the institutionalization of many aspects of private and professional life - has detracted from the importance of inter-human reality. Still, now more than ever before, new forms of human relationship are developing particularly among the young. We notice new and justified opinions concerning the values inherent in this reality, and there is a strong desire for taking part in it.

Attempts are being made to put an end to the isolated way of living, to experiment with new forms of living together - mainly in groups whose members are of the same age, and often in contact with nature or art. Particular emphasis is placed on experiences which allow an extension and deepening of contacts. All these tendencies reflect the present desire for "living together", they reflect the protest against a characteristic of mass civilization - the isolation of the individual.

However important all this may be, "living together" is not the only form of satisfying the human desire for contacts and interaction. Man can also satisfy this need by taking part in activities directed towards the whole society, towards the nation or towards mankind as a whole. Every individual belongs to his nation in the same way as a child belongs to his family, everyone belongs in some way or other to the great human family, to mankind. In this constantly expanding field lie the spheres of *human* responsibility and *human* tasks, where a person's triumphs and defeats are registered and memories of his deeds and of himself are passed on to later generations.

Education is a powerful instrument for enabling man to take part in a form of social activity which goes beyond the personal level of contacts between a few individuals.   can stimulate him to participate in the kind of social activity which links individual existence to that of "mankind" - in his nation and in the world. In this connection historical and social education becomes one of the chief objectives of educational activity. Many efforts are being made to render this education lively and authentic. Man's relationship with tradition on the one hand and with contemporary society on the other is a very complex one. With regard to the past, one can assume the attitude of the visitor in a museum;

with regard to the present time, one can assume the attitude of the spectator
of a stage-play. But these ways of looking at the world make life shallow,
boring, fatiguing, and tiresome. If the past is felt to be an abundant source
of events which broaden our horizon and further our dialogue with our history,
if the present is understood as a time for responsible commitment to our tasks,
human life will gain both in spiritual value and in social quality.

   In this concept of education special attention must be given to the role
of art. Art initiates, moulds, and develops a feeling for social values. Whether
it creates an imagined world of human situations and events or appeals to us
only by sounds, colours, and form - in either case it is an important sphere for
social contacts and human interrelations. Aesthetic education - or, using a more
common term, education through art - is not limited to developing aesthetic sensibility for its own sake. It can make this sensibility a factor in the process
of extending and enriching human interrelations, human cooperation and mutual
understanding.

   This complex programme of a modern historical, social and aesthetic education justifiably stresses that human interaction cannot be restricted to communication and empathy between two individuals. It must also include various
values and objective tasks outside this personal sphere to unite the interests
of men and help to strengthen the links between them.

                                    XIX

   Communication between human beings, previously neglected, subsequently
yearned for and finally, in a certain sense, realized in modern civilization,
represents new and important aspects of the orientation of human life as a whole.
It is important that social values should act as a challenge to man's commitment,
his exertions and, if necessary, his devotion to the point of self-sacrifice.

   Acceptance of this principle of life is not as exceptional as most people
may think. On the contrary, for many it is the only one that seems attractive.
It can be regarded as the expression of man's dual nature: on the one hand he
tries to exploit certain mundane possibilities which life offers to him; on
the other, he tries to devote his life to those values which he considers important and essential.

The motives vary, but they are all based upon the acceptance of life as a field for the realization of certain values. Life in itself is not valuable, only certain principles render it so. Valuable in this sense is an existence devoted to work or to the search for truth, to the fight for national freedom or to social justice, to art, to educational activity. The values differ, but the ways of life connected with them are similar. The more our actions and aims tend to exceed our horizon and achievements, the more does our existence deserve the epithet "human".

The notion of a valuable life does not promise continuous tranquility, it does not offer permanent happiness. It is not exclusively the lyrical element in life; it can also include elements of tragedy. This concept of a life worth living requires effort, willingness to take risks, and sometimes to fight. On the whole, this concept of life does not guarantee success; it even forces us to consider the possibility of being defeated. If need be, it may also include heroism. These features may seem characteristic of a rather old-fashioned way of life, because Europe today has apparently lost the sense of tragedy as an aspect of human fate. It has been replaced by the notion of unhappiness. This idea has brought about an orientation of life which differs radically from the principle of life manifest in Greek tragedy - to go back to the sources of European culture. Greek tragedy was based on the idea that man's greatness and freedom are founded on his courage in taking decisions which seem to him right, even if he knows that as a consequence his life may be destroyed by gods or men. We learn from Greek tragedy that man has to fight against misfortune, and if necessary to submit to its heavy blows. We learn what constitutes the notion of "tragic guilt" - a deed carried out in full awareness of the consequences it entails.

In the course of the later development of European culture the feeling for truth inherent in the Greek idea of tragedy was lost. Christianity burdened the whole of mankind with the principle of guilt, of original sin requiring penitence and redemption. In our modern secular culture this notion of guilt innate in the human race has been replaced by the ideas of defeat, of calamity and ill luck. Only psychoanalysis has aimed at substantiating these ideas by investigating the mysterious field of the human psyche tortured by complexes. These were the fetters from which we had to free ourselves.

However, the classical notion of guilt, one of the basic ideas in the old European tradition of tragic guilt, is inseparably linked to the notion of freedom. It is connected with responsibility for one's deeds, which are always the consequences of decisions based on an act of selecting our particular way of life out of many other possible ways of life. Actually, every step we take in our everyday lives is such an act of selection, since it implies the rejection of all alternative ones. At every moment we find ourselves at the crossroads, are called upon to take a decision which determines our future. The classical notion of guilt emphasizes the sense of responsibility. Responsibility has to be taken not only for one's own deeds - it is easy to see how they stem from one's intentions - but also for the remote past in which our life originated. The past is in a certain sense burdened by the fate which determines that we shall find ourselves in situations of exactly the same kind, faced with dilemmas of exactly the same nature. Responsibility must also be taken for the future, because our deeds will have unforeseen and unintended consequences. Is not the ancient Greek notion of responsibility clearly a tragic anticipation of modern society, which is loaded with the whole heritage of history, yet courageously and actively faces the future?

Modern man is fully aware of the fact that his actions may - or inevitably will - lead to consequences that are completely different from what he intended. We might say that man "casts his deeds upon the world" - a truth which is very adequately expressed in the notions of tragedy and tragic guilt. This may sound like a metaphysical echo of the remote past, and it may seem strange in our age of reason, intellect and technological power. Yet, thinking in terms of tragedy can certainly be regarded as the most profound understanding of human greatness and human conflicts. In other cultures the same idea probably exists in some form. These perspectives can be interpreted as characteristic of the destiny of modern man who, searching for a way out of the production and consumption-oriented civilization, comes to the conclusion that even the learning society will not enable him to lead a valuable life, and that the essential values of human existence surpass not only the spheres of production and consumption, but also that of education.

We are using the notion of Humanism in the modern sense. It is connected with the classical European tradition, but its essence consists in the conception of the world created by man and for man.

5. Humanism as the Philosophy of Lifelong Education

XX

The reflections in the preceding passages were in some ways concerned
with the social and anthropological foundations and conditions for the realization of a programme of lifelong education. These reflections revealed a
convergence of tendencies. The future development of lifelong education depends on whether man will be successful in his efforts to render civilization more humane and to base his happiness on a way of life which really
deserves the epithet "human". Our modern civilization is a difficult form of
social existence. To a superficial observer it may appear to be a "press
button" culture. But in fact the term "thinking machines" can be used only
metaphorically, for it is man who controls the machine and acts through it;
it is man who thinks with the aid of instruments, and who perfects them. And
it is man who has to master the vast social and technological reality he has
created and continues to create. That is why he is not only an "operator" in
the world of machines and organization. He is at the same time its "helmsman".

To us the debasement of man by modern civilization must be seen in connection with his increasing responsibility. The structure of future civilization will result from the dialectically interrelated measures which must be
taken in order to organize the chaos existing in the world of material things
and in man himself. This requires reconciling technological with organizational culture. In the course of this reconciliation man will have to adapt himself to the new conditions of life, but at the same time these conditions must
be adjusted to man's need for creating values and satisfying them. We have to
change both conditions and people - an ambitious undertaking. But if we fail to
solve these problems, it will be the ruin of mankind. It is hard to say which
of these "bottlenecks" is now the narrower one: man or conditions. We must
become aware of the bounds limiting the further development of civilization;
inventors must use their technological and scientific resourcefulness to spread
and preserve the civilization they have created. We must also take into consideration the social and psychological barriers which restrict the development
and the preservation of civilization. If all these factors are taken into account
we shall discover new objectives and tasks for cultural life, and its role in

the development of motivations and values will be seen more clearly.

Perhaps what is needed is a new kind of belief, a spirit common to all mankind, beyond all regional differences.

XXI

Irrespective of the feasibility of these prospects, we can without hesitation say that they are based on a twofold realization. Firstly, the social sciences have to serve politicians and administrators to organize social life and to control its development. Secondly, they should serve to mould or transform the consciousness of modern man by forming his outlook on life and on the world. This implies that sociology should try to improve his ability to organize his living conditions and at the same time help him to adjust better to the civilization he has created; it also implies that sociology may deepen the feeling for the meaning of life and its essential values.

Human hopes and aspirations are essentially formed by the ideal of efficiency on the one hand and that of freedom on the other. The superiority of our epoch to the past is due to its greater efficiency, which has become a powerful influence on man. In technology and sport the modern ambition to achieve greater efficiency is particularly evident. Organization and administration also aim at increasing efficiency.

But at the same time one of the fears affecting man in modern civilization is the general threat to his freedom; the main object of our dreams is freedom in its different dimensions. The fact that these problems are felt more and more urgently and have begun to influence parts of life never before affected, bears witness to the restlessness characteristic of people who are aware of their alienation. It is also evidence of the great expectations set on the reconstruction of the fundamental unity of all men on the one hand, and of the unity of the individual and the material world on the other.

However, the interrelationship between efficiency and freedom - the ideals of modern man - is a very complex one.

There is some reason for the view that efficiency leads to freedom: the organizational and technological progress entailing improvements in the material world and in human relations prepares the way for human freedom. Although this progress is of limited importance, it is undoubtedly more conducive to freedom than is chaos. In the same way that effective traffic regulation ensures greater mobility to all road users, effective control and organization of work processes and social cooperation provides more possibilities of freedom for every individual.

But we could also muster facts which support a different thesis. One may take the view that only freedom can improve the conditions to achieve maximum efficiency of human work. While we can increase the efficiency of machines and people, with the help of computers, this will not help to solve the problems arising from the fact that in certain fields human work exceeds "functionality".

If it is true that man is not merely a mechanism but a living being whose education cannot be predetermined, this would imply that the model of "controlling and directing" things cannot be applied to guiding and steering people. Insufficient organization is also dangerous. For human beings motives and aspirations are important, as opposed to the world of things which are mere mechanisms fulfilling certain precisely defined functions. Under these conditions freedom becomes an important factor in encouraging initiative and commitment, it becomes a precondition for efficiency in all activities and at the same time a source of harmony and order.

If, in regard to science, technology and humanistic values, we consider the future of our civilization as a process of reconciling the requirements of efficiency and freedom, it implies that we believe in coordinating the two strategies of "directing and controlling" mentioned above, although this coordination may be difficult and full of tension. In this perspective the social sciences will have a very important role to play.

The social sciences will have to lay the foundations of "socio-technical" sciences, which will guarantee the efficiency of human activity not only through improvement of methods, but also through profound changes of human aspirations. They will influence the outlook on life and on the world, and they will also create a new kind of social consciousness; they will form community feeling, and they will increase individual freedom through the cooperation of all. Contributing to the simultaneous and equal development of efficiency and freedom will be the great task of the social sciences and of lifelong education.

XXII

From another point of view, the problems of efficiency and freedom can be regarded as the correlation of, and intrinsic contradiction between, the concept of life as the entirety of all means and methods which help us to achieve more and more new aims, and the concept in which life has an immediate value of its own because of its inherent qualities and not because of its future prospects. It is a well-known fact that this is one of the basic forms of dualism in modern life.

A great number of factors are responsible for the phenomenon that social policy as well as the life of the individual are dominated by the principle that the present is only a means of reaching a well-planned future. Under these conditions life consists entirely of collecting means of living; it loses its independent value and becomes merely a means to an end.

There is, however, a strong trend towards an orientation in which life has an immediate value of its own. In contemporary society, art is steadily gaining importance, and this development is closely connected with the belief in non-material values. In the same way other values can be experienced. Science for example, need not be treated exclusively as a means of strengthening the power and control which man exercises over natural and societal processes. It can also be regarded as an end in itself. We can appreciate science as a means of satisfying the unselfish, non-utilitarian desire for new insight and new knowledge. We can appreciate science as an adventure capable of arousing passionate interest in the human mind and bringing man face to face with the universe.

Lifelong education is very closely associated with these tendencies. As already shown, it encompasses not only the dimension of utility represented by the processes of vocational and supplementary training, but also the dimension of values exceeding the sphere of utility. Regarding the latter dimension it is very important that education should not serve as a means of improving the function of human beings in the mechanisms of production required by the society, but should enrich people's present existence and their personal development in the future.

This orientation, which includes two contrasting yet complementary tendencies - efficiency and values instrumental in reaching a certain practical

purpose on the one hand, freedom and "independent" values on the other -
represents the basic problem of modern humanism.

XXIII

What is the essence of this problem? It is rooted in the desire for
an existence which will be really fit for human beings, for a life made
worth living by the happiness that comes from a variety of experiences and
activities. This problem embraces the most urgent and acute questions of our
epoch - the questions concerning alienation, boredom and indifference, and
the conflicts arising from rivalry. These are the problems confronting us in
the search for a way of life which will be free from the simple conformism of
consumption, the banal diversions of leisure time, the dull uniformity of mass
ideals promoted by the "culture" industry.

This leads us to the diagnosis of our situation. Humanistic culture proves
to be the object of an independent and separate desire characteristic of an
epoch which puts our practical abilities to the most severe test, and in which
the control of material and social developments requires not only up-to-date
information, but also up-to-date people. In our hard and difficult times, the
personalities of individuals are more important than their skill levels.

But at the same time modern civilization offers people more leisure, more
diversions, more sports, more tourism. The mass media facilitate access to the
art of all epochs, including the contemporary one, and to science and philosophy.
In the so-called "mass culture" there are latent sources of the desire for
authentic experience and genuine values: the desire is formed and stimulated
by the increasing possibilities for its satisfaction. Man does not merely perform a certain "role", he does not merely "function" in a certain way. He also
wants to lead a life not governed by the criteria of utility, he wants to live
for himself, for his friends, and he wants to experience the values he esteems.

These are the two aspects of the perspectives of a modern kind of humanism and of the position of humanistic values in the concept of life. Consequently there are two ways leading to the realization of man's prospects in this
domain. One of them is represented by the assumption of responsibility for
controlling the development of modern civilization, the other by the search for

modern values and by the effort to develop a new feeling for the essentials
of life.

The great rivalry between the two types of socio-economic system - the
"producing" and the "consuming" society - will also extend to these spheres.
The efficiency of production and higher standards of living will no longer
be the most important aspects of this competition. Instead, the emphasis will
be shifted to life styles, to life values, to the everyday existence of the
masses. In these perspectives humanistic culture will be of incomparably
greater relevance than the exploitation of all possibilities of leisure activities, of "decent" diversions and recreation. Humanistic culture will become an integral part of the substance of human life. In this connection lifelong education will not be merely an adaptation to changing conditions but
the most important factor of liberation, of courage, of a true life.

Let us take one more step towards an analysis of the future. The use of
the term "humanistic culture" for a kind of existence which is complete in itself and free from the influence of utilitarianism implies that we do not build
up a separate, exclusive "kingdom", but on the contrary treat with due respect
all that has been the foundation of human life through the centuries, everything that has enabled man to take all the risks connected with harnessing
nature and creating civilization. The ancient Romans were right in saying that
man does not have to live, but that he has to steer his ship. And it is this
complex process of courageously "steering the ship" that has formed the substance of human development in the course of centuries.

This has been, and still is, an inexhaustible source of humanistic culture. It is true that our epoch is characterized by the important role science
and technology have assumed. Nevertheless the final and most crucial decisions
that have to be taken to organize social life on the basis of justice and
equality require criteria which surpass the level of doctrines useful to administer the world but offering no answer to the fundamental question: Why
do we take these particular decisions?

And even though in our epoch the organized worlds of work and leisure
seem to exploit all the possibilities of human life, this formalized system of
interdependencies and obligations pays no attention to the most profound human
motives and aspirations. It includes neither man's desire to create nor his
feeling for beauty.

Many centuries ago Aristotle in his Ethics made a distinction between the practical and the poetic element, between activity and creativity. He understood "activity" as a moral action, and "creativity" as "inventive thinking and originating" of action. The tradition of later centuries has changed the meaning of these distinctions: "Praxis" has become a category of the social and material reality, "creativity" has become associated with poetry. But this change has not eliminated the fundamental dualism by which every human action belongs either to the category of "necessity" or to that of "freedom".

Linking art with science, Aristotle distinguished them by saying that "art deals with the origin of things, whereas science deals with their existence". In later centuries, when science became an important instrument of reorienting and reforming reality, this distinction was weakened, but its fundamental sense has been preserved: Man has the power to gain insight into the nature of things, and the power to create things as a means of self-realization.

Essentially humanistic culture is "creation", which lies at the source of any "activity" and becomes the "poetry" of life, a "poetry" permeating the whole existence.

That is why humanistic culture represents the fundamental power and the basic value of human existence. The same idea is found in Marx's *Critique of Political Economy* (1859): the true sense of economics consists in "economizing", i.e. it requires an organization of production which allows full development of man's faculties. Leisure time is - as Marx put it - a time of freedom and a time of higher activity. It completely changes those people who possess it. Thus changed, they also become more active in the process of production, and here their activities are reinforced and their creative power is developed. If "economizing" becomes the ruling principle in our strategy of shaping material and social reality, it will lay the best possible foundation for the development of freedom. Humanistic culture adds to this freedom the quality of commitment to a task, and this protects freedom from degenerating into idleness and shallowness. Thus humanistic culture creates man's true and essential "wealth".

NOTES

1. Final Report of the Ministry of Reconstruction, Adult Education
   Committee. London, 1919.

2. Yeaxlee, A. B. *Lifelong Education. A Sketch of the Range and
   Significance of the Adult Education Movement.* London: Cassell,
   1929.

3. Lengrand, Paul. *An Introduction to Lifelong Education.* Paris:
   UNESCO, 1970. p. 59.

CHAPTER 3

HISTORICAL STUDIES AND THE
FOUNDATIONS OF LIFELONG EDUCATION

P. N. Kirpal

1. The Emerging Concept of Lifelong Education

The roots of lifelong education as an emerging concept of the nature
and role of man, the functioning of his society and the transcendence of both
man and society to higher levels of attainment lie in a new situation that has
arisen in our times.

The dominant factor in the making of civilizations and the shaping of
the course of history is the *spirit of man*, operating in love and fear, greed
and altruism, selfishness and idealism, conservatism and adventure, reform
and revolution, and in so many other diverse and fascinating ways. In man's
strivings, his magnificent successes and tragic failures, his spirit is ever
at work in history, creating, destroying and preserving, adapting, renewing
and exploiting, responding in often unpredictable ways to its own creations and
to the circumstances arising from his works and aspirations. The course of
history appears to be a perennial story of interactions between the spirit of
man, the organization of society comprised of numerous institutions, establishments, laws and moralities, and the complexity and power of technology, developing from his own creations and also from its automatic, relentless growth.
Man, society and technology are always in some state of balance and poise, man-
ifesting in changing forms and varying degrees the elements of security, ela-
tion and peril in all civilizations known to history. The balance is often
precarious and uncertain, calling for the utmost care, vigilance and ingenuity;
the instinct for survival, the spark of creativity, and some mysterious itch

for adventure are at work together, determining the health and strength of
a civilization and the nature and pattern of its problems and challenges;
also lurking around is the possibility of destruction and disaster through
the fatalities of choice or accident. In this ceaseless flux of time and
events the drama of history is endless and the stage appears to be set for
ever, with the same actors playing many changing roles, often destined to
the same fate of growth, creation and disintegration.

1.1 A crisis of contemporary civilization

Our present age, witnessing for the first time the emergence of a
global civilization, is confronted with a challenge of unparalleled dimensions. Man's technology and the social organization have far outstripped
his spirit, resulting in a state of confusion and chaos, the loss of moor-
ings and directions. What we need now is a great renewal of the spirit of
man to redress the balance of the three inter-acting forces in the making
of civilization. The worth and dignity of the individual person are threat-
ened by the brute force and senseless behaviour of the impersonal mass of
machine and society. Human values and aspirations cannot survive without a
fresh strengthening of their sources and the enrichment of their content.
The urgent need for a renewal and resurgence of the spirit of man calls for
a revolutionary transformation of education along with other developments
and creations. The concept of lifelong education arises from a growing crisis
of contemporary civilization; lifelong education is required to fulfil the
need of contemporary man to control, adapt and create the relevant technology and social organization for a new quality of life and for a meaningful
quest of more effective and appropriate values of the spirit. At the same
time, lifelong education owes its very existence to the human and technological achievements of a global civilization.

1.2 The concept of lifelong education

From its origins in the changing conditions of our time emerge the broad
outlines of lifelong education as a new concept. Much has been written about
it in recent years, but educational thought is still groping toward a new
theory, based on sound foundations and capable of sustaining concrete practices.
A great deal of research and experimentation is needed to construct a compre-

hensive and viable theory.

The emerging concept of lifelong education can be summed up in three words indicating the main directions of change and emphasis: *expansion, innovation, and integration.*

1.2.1 *Expansion*

Above all, lifelong education is the expansion of the learning process in time, both in the range and content of learning, and in the multiplication of learning situations. Covering the entire life-span of the learner, education is viewed in its totality, encompassing and unifying all its stages and forms, generating new motivations and offering all kinds of opportunities. The universal right to education and to participation in the cultural life of the community are joined together. Traditional education as practised in the past is to be expanded immensely in scope and content. The massive opportunities of non-formal education are to be added to the methods and structures of formal education. The horizons of expansion are vast and staggering. The learning process becomes the attainment of the quality of life through the understanding and renewal of value systems, the continuous enhancement of personal, social and professional growth, the conscious utilization of intergenerational, family and community learning, and the employment of all possible ways and means of developing a learning society that accords high value and priority to the continuing pursuit of enlightenment. Such an expansion of education calls for new attitudes to work and leisure.

1.2.2 *Innovation*

The principle of expansion gives rise to the need for innovation which opens fascinating vistas and new modalities. The emphasis on creativity and innovativeness is essential for finding alternative structures and patterns of learning, providing meaningful inter-relationships between general and professional education, and adapting present practices to new needs. The creation of learning opportunities for the choice and use of learners generates a climate of learning in which innovations are encouraged and valued and the three major prerequisites of opportunity, motivation and educability are realized. Flexibility and diversity in content, appropriate use of learning tools and techniques, and viable options for the time and place of learning are consciously sought and boldly adopted in the innovative process. The emphasis on self-directed learning gives rise to new and promising forms of self-learning, inter-learning, self-evaluation and cooperative evaluation. The individualization of learning and evaluation solves many problems and mitigates the inequities of the past. Most of the innovations contribute to the elevation and liberation of the spirit of man, giving a better deal to all and creating new ways and means of self-expression and self-fulfilment.

1.2.3 *Integration*

The principle of integration is the third dimension of lifelong education. It facilitates the process of expansion and the introduction of innovations by adequate organization and meaningful linkages. The haphazard growth of social organization and the lopsided character of a fast developing technology have led to proliferating elements of confusion, waste and fragmentation. Here again a fresh assertion of the spirit of man is sorely needed to rationalize, unify and devise new relationships and methods of action. Integration is both necessary and possible. Without it expansion is costly and wasteful, and innovation is difficult to achieve. Integration acts as a unifying and organizing principle for all education. Its search for the unity of knowledge leads to interdisciplinarity, order and discrimination mphasizing the value and quality of knowledge in the midst of its exploding quantity. The scope for integration is vast and challenging. Apart from interdisciplinarity, the educational potentialities of the home, the local community, the larger society, the world of work and the mass media need to be linked together or integrated in order to make the educational process more effective and to create new learning situations. The different aspects of development, such as the physical, the moral, the aesthetic and the intellectual, also offer many opportunities of integration. Isolation of different stages of learning (pre-school, school, post-school and recurrent) is no longer feasible, and it is also necessary to articulate different levels and subjects within a particular stage. New links need to be established between changing roles during the life-span. These possibilities indicate the range and scope of integration, calling for great ingenuity and improvisation.

The broad features of the emerging concept of lifelong education implicit in the three principles of expansion, innovation and integration are described above in general terms. This brief outline is based upon some recent statements and publications sponsored by UNESCO, notably the publication *Learning to be*, the report of the International Commission on Education headed by Edgar Faure.[1] Of special value are the materials developed by the Unesco Institute for Education in Hamburg.[2]

From the concept of lifelong education we can now proceed to its origins in history, and the relevance of the historical sciences to the building of the foundations of lifelong education.

1.3 The origins of lifelong education

The introductory remarks on the crisis of contemporary civilization refer to the need for lifelong education. As the concept is a product of history and a phenomenon of the present time, a clear understanding of its origin in history is essential to any scientific construction of a comprehensive theory. In the following paragraphs the important historical factors contributing to the emergence of lifelong education are examined briefly.

Historical movements become realities by the conjunction of felt needs, viable modalities and clear objectives. The movement toward lifelong education which is now assuming a concrete form has been assisted by such a conjunction of forces.

1.3.1 *Needs*

The Explosion of Knowledge. The growth of rationalist thinking and attitudes followed by the scientific and technological advances of the last two centuries created what could be described as an intellectual revolution, accelerating the pace of creating new knowledge and expanding its range immensely. The explosion of knowledge continues unabated, posing a challenge to education which calls for an adequate edifice of lifelong learning resting upon some basic cycle of studies to motivate the learner to adapt himself to the fast changing needs of his life-span by making his own choices for the pursuit of skills, assimilation of new knowledge and practice of relevant values. Suitable forms of adult education, recurrent education and self-

education accompanied by some reorganization of knowledge are urgently
needed and existing systems have to respond to those needs.

Democratization. No longer can this fast developing knowledge be confined to the privileged classes. The principle of democratization has been
at work in modern times, changing education from an elitist to a mass activity, and from the narrow base of privilege to a fundamental right of man.
The American, the French and the Russian revolutions were conspicuous highlights of an historic process of the liberation of the mind of man and of
the fabric of social organization. Belief and dogma, privilege and authority,
faith and tradition, and all the stabilizing elements of a social order rooted in the past began to be questioned and the spirit of scepticism developed alongside the economic and political changes arising from the Industrial
Revolution, the advent of democracy and the rise of that new form of Western
dominance which is popularly labelled as modernization. Western societies
were often in the vanguard of progress towards democratization, but the movement has become truly worldwide and the trend is evident everywhere, although the measure of change reflects a great diversity, and nowhere has
class and privilege been completely eradicated. Equality of access to education and culture became the socially accepted goals, calling for new policies, programmes of action, and institutional changes. The formulation of
human rights is a significant product of our own times and has been assisted
by historical movements and forces, carrying the concept of democratization
far beyond the emotional slogans of liberty, equality and fraternity. The
implementation of human rights calls for the means and modalities of lifelong education, and the principle of democratization has to be applied to
education and culture as well as the working of the political systems and the
economy. The essence of democratization in our times is the measure of participation of man in all his activities and the broadening of his scope and horizons in all the directions of his own choice. Such participation is still an
ideal and all societies, the materially affluent as well as the economically
backward, have a long way to go toward its achievement. It sets new tasks to
education and calls for stupendous efforts of expansion, innovation and integration to evolve lifelong patterns, programmes and objectives. It calls for
a radical change from the elitism of the past based on privilege, stability
of established orders, social hierarchies, explicit or implicit belief in

inequalities, white-collar job superiority, high esteem for intellectual
work, sophistication, social snobbery and diverse forms of exploitation.
The explosion of numbers resulting from the increase of populations raises
the costs of formal education and leads to urgent search for non-formal
education, which is also required for the diversity of needs and aptitudes.
Economic, financial, sociological, and cultural factors contribute to the
transformation of education.

Development. Such a transformation is also required by the needs of
development, a concept peculiar to our time. That the improvement of the
human state and progress of society are desirable and possible was believed
and acted upon in the past; but the idea of conscious, planned and overall development in a global context is a product of modern times, and its
many aspects are still not fully understood; they need to be probed further
and integrated into a theory of development. The sense of urgency and the
efforts needed to raise the living standards of the economically backward
sections of humanity within a comparatively short span of time require application of knowledge in a planned and systematic way and a much greater
stress on non-formal education. Like lifelong education, the pursuit of development is marked by compulsions of expansion, and opportunities of innovation and integration. Participation in the process of development is both
its means and aim, and democratization is its main motive force. The plural-
ity of aims and diversity of models of development, comprehending economic,
social, cultural and ethical elements, call for the values, attitudes and
skills which lifelong education generates and promotes. Development and lifelong education are closely inter-woven. Both are essential components of the
contemporary scene, in which the assertion of one's own roots is accompanied
by a striving for universality, reflecting the search for a new balance between freedom and technological realities, tradition and innovation, material
welfare and a higher quality of life.

1.3.2 *Modalities*

The Media of Mass Communication. The emergence of new needs for dealing with the explosion of knowledge, the march of democracy and the pursuit
of development are now matched by other historical factors that offer modalities for educating all persons in all possible ways all the time. By far the

most important modalities of action are provided by the mass media. The
recent advances in educational technology, such as radio, film, television
and computers, and the fantastic potentialities of newer developments will
surely make powerful contributions to the spread of lifelong education in
all societies. The audio-visual possibilities of projecting and assimilating knowledge systematically and spreading culture widely are still to be
exploited effectively even in economically developed societies. To the
developing countries they offer powerful ways and means of mass education
and social integration, in order to narrow the knowledge gap, which is even
more formidable than the economic gap between the rich and the poor. Without the new technologies of communication the concept of lifelong education
could not enter the realm of realistic action. The communication revolution
is the product of history, resulting from the complexity and conjunction of
scientific, technological, economic, social and cultural developments in
modern society. These developments have profoundly affected the worlds of
work and leisure which are fast becoming important means of advancing lifelong education.

The World of Work. The traditional systems of the past, almost wholly
confined to formal modalities, trained the elite for certain recognized professions and imparted general education for elitist leadership. Mass education was directed to the inculcation of attitudes and skills for sustaining
hierarchical societies in which the upper classes dominated the masses. The
new forces released by the explosion of knowledge, the compulsions of democratization, the pursuit of development, and the application of science and
technology to production and social organization radically changed the patterns of work, the role of workers and the life styles and goals of society.
The explosion of numbers reflected both in the rapid increase of populations
and the enrolments of students at all levels contributed to the search for educational situations in the world of work, which itself calls for the renewal
and recurrence of opportunities for fresh knowledge to cope with changing
technologies and new modes of production. The growing alienation of traditional education from the world of work resulted in massive waste and irrel-
evance, especially in developing societies which could ill afford the luxury
of so-called "liberal education" that contributed neither to economic productivity nor to social change. The search for educational opportunities and viable

modalities in the world of work has now become imperative, and a closer relationship between work and education contributes to the theory and practice of lifelong education.

 Leisure-time Activities. Equally important and even more promising in
their potentialities for lifelong education are the uses of leisure, which
has now increased in length and in creative possibilities. The integration
of culture with education and the advancement of the objectives described
in the following paragraphs enhance the scope and value of leisure. Automation and sophisticated technologies of the affluent societies as well as
the growing mechanization of production and distribution in the economically
backward countries increase leisure, and the mass media offer the means of
carrying artistic forms and cultural messages to the masses everywhere. The
organization and use of leisure-time activities give rise to fascinating
challenges and opportunities for lifelong education.

1.3.3 *Objectives*

 The Quest for Peace. Objectives are to some extent implicit in both
the needs and modalities described above. All the main components of lifelong education serve in varying degrees as needs, modalities and objectives.
Development is an objective as well as a need; so is the quest for peace.
The objectives stated here are marked by their global character; the essence of lifelong education is the universality of its objectives. Both in
time and space lifelong education comprehends the totality of one's existence
in the life-span, linking even man's home on earth to the neighbouring cosmos.
The necessity of peace in our times is the result of the historic process by
which war, hitherto a normal state of human existence, has suddenly become an
imminent danger to man's survival. The nuclear horizons of utter destruction
and the perils of a deeply-rooted barbarism latent in the nature of man led to
the birth of the United Nations system. Historic documents such as the United
Nations Charter, the constitution of UNESCO and the Declaration of Human Rights
mark the age of universality in which man is striving to become truly the citizen of the One World of tomorrow. The way may prove to be long and tortuous,
and old habits and instincts will not be eradicated easily; but the necessity
for a global order ensuring peace and gradually undertaking planetary tasks
and responsibilities is now beyond question. Education for peace and world-

mindedness must permeate the life-span and employ all possible modalities. From being located on the fringes of traditional systems, education for peace and international understanding has to become an essential element at the heart of the educational process. Peace is also essential to the promotion of democratization and development. Education for a non-violent social order is a viable form of lifelong education and essential to the building of the foundation of peace in the minds and hearts of men.

The Quality of Life. Such a foundation of peace and human brotherhood must be built on a new fabric of values to live by. The material power of man emanating from the fruits of science and social organization and fed by the acquisitive instinct rooted in both greed and adventure often leads to unbridled affluence and waste, self-centredness, aggression, sense of insecurity, triviality of action, and vulgarity of taste. These pitfalls of material opulence need to be eliminated by the pursuit of a quality of life based on the practice of humanistic values. The concept of quality of life is an emerging vision of our times, specially reflected in the spirit and attitudes of youth. The change in the role and cultural values of youth is a contemporary phenomenon about which little research has been attempted so far. There are also signs of revulsion against obsession with economic growth, conspicuous affluence and gross consumption. The measure of GNP as an indicator of development is being questioned and new ways of attaining and evaluating happiness are stressed by creative people in all walks of life. The concept of quality of life needs deeper exploration, but it has undoubtedly become an important goal of development. Each society must seek its own quality of life from the roots of the past, the strivings of the present and the vision of the future; but there are certain humanistic values which should be sought and shared by all. The concept of quality of life is in essence the vindication of the human spirit which was weakened by the worship of mammon and machine.

Transcendence. The human spirit is now fortified by the attitudes and fruits of science and a new assertion of humanism. The humanism of the past was based upon man's discovery of himself, followed by liberation from taboos and dogmas accepted in fear and superstition. The humanism of tomorrow seeks to substitute love for power, stresses the brotherhood of man and his common humanity, and probes toward a new relationship of man with the cosmos. It aims

at an act of transcendence which is within the reach of man, who is now
more than ever the maker and arbiter of his destiny. The final aim of
lifelong education is transcendence from the confused and troubled state
of contemporary man to a new humanism, both human and cosmic, free, wise,
compassionate and loving.

Such a vision of the future is implicit in the contemporary idea
of Evolutionary Humanism, so well described by Julian Huxley,[3] the first
Director-General of UNESCO. Let me recall his own words written in 1957:

> If asked to name the most remarkable developments of the
> present century, I suppose that most people would say the
> automobile and the aeroplane, or the cinema, the radio and
> TV, or the release of atomic energy, or perhaps penicillin
> and the antibiotics. My answer would be something quite
> different - man's unveiling of the face and figure of the
> reality of which he forms a part, the first picture of human
> destiny in its true outlines.
>
> This new vision is based upon the enlargement of knowledge,
> not only or even mainly (as laymen, and I fear also many
> scientists seem to think) in the natural sciences, but equally
> in the social sciences and the humanities.
>
> During my lifetime, I have seen its gradual emergence, piece
> by piece.
>
> From these bits and pieces of new knowledge, new realizations
> and new understandings, man is capable of forming a new picture
> of himself, of his place in nature, his relations with the rest
> of the universe, his role in the universal cosmic process - in
> other words, his destiny; and on that, in turn, building new
> and more adequate beliefs.

The most important of these beliefs built on the new concept of man's
destiny is the possibility of lifelong education to make an education-oriented society which is permeated by the idea of evolutionary humanism.
Huxley describes his own living experience of evolutionary humanism in the
following words:[4]

> The primary function of earlier systems was of necessity to
> maintain social and spiritual morale in face of the unknown.
> But the primary function of any system today must be to ut-
> ilize all available knowledge in giving guidance and encourage-
> ment for the continuing adventure of human development ... The
> present is the first period in the long history of the earth in
> which the evolutionary process, through the instrumentality of
> man, has taken the first step towards self-consciousness. In
> becoming aware of his own destiny, man has become aware of the
> entire evolutionary process on his planet; the two are inter-
> locked.

Towards the close of his life Huxley asserts his faith in transcendence with a clear and forceful conviction:

> Man's most sacred duty is to realign his possibilities of knowing, feeling and willing to the fullest extent, both in individual achievements and social development, in the further evolution of mankind ... This will be the most powerful religious motive in the next stage of our evolution.
>
> The human species can, if it wishes, transcend itself, not just sporadically, in individuals here and there, but in its entirety, as Humanity.[4]

1.4 The relevance of history

The nine historical forces outlined above point the way to the understanding of the concept of lifelong education and its further evolution. The discipline of history is undergoing significant changes. No longer is the historian obsessed with political and national developments and the study of isolated events and movements of the past. UNESCO's noble attempt at the preparation of a scientific and cultural history of mankind, more significant in conception than in execution, is a pointer toward the writing of history relevant to our time. Each generation creates its own image of the past. So far history has been confined to the limited horizons of the tribe and the nation, and the historical method has conformed predominantly to the requirements of scientific truth and objectivity for establishing historical facts. Recent developments broaden the horizons of history and open out new lines of investigation and new ways of synthesizing the fragmented knowledge of the past into more significant patterns for a fuller understanding of the nature of man and his society. The evolution of lifelong education needs to be guided by the method and spirit of history, and enriched by historical thinking and knowledge.

In the pursuit of the objectives of peace, universality, quality of life and humanism, the study of history has an abiding role and relevance. We need to develop the sense of history which is a kind of habit, flair and capacity for seeing and understanding events in their larger context of past roots and future trends, thereby acquiring the insight and wisdom for making right choices and decisions. We need to nurture the spirit of history in its sense of wonder and vision and its perpetual consciousness of time as a river of experience and awareness, comprehending at each moment the past, the present and future. With

the sense and the spirit of history we need to search for the meaning of history
beyond what is trivial and transitory, emanating from that pursuit of the
strictest scientific truth enriched by imagination and wonder which brings
wisdom and humility.

2. History and Lifelong Education

2.1 The idea of lifelong education in history

In the first part of this essay the emerging concept of lifelong education has been attributed to a conjunction of historical developments and
forces peculiar to our times. It is true that lifelong education as an overall system, consciously planned and systematically operated by a society for
the good of all its members, has never existed in the past, and even in our
present time it is still only a concept, waiting to become a reality through
far-reaching changes of content, scope, methodology and organization of education. A profound and comprehensive transformation of institutions, practices
and objectives remains to be achieved; at present we are merely groping toward a viable theory that could guide the changes to come. The novelty of lifelong education as a new way of education offered by a society to all its members through all possible modalities and diverse choices is obvious. But this
should not make us forget the existence of the idea of lifelong learning in
various forms in all civilizations known to history. The transmission of culture from generation to generation and people's participation in traditional
cultures lead inevitably to ways and means of learning far beyond the limited
span of formal education, embracing more or less the totality of the life-span.

Discussing lifelong education with groups of educationists in India, I
have often heard the comment that it was not really anything new but had always
existed in all civilized societies, that the very process of living and participating in any manner in the life of the community entails continuous learning.
This view is heard not only among sophisticated groups in metropolitan cities,
but also in the remote countryside among those involved in programmes of rural
development for poor agricultural and traditional communities. This is natural
in societies where culture reigns supreme and tradition holds sway while education is neither universal nor relevant and modern, and the new developments

described earlier have not yet penetrated the masses and the general life of
the community. The continuity of traditional culture and its isolation from an
alien form of education in India and elsewhere in several developing countries
provides opportunities of lifelong learning to the masses. Such opportunities
are, however, casual and sporadic, chancy and incidental, and almost always
limited to the preservation of a traditional past, rarely preparing people for
rapid change in all sectors and dimensions of life. It is clear from what has
been said earlier that the emerging concept of lifelong education, derived from
the crisis of our times and the new developments confronting man, is not a product of the past but a possibility of the future, largely assisted by the reality and vision of evolutionary humanism. It calls for new transformations in
both education and society and responds to needs that did not exist earlier.

While it is important to distinguish between the lifelong education of the
emerging future and the cultural learning of traditional societies, it is also
of the utmost importance to understand and appreciate the idea and ramifications
of lifelong learning in history, and especially their relevance to the modernization of education in the developing countries. All civilized societies seek
stability and the perpetuation of beliefs and insights on which the social order
is based. Religion and philosophy offer explanations of existence and its goals,
and enjoin upon individuals duties and responsibilities for maintaining the social order and its ideologies. Social institutions such as religion, caste, community and family impose their own disciplines and provide facilities to their
members to imbibe types of knowledge and experience projected by these institutions. The process of human growth through the traditional stages of life is always an educational experience. It is the lot of all individuals to experience
suffering and satisfaction, pain and pleasure, success and failure, and be school
ed in the whims and tests of fate and fortune. To a few it may be given to experience love and ecstasy, the essence of beauty and the poetic vision. All these
are precious elements of lifelong cultural learning.

Traditional societies inherit from their past of faith and religious belief, from their myths and history, ideas and forms of cultural learning which
continue to guide and educate. Religious scriptures and classical literatures pro
vide numerous injunctions and inspiring utterances for the training of the mind
and the refinement of the spirit for all believers. An anthology of such sayings
and writings bearing upon the idea of lifelong learning would have more than mere

historical interest.

The Hindu idea of lifelong cultural learning is abundantly reflected in the religious scriptures and literary classics: For example, in the fourth discourse of the *Bhagavadgita*, entitled "The Yoga of Wisdom", Lord Krishna says to his friend and disciple Arjuna:

> All actions in their entirety culminate in wisdom. Learn thou
> this by *discipleship*, by *investigation*, and by *service*. The
> wise, the seers of things, will instruct thee in wisdom. And
> having known this, thou shall not again fall into this con-
> fusion ... Verily there is no purifier in this world like wis-
> dom; he that is perfected in Yoga finds it in the self in due
> season.[5]

Thus the attainment of wisdom is the ultimate end of lifelong learning and the way is the science and art of Yoga which the Bhagavadgita expounds in its various aspects. In modern terms discipleship, investigation and service comprehend both formal and non-formal education, stressing the role of great teachers, free enquiry, social service, work experience etc.

Again the Taittiriya Upanishad expresses the joyful spirit of students seeking knowledge together through both study and action:

> Let us live together. Let us dine together,
> Let us do daring deeds together. Let us
> beget inner energy by our joint study.
> Let us not indulge in mutual hatred.
> Om! Peace, Peace, Peace, Peace.[6]

The Upanishads, the Jatakas, and other ancient Indian works underline the superiority of knowledge to material acquisition, and there are many writings, such as the fable of Shvetaketu, that express some surprisingly contemporary concepts of lifelong education. Thus according to Apastamba, Shvetaketu lays down: "He who desires to study more after having settled as house-holder shall dwell two months every year with collected mind in the house of his Teacher".[7]

The Buddha preached:

> The teacher, brethren, should regard the pupil as his son. The
> pupil should regard the teacher as his father. Thus these two,
> by mutual reverence and deference joined, dwelling in community
> of life, will increase and win growth and progress in this Norm-
> Discipline. I do enjoin, brethren, that ye live ten years in
> charge of a teacher. Then he who has completed his tenth year of
> discipleship may have a charge himself.[8]

The *Car of the Norm*, symbolizing the objectives of education, is described as follows:

> Whoso the Faith and Wisdom hath attained -
> His states of mind, well-harnassed, lead him on.
> Conscience the pole, and Mind the yoke thereof,
> And Heedfulness the watchful charioteer:
> The furnishments of Righteousness, The Car :
> Rapture the axle, Energy the wheels,
> And Calm, yokefellow of the Balanced Mind :
> Desirelessness the drapery thereof:
> Goodwill and Harmlessness his weapons are,
> Together with Detachment of the mind.
> Endurance is the armour of the Norm,
> And to attain the Peace that car rolls on.
> 'Tis built by self, by one's own self becometh -
> This chariot, incomparable, supreme:
> Seated therein the sages leave the world,
> And verily they win the victory.[9]

The watchful charioteer of the Buddha's Car of the Norm is Heedfulness that is comprised of curiosity, alertness, and awareness of the total situation in all its aspects, the unifying and directing force of all action. The last words of the dying Buddha are significant:"Come now, brethren, I do remind ye: 'Subject to decay are all compounded things'. Do ye abide in heedfulness."

The religious literature of all cultures abounds in similar examples of the importance of the idea of lifelong cultural learning and the overriding value of education. The prophet of Islam recorded: "Verily God does not alter the fortunes of a nation until they bring about a change in their own psychology".[10] Guru Nanak, the founder of the Sikh faith sang:

> Make wisdom thy mother, contentment thy father
> Truth thy brother - this is best.
> Make divine knowledge thy food, compassion thy store-keeper.
> And the voice which is in every heart the pipe to call to repast.[11]

The ideal of service to fellowmen is proclaimed in words inscribed in stone by Emperor Asoka more than two thousand years ago: "I am now attending to people's affairs at all places ... I consider it my only duty to promote the welfare of all men." (Inscription of Asoka). Kautilya defines intellect: "Inquiry, listening, perception, retention in memory, reflection, deliberation, inference and steadfast adherence to conclusions are the qualities of mind."[12] The *Naladiyar* states:

> Learning is the best legacy. It cannot be taken from its place
> of deposit; it does not perish anywhere by fire; if kings of
> surpassing grandeur are angry they cannot take it away; and
> therefore what any man should provide for his children as a
> legacy is learning. Other things are not real wealth.[13]

And now listen to the voices of two prophetic poets of modern India
both steeped in its composite cultural tradition and inspired by the vision
of the future that stems from the past. Mohammad Iqbal wrote:

Life is preserved by purpose
Because of the goal, its caravan bell tinkles;
Science is an instrument for the preservation of life,
Science is the means of establishing the self,
Science and art are servants of life.[14]

And the following comes from a Bengali song of Rabindranath Tagore:

On the shores of Bharat
Where men of all races have come together
Awake, O my mind
Standing here with outstretched arms
I send my salutation to the God of Humanity.
None live forever, brother. Keep that in mind and rejoice:
Beauty is sweet to us because she dances to the same fluting tune
as our lives,
Knowledge is precious to us
Because we will never have time to complete it.[15]

The traditional writings and verbal tradition preserve for the Indian
peoples their notions and values of lifelong learning. The same is true of
other cultures, especially those which still keep traditions alive and pul-
sating. The idea of lifelong education in history is of paramount importance
for planning the transition from existing systems to the emerging structures of
lifelong learning in the developing countries where traditional forms and modes
can facilitate the change and carry the new idea to the masses of people.

The missing link between the idea of lifelong cultural learning in history backed by numerous traditional rituals, practices and institutions surviving into the present times and the emerging concept of the new systems of
lifelong education based on the contemporary developments and possibilities described earlier is an adequate history of education. It is surprising that the
large and often the most expensive operation of public spending, education, in
almost all societies is seldom assisted by sound historical foundations. Until
recently very little research was devoted to the history of education, and published works of sufficiently high standard are few and far between. Historical and
sociological approaches can make immense contributions to the identification and
solution of educational problems and guide the transition to new systems of lifelong education.

Fortunately, signs and trends in contemporary historiography point to the

growing interest in the history of education both among historians and the
larger readership now getting involved in the numerous facets of education in
the broadest sense. Partly this new interest stems from the recent popularity
of social history and the development, especially in the USA, of what may be
called intellectual history concerned with the interaction of ideas and individual thinkers with the society at large; partly it is the growing need of
planners and scientists concerned with development who have begun to emphasize
social change instead of mere economic growth, and consequently need to know
how education has helped or hindered the process of making people attuned to
conscious change and planned action. For the educationist who will teach, administer or plan in the context of lifelong education, adequate knowledge of
the history of education is essential. Its insights can contribute significantly
to the innovative and creative action required for the renewal and transformation of education.

    At present historical research in the field of education lags sadly be-
hind. New initiatives are more evident in the developed countries, especially
of North America and Europe, than in the developing countries which need this
type of knowledge for planning and launching educational reforms. Even in the
West much of what passes for history of education is only histories of specific
institutions or pedagogical reformers. What is needed is a systematic and broad-
based history of education with its various ramifications in society. We need to
study the effects of education in perpetuating particular class structures and
maintaining certain forms of social stratification. The relationship between education and politics is of special interest for the study of elitism and the
power-structure of newly independent countries. New types of historical works on
education can exercise considerable influence upon the study of politics, economic development and social change. Care must, however, be taken to develop the
history of education as a part of the larger organic life of the entire society;
the tendency to make it a narrow and specific area of study should be avoided.
Interest in the history of education could be stimulated and new insights of
great value gained by a new UNESCO initiative for the writing of a world history
of education on the lines of its "Scientific and Cultural History of Mankind".
Such a task is appropriate to UNESCO's objective and its present programme
priorities, which stress the need for educational change in the context of the
quest for peace and development.

2.2 Contemporary patterns and problems of historical studies

The need for historical studies of education and society is evident and present trends are encouraging, although far greater interest in this field should be evinced by Asian historians. In recent years, there have been other developments of historical studies giving rise to a number of problems and opportunities. Since the end of the Second World War an immense increase in the bulk and range of historical knowledge has taken place and both the sources and the vistas of the historian have expanded far beyond the conditions and expectations of earlier generations which concentrated on exploration of the past from the angle of the nation-state and the supremacy of the West. The historian's time-span has been extended fantastically by the work of pre-historians, geologists, biologists and archaeologists, and the sciences of man and nature yield new insights and riddles concerning the past of man on our planet. The last two decades have witnessed a remarkable shift of interest from Europe-centred history to the past of peoples and civilizations of Asia, Africa and Latin America. New branches of history, such as the history of science and technology, have opened up. The close relationship between history and the social sciences is a subject of growing interest to both historians and social scientists. Along with the rapid growth of the content and range of historical studies the philosophical questions of the meaning of history and the interpretation of the historical process pose problems of fresh perspectives, organizational principles and adequate frameworks projecting into the prospects of a world history on a more systematic and scientific basis. For the purposes of this essay there is no need to go into the details of recent developments of historiography and historical knowledge, but brief reference to them is necessary in order to understand the role of history and its uses for the emerging systems and patterns of lifelong education.

The work of Toynbee, the German historicist school, and Marxist history merely indicate the vast scope and diversity of the historical thinking and writing of our own time, and the emergence of issues and problems that claim the attention of a new generation of historians. It is not only the nature and meaning of history that leads to debate and controversy. The historian's craft and methodology also experience profound changes resulting from the enormous explosion of source materials.

The expansion of documentation in the post-war years which proceeds at a fantastic rate has created a situation calling for revolutionary changes in the historian's method and style of work. Everywhere the bureaucratic nature of modern government, corporations and international organizations, assisted by the typewriter, printing, stenography, dictating machines and other mechanical devices, produces a massive array of papers destined for historical archives. This traditional form of documentary material is further supplemented by new forms of recording, such as photographs, films, tapes, and by oral traditions and interviews. The shift of the historian's interest from political to economic history adds enormously diversified materials of social history, flooding every archive and defying all efforts to analyse and calendar such materials in any detail. All this makes the individual historian's task of compliling a manageable documentation for answering his questions almost impossible. From around 1950 a host of newly-independent countries of the so-called Third World have organized their national archives on a scale far surpassing the efforts of their colonial masters, placing new materials at the disposal of the historian.

Nor is the recent extension of history confined to sources and methods alone. Even more important is the developing relationship of history with other disciplines and new knowledge. Predominantly in the United States the use of quantitative techniques, data analysis, ecological correlation, econometrics and several other conceptual tools began to be employed in the historian's work. From these methodological developments and the special features of North American society a new alignment between history and the social or behavioural sciences emerged and spread to other parts of the world.

The impact of the social sciences has broadened the range of historical materials, enhanced the scientific objectivity of the historian's work, multiplied the tools of investigation, diversified the methods of study, and added new concepts and interdisciplinary possibilities. But the significance of history as a mode of thought and as a comprehensive, synthesizing and unifying system of the science of man has not diminished in any way. As the American historian Page Smith[16] sums up:

> History is and must remain pre-eminent among the social sciences, for it is history that brings together the results of the inquiries that the various social sciences carry on and shapes them into a comprehensive account related to the course of historic events.

2.3 New dimensions in history: the larger view

The impact of the social sciences has indeed been fruitful and creative both for the methodology of historians and the nature of their subject-matter and sources of knowledge. Historical studies have been further marked by an interdisciplinary approach and the extension of the historian's field of vision both in time and in space.

The most important development which we are still witnessing is the gradual abandonment of the Europe-centered view of history and the opening of new vistas not only to comprehend the great civilizations of China, India and Islam, but also those traditionally regarded as "outside history", the cultures of Africa, the steppe-lands of Central Asia, the mountainous regions of Burma, Thailand and Vietnam, and pre-Columbian America. The historian's drift is clearly towards a larger view of all mankind, and in this process history joins hands with archaeology and anthropology. "Without world history there is no sense in history", as Reinhard Wittram has written.[17]

The widening of the range and vision of history acquired speed and urgency as a result of the great change in the world situation since 1945 and especially since the rapid advance between 1957 and 1960 of the process of decolonization. At the 13th International Congress of Historical Sciences in Moscow in 1970, L. Elekee remarked pertinently: "In the contemporary epoch a living history demands a concrete revision of universality and a more consequential and far-reaching application of it in historical research."[18]

This implied that institutions everywhere should transcend their national and ethnographic limitations. While the Europe-centred approach began to be abandoned in the West, new schools of nationalistic history developed in the newly-independent countries of Asia and Africa. This was necessary to correct the colonialist interpretations of European scholars of preceding generations, but it also posed the possibility of replacing the old colonialist myth by a new nationalist myth. The modernization of historical studies in the countries of Asia owes its impetus to the assimilation of Western methods and concepts. Initially the main concern was to adopt and assimilate the methods of internal and external criticism for thorough research and scientific accuracy, largely under the influence of the German historical school of the 19th century. From 1920 onwards the influence of Marxism and of historical materialism gathered strength in China, India and elsewhere in Asia. The most recent trend is towards the assimilation and adaptation of

the sophisticated techniques of analysis developed in the West during the last
twenty years.

Undoubtedly an important reason for the upsurge of interest in the history of the countries of Asia and Africa among Western historians was political. It reflected a new awareness of the growing importance of the countries
of the Third World in the contemporary scene and the consequent need for a
better understanding of their traditions and historical evolution. The independence of India in 1947 and the Communist victory in China in 1949 led to
an increasingly active concern with the history of the non-western world. These
events, as K. M. Panikkar pointed out, marked the end of the European epoch
and the advent of a new stage in world history in which the civilization of
China, India and Islam became as important to historical thinking as the civilization of the West.[19]

The abandonment of Europe-centrism accompanied by the establishment of
new branches of study, such as the history of science and technology, the extension of the historian's time-span through pre-history and archaeology and the
insights and methods of the social sciences, resulted in the emergence of many
problems and opportunities for history, and gave rise to the question of finding a relevant framework. The national and political framework of the 19th and
early 20th centuries was obviously inadequate and by the middle of this century
there was wide-spread discontent with old patterns. New knowledge and perspectives called for fresh integration and more meaningful organizing principles. However, the continuing reality of the nation-state, the search for national identity
by newly-independent societies, and the habit and inertia of the historians kept
the old patterns alive. But new forces are at work and there is a growing tendency among contemporary historians to turn from a national to a regional framework.
Braudel's history of the Mediterranean world,[20] Stoianovich's work on Balkan
civilization,[21] Hall's *History of South-East Asia*,[22] G. H. Kimble's *Tropical
Africa*,[23] several regional histories of the Middle East and Latin America and
the increasing popularity of area studies are examples of this tendency to work
in a regional framework. But such efforts are regarded only as a stage on the way
to a larger conception of world history which must be universal in spirit and
concept and regard all mankind as the subject of its study.

The Dutch historian Huizinga pointed out in 1936 that "Our civilization
is the first to have for its past the past of the world, our history is the

first to be world-history".[24] The emergence of new forces outlined in the
first part of this essay reflects a new phase of global integration calling for a wider view of the past. But between need and response, ideal and
reality, there is still a large gap. Even in 1955 E. G. Pulleyblank had to
plead that China should not "be regarded as outside the mainstream of human
history".[25] The difficulties of writing universal histories proved to be
almost insurmountable. After the appearance in 1963 of the first volume of
the UNESCO six-volume *History of Mankind* many similar cooperative efforts
appeared without achieving any notable success. Loosely linked chapters or
monographs contributed by teams of specialists are no substitute for the
unifying vision of an individual historian.

The difficulties of constructing a world history are not only practical ones which could be surmounted with greater experience and better
organization of materials. There are more serious theoretical difficulties.
As W. T. de Bary has pointed out: "We have no convenient and accepted framework in which to present world civilization as a whole".[26] The views of world
history are different from New York, London, Paris, Moscow, Cairo, Peking or
Delhi. Equally elusive is the search for an organizing principle of world
history. Idealistic premises such as Lord Acton's conception of liberty as the
central thread of all history, or the unifying factor of Divine Providence
seen by Christian writers such as Christopher Dawson and Herbert Butterfield,
make less sense than the materialist position of Marxist historians. The theme
of Man's conflict with his environment has often yielded good results. For
William H. McNeill the key factor in human development is technolgocial advance,
while J. H. Plumb pins his faith on the material progress of mankind as the one
element of the human story that makes sense. Both the influence of Marxism and
the applications of archaeology and pre-history strengthen the current fashion
of a materialist interpretation of world history. Marx himself took the view
that world history was only gradually produced by "intercourse and the division
of labour between nations". As R. F. Wall has written, in taking a world view,
"history becomes not a study of facts, but a study of interrelationships:
cultural, social and commerical, as well as diplomatic and religious".[27] Indeed,
the problem of world history can only be solved by breaking into a new dimension
and adopting a global instead of a national or local approach. This is best
achieved by a comparative study of the institutions, habits, ideas, beliefs and

assumptions of men in all times and places. The stuff of world history is
the perennial problems that confront all societies and civilizations. But
we have to go a long way to give to world history the unity, coherence
and meaning undoubtedly required by an emerging global order.

2.4 The place of history in lifelong education

The preceding sections attempted a bare outline of the developments
in historical studies during the last quarter century. The situation is complex and still fluid, as is the larger problem of reorganization of knowledge
into disciplines and areas of study in conformity with present-day needs and
in the context of the great explosion of knowledge that continues unabated.
Traditional divisions and relationships are no longer relevant; and requirements of both specialization and broad synthesis point to the need for new
arrangements and interdisciplinary approaches for solving concrete problems
of mankind. The transition to a global order, the new vistas of development
and the fascinating possibilities and implications of evolutionary humanism
call for adequate systems of lifelong education reflecting the diversity of
cultures and the unity of science. Each society will develop its own pattern
of lifelong education from its historic roots and experience and the uniqueness of its culture; and such patterns will also be influenced by the uniformity of science, which is valid for all and can be made available to all. A new
global humanism must be made the overall quest of lifelong education. It has
to be based upon a synthesis of knowledge and wisdom, of science and the human-
ities, of reason and mystery, with man himself remaining at the centre of the
dynamic process of change, retaining his value and dignity as the creator of
knowledge and also as the sole arbiter of its application. To the power of
creation we shall need to bring the quality of discrimination and the virtue of
"heedfulness" which the Buddha recommended to his disciples. Only in this way
can we bring the spirit of man into the centre of the planetary civilization
of tomorrow and thus overcome the crisis of our times mentioned earlier.
Humanism requires a unifying core of values. How far can history provide such a
core? In other words, what can history contribute to the foundations of lifelong education?

I believe that historical studies can make very significant contributions
to the evolving concept of lifelong education by defining and promoting its

objectives and enriching its content. More than any other discipline,
history can help in giving a concrete form to the essence of humanism.
By spreading the humanist outlook, which is essential to the emergence
of an education-oriented society, it can promote conditions and attitudes
congenial to the growth of lifelong education. An education-oriented society is necessary for lifelong education. Perhaps we are already at the
threshold of such a development in human affairs. To sum up briefly, the
following nine aspects of history are relevant to the foundations of lifelong education:

2.4.1 *The idea of lifelong education in history*

Reference has already been made to the idea of lifelong education
implicit in the concepts and modalities of cultural learning in almost all
civilizations of the past. We can surely profit from a deep understanding
of the beliefs and practices of the past in systematically building relevant
structures and systems for the future. The history of education can yield
insights and lessons for wise and realistic planning of education for the
future.

2.4.2 *History and the search for the meaning of life*

From the examples given from the cultural heritage of India to illustrate
the idea of lifelong cultural learning, it is evident that such learning was
closely related to the search for the meaning of life. The historian's quest
for the re-creation of the past arises out of the self-time-space relationship,
a dimension through which saints and sages, philosophers and scientists have
often probed into the mystery of life and its meaning. Historical thinking has
been directed to this quest. The present search for a universal history and the
new awareness of the state of mankind groping towards a global order are parts
of a larger quest of the mind to comprehend the meaning of life.

2.4.3 *History and human affairs*

As history deals with human affairs, with men in action in concrete
situations of thought and feeling, reason and unreason, faith and impulse,
wisdom and folly, its subject matter helps towards an understanding of human
nature and an appreciation of man's immense potentialities as well as his tragic

limitations. History has always been considered an essential part of the
training of those who are called upon to lead their fellow-men in the
ordering of societies; philosophers and thinkers have also drawn upon it
for constructing beliefs and ideologies to hold groups together and inspire
people to action. For citizenship and the art of politics knowledge of history is considered essential. This will be even more important when the
process of democratization calls for the participation of all in the
governance of society and its institutions. Learners in lifelong systems of
education will need to understand the complexities of human nature and the
working of human institutions in order to adapt themselves to rapid changes
in the human and social environments.

2.4.4 *History as a discipline of the mind*

History as a branch of knowledge concerned with the past of man and
his societies and the interactions between them has the dual burden of sub-
jectivity of interpretation and objectivity of scientific knowledge. The
discipline of history, therefore, partakes of both art and science. The historian must follow the scientific method to collect his evidence for establishing facts as they really happened and conform to the highest standards of
objectivity in this search. He must shed his own preferences and prejudices
and try to recreate the past as it actually existed. The poetic element infuses
into dry facts and dead skeletons the meaning and throb of life. Beyond the
scientific labour and artistic exposition, there may be the contemplative and
philosophical effort to relate the patterns of the past to some larger scheme
or process in time and reality. This is the historian's vision. Objective
truth, subjective interpretation and poetic vision are thus combined in the
discipline of history, which affords to the mind a unique form of experience and
a most valuable type of training. A great historian combines knowledge with wisdom, realizes the immense value of science and also its limitation, and attempts
to bring back to life what is dead and gone and could never be experienced
directly. He must be a bit of the scientist, artist, poet and philosopher all
rolled into one.

2.4.5 *History and human growth*

Lifelong education is a consciously planned process of growth throughout the life-span. The idea of stages of life such as the four *ashrams* of
the Hindus - student, house-holder, teacher and philosopher - is familiar
to many cultures. The Hindus believed in the cosmic path of the essence of
the living organism from its mysterious origins through manifold forms into
the equally mysterious godhead. Likewise, the individual grows from childhood
to youth, adulthood and old age, seeking knowledge, practising the arts and
gathering wisdom through experience. Historical studies contribute effectively to the process of individual growth as well as to the general health and
enlightenment of societies. The heritage of the past, acquired through a long
and elaborate process of cultural transmission, is a source of pride and stability, projecting values and standards to be attained with vigour and deter-
mination. The lives of great men and women show how success and merit can be
achieved. Historical biography is a powerful source of motivation and inspiration for the individual's growth.

2.4.6 *History and learning motivations*

Interest and pleasure strengthen the motivation of learners. History
can afford these in ample measure. Once the teacher has aroused curiosity
about the origins of present things and the mystery of the past, and has spark-
ed off the imagination of the pupil, there is enough to explore all through
the life-span, and the exploration can be so exciting and delightful, so simple
and rewarding. The avenues of history are many and one can choose according to
one's need or fancy. So many living things, monuments and historic sites evoke
the past; earnest and enthusiastic students can go to books and documents,
archaeological finds, museums, and films to satisfy their curiosity. Few subjects attract the imagination of the young and the curiosity of the adults as
history does. It is, however, necessary to evolve new learning schemes and
identify materials of study. Historical studies have a powerful potential for
correcting some serious faults in the motivations of young people, such as self-
centredness, intolerance , absence of imagination and understanding, an overriding concern with the present, lack of balance of mind, false assurance of
rightness produced by an insufficient range of experience and obsession with
one's own preoccupations and needs. History can correct these errors by creating

doubt about existing evidence and theories and by instilling wide understanding and real awareness of the range of human experience. It can create a
lively awareness of differences and diversities in both space and time, an
und standing of civilizations and cultures other than one's own. If the historical foundations in general education feed the imagination, enlarge mental
capacity, broaden vision and generate the beginnings of universal sympathy,
the basic motivation for lifelong learning will be well and truly established.
From lore of the past and the lessons of history one could enrich other quests
of the min , both human and scientific.

2.4.7 *History as a mode of thought and guide to action*

Lifelong education will not be limited to the present formal division of
knowledge into a number of disciplines. It will rely more and more on the
solution of real problems, the understanding of complex and changing situations
and the creation of new ideas and relationships relevant to the needs and preoccupations of the life-span. The learner will learn from experience, but the
manner and method of learning will be conscious, dynamic and systematic, and
not passive and sporadic. For such learning which leads to problem-solving,
history as a mode of thought and the method of history are of utmost relevance.
To understand problems and to penetrate through their complexity it is essential
to apply the method of history and see things in their true perspective in time
and space. All life is flux, and the past, present and future are reflected in
each moment of experience. For true understanding we must view problems and
situations in their historical context. Correct knowledge and adequate appreciation of roots and origins illuminate present reality and forecast the future, revealing diverse trends and various possibilities for our choice and decision. In
this way history becomes more a mode of thought to guide action and life-experi-
ence than a well-defined and limited discipline of knowledge. It is in this way
that it will be best used in lifelong education.

2.4.8 *History and cultural learning*

Cultural learning imparted through history produces a cultivated mind, refinement of spirit and keen sensitivity to all that is noble and beautiful. Its
brightest ornament is the sense of history which brings a balance and poise of
personality, breadth of outlook, warmth of sympathy, imaginative understanding

and appreciation of others, compassion, humility and love of life. The sense of history is not acquired merely by academic learning and wealth of scholarship; it comes from a deep contemplation of the past, and from the capacity to identify oneself with characters, events and movements. It is a product of the humane, artistic and poetic elements of history, a kind of luminosity of the mind attained through the combination of the dedicated pursuit of truth with the poignant feeling that the whole truth will never be known.

2.4.9 *History as personal experience*

Finally history has meaning and value because it becomes a personal experience. The past can never be resurrected in its original reality. With the exception of contemporary history, no historian has direct experience of events in history. The absence of perspective detracts from the value of what is described as contemporary history. To recreate the past from our present moment in time - and we can never shed this point of vision - the persons, events and phenomena of the past must enter our personal experience in order to enable us to understand them fully and to weave a meaningful pattern. The historian's personal experience of the past achieved through a synthesis of objective truth, rational analysis, imaginative perception, and the sense and vision of history draws him close to the essence of humanism and offers a way of lifelong learning that can contribute significantly to the making of the education-oriented society of tomorrow. The relevance of history to lifelong education is perennial and inexhaustible. The change of perspective alters our view of the past, and each age will construct its own image and pattern of the past. The urge for history is rooted in the nature of man. Only in the knowledge and awareness of the past and the throbs and glimmers of the future that accompany this experience can we escape the narrow temporal prison of the present, and enter the experiences and aspirations of our fellow-beings in all ages. Only in this way can man become not merely a citizen of this world but also a humble participant of the cosmos that is revealed to him progressively by the collective effort and vision of his whole species.

NOTES

1. Faure, Edgar, et al. *Learning to Be*. Paris: UNESCO, 1972.

2. Dave, R. H. *Lifelong Education and School Curriculum*. Hamburg: Unesco Institute for Education, 1973. (uie monographs 1).

3. Huxley, Julian. "New Bottles for New Wine". In Huxley, Julian (Ed.). *Essays*. London: Chatto & Windus, 1957. pp. 11 - 12.

4. Huxley, Julian. *Memories*. 2 vols. London: Harper & Row, 1972.

5. *Bhagavad Gita: The Lord's Song*. Text in Devangari and English transl. Annie Besant (Transl.). Madras: The Theosophical Publishing House, 1949.

6. "Taittiriya Upanishad" (late Vedic scripture). In *The Thirteen Principal Upanishads*. Robert Ernest Hume (Transl.). Oxford: Oxford University Press, 1921.

7. Kausalayan, B. A. *Jataka Stories*. Allahabad: Prayag Hindi Sahitya Sammelan, 1946.

8. "Mahavagga iii I" (one of the five parts of the *Vinaya Pitaka*). In Henry Clarke Warren (Transl. and Ed.). *Buddhism in Translations*. Cambridge, Mass.: Harvard University Press, 1906.

9. "Dhamma ratha from Samyutta Kikaya" (Buddhist Pati Canon, part of the *Sutta Pitaka*). In Conge, Edward (Ed.). *Buddhist Texts through the Ages*. Oxford: Bruno Cassirer, 1954.

10. *The Glorious Quran*. 2 vols. Arabic text and English transl. Marmaduke Pickthall (Transl.). Hyderabad Decca: Government Central Press, 1938.

11. Guru Nanak. "The Psalm of Life". In *Guru Nanak's Japji Sahib*. Gursharn Singh Bedi (Transl.). Amritsar: Jawahar Singh, Kirpal Singh, 1952.

12. *Kautilya - Arthastra*. R. Shamasastry (Transl.). Introduction by J. F. Fleet. Mysore: Mysore Printing and Publishing House, 1960.

13. "Naladiyar". Composed by a Jain saint of 8th century A.D. In *Tamil Sacred Literature*. Pope (Transl.).

14. Iqbal, Mohammad. *Aspects of Iqbal - A Collection of Selected Papers*. Read on the occasion of the 'Iqbal Day' Celebration on 9 January, 1938. Lahore: Quami Kutub Khana, 1938.

15. Tagore, Rabindranath. *Gitanjali* (Song Offerings). Introduction by W. B. Yeats. London: Macmillan, 1953.

16. Smith, Page. *The Historian and History*. New York: Knopf, 1964.

17. Wittram, R. *Das Interesse an der Geschichte*. Göttingen: Vandenhoeck und Ruprecht, 1958.

18. Quoted in *Main Trends of Research in Social and Human Sciences*, Part II, Chapter III - History by Geoffrey Barraclough. Paris: UNESCO. (In preparation)

19. Panikkar, K. M. *Asia and Western Dominance*. London: Macmillan, 1969.

20. Braudel, F. *The Mediterranean and the Mediterranean World in the Age of Philip II*. New York: Harper & Row, 1974.

21. Stoianovich, T. *"Balkan Civilization"*. Philadelphia, PA: Philadelphia Book Company, 1967.

22. Hall, D. G. E. *History of South-East Asia*. New York: St. Martin, 1968. (5th edition).

23. Kimble, G. H. *Tropical Africa*. 2 vols. New York: 20th Century Fund, 1960.

24. Huizinga, J. "A Definition of the Concept of History". In Klibansky & Paton (Eds.). *Philosophy and History*. Gloucester, MA: Peter Smith, 1936, p.8.

25. Pulleyblank, E. G. *Chinese History and World History*. Cambridge: 1955.

26. De Bary, W. T. & Embree, A. T., (Eds.). *Approaches to Asian Civilizations*. New York: Columbia University Press, 1964.

27. Wall, R. F. "New Openings: Asia". In *New Ways in History*. London: Times Literary Supplement (April, 1966).

ADDITIONAL SOURCES

Ballard, Martin (Ed.). *New Movement in the Study and Teaching of History*. London: Temple Smith, 1970.

Barnes, Harry Elmer. *History of Historical Writing*. 2nd edition. New York: Dover Publications, 1963.

Barraclough, G. *An Introduction to Contemporary History*. London: Watts, 1964.

Butterfield, Herbert. *History and Human Relations*. London: Collins, 1951.

Daedalus, Journal of the American Academy of Arts and Sciences. 1970/71, No. 1: Historical Studies Today. - 1971, No. 2: The Historian and the World of the 20th Century.

Dilthey, W. *Pattern and Meaning in History: Thoughts on History and Society.*
  London: George Allen & Unwin, 1961.

Hairani, Albert. *Vision of History: Near Eastern and Other Essays.* Beirut:
  Khayats, 1961.

"History and Social Science". *International Social Science Journal* 5,
  17.4.1965.

Hughes, H. Stuart. *History as Art and as Science.* (World Perspectives, Vol.32).
  New York: Harper and Row, 1964.

Transactions of the Asian History Congress. New Delhi: Indian Council of
  Cultural Relations, 1961.

Issawi, Charles. *An Arab Philosophy of History — Selections from the Prole-
  gomena of the Khaldun of Tunis (1332 — 1406).* London: John Murray, 1950.

Meyerhoff, Hans (Ed.). *The Philosophy of History in Our Time.* An Anthology.
  New York: Doubleday, 1959.

Mukerjee, Radhakamal. *The Destiny of Civilization.* Bombay: Asia Publishing
  House, 1964.

Plekhanov, G. V. (N. Beltov). *The Development of the Monist View of History.*
  Moscow: Foreign Languages Publishing House, 1956.

Stern, Fritz (Ed.). *The Varieties of History from Voltaire to the Present.*
  London: Macmillan, 1970.

Toynbee, Arnold J. *A Study of History.* 8 Vols. Oxford: Oxford University
  Press, 1961. - *An Historian's Approach to Religion.* Oxford University
  Press, 1956. - *Surviving the Future.* Oxford University Press, 1971. -
  One World and India. New Delhi: Orient Longmans, 1960.

Widgery, Alban G. *Interpretation of History: Confucius to Toynbee.* London:
  George Allen & Unwin, 1961

————. *The Meaning in History.* London: George Allen & Unwin, 1967.

C H A P T E R   4

THEORETICAL FOUNDATIONS OF LIFELONG EDUCATION:
A SOCIOLOGICAL PERSPECTIVE

Henri   J a n n e

> *"Plus est en vous!"*
> Motto of the Maison Gruuthuse,
> Bruges, 16th century

1. Sociology and Lifelong Education

1.1 The challenge to sociology

The fundamental significance of lifelong education lies in its final
implication: the abolition of systems which confine education for a man's
whole lifespan to his youth (even if some additional training is found
necessary at the adult stage). In lifelong education, learning and development of the personality become a *normal, constant* dimension of man's entire
life, a component - varying in explicitness and importance with each person
and each period in an individual's existence - of the "time budget" of
every man and woman, *at every age of their lives. It becomes an essential
part of culture*. The entire field of education, and particularly education of
youth, must, therefore, be designed on the basis of this break with the old
tradition of schooling (in which term we include the university): education
in youth must produce people motivated and able to learn throughout their
lives.

On the other hand, if education is to constitute an aspect of every phase
of life it must necessarily enter into *all* human activities *wherever they may
take place*. Thus society itself becomes educative. Education will no longer be
confined in time and place to youth and school: it will be "diffused".

Sociology is, therefore, called upon to furnish specific criteria that may help to elucidate those implications of lifelong education that touch upon its domain. It will have to mobilize its methods and experience, provide action schemes and direct research towards appropriate educational techniques. This is the challenge to sociology. To this end an effort should be made to draw up a theoretical and methodological inventory similar to the one attempted by Jack London (1964), who investigated whether sociology could contribute useful elements to *adult education*.

Of course, adult education is not the same as lifelong education. Although application of the principles of lifelong education will certainly entail an intensification of education for adults, this will differ fundamentally from adult education as understood at present, namely as a complement to or a prolongation of youth education. As such it is already expanding and has produced its own "school" tradition. Hence, while many of the aspects stressed by Jack London (1964) are of relevance to lifelong education, the distinction just made should be kept in mind. Furthermore though London rightly attaches importance to the interpersonal phenomena of sociology, which are especially pertinent to education, he does not, in our opinion, give sufficient weight to the *macrosociological* level of the social system. This is quite understandable considering that it is not the traditional type of education but the principle of lifelong education which reflects changes in the larger society and at the same time questions basic societal structures, such as the principles of social hierarchy and the concept of adult education as essentially vocational training.[1] In its traditional meaning adult education plays only a compensatory or complementary role and, no matter how widely spread, does not constitute a factor of fundamental change of the larger society.

1.2 Potential contributions of sociology in the field of social relations

Some sociological findings are relevant to the technical approach to lifelong education; they can serve as explanatory elements and as a theoretical framework. They have, as yet, not been adequately explored from this point of view. An exhaustive study would far exceed the scope of this paper, but it is suggested that one should be undertaken. Here we must limit ourselves to a definition of these elements as *initial* terms of reference.

1.2.1 *The theory of interpersonal relations*

In sociology interpersonal relations are regarded as vehicles of the "social force" (defined as the capacity of each of the two poles to influence the thoughts and/or actions of the other one, as the case may be). But these relations are also regarded as "communication channels", as vehicles for "messages" and information conveyed by means of "repertoires" and "codes" of which language is one of the factors in human societies. Of course the signs and the content of a message can themselves exert considerable influence, since a message may express a threat, a proposal of exchange, or an argument of persuasion.[2] Thus the interpersonal relationship implies a *potential educative or miseducative influence* on the weaker *individual or group* by the stronger. This notion is fundamental for the pedagogical and educational relationship, the major characteristic of which is that it makes social relations - which are otherwise *latent* or *imposed by myth or illusion* - manifest and controllable.

Further, sociology has developed an approach of great significance in this context: *typology*. It consists in classifying social relations according to definitions based on the criterion of similarity or analogy. The prototype of this method is botanical *taxonomy*. In sociology, binary or polarized typology is particularly important. Some pertinent types of educational relationship are the following:

- community or societal relations (especially the opposites "statutory" and "contractual", or "spontaneous" and "organized")

- primary and secondary relations

- manifest and latent relations

- normal and deviating relations

- competitive and cooperative relations

- relationships of intuitive understanding and rational explanation[3])

1.2.2 *The theory of social groups*

This concerns characteristic group structures, their methods of integrating members, their ways of exercising power, their systems of organization, the coherence of their action with the values inspiring them. The word "group"

is here understood in its widest sense:
- from informal groupings of individuals (a crowd, the "general
  public") to rigidly formal institutions;

- from the micro-group of the family to the macro-groups of
  social classes;

- from local communities to nations and international
  communities;

- from parishes to religious powers aiming at universality;

- from craftsmen's workshops to multinational businesses;

- from local municipal administrations to national-level
  central state administrations;

- from film clubs or individual commercial cinemas to the
  large systems of public or private mass media.

As Jack London (1964) points out, the findings of the sociology of
organizations would be of special interest in this connection, since they may
involve educational activities or provide explicit or implicit "models" for education. This is a field which the principle of lifelong education should
encourage educational sociologists to enter, for we still have some way to go
before we can organize the new system.

1.2.3 *Theories of personality*

Of particular interest in our context are the theories on personality as
a product of social life (interpersonal and group relations) and as a factor
affecting, or capable of affecting, interpersonal relations and group life, the
initiating mechanism being self-awareness, an essential goal of education if
we reject the behaviourist objective of conditioning.

These aspects are extensively covered by the contributions from A. J.
Cropley (Chapter 5) and C. De'Ath (Chapter 6), but as the boundaries between
sociology, psychology and social anthropology are difficult to draw in a study
of personality, an interdisciplinary approach to the subject seems particularly
important. To give merely some examples, use should certainly be made of the
following approaches:
- the *sociological* theories of Georges Gurvitch (1966) (the "depth
  levels" and the action of "ideologies");

- the observations accumulated and theories drawn up on the subject
  of "roles" and social status, especially the work of Talcott
  Parsons (1964) (see also Henri Janne 1968);

- the *psychological sociology* of George Herbert Mead (1965). As
  Jack London (1964) points out, several of Mead's theories are
  relevant to education, e.g.: his theory of the process by which
  the individual assimilates the view of the world held by the
  groups to which he belongs; the problem of the meaning of *"self"*
  in the context of social behaviour (man acquiring his "self" by
  making it the object of his own activity, and by enabling himself
  to act towards himself as he does towards others); the connection, in this perspective, between *self-control* and *social control*
  (integration in a group); and finally the defence mechanisms
  of the individual depending on his - correct or incorrect - self-
  evaluation in a given situation;

- *the American psychodynamic school* (Ruth Benedict, Abram Kardiner
  (1966), Margaret Mead, etc.), which in turn utilizes psychoanalysis to the extent that the latter has socio-cultural
  implications and thus represents a form of social anthropology;

- the *neobehaviourist school* and its application to education
  (especially by Skinner);

- the *sociometry* of Jacob Moreno (1954, 1965), and his school, which
  permits qualitative and quantitative definition of the structures
  and characteristics of relationships in small groups. Also, of
  course, the work done on group dynamics (overlapping with sociology and social psychology) by Kurt Lewin (1947, 1948, 1959) and its
  extension, especially by Solomon Ash (1952) and Bales (1950), opening up most interesting perspectives on problems relating to educational groups of limited size (microsociological level);

- the *Geneva school* of Jean Piaget (1969) and his disciples, such
  as Pieron and Reuchlin (1973), who are already dealing directly
  with educational problems, as are Basil Bernstein (1961) (1965),
  Bloom (1965, 1971) and many others.

The most comprehensive genuinely sociological approach to the subject of
personality would seem to be Talcott Parsons' (1964). These findings, pertinently applied to the social personality in an "educational situation" (formal or
informal), have as yet hardly been tapped for the purpose of creating a real
social psychology of education. It is still in its infancy. One only has to
think of the progress made, for obviously utilitarian reasons and for the
resolution of conflict situations, by the *psychology of work* (from Wilbert
Moore to Georges Friedmann).

1.2.4 *Theories and research relevant to some key phenomena*

- *division of labour* (without neglecting the Marxist perspective connecting it with the relations of production and the *social class* dialectic);

- *industrial relations and trade unionism* which include in their development itself phenomena of education in dialectic resulting from the confrontation of social forces (the reports and other work produced by or for the ILO provide the best basic documentation);

- *social mobility* (again overlapping with Marxist views, with the contributions of "technocratic" analysis of social systems and with research on social stratification);

- the research on *"time budgets"*, in particular the extensive international investigation coordinated by Ed. Szalai (1972).

There is no need to stress the weakness of theory in explaining the above phenomena, *since we will attempt to apply these theories to examine phenomena in education.* We only have to remember the failure of the manpower approach when used to define the quantitative and qualitative economic requirements of education (the difficulty arising from the lack of useful theories and data concerning the division of labour); or the absence of links between the theories about "equal opportunities" or "democratization of education" and those on social mobility.

Of course sociology cannot provide theories and ready-made data which may be used to solve such problems - far from it - but it does offer usable theoretical and methodological bases for indispensable developments. And these bases have been neglected, even ignored, by the theoreticians, policymakers and practitioners of lifelong education.

1.2.5 *General mechanisms for the maintenance of social relations*

This is a fundamental contribution of sociology together with social psychology. We refer in particular to the effects of initial social integration of newcomers into groups[4], shown by Eugene Dupréel (1947). Prime social integration - especially important in the educational context - is the condition of the *new* member of a group: the newborn child, the immigrant arriving in a strange society, the young worker entering employment. As we join new groups several times in the course of our lives, we undergo a process of assimilation to the specific values and relations of each of these groups. In every case the process consists, more or less consciously on both sides, in making the new entrant more similar to the members of the group than he was before joining it, since the newcomer wishes to be accepted and the group wants to maintain its equilibrium. There is even anticipated assimilation when an individual hopes to join a group he considers to be on a higher social level but not beyond his reach. Social integration is a mechanism for maintaining the existing order of social relations, and a concept essential to a sociology of education.

Social integration of new entrants is only an example - important, no doubt, but only one of many - of the mechanisms of *social pressure*. A long list of other mechanisms could be drawn from studies in social psychology and sociology:

- systems of meaning, prejudices, stereotypes, normative expectations, affective clichés, group standards, preconceived moulds, cultural models, inspiring or accelerating predictions, myths, psychoanalytical processes (all these being the more specifically psychological aspects);

- social role, fashion, language, social force (more specifically sociological aspects bringing functional mechanisms into play);

- advertizing, propaganda, persuasion, change (more specifically cultural or economic aspects involving more or less institutionalized groups).

The list, which may seem too long to some and incomplete to others, could, of course, be drawn up on quite different lines. But that is of no particular importance here. The point is that these processes and mechanisms of social pressure play a significant part in education.

1.2.6 *Sociological findings concerning "social change"*

London (1964) has shown how important these are for adult education. In this respect there is a paradox in sociology in that any social system consists of processes and mechanisms of resistance to change and assimilation of individuals to its traditional values and structures, while at the same time it bears within itself factors of change.

Before the Industrial Revolution, societies were characterized by their rigidity and their *sense of tradition*, but history shows us that they changed nevertheless, sometimes by very slow evolution, sometimes by sudden leaps (the

rapid appearance and expansion of the Communes, the Renaissance, the Reformation), or by "massive" uncontrolled events (the plague epidemic of the
1350s). But on the whole a man did not experience any personally significant
changes in the course of his life (partly because the slow means of communication restricted diffusion). In contrast, post-industrial-revolution societies are characterized by far-reaching changes affecting most individuals
many times in their lives. We are truly living at a "time of change", in
knowledge, communications, political, economic, social and cultural conditions,
technical development, hygiene, etc. While large-scale upheavals still occur
(the two World Wars, the Russian and Chinese revolutions, the emergence of
Japan as a world power), it is this "discontinuity" that affects the *individual*
far more frequently and creates internal conflicts in social systems. This is
an era of "conflictual discontinuity". This erratic and chancy type of change
is also typical of the so-called developing societies, where traditional
structures and values clash with those deriving from industrialization and
urbanization.

We therefore agree with London (1964) that this situation demands new
educational processes and calls for a revision of all educational systems,
even though these are a product of the Industrial Revolution (compulsory schooling, technical education and expansion of job-oriented universities). But the
concept of social change and the sociological findings on the factors and
mechanisms of this change should be used to understand, and to institute in
improved conditions, changes in education in the "lifelong" perspective which
will save individuals and social systems from painful or even disastrous upheavals (Ogburns's "cultural lag" theory (1922) still offers an excellent starting point). On the other hand, London rightly points out that on the microsociological level community development and lifelong education go hand in hand.
This is increasingly happening not only in the Third World, where such projects
started,[5] but also in the less developed regions of Europe, such as the province
of Bari in Southeastern Italy (the Social Centres of Lifelong Education set up
by Professor Gaetano Santomauro (1974) or in the region of Lorraine in France
(the remarkable work of Bertrand Schwartz (1973)).

1.2.7 *Some "specialized sociologies"*

We will limit ourselves to some disciplines that have a particular bearing on lifelong education.

   a) Urban sociology. The pertinent problems are the following:

- space utilization and housing: individual houses, flats, social units, satellite towns, etc.;

- changes in interpersonal relations and outlooks (resulting from the specific characteristics of urban life, especially family sociology);

- changes in the occupational structure (expansion of the tertiary sector, female labour force participation and its implications, especially for the role of women and sexual taboos);

- youth revolt (not confined to cities but most evident in urban areas);

- the freedom resulting from the anonymity of individuals in a mass society or in big organizations (social, political, economic, administrative organizations, cultural markets). This freedom encourages innovation, but also results in anomie (symptoms: increase of mental illness, use of drugs, delinquency) or, on the other hand, in restructuring of a neighbourhood according to community aspects (symptoms: increase in "local committees" and their initiatives);

- air and water pollution, not to mention noise and advertizing.

   b) The sociology of mass communication. Lasswell (1949), one of the founders of this branch of sociology, has become famous through his scheme: "a) Who? b) says what? c) to whom? d) in what circumstances? e) what are the results?". London (1964) points out that the sociology of mass communications has since advanced in several directions:

- the reaction of the "recipient" of the message is no longer considered to be largely rational or mechanical (as it was in the behaviourist S-R pattern) but *interpretative,* depending on the situation (a larger perspective than rationality because it involves attitudes in areas other than that of the message, and also the emotions, values, interests in the wider sense and loyalties);

- importance of the concept of the "reference group" (the communicator and the recipient respectively);

- the central notion of opinion leader (local or cosmopolitan) influencing both the communicator and the recipient.

Moreover, it has become clear that the overwhelming power of mass media is a myth. The television viewer, e.g., is not an isolated "recipient"; he reacts according to the social set-up to which he belongs, he makes choices. The original prediction of homogenization has therefore given way to a concept of different milieus. It has also been realized that TV tends to strengthen existing opinions rather than change them![6]

These are but examples. This branch of sociology and the techniques it uses have themselves benefited from the findings of the theory of interpersonal relations (see 1.2.1 above). Clearly both in theory and practice this branch of sociology is relevant to the development of the concepts and methods of lifelong education. The Open University formula is only one example of its application to educational processes in this perspective.

c) The sociology of culture. This is a vast field in which sociology so frequently overlaps with philosophy (see Chapter 2), social anthropology (see Chapter 6), and social psychology (see Chapter 5) that it is difficult to delimit its specific area. In order not to get lost in this immensely wide domain, it seems, therefore, advisable to confine ourselves in this paper to the subject of *leisure*, the most interesting in our perspective. The works of J. Dumazedier (1966, 1967) are recommended to readers desiring further information, and the aforementioned research papers on time budget offer a basic framework.

d) The sociology of education. Existing work in this discipline shows how very young and fragmentary this branch of sociology is. In fact, many books claiming to belong to the sociology of education are actually interdisciplinary efforts applying to the study of education not only sociological concepts (e.g., equality of opportunity), but also concepts from political statistical theory, social economy, the administrative sciences, pedagogy, child psychology, history of education, etc. The result is a "field" discipline. This interdisciplinary aspect explains the collective nature of many of these writings. A true sociology of education would utilize for the interpretation of educational phenomena all those sociological approaches of which we have attempted a - perhaps too general - definition when we suggested

the lines along which the principle of lifelong education could be
scientifically developed. For further reading on the sociology of education, the bibliographies of Torsten Husén (1969) and of Dr. Coster,
Sylvain and Hotyat (1970) can be recommended.

Particular attention is drawn to Ivor Morrish's book (1972),
which deals in a remarkable if condensed way with most of the problems
referred to in part 1.2 of this paper and also opens up new perspectives at the level of the larger society (see 1.3). Morrish modestly
calls his book "Introduction"; in fact it is a first comprehensive
concept of what sociology of education could and should be.[7]

1.3 Potential contribution of macro-sociology

1.3.1 *Systems approach*[8]

In systems theory the educational system is regarded as a sub-system of society. It is beyond the scope of this paper to give a full account of the systems
approach (of which there are several variants), its theories and methods. The intention here is merely to show why this approach is essential for a sociological
understanding of lifelong education. For this purpose the concept of "system" must
be defined. It is a paradigm of a general nature: the phenomena that constitute
reality in any field (physical, biological, social) are organized into aggregates
of interdependent factors, the dynamic inter-relations of which are at the same
time the result and the cause of the existence of each aggregate. Such aggregates
are systems. Any modification of one factor implies one or several modifications
of one or several other factors, and these modifications serve to maintain the
system by adapting it to changing conditions (internal or external ones). This adaptive interdependence derives from the integrative force inherent in any system
and can be translated into "laws" or, if you like, "constants", "regularities"
that are the subjects of scientific research. The life of a system consists of successive restorations of equilibrium by processes of self-compensation. Between the
"whole" and its parts there is thus a reciprocity of influence, but it is the whole
that ensures the coherence of the aggregate: if the influence of the parts (their
modification) exceeds the *limits* within which the system can remain what it is,
the system will be destroyed. Conversely, if integration can totally prevent
any transforming action of the parts, the system will finally become rigid

and static. The most stable and change-resisting of all the factors constituting the system form networks of relations (a kind of skeleton) representing its *structures*.

This paradigm has proved most useful to explain social systems, whose
constituent factors are *social relations*. In fact, social relations, and
nothing else, are what constitutes sociological reality and the subject of
sociology. Some of these networks are particularly stable and so become
structures.

Societies at the global level are the most clearly delimited systems,
but their complexity is such that they always contain sub-systems (types of
macro-structure): the political, economic, social, cultural and educational sub-systems and the "community" (the typical sub-system of interpersonal
relations).

*Seen from the macro-sociological level education must thus be con-
sidered as a sub-system.* It consists of relations that are stable enough to
be called structures and of more flexible ones, the conscious or unconscious,
formal or informal objective of which is acquisition of knowledge - scientific,
technical, cultural (e.g., history), moral, role-playing and use of status,
practising communication (e.g., writing) - by means of progressive and coherent intellectual, physical or sensory assimilation. Knowledge derived
from occasional or incidental information which does not involve a specific
process of acquisition thus does not form part of the sub-system education.

1.3.2 *Two major orientations of the systems approach in
sociology (functionalism and Marxism)*

Again it is necessary to be as concise as possible. The first of the two
orientations is a functional one. It sees the constituent factors of the social system - social relations - as "functions", i.e., as having to contribute
to the maintenance and continuity of structures. This analytical method -
first employed by social anthropology - explains why social systems and their
structures tend to last and to resist change, mainly by adaptation that remains
strictly within the systems' margins of tolerance.

As regards education, it may be said that the function of educational
systems is to socialize the young, i.e., to make them fit to live in the so-

ciety as adults. To that end they must be taught the language of their society and its other signs and means of communication, and be equipped with
technical competence commensurate with their aptitude so as to be able to
contribute to the production of goods and services in the framework of the
division of labour; they must be prepared to assume the roles necessary to
establish a family and to participate in social and political life, and
finally, to share the values on which the culture of their society is based
and which will direct their entire lives. Education is thus seen as a complex
process of "enculturation" - conscious and unconscious, partly organized and
partly incidental.

In this view the principle of lifelong education, a concomitant to the
development of adult education, will be interpreted *functionally* as an adaptation to the rapid changes in technology and scientific knowledge and to the
increased cultural needs due to the growth of leisure and the facilities
offered by the intensification of mass communications. The problems arising
from this great change in educational needs are, therefore, essentially
problems of adaptation. They will be seen from the viewpoint of *system maintenance* (the neo-capitalist society of consumption and its values), and hence
of the sub-system of education which will, as far as possible, remain "schooling" in its established structures though incorporating the new teaching
methods required to achieve these adaptations. Education will remain functionally organized to prepare youth for, and adapt adults to, the occupational and
social roles the system expects them to assume. The perspective will, therefore,
continue to be predominantly vocational and utilitarian. Cultural education of
adults will remain separated from the "true", "real", "sanctioned" educational
system. The functional systems approach helps us to understand this very real
trend of lifelong education.

The second orientation is the Marxist one. It defines constituent elements
of the social system in terms of *opposition* to the system. The "parts" are no
longer considered under their functional and positive aspects in regard to the
system, but under their critical and negative ones. It is the logic of contradiction[9] as against the logic of identity. Consequently Marxist sociology,
based on "social classes", proceeds in the opposite direction from the sociology
based on "social order". Actually each of the two logics sees only one side of

social reality; one might be more significant than the other in a particular situation, but to some extent both are always present.

The Marxist approach thus consists in looking for the tensions which, in principle, exceed or aim at exceeding the system's margins of tolerance (disintegration, revolution). The nature of the system itself is fundamentally dependent on the "relations of production", i.e., relationships among people which, as far as the production of goods and services is concerned, are determined by the rule of private ownership of the means of production, and this establishes at the same time the distinction between the ruling class (the bourgeoisie) and the dominated class (proletariat and wage-earners). The relations of production are technically dependent on the "productive forces", in particular on those techniques that demand a "division of labour" - not to be confounded with the relations of production. The latter depend in fact on the power system prevailing in the society concerned and on the distribution of the national product, proportionate to socio-occupational levels and governed by modalities such as profits and wages.

The relations of production constitute the "material base" of society creating a social edifice within society: the superstructure. This includes law, the state, science, religion, culture, ideologies - and education. The superstructure aims at maintaining the social system and is built for that purpose.[10]

In this perspective educational institutions are a reflection of the relations of production and at the same time the mechanism designed to reproduce them from generation to generation, each individual being taught above all to play the social roles characteristic of the class from which he originates. In Bourdieu and Passeron's words (1964a), education is an instrument of "reproduction" of the social system. Biological reproduction, which places an individual into a definite class by his birth, is immediately followed by social reproduction which conditions him to remain in that class through his occupation.

In fact, the Marxist interpretation correctly applies functional analysis to the particular case of class societies. It has the merit of drawing attention to the fact that in reproducing existing social relations, education reproduces the power systems, the rules governing the distribution of the national product, and hence the social hierarchy.

This is where the class struggle comes in. If it is true that in the capitalist system the relations between the "material base" and the "super-structure" serve to maintain the system, the organic tension between the opposed parties, the (closely integrated) classes and the (shaken) larger society, becomes the most significant phenomenon. From the Marxist point of view the dominated class, becoming aware of its condition, organizes itself to change the relations of production and the society. This is the origin of the class struggle. Can it fail to affect the educational system? Is not the educational system a field predestined for class struggle, since its role is to maintain the status quo? And, therefore, must not this system, as one of the "arenas" of class opposition, break down and undergo changes commensurate with any success achieved by the dominated class or with the steps taken by the ruling class to reduce tension by making concessions or adapting the sub-systems of the social order?

On the other hand, Engels admitted in his letter to Starkenberg (1894) that, although the fundamental course of history consisted in transformation of the superstructure as a result of changes in the productive forces and the relations of production (the material base of a society), at certain stages in the social evolution the superstructure - in particular the state - may become an *agent of change* of the relations of production and the productive forces. Though the fundamental long-term course runs in the direction of "economic determinism", there is in the short term an interaction between the economic base and the superstructure, i.e., a dialectic relationship. All this is far removed from the popular Marxism which regards education as purely an instrument of the ruling class, a system of manipulation, reproduction, re-pression and mystification (even in its permissive aspects). According to its own logic the Marxist approach thus has to take into account the educational system as a *factor of change,* be it to determine the causes and consequences of changes that have taken place, to work out strategies for future change in the framework of class struggle, or to consider the "cultural lags" created by the tension between the force of tradition in education (rigidity of the superstructure) and the more fundamental factors of social change (logic of contradiction).

Functional sociology, on its part, should not restrict itself to static analysis; it should take conflicts and dysfunctions into consideration. It should investigate to what extent the educational system *in a changing society* is capable of effectively playing its role as a mechanism ensuring the maintenance and continuity of the social system despite these conflicts and dysfunctions. For society is far from being a perfectly and transparently functioning machine. It contains faults, evils, ambiguities, deterioration as well as - often latent - compensatory mechanisms. Essentially, the subsystems making up the larger system are out of harmony with each other to a greater or smaller degree according to their respective evolution, each of them obeying to some extent their own laws (Ogburn's "cultural lags", 1922). Dysfunctions and conflicts (including those of the class struggle type) are the raw material of history and agents of social change. Why should we be mechanists and exclude education from such critical sociological examination, and categorically assign it the task of serving as an automatic instrument to reproduce social structures?

Though the explicit function of the educational system may be maintenance of the society, social reality turns it into a hidden, more or less intense factor for changing society. In certain historical situations the innovating function of the educational system even becomes explicit; it is a question of awareness.

When a social system is more or less in a state of crisis and therefore subject to internal or external conflict, the educational system is bound to get involved; it becomes less a "reproducer" of the established social order and more a generator of change.

It is in this general framework that we can place lifelong education, which thus appears as a critical theory to integrate the "lags" and conflicts (including the organic class conflicts) in educational practice. It becomes a new educational sub-system, a factor of radical change not only of education but also of the society as a whole.

All we have wanted to show here is to what extent the systems approach and its two major orientations can provide useful theoretical foundations for an overall study (or, if preferred, a general theory) of education, and hence of lifelong education, which claims to be its future form.

1.3.3 *Use of models*

A model is merely a theoretical representation of a system in one of the following forms:

- verbal type

- mathematical type

- homologous type.

It is a simplified representation of real phenomena and should, therefore, include - at least implicitly - all known elements of the phenomena under consideration in order to avoid any error through omission. It should also project these elements accurately, i.e., reduce them by identical rules in the sense that a black and white filmstrip is a faithful representation of reality although the colours and the third dimension are missing. Omission and inaccurate transposition are the two potential sources of error. There should be a very simplified but *implicitly* complete projection consistent in its approximation to reality.

The point of departure is, of necessity, the verbal model, the first approximation. This is evidently the stage we have reached regarding the design of models of the essential changes in larger societies. From the outset the model should exclude anything incidental or contingent and represent what is essential or "significant". Significant means going beyond description and expressing the fundamental implications of the constituent elements of the model. At this first verbal stage the model will serve its purpose if it is capable of providing an effective problematization of the phenomena to be investigated. The validity of a set of problems can be measured by the range of information their dialectic investigation will yield. It is a range open to theories about concrete facts.

Typological representation by means of models is particularly pertinent for global societies. For contemporary societies some models are:

- neocapitalist consumer societies (both the predominantly capitalist[11] and the welfare state[12] versions)

- centrally planned socialist societies (both the techno-bureaucratic version[13] and that embodying a factor of politico-cultural change[14])

- so-called developing societies (both capitalist[15] and
   socialist[16], and in various stages of industrialization).

One of the elements that should be incorporated in these models is the
educational sub-system considered in its two aspects: as function and as
factor of dialectic tension. In the first case it should be regarded as an
independent variable, but it should also be studied as a dependent variable
of other functions. In the second case the educational sub-system must be
polarized with other social factors to interpret their tension.

In addition to permitting all factors concerned to be fitted into a
coherent system including both the forces of preservation and those of change,
this methodology offers a very efficient means of building up an image of the
future taking into account present intentions and heavy trends. This can be
done by studying the forward projection of certain factors - quantified or
unquantified - or conversely, of the effects of a proposed course of action,
taking account of given facts not open to action and of powerful trends producing massive but extremely gradual changes, hardly open to short-term or
even medium-term intervention.

Such scientific prognostication should precede all educational planning.
And planning is indispensable in view of

- the inertia of the system

- the necessity, imposed by the great increase in needs,
   of determining priorities

- the massive financial and human resources required.

The Appendix to this paper showing some models of European global societies
including their educational sub-systems, may be found useful to illustrate
this methodology.

2. Outline of a Sociological Theory of Lifelong Education

2.1 The crisis in industrialized societies

As these are "changing societies" the criteria used by the *sociology of
social change* (see 1.2.6) must be applied to them. As far as social relations
are concerned, it is impossible to understand the implications of a transformation of the traditional educational system in industrialized societies

towards a system of lifelong education without recourse to that branch of
sociology. The study of social change shows that education would have to
change from an organized school-based type into a less structured, flexible
one. The global perspective of this transformation can in turn only be
perceived by recourse to the two orientations (functional and Marxist) of
the systems approach (see 1.3.1 and 1.3.2). Finally, the methodology of
"models" and its use as an instrument to interpret the constraints and the
choices about the future should make it possible to design a blueprint of
lifelong education (see 1.3.3) which is, on the whole, still in the form-
ative stage. These are our epistemological categories.

Without going too deeply into methods and details which we have only
begun to explore, we will try to extract from the specific nature and the
crisis situation of industrialized countries the most significant factors
capable of providing a sociological "model" of lifelong education. At the
present stage we can only hope to establish general theoretical foundations,
and the following will be no more than a sociological sketch including many
hypothetical elements.

The industrialized societies are closely linked with the ideology of
progress, which lends them historical legitimacy and at the same time draws
its own justification from their spectacular achievements. But this ideology,
a socio-political expression of scientific rationalism and a scale of values
extolling the rationality of societal organization, is to-day under fire from
many quarters. And the mental climate is changing: optimism is being succeed-
ed by pessimism. The certitude of the *projet humain* has given way to uncertainty about the future. It is a period of incertitude, of awareness of the
contrast between man's power over nature (which he is capable of transforming)
and over society (which he is capable of manipulating) on the one hand, and his
inability to decide his own future, to conceive a new *projet humain* and to free
himself from the "power of things" on the other.

Everything has become uncertain: values, power systems, distribution
of the social product, even the purpose of industrial production.

Against rationality and organization are set the irrational components
of human nature and the richness of interpersonal relations founded on man's
spontaneous, affective needs.

Against the artefacts created by man (especially the city and industry) nature is juxtaposed.

Against utilitarian purposes (depriving man of the possibility of expressing himself in his work) is set the overriding need for personal fulfilment implying democratic "participation" in work.

In this spirit, commercialized culture (merchandise, even if of good quality) separated from the real world (because confined to leisure hours) is being opposed by a culture of creative participation (even if mostly of mediocre quality, so long as it is the product of each and everyone) and integrated into the *whole* of social life.

Having (consumption, property, power meaning possession and "consumption" of one's fellowmen) is opposed by *being* (development of individual and general potentialities, the natural life, knowledge for its own sake, importance of happiness). Instead of personal involvement, detachment (a kind of ataraxy) not without affinity to stoicism is becoming the ideal.

Here the contradiction in the objectives of learning activities (education) becomes apparent: on the one hand, we have cumulative knowledge with the aim of acquiring possessions and access to hierarchical power, competitive selection for education, careers, the knowledge to improve the production of goods and services, to dominate nature still more and increase the military power of the society; on the other, non-cumulative knowledge acquired by personal choice, contempt of hierarchies and desire for collective and spontaneous self-management, refusal to accept selective barriers and "careers" (to be replaced by non-alienating activities offering much leisure time, security and adequate remuneration not to be spent on senseless consumption), a science of humanity, critique of society, and cultural activity. "Natural" wisdom is being opposed to reason.

In real life we meet this contradiction in its pure form only in the conflict between the upper middle classes and the technocrats of the neo-capitalism of consumption on one side, and the countercultures (e.g., Hippies) and revolutionary leftists on the other. But in some aspects and to some extent it exists everywhere. It exists in nearly all mentalities, it exists in the generation gap since the young believe less than their elders in present society and its future and are far more receptive to new ideas opposing the old order.

But everywhere ambiguity and incoherence are growing: many of the "young" who claim to be against the system are large-scale consumers guided by the advertizing put out by the system, many of the "old" who are conservative seek quality of life, nature, creativity; the regime makes cultural concessions even in its mass communications and, espousing "natural wisdom", turns "environment" into a kind of social ideology - without going so far as to let this interfere with the functional mechanisms of the system.

The class struggle is being increasingly influenced by the *new* contradictions engendered by the evolution of the capitalist system (neo-capitalism): a neo-socialism (an opposition - Marxist or otherwise - trying to go beyond classic socialism) is being sought which will also give a new meaning to the controversy on reform: improvement of society as it is, by an efficient and socially-minded management, or revolution transforming society through conflict and revolutionary behaviour.

This is the general sociological context. Its functional implications for education are evident both in theory and practice. Now we will attempt to see how they apply to lifelong education.

2.2 Dead-ends and limits of the traditional educational system

2.2.1 *Function of the system: reproduction of social structures*

By institutionalizing the educative function, pre-industrial and subsequently industrialized societies more or less consciously turned it into a process of "enculturation" or "socialization" of the young to make them resemble their elders as closely as possible. Hence they had to be taught to live, each one in his proper, strictly defined place, in harmony with a society considered to be hierarchic and non-egalitarian. In this perspective every young person had to be provided with an education, with a package of social and technical "recipes" allowing him to assume during his entire life (with perhaps possibilities for some to acquire additional *technical* knowledge) the roles conforming to the values and culture education had taught him to imbibe and respect. Thus the educational system of the industrial societies aims in principle at reproducing in each generation the hierarchic structure of the larger society. Each of the channels and levels of the educational structures is designed for children from a fairly well defined social category. These channels and levels lead to occupations of different hierarchic rank within the working population, different shares in the social product, different degrees of power and prestige and different types of cultural activity. Of course, no child is at every level of his studies assigned to a particular school or a definite type of school; he is not formally excluded from any channel or level provided he achieves the required standard. But in *actual fact* all educational institutions seem to prepare the vast majority of children for remaining in the social class into which they were born, *by equipping them for precisely the kind of studies that will lead to that result.*

2.2.2 *The dead-end of equality of opportunity*

Ever since the 19th century or at least since the First World War, most industrialized countries have been trying to bring about equality in education and to make education a means of social mobility depending on intellectual aptitude. But all the endless reforms, from compulsory education to general eligibility for scholarships, from the creation of new "secondary modern" schools to the flexible structure of the "comprehensive" school and the shifting of choice or selection to ever higher age levels, from the deliberate policy of increasing enrolment at schools to wider access to universities, have not prevented the "educogenous" level or the cultural level of families and cultural milieux from retaining, by and large, the hereditary character of the social and occupational hierarchy, and so from preserving the class structure of the society. In this respect reform of the traditional educational system is at a dead end, and only the principle of lifelong education can bring progress. However, the considerable efforts made by the industrialized countries have borne some fruits:

the educational level of the entire population has risen

social mobility though still limited[17], has increased significantly (e.g., a far greater number of workers' children enroll at university)

equality of opportunity is growing overall, though at a very slow rate for the lower classes.

This process is not gathering speed. In particular it does not impinge on the privileges of the ruling class nor modify the hierarchial structure of society.

In societies where class conflicts and pressing demands for democracy tend to create fairer conditions of socio-economic equality, the serious significance of the deadlock equality has reached in education and the "challenge" it presents demand attention. Once again only the principle of lifelong education could help to deal with this problem, which is fundamental to the equilibrium of modern societies, and rekindle the enthusiasm of the first reformers. It is no longer a matter of piecemeal reform but of a total and imperative change of the education system through new ways of action, explicitly designed to compensate for socio-cultural inequalities (so-called positive discrimination). The political significance of this principle is evident.

2.2.3 *The changing requirements of the system regarding technical and scientific skills and their educational implications*

As a result of the progress of ideology, the system needs to develop human aptitudes and make better use of the "pool of talent" necessary for industrialization and the development of science and technology on which, in the last analysis, industrialization depends.

The recent structural developments of neocapitalism and its typical production forms - multinational companies and large national ones (usually created by mergers) - correspond to extremely rapid and far-reaching changes in science and technology. Among these may be mentioned the progressive mechanization of industrial processes (right up to automation), the wide application of electronics, new chemical processes (substitutes for raw materials), power production, expansion of the automobile, radio and television industries, mechanization of agriculture, office work and domestic work. In all fields scientific research, technical control and new forms of organization are transforming work.

How does this transformation affect the structure of the working population? Two processes cut across each other in some way (we shall see a similar development in the tertiary sector): On the one hand, the growing demand for qualifications (in number and level) in the top layers of the pyramid, and on the other, on the level of the skilled worker, a trend to lower qualifications due to advances in mechanization replacing human skills and consequently an increase in repetitive types of work. The unskilled worker for his part is required to give less physical strength and more attention (as conditioned as possible); he becomes an "operator" rather than a "worker" (in the etymological sense).

There is now, and will be in the future, a growing need for more university graduates and highly qualified technicians,[18] more competent and versatile shop stewards, industrial designers and men able to adjust or repair automatic devices, while there will be fewer skilled workers of the traditional type, such as fitters and turners. Of course fitting and turning jobs will not disappear from the metal industry, but self-adjusting machines do not require qualified personnel (the five senses and manual dexterity become electronic qualities - with machines achieving suprahuman perfection). The best among the skilled workers can, of course, become "technicians" if they make the effort to get trained, and obtain promotion. The older and less gifted ones will be down-graded. Instruction of the young in technical schools has difficulty in keeping up with the advance of technology, above all with the new skills it entails; *that is why the most advanced companies are themselves taking over the function of basic and further training and recycling.*

At this point a closer examination of the educational implications of the frequent and often profound technological changes characteristic of industrial societies seems necessary. Jobs, whether skilled or unskilled, are already requiring re-adaptation or will be totally changed in their knowledge and skill components, and this trend will accelerate. Old trades and specialities are disappearing while new specialized jobs have to be filled. This means that training must become a fundamental factor of work organization and study a recurrent activity of a large number of workers. Therefore, school education cannot continue to supply youth with clearly defined knowledge, very specialized competences or skills *relating to definite types of work*. The "encyclopaedic" character of traditional schooling beyond the level of general elementary education (language, mathematics, manual skills, moral education) must be replaced by wide and versatile but in-depth education in the mastery of certain types of "logic" and languages constituting a sufficiently homogeneous epistemological approach to a given *field*: mathematics, a sector of technology and its scientific bases, communication, languages, history and culture, etc. That kind of education should aim not so much at acquisition of knowledge and information as rather at intellectual ability and practice in solving new problems in a given sector.

Since the available information on any subject is too vast and fast-changing to be committed to human memory, and besides, is stored and retrievable by means of several documentary or electronic processes, there is less need to know the content of information, which in any case will soon be out of date, than to know how to identify and collect the required information. It is more important to be able to formulate questions correctly than it is to know the answers (the traditional objective of all teaching). But formulating questions correctly implies the capacity to place them into their precise context. It is, therefore, necessary to assimilate in one's memory large but solid *reference units* for the chosen field, i.e., major classifications, "models". Apart from this basic knowledge which, though limited in volume, must be perfect, the intellect and the critical faculty are of greater importance than memory, which is not critical because it is merely concerned with retention. Moreover, rather than applying themselves to learning, people must "learn to learn" (to use a phrase that is getting a little worn but remains nevertheless valuable). And they will have to *"learn by doing"*, not by storing up theoretical knowledge. Here we come back to Gian Baptista Vico: "Man can only know what he is doing. Man makes it true by living it." (1725).

The changing nature of scientific and technological developments thus affects not only the time of study but also the purpose (abilities to be acquired), the method (the "act" of studying), the content (the types of knowledge and competence) of the educational system. Teaching the young is no longer an end in itself (an accomplishment), it is a means of attaining ulterior ends that change ceaselessly throughout an individual's life. Since the moral and cultural values of the society are also in dispute, uncertain and in a crisis, education must enable everyone to make a critical choice of values rather than internalize "prevailing" ones. This is education to meet uncertainty.

Having now outlined the functional principles of lifelong education, we may say that, essentially, the new educational system should produce adults not only intellectually capable of studying but desiring to do so ("motivated"). Going back to study should not be a "sad return" (the "unpleasant recollections" school evokes at present), but a response to a normal need. Study should no longer be of a competitive nature depending on "examinations" or "competitions" (barriers); if it were, lifelong pursuit of it would become a nightmare worthy of Kafka.

2.2.4 *The growing and diversified needs of the tertiary sector*

In the second phase the need of neo-capitalist societies for specialized knowledge (i.e., *educated intelligence*) must be adapted to the expansion of the tertiary sector, which has become the most important one in a
society characterized by a proliferation of services, especially in connection with the increasingly complex distribution of goods.

Hence the demand for ever more diversified skills in:

- organization: expansion in the size of a great many economic
  units and, within these, of the function of organization

- administration: bureaucratic way of management and of
  functional relations

- information: internal to the economic units and external

- distribution: necessity of distributing ever vaster and more
  diverse quantities of goods and services, mechanization, control,
  accounting, conditioning of customers (self-service establishments), advertizing

- allocation: transfer mechanisms: taxes, social security;
  distribution of risks (insurance systems)

- communication: mass media, telephone, mail

- transport: from the motorcar to the aeroplane

- diffusion of culture: by commercialization (from tourism to
  cinema and pocket book, from variety shows to records) or by
  public service (cultural centres)

- education: developments in schools and universities; "re-
  cycling" of adults and further vocational training; lifelong
  education

- scientific research; expansion of research in the universities,
  the public sector and the large companies.

The tertiary sector already employs the majority of the working population and multiplies service functions, and the number of posts for technicians with high or specialized qualifications within the sector and in the
industries supplying and maintaining its infrastructure and technical equipment is still on the increase. On the other hand, the new techniques of office

work and the new giant types of organization transform many employees into "operators" doing work that they find alienating.

This tertiary sector tends to offer new openings for graduates in fields of study where prospects were deteriorating, such as certain branches of teaching that were becoming saturated after having been an expanding source of employment. Among them are culture and literature, languages, communication, social relations, psychology, the social and political sciences, all of which open up jobs in trade, advertizing, tourism, promotion of culture, political propaganda, trade unions, public relations, the cultural market etc. However, this upgrading of studies that are in general "non-cumulative" (in the sense meant by Maurice Reuchlin[19]) does not bring them anywhere near the remunerative level or the prestige of "cumulative" higher studies for a specific profession (medicine, law, engineering). Besides, there are signs that the labour market is reaching saturation with certain university degrees (in particular in the social and political sciences).

One of the causes of the expansion of the teritary sector is the continuous increase in leisure brought about, in the last analysis, by the higher rate of productivity: daily leisure (catered for by the mass media and shows), weekly leisure (automobile industry, weekend travel, the industry of the "second residence", sports organizations and the catering trade), annual leisure (tourism and holiday amusements), the leisure of retirement prolonged by longevity (ever more commercialized hobbies and ways of life offered to the "third age"). All these new openings in the "leisure industry" have an educational dimension at the level of youth and at the level of adults. They create "demand" from commercial companies and from job-seekers. Culture is becoming a business and an occupation.

Yet another aspect of this rapid evolution merits attention. The growth of "tertiary" activities opens up outlets for women in areas for which they show special ability: clerical work, accounting, human relations, information, culture, languages, social services. Contrary to widespread belief the total proportion of women working in the economy has not increased since the beginning of the century, when a very large number of women were employed as unskilled labourers or domestic servants. The present situation is characterized by decreasing employment of women in industry and the domestic sector (their jobs - the least remunerative - are carried out by machinery or by young foreign girls)[20] and growing employment in the tertiary sector with a

wider and, on the average, higher range of qualifications.[21] This development
is the reason why women's demand for education is expanding at all levels of
post-compulsory education, including to an increasing extent the adult level.
The majority of adult women have, however, remained faithful to their traditional "image". It is the new generations that shape and live the new image
of the "liberated woman". Thus they tend to reduce the significance of the
nuclear family and their parental role in the family.

In fact the age structure of women's employment shows that marriage or
motherhood have reintegrated many women into their traditional status. Their
experience of society and outside work has, however, made them different from
the model represented by their mothers. So up to a point they remain a factor
of social change and, in many cases, potential candidates for some form of
adult education. Regular provision should, therefore, be made for re-cycling
young mothers whose children have reached school age, and who would like to
resume outside work.

2.2.5 *Structure of the educational system and structure of the working population*

In general one may ask whether the present educational system, which
caters essentially for the young, is producing a type of education suited to
the quantitative and qualitative structure of the working population. This
structure undergoes unforeseen changes at the same time that teaching programmes
built on the needs existing prior to these changes are being drawn up. In other
words, schools tend increasingly to produce qualifications that are one technological stage out of date at the moment they have to be put to use.

It should also be realized that the goal of meeting the requirements of
the labour market (categories, numbers, technical contents) is not the only one
inspiring educational policy, or even its "technical" side. Another immediate
objective is to meet the social demand, i.e., the aspirations of individuals and
families, who are even less well informed about the situation on the labour
market than are the educational authorities. Not only through ignorance, but
also through tradition, through the desire of certain families or groups to
climb up the ladder, through the effects, real or presumed, of selection at
school, social demand is far from corresponding to actual opportunities. *Consequently, the levels of education produced by the school system, including the*

*university, do not correspond to the levels of available occupations (hier-
archy of status).* Torsten Husén (1969) has shown that the distribution of
the working population *by level of education* can be illustrated by a
pyramid:

FIGURE 4.1

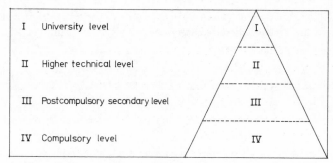

I	University level
II	Higher technical level
III	Postcompulsory secondary level
IV	Compulsory level

From Torsten Husén, *Lifelong Learning in the Educative Society*

But the structure of this pyramid is under strong pressure: the proportion
of the working population at levels I and II (with internal variants) is growing with each generation. The number of people with *only* secondary education
(level III) seems to diminish slightly in the long term, whilst the proportion
of those reaching only the compulsory level decreases from one generation to
the next (level IV). As a long-term forecast, Torsten Husén illustrates
(Figure 4.2) the future structure of the working population *in terms of
educational level* (not to be mixed up with the *level of qualification actually
required for the job they do*) by the shape of an up-turned egg:

FIGURE 4.2

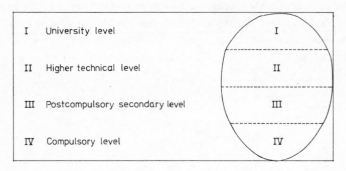

I	University level
II	Higher technical level
III	Postcompulsory secondary level
IV	Compulsory level

From Torsten Husén, *Lifelong Learning in the Educative Society*

This seems a very likely trend if one looks at developments in the United States, where more than 60% of the 18 - 25 age group receive post-secondary education (some 20% in the European OECD countries and close to 30% in the USSR).

The raising of educational levels tends to reduce the number of persons having only primary education *in the cultural sense of the term* because, first-ly, this level is being progressively raised by the addition of 2 to 4 years of compulsory additional study (lower secondary level), and secondly, an increas-ing number of children reach at least the higher secondary level.

The result of this rise in the level of education, living standards and habits is that unskilled industrial jobs - the most uninteresting, hardest and dirtiest - will not be taken by the nationals of highly industrialized countries. This void attracts masses of foreign workers from less developed or plain under-developed regions or countries (e.g. Italians from Southern Italy, Sardinia and Sicily, Spaniards and Portuguese, Antillians, Greeks and Turks, North Africans). These migrant workers and their children (high birth-rate) make very special demands on education (language, social assimilation, vocational and trade union training; right of the children to an education equal to that of the nationals; right to maintain their own language and culture). Incidentally, the lower the status of these workers, the more does their employ delay the elimination of "repulsive" industrial work through technical progress.

In this obvious case the educational system does not provide an adequate answer to the *internal* needs of a country in terms of its labour force. But do the other levels of education form a dynamic structure matching that of the working population? It does not seem so.

Though at levels I and II the growing need of industry for higher qualifications and, to a lesser degree, the revaluation of certain university studies resulting from the expansion of the tertiary sector, i.e., the overall increase in openings, has for a long time corresponded to the increase in the number of graduates, the distribution of specialized qualifications has not matched the demand, and some intellectual unemployment, a devaluation of certain degrees and their utilization for other than their real purposes have been causing problems. At present the overall turn-out of higher diploma holders seems seriously to exceed the capacity of the market.[22]

As regards level III, the number of men and women receiving this education has increased considerably, but the lowering of qualifications needed for industrial and office work at the medium level that has been described raises extremely serious socio-psychological problems as well as problems of promotion. Here we have not so much a question of employment as one of "over-education" - at least on the cultural plane - and status.

On all these problems there is a serious lack of statistical data permitting clear interpretation. Moreover, such data as do exist are out of date as they are classified by categories no longer valid.

2.2.6 *"Isolated" education in "isolated" culture*

When we speak of culture an immediate difficulty arises: the diversity of definitions of this social phenomenon.

We consider the following definition adequate: culture means any act, knowledge, creation, modality of action or relationship, consciousness, that does not serve an essential function in meeting normal basic needs; culture is thus the opposite both of nature and of purely utilitarian technology. Hence culture impregnates the *whole* of social life from the point where basic needs are satisfied. It is present in the gestures of relationships, in the ornamentation or shape of a tool, in the seasoning of a dish, in the expression of sexual desire and the image of male and female roles, in the explanation of natural phenomena, in celebrations and games, in man's awareness of himself, in the peculiarities of language, in the way of walking, in any variety or refinement of clothing, in artistic and poetic creation. Culture exists in work, leisure, knowledge, love, friendship and in objects. And since it expresses itself in creative activities according to the explicit or implicit values of social groups, it represents the *specific* aspects of these groups (constituting the essential difference between them and others, and giving them their identity). It goes without saying that the way of bringing up and socializing children and young people, i.e., the process of education, is part of the culture of a society. In traditional societies the educational system is diffuse: the entire life of a young person is governed by the perspective of education.

But what characterizes culture in industrialized societies is precisely that it tends to be compressed into definite periods of time: *leisure times* and definite areas of space: the *places* (public or commercial) *where cultural products are consumed* (cinema, theatre, sports ground, family television corner, etc.). In industrialized societies culture is almost divorced from an individual's work; it plays a role of antidote or compensation. *It is thus isolated from real social life, like a sector of socio-mental "health", and tends to consist of passive consumption of professional activities*. These activities are partly commercialized and partly provided by public services. This is what we call "mass culture".

Cultural consumption in our societies is thus unconnected with any socially responsible activity: the ideas it offers and the critical comments it supplies have only the impact of a "game" within a sector neutralized in time and space. That is the reason for the permissiveness - involving no risk - prevailing in these societies in regard to ideas and morals (see H. Marcuse, 1955). Everything seems to be of no consequence - no more serious than a show or at best a sport. Culture offers man the possibility not only of resting from work and collective obligations, but also of enjoying the illusion of liberty by consuming *criticism of society*. Culture plays the role the "carnival" plays in traditional societies, a diffuse and passive carnival. *Being a part of culture, education naturally shares in this "isolation"*. As the cultural function of the modern family or couple is constantly declining, the educational process tends to be confined to "school", a microcosm also divorced from life. In fact school artificially reproduces, in isolation, the relations of outside life for didactic purposes, and the young at school consume education in a very organized and directed way. Like cultural activities, the provision of education is *professional work*, the job of teachers; the pupils consume the services the teachers provide.

The faster the rate of change in knowledge, technology and ideas, the wider grows the gap between school and real life. The highly structured educational system displays growing inertia preventing it from being in step at least with socio-economic life as it is. This is the result of its "isolation": school education cannot go to the real "resources" of education (see Bertrand Schwartz, 1973) in the public services and private enterprises. Moreover, school has a rival in the massive diffusion of extremely variegated information which contemporary culture provides through the *mass media*. It is not surprising that the young seek and find in these "informal resources" compensation for unadapted school knowledge, just as adults compensate for the negative nature of their work by consuming cultural resources. But like their parents, the young thus receive an "isolated" culture, in the neutralized, socially aseptic field of "leisure".

Application of the principle of lifelong education would have the essential result of *reintegrating culture and education into real social life*. That is why it would constitute an authentic revolution, for through this integration it would introduce individual responsibility into culture and education. It implies cultural creativity and self-education, one following necessarily from the other. It must be clear to everybody that this fundamentally threatens the very structure of a neocapitalism based on consumption.

But is not lifelong education, in this perspective of confrontation, a means of preventing the necessary revolution from generating violence and technical deterioration which would victimize at least one generation? However that may be, the revolution, if it does occur, will be a cultural one.

2.3 Necessity for and significance of lifelong education

2.3.1 *Industrialized societies*

In the highly industrialized world, there is a crisis in society and a crisis in education. The structure of the educational system for the young does not match the structure of occupations. We have already referred to some of the consequences that frequent technological changes entail for education.

Altogether these developments demand a revision of the fundamental concepts of education. Education of the young should cease trying to turn out a *finished* person and adopt instead the model of an adult who *develops* and has been *rendered capable of doing so*. Obviously this is possible only if *in the process* of education of the young their capacities for readaptation, search, decision-making, and responsibility are trained. This implies a reversal of the respective positions of adult education and education of the young. Up to now adults wishing to resume studies have had to start from the level they had reached at school, and a resumption of study could only mean to them "returning to school". Thus school projects into adult age. In fact, the response to the needs of adults has been a recourse to professional teachers, i.e., to school, and to the use of school facilities (buildings, teaching methods, etc.). If, however, there is going to be lifelong education in order to facilitate the necessary adaptations, the way of teaching applicable to the adult (assisted self-learning and its implications) must project into basic education, which must be designed to lead to it. Instead of the "adult going back to school", school should be attuned to adults. The classroom system (units of *fixed numbers* of children *of the same age,* designed to make all of them successful *in every branch* of a *curriculum*) is virtually doomed. Actually, is it not plain logic that Smith minor in accordance with his aspirations (centres of interest), his specific abilities and learning rhythm, should be in Form 2 for mathematics, in Form 4 for his mother tongue, in Form 3 for history etc., instead of taking every subject in the same "form" (at the same level)? If the answer is yes, it would mean projection of the principle of self-education for adults into school education, and this would explode the traditional age-graded system.

Sociologically this change of perspective corresponds to the changed status of the child in industrialized societies. In the traditional world the child was entirely dependent and without responsibility under the hierarchic authority of his father (a situation paralleled in religion: the relationship between the faithful and "God the Father").

Now a change has taken place. From the age he can speak coherently the child is listened to; he very soon has a voice of his own in matters directly concerning him, and can make personal choices; his individuality is respected; he makes his own decisions - to the horror of the traditionalists. His opinions, nourished - if in a chaotic manner - by the mass media, are received with interest by the family circle, and he is encouraged to express them; at a very early age he takes part in family discussions. The reason is that in industrialized societies the low rate of infant mortality and birth control have made the child something precious and, therefore, respected. Moreover, as children now attain puberty and psychological as well as sexual maturity at an earlier age, the period during which the growing number of those receiving longer schooling resent their dependence is extended, and the authoritarian paternalism of school becomes increasingly unbearable to them. Furthermore, at a time when, as has been shown, the mass media provide children with extensive if haphazard information on the world, school seems to them divorced from reality.

These feelings are strongest in the intermediate, transitional period represented by the age group 15/16 to 18/19. For those in this age group that are still at school this phase represents the final school years preceding higher studies or entry into an occupation; for those no longer at school it is the start of working life, at a non-qualified level, with or without further studies. Lifelong education will change this dichotomous situation: it will transform that phase from the *"final school period" for some* into the first period of adult education *for all* and the *first* - progressive - working activity. Some reforms are already aiming at alternating study and work.

The principle of lifelong education is based on a fundamental premise: the adult must be *motivated* to pursue educational activities (studies) continually, he must have an *aptitude* for assimilating new knowledge and be *able* to make responsible decisions on his orientation when faced with change.

Here the instrumental values governing social life assume paramount importance: full self-awareness, a sense of responsibility, respect of other people's identity, capacity of self-evaluation, ability to cooperate in groups for common ends; without these action values, the central values - or goals - of democracy, humanism and total development of the personality will remain but pious hopes in education.

Thus lifelong education becomes the essential objective of compulsory primary education. In any society the role of education is to prepare the young for social life by providing them with the skills necessary to acquire later the techniques of production then in use, and to fit normally into existing social relations (which implies respect for the values justifying and legitimizing them). As has been explained, in industrialized societies this basic education covers mastery of the mother tongue (speech, comprehension, reading and writing), elementary practice in quantitative logic ("mathematics") and moral education (including both the political and civic aspects). The goal of lifelong education demands, however, that in addition appropriate attitudes and behaviours be inculcated: study becoming a dimension of the *entire lifespan*, aptitude for self-learning (self-education - *assisted*, of course), capacity to make responsible choices. This new perspective radically modifies the role of traditional education, which consisted in furnishing a stock of basic knowledge to serve for the *whole* lifespan, and in inculcating modalities of social relations to be considered as "normal" throughout life in order to ensure acceptance of the well-established roles and statuses in the family, at work, and in the civic and cultural order.

As already stated, this perspective is based on the fact that the man of tomorrow must be educated to cope with *uncertainty; his essential capacity must be to make choices.*

2.3.2 *Developing societies*

Again we come across an apparent paradox: the most advanced type of education, often considered "futurist" or even utopian in highly industrialized societies - the "lifelong" system - , also offers the best and relatively easiest solution for developing countries! Up to now these have striven, with the encouragement of Western Technical Assistance representatives, to copy the traditional structures and methods of *school education* in the most advanced countries ... But the shortcomings of this system, of which the industrialized countries themselves have now become aware, are aggravated by the conditions prevailing in developing countries. This applies in particular to the following points:

- the crippling financial burden (capital expenditure and extremely high unit costs) on a system which was very inadequately developed by the colonial regimes and has to cater for demographically very large age groups;

- the absence of a structured solution for an adult population that is technically very backward, in many cases even illiterate;

- the difficulty - which is even greater in developing countries than it is in Western ones - of matching education to the needs of an embryonic economy and of individuals whose occupational prospects are uncertain (hence the paradox of diplomas that are of no value in economic life because they do not correspond to actual requirements);

- the problems of recruitment, training and status of teachers (competing for priority with other administrative and technical needs);

- overall, the cultural "isolation" of school from social life, which is still more pronounced than it is in our countries (lack of family support for school work, and the "uneducogenous" nature of a background unfavourable to formalized, selective education).

From these points of view the principle of lifelong education is better suited to developing societies, for it offers the following advantages, among others:

- the field is not saturated with traditional school structures; there are still voids to be filled;

- the far more flexible nature of lifelong education enables it to meet actual needs more progressively and specifically;

- in developing countries the educational system must cater for *all age groups*, and lifelong education is by its nature much more capable of doing so;

- since lifelong education takes place where educative activities are actually carried on (the educational "resources"), it requires less didactic infrastructure and adapts better to real needs, at the same time motivating people through better comprehension;

- from the start the educational dimension can be made a *normal function* of companies, administration and newly created institutions; their entire personnel can be utilized and trained to perform part-time educational activities connected with their technical responsibilities;

- the international "technical aid" programme can be conceived
  as integral development covering at each step the educational
  requirements involved (a technical advantage for the planners).

In view of all this it should be possible for developing countries to establish,
even sooner than industrialized countries, an educational system based on the
principle of lifelong education.

2.4 The dilemma of lifelong education: to condition man or free him

There is a dilemma facing lifelong education: it can either respond to
the currently apparent needs of a changing society by subtly conditioning man
(this is a general tendency in Skinner's work) acting as a handmaiden to production in the utilitarian perspective of returns on investment, i.e., aiming
primarily at efficiency,[23] or it can endeavour to produce individuals able to
make responsible choices in a changing world by placing these changes in the
perspective of personal and collective *achievement*, i.e., make liberty its
principal goal. It is a fundamental choice between two value systems, a choice
which will determine future history since it involves the very nature of power:
the power of man (democracy) or the power of the social system (totalitarian-
ism). Will the "change" bring about the liberation of industrialized man, or
will it result in his final and total alienation? Although traditional societies did engender various forms of alienation, they remained nevertheless
based on a type of responsibility which mitigated that alienation: *the
individual fulfilled himself in the way he performed his roles, which were
deemed to be as "given" an element of life as was his natural background:* to
that extent he was secure. By contrast, perfect adaptation to the changing
"needs" of a highly technicalized society would imply conditioning in accordance with implacable neobehaviourism ... We are thus confronted with a
challenge to human nature.

There is no uncertainty about the choice of the self-aware man: lifelong education must be based on the development of fully aware personalities,
carrying individual and collective responsibility for the manifold choices with
which a society in rapid and continual change confronts them. Each choice that
has to be made when readaptation of individuals, groups and even whole societies becomes imperative requires a personal search, a "study" in the fullest
meaning of the word. It is the task of the educational system to equip individ-

uals for such renewed participation in studies and to place at their disposal
an organization which will enable them, at every level of aptitude, to acquire the knowledge necessary to adapt ways of thinking, skills, social relations and practical choices to novel situations. This is what "studying"
and "learning" should mean. And it is what lifelong education means. Founded
on responsible choice, *a genuine choice thanks to education*, lifelong education is essentially democratic, whatever the institutional modalities of a
democracy which, we *must* fervently hope, will be authentic and not just formal.

If lifelong education were to be based on the efficiency and facility of
learning methods (conditioned intellectual and motor reflexes) with the aim of
increasing the yield of business enterprises and economic growth, it would
merely serve to establish a totalitarian, one-dimensional society which would,
for the first time in history, be irreversible. It would be the "closed" society, Henri Bergson's "insect society". And there would be no way of return.

This implies no judgment on the "happiness" of the social units in either
case. It is simply - and that is quite enough - a matter of fundamental choice
concerning the meaning of human nature, a choice all types of society, industrialized or developing, must make for themselves.

2.5 The guidance principle and lifelong education

We have seen the great differences between the structure of education and
that of the working population. We have also underlined the great changes
occurring in numerous occupations.

Attempts at reconciliation of the two structures have produced no useful
method of readjustment. In this respect the organizational deficiencies of the
industrialized societies are most obvious. Not even the magnitude of the
problem has been determined, nor has an instrument of prediction been devised.

This situation is one cause of both the malaise of the young, whose
choices of orientation - school or job - are aleatory, and the frustration of
many adults, who are better motivated than the young but unable to fulfil their
aspirations by resuming studies that would not merely entitle them to promotion but actually ensure it.

There is an urgent need for setting up a mechanism that will satisfactorily coordinate educational objectives, individual choices and occupational

opportunities offered by the economy. The idea that the "labour market" or
the law of supply and demand are sufficiently effective is socially and
scientifically obsolete. A concentrated effort must be made to bridge the
gap between individual aspirations and working activities. The only way to
achieve this is lifelong education, which alone can enable people to effect
the frequent adaptations necessary in the course of a working life. They must
answer the needs of the economy and those of the individuals by means of
innumerable successive adjustments.

In any case it is evident that individuals of all ages will be unable
to make *responsible* choices regarding study unless a dimension of counselling
and guidance is integrated into education as a corollary to the principle of
self-education. Education must, therefore, include a process "locating" the
student at every stage according to his aspirations (clearly defined and well
motivated), his aptitudes (adequate for the studies undertaken and for his
future occupation) and the openings available (more reliable pragmatic
information). This implies that guidance should be an inherent part of teaching.

The term guidance should not be misunderstood. It does not mean manipulating choices; on the contrary, it means rendering them fully conscious
and responsible, in awareness of the dilemma we have referred to above (see 2.4).

There can be no lifelong education without responsible choice; no
responsible choice without awareness of self (aspirations and abilities) and
adequate information on the nature of the various occupations and the possibilities they offer. Since this is in practice a question of *individual* capacity
to situate oneself, the operation is by its nature inseparable from self-learning; it is an integral part of it. Lifelong education must include guidance if
it is not to be chance competition and a source of frustration.

Guidance integrated into the act of learning, with the help of teachers
who are also "counsellors", accentuates the individual character of assisted
self-learning. Through orientation every young person or adult can, at every
stage of his studies, "locate" himself according to his personal characteristics
and his present position in society. In a flexible system of options he will be
able to choose, in full knowledge of all factors, the next stage he is most able
and most motivated to cover. Thus orientation is substituted for the *negative
selection* of traditional examinations which either confer a graded right to

continue, or refuse it without providing any alternative.

Does this mean that in future there will be no more selection? Certainly not, because "locating" pupils or students implies placing them at a certain level, before a certain choice - commensurate with their abilities. Therefore the process in itself *is* a selection, but a *positive* one. Instead of *barring* a candidate from further studies, it shows him where he stands: it creates a pyramid according to aptitudes. Those at the top are, in fact, products of selection. But in lifelong education orientation constitutes a procedure ensuring real equality of opportunity. What opportunity? The opportunity for every individual to fulfil himself in accordance with the - at last well-defined - personal and social coordinates.

If this general solution is not accepted, the only help can come from initiatives of the big commercial and industrial companies which could provide training leading to change of job and promotion *within their own organization*. But this involves the danger that the individual might become totally dependent on "his" company, and that the training would be preponderantly of a pragmatic, one-sided kind designed to meet only the immediate interests of the company and the apparent interests of the individual without taking the development of his personality into consideration. The latter can in fact only be achieved by a wider education which, incidentally, contributes to autonomy in work (necessity of versatility to cope with frequent technical changes).

Whilst business companies certainly have a role to play, it is one of "finalization" of learned skills, since their nature and their objectives are incompatible with an education centred on the liberation and promotion of man. Harmonization of the educational role of the place of work with the objectives of the global educational system will be one of the touchstones of the significance of lifelong education. Education organized by business postulates a form of economic democracy which will enable it to be controlled by the base. In particular, the trade unions must ensure that no great differences of level arise between the respective educational goals of business companies.

It will, of course, take time for orientation and guidance to attain their objective. They should, therefore, be incorporated in education as rapidly as possible by providing it with the scientific, technical and human resources required for the purpose.

2.6 Decentralization, central coordination and lifelong education

In all advanced countries educational systems are controlled by the
state by means of direct management (total or partial), legislative provisions, or various kinds of financial control. If lifelong education
postulating flexibility, options, individualization and self-learning becomes the guiding principle, the educational system cannot possibly be a
centralized and monolithic one. Neither can it dispense with private
initiatives or the freedom to teach (which is, actually, expressly
embodied in some political constitutions). On the contrary, in order not to
thwart its own possibilities of renewal, it will benefit from being
pluralistic and free from any monopolist spirit.

However, there is also a need for central coordination. It derives
from the necessity of comparing initiatives with results, and also from the
need to control and safeguard the level and quality of teaching, to maintain
conditions ensuring equal access and chances of success, respect for democratic values and procedures (principle of choice and self-learning), and to
institutionalize the diffusion of innovations and information in education.

In education a monolithic structure is completely unacceptable as it
creates organizations that, owing to their homogeneity and their ineluctable
bureaucratic nature, are averse to change and to individual or local adaptation. Decentralization of the greatest possible number of decisions is
indispensable in a system founded on responsible choice, on individualization
and education defined as *"learning"* rather than *"teaching"*. This spirit must
be fully reflected in the educational relationship, in the dynamic democratic
processes of small informal groups varying with the subjects, the levels and
the rhythms of learning.

An educational system capable of providing the flexibility needed to
offer a maximum of options in the form of "study units" (or "credits"),[24] the
possibility of "going to the resources"[25] (i.e., of organizing education where
the relevant activities take place), and mobile structuration of self-learning
in small, changing and diversified groups, requires decentralized regional
organization divided into "educational and cultural districts",[26] in which all

human[27] and material educational instruments can be made available to the
local population to meet its educational needs. The *functional severity* of
this organization will replace the *structural rigidity* of the present system.
This decentralized system must be built on democratic participation of the
base and on the principle of individual choice, but its technical side must
be tightly integrated.

The danger of formalistic, authoritarian centralization is, and will
be for a long time to come, all the more serious as every educational system
harbours a strong force of inertia. This is inherent in the very nature of
the educational relationship - a fact that is often overlooked. From the outset, every teacher is aware of the delicate and precarious character of this
relationship, because the equilibrium of his professional life depends on it.
When a teacher has established harmony with his pupils - be it only relative
but passable - any reform asking him to introduce a significant change arouses
in him a more or less conscious panic. He feels that he is somehow being "put
to the test" again. That is why even the best educational methods so easily
degenerate into routine. Besides, owing to the huge apparatus it has to
penetrate,any really profound change in the educational system takes considerable time to progress from conceptualization to practical application. Changes
in education proceed more slowly than technological changes. This difficulty
can only be overcome if initiatives are decentralized and made the joint responsibility of units of limited size enjoying functional autonomy and managed
collectively by a team of teachers, provided there is a centralized agency to
diffuse such innovations as have been proved successful by scientific evaluation.

Here we have another paradox in the educational system. Though conservative through inertia and partly also through tradition (transmitting what has
been "acquired", i.e., the past), it is at the same time a milieu generating
violent criticism of the social order. As a result of the essentially intellectual training of teachers combined with their lack of social pragmatism due
to their comparative remoteness from economic life proper, which inclines them
towards theoretical or doctrinaire views, their work of transmitting to the
young the "state of knowledge" (a psychological situation involving a risk of -
fully or partly - conscious dogmatism), and the frustration engendered by a
relatively unsatisfactory professional status giving rise to militant trade

unionism, the members of the teaching profession form a critical-minded group
in society. Teachers tend to be opposed to the established order, to hold
revolutionary opinions as citizens. In the Latin countries this trend is more
pronounced than in the Nordic ones. No judgment on this situation, which has
its positive as well as its negative aspects, is implied here. It is simply
a statement of fact. In the schools, this tendency among teachers meets the
tendency towards protest among the young.[28]

As a factor of *radical change of society*, lifelong education is therefore finding an echo among teachers. But as a factor of change of the school
system it comes up against its inertia and the rigidity of teacher mentality.

To start with, lifelong education is a matter of political persuasion
and involves a stage of democratic confrontation. Its strength, as far as
teachers are concerned, lies in its being able to make them realize that the
traditional classroom constitutes a system generating teacher frustration,
and that the change in their role from *teaching* to assisting pupils in their
self-education *(learning)* will at last erase the ambivalent - both despised
and respected but now outdated - image of the "schoolmaster". Moreover, in a
system of lifelong education, progressively more *non-professionals* will join
the cadres of professional teachers. This situation, combined with the end of
age-grading and involvement in social life through "going to the resources",
will help to make the criticism emanating from the educational system less
dogmatic and bring it more into line with social reality. The very function of
the teacher will change radically: instead of being "responsible" for a homogeneous age group to whom he furnishes explanations or demonstrations, he will
become an individual within a heterogeneous age group, an orientator, animator,
a counsellor.

The first step in introducing lifelong education must be to apply its
principles in full to the teaching profession; this requires restructuring the
"time budget" and the remuneration of teachers.

2.7 Conclusion

2.7.1 *Changing the "condition humaine" through lifelong education*

The increasing significance education is gradually assuming in the

activities of people at all stages of life is one of the most essential
factors of the social change we are now experiencing. For lifelong education
does not consist, as some thought or are still thinking, in simply providing
adult education for everybody who has completed a basic school education. Its
"lifelong" nature is now clearly seen to be the agent of total change of the
educational system, and in particular, as we have shown, of education of the
young. The basis of this radical change is recognition of the fact that the
acquisition of a stock of knowledge is an encyclopaedic exercise rendered
increasingly futile by developments in science and technology. It is, therefore, necessary to master not so much knowledge as all-round "know-how"
(approaches, methods, logics, "languages") representing intellectual tools for
the solution of certain types of problem.

We have already seen that the structures of education must be more decentralized, more flexible, and more optional. That means deschooling education and abandoning the classroom system. The educational system will then
become a functional organization, centrally controlled for the reasons indicated (see 2.6), in the sense that education becomes a *normal function* of any
group (commercial company or institution) and any activity, which must, of
course, find the necessary means of action (the answer to learning needs)
through technical help and establishment of specialized centres for the diffusion
of knowledge staffed with qualified personnel (guidance experts, counsellors,
animators, communication experts, etc.). It will cease to be a closed system
divorced from socio-cultural life. Lifelong education therefore implies an
entirely *different* type of organization and integration of individuals of both
sexes and of all ages in accordance with their individual learning needs.

Such a heterogeneous organization not tied to age (except perhaps in
youth to make allowance for the different psycho-physiological phases of growth)
and liberated from space ("school"), since the "resources" of knowledge, from
commerical firms to the civil service, must be utilized where they are, leads
of necessity to a functional organization divided into "educational districts"
(Schwartz) where every individual should in principle find a possibility of educating himself in any field (vocational, technical, cultural). Only the top-
most scientific and cultural levels of education would cover geographical areas
larger than the "district", the basic operational unit for "normally" distributed aptitudes even on rather high levels.

The views that have been expressed here are not dreams. Under the
pressure of an irreversible evolution, the "Open University", (Britain), the
"Tele Kolleg" (Federal Republic of Germany), the University Without Walls
(USA), general correspondence courses in line with technical and university
teaching (USSR), not to mention the improvements in medical education (unity
of theory and practice, simulation activities such as dissection and laboratory work, internships with *real* work and carrying responsibilities) are developments we are already witnessing. And these are only some examples.

The two new characteristics thus are:

- "Time-free": no more age grouping, no more necessity for
  full-time work (not even for teachers), no need to complete
  all formal education at a stretch (new systems of alterna-
  tion and recurrence)

- "Space-free": learning where knowledge is actually produced.

Education becomes a dimension of the whole life, (the individual seen as
"receiver"), of all activity (the collective whole seen as the "place") of
any occupation (the individual seen as "donor"). Just as work and leisure,
with their defined objectives, are periods devoted to recurrent activities,
self-learning appears as a new item in the "time budget" with its own ends and
activities. In the perspective of lifelong education, study after the period
of compulsory education and full time schooling can no longer be regarded as a
form of leisure or something that has to be done in leisure time. This sociological view is already implicit in the growth of legislation and social con-
ventions on paid study leave. Further, there is increasing demand for a
special work schedule for trade union representatives which will allow them to
study during factory or office time. Paid periods of "recycling" for certain
categories of staff in big business (usually the management, sales personnel,
etc.) are further signs of the recognition of the "third dimension".

Indeed, lifelong education is a principle of change in the meaning of
social life.

Up to now the developed societies have divided the life of man into three
distinct stages:

The school phase:

- main activity: study

- concern: examinations

- no occupational, social or political responsibility, and in
  particular, no real work.[29]

The working phase:

- main activity: work

- concern: career

- full responsibility in each domain

- in exceptional cases, studies of a supplementary nature.

The retirement phase:

- main activity: passing the time

- concern: health

- decline of responsibility, which is confined to voting in
  public elections.

The way of life which is beginning to take shape, one of the most significant components of which will be lifelong education, is going to abolish
these distinctly divided phases. After the age of discretion, living will involve making choices and taking on responsibilities; learning will be an ever-
present dimension, and so will real work. In youth, there will be work as a
preparation for later vocational activities linked with recurrent studies and
vocational and cultural adaptation. In old age, work will continue because the
increase in longevity, the longer maintenance of good health and the greater
number of occupations not requiring too much energy render abrupt cessation of
any vocational activity at a fixed age absurd and impossible. At all ages there
will be more leisure to develop *creative and active* attitudes (putting an end to
almost exclusively passive consumption in leisure time), which the practice of
self-learning in what will have become recurrent education will have engendered.

From the age of discretion to senility the life of an individual will thus
evolve along a continuum where study, work, leisure, responsible decision-making
will at all times be present, any one of these preponderating temporarily and
largely irrespective of age. Assisted self-learning, changing vocational activities, creative expression in leisure time, participation in decentralized democratic decision-making procedures (orientation) - these will characterize the
human condition in a society whose educational system is based on lifelong education.

Sceptics might call this prospect utopian, and they will not be wrong.
Today's reality was yesterday's Utopia. Condorcet's famous report envis-
aging compulsory education was a Utopia at the time, yet it has become reality.
Who but minds inspired by revolution would have believed at the end of the
18th century that it could come true?

2.7.2 *The methodological aspect*

The sociological foundation of the theory of lifelong education which we
have attempted to set out in this paper has been derived, as far as its global
aspect is concerned, from the critical analysis that has been synthesized in
the first paragraph of Part 2 (see 2.1). Throughout our method is based on the
sociology of change (for definition see 1.2.6) and on systems analysis (see
1.3). We have used the criteria of the latter to examine the global society,
and in particular its social stratifications, its social order, division of
labour (structure of the working population), and educational sub-system. To
explain the functioning and maintenance of the social system and its sub-
systems, the methods of functional analysis (synchronic aspects) have been
employed. The *critical review* of the system and the interpretation of the dynamics of change have been based on dialectic analysis (dysfunctions and contradictions; diachronic aspect).

In conclusion a new prospective model of the global society (2.7.1) has
been presented. This has been inspired by the results of the preparatory studies
for *Project I* (education) of Plan Europe 2000 sponsored by the European Cultural Foundation (Amsterdam). However, the base for our reasoning has at no
point been explicitly stated, since the object here was not to present an
exercise in applying a methodology. That approach would have made the text
rather unreadable.

We should, however, like to draw attention to the specifically sociological aspect of our approach. Any reader prepared to take the trouble can
trace it without much difficulty.

Future research on the application of sociology to lifelong education,
which should be undertaken as a matter of high priority in order to establish
its theoretical foundations, might make use of this contribution as an initial
"list of contents", to be enlarged and critically reviewed for the purpose of
finalizing each of the elements it contains. This will be a full job for a

team of specialists representing the various branches of sociology mentioned
in this paper. The final result should be a basic hypothesis and a framework
for a new sociology of education. It would be an indispensable tool which, we
believe, the present development of sociology can provide. But however that
may be, the major orientations will be governed by political choices. And
everything possible must be done to ensure that they are enlightened.

NOTES

1) It may be argued that Oxford University has become "the" symbol of gener-
alist education. But this is exactly where its vocational objective is
most evident: the purpose of the general, cultural and psychological education it provided was to turn out leaders of the Empire in all fields.
Its function was thus clearly a vocational one: to train its students as
members of the ruling class at its various levels.

2) According to Dupréel, Eugène (1947) the "social force" works in three
ways: by coercion, persuasion and exchange. According to Etzioni, Amitai
(1961) there are also three ways of exercising power (each relationship
being formalization of a social force): coercive, remunerative and normative. As regards persuasion - perhaps the most important aspect of the
educational relationship - use might be made of the theories on the *logic
of argumentation* (which, as shown by Perelman, Chaim (1958), varies with
the "audience" and its consensual context).

3) On the method, see Janne, H. (1968), the section on the typological approach. On definition of particular types, see references in the bibliography. See also Lazarsfeld, P. (1971), p. 39 ff.

4) In French "situation de survenance".

5) In certain countries, e.g. India, such local communities are traditional features; the problem is how to base on their typical human relations
educational developments that will effectively meet present needs.

6) See Cazeneuve, J. (1974) and MacQuail, D. (1969).

7) At the end of each chapter the book gives a carefully selected bibliography which is an indispensable complement to the bibliography annexed
to this paper.

8) For further data and sources see Janne, H. (1968).

9) For the dialectic see especially Perroux, François (1963).

10) The Marxist approach thus attributes to the system a functional rationality which constitutes its coherence and its way of resistance to change.

11) e.g. the United States, the Federal Republic of Germany and France.

12) e.g. Sweden. Great Britain is in an intermediate position between 12) and 11).

13) e.g. the Soviet Union. Jugoslavia is in an intermediate position between 13) and 14).

14) e.g. The People's Republic of China, which is the true "model" of this type of society. In some respects, however, it also belongs to type 16), though in view of its high civilization it cannot be classified as "developing".

15) e.g. Iran and Brazil.

16) e.g. Cuba.

17) For instance, the large majority of university degrees giving access to leading positions are taken by sons of the elite class. The few children of economically weak background who obtain such degrees certainly manage to obtain higher positions but, generally or for a very long time, subordinate ones. The children of middle class background walk straight into top management. ... Only civil service careers are without this inequality, though at the price of lower financial returns and the risk of being passed over for political reasons.

18) This development and its implications are extremely well analyzed in the preparatory reports, discussions and conclusions of the OECD Conference on "Utilisation of Highly Qualified Personnel" held in Venice in October 1971.

19) "Cumulative" studies cover a very coherent, specialized field comprising absolutely necessary sequences of increasing difficulty. "Non-cumulative" studies cover more diversified areas offering wide options; they explore more extensive matters, and the techniques applied are generally less difficult. See "L'Evolution des Structures de l'Enseignement". In *L'Enseignement en l'An 2000* (1973), p. 90 ff.

20) Also, an increasing number of domestic chores are done by mechanical gadgets or service organizations (laundries, dry cleaners, with the self-service variant).

21) It must, however, be realized that the majority of women in commercial or service establishments do work that requires no specific qualification - except, perhaps, a certain amount of culture - and is relatively badly paid; besides, there is as yet no equality with men doing similar jobs, though the difference has become smaller.

22) All this has been clearly shown by the Venice Conference already mentioned (Note 18).

23) This propensity is evident in all industrialized countries, whether socialist or capitalist. It becomes particularly alarming when it manifests itself in an integrated form on the international level - in actions taken by multinational companies.

24) See Schwartz, Bertrand (1973), pp. 276 - 281.

25) See ibid. pp. 60 - 61 and especially p. 68.

26) See ibid. Chapter IX, pp. 211 - 226.

27) Potentially this approach to the problem leads to the principle that any technical occupation should in future include some educational activity.

28) See 2.1. The crisis in industrialized societies.

29) This rule, which has seemed so natural, contrasts with the practice of historical societies (built on agriculture or crafts), where children were treated as "helpers" in the large patriarchal family and later as "apprentices", so that from a very early age they were progressively trained for the activities and techniques of production.

REFERENCES

Asch, Salomon. *Social Psychology*. New York: Prentice Hall, 1952.

Bales, Robert. *Interaction Process Analysis. A Method for the Study of Small Groups*. Reading, Mass.: Addison-Wesley, 1950.

Bernstein, Basil. "A Socio-Linguistic Approach to Social Learning". In Gould, J. (Ed.). *Survey of the Social Sciences*. London: Penguin Books, 1965.

————. "Social Class and Linguistic Development: A Theory of Social Learning". In Halsey, A. H. et al. (Eds.). *Education, Economy and Society*. New York: The Free Press, 1961.

Bloom, B. S. et al. *Compensatory Education for Cultural Deprivation*. Research Conference on Educational and Cultural Development, Chicago, 1965. New York: Holt, 1965.

————. "Mastery Learning". In Block, J. H. (Ed.). *Mastery Learning: Theory and Practice*. New York: Holt, 1971.

Bourdieu, P. & Passeron, J.-Cl. *La Reproduction*. Paris: Ed. Minuit, 1964a.

Bourdieu, P. & Passeron, J.-Cl. *Les Héritiers. Les Etudiants et la culture.*
Paris: Ed. Minuit, 1964b.

Cazeneuve, Jean. *L'Homme téléspectateur.* Paris: Denoel/Gonthier, 1974.
(At the end: List of works by the author.)

De Coster, Sylvain & Hotyat, Fernand. *Sociologie de l'Education. Bibliographie.* Brussels: Institut de Sociologie de l'U.L.B., 1970.

Dumazedien, Joffre. *Loisir et Culture.* Research at Annercy, in collaboration
with Riper, Aline. Paris: Le Seuil, 1966. (Classic piece of research in
this field, very interesting for lifelong education.)

——. *Espace et Loisir dans la Société française.* In collaboration with
Imbert, Maurice. Paris: Centre de Recherches d'Urbanisme, 1967.

Dupréel, Eugène. *Sociologie générale.* Paris: P.U.F., 1947.

Etzioni, Amitai. *A Comparative Analysis of Complex Organizations.* Glencoe:
Free Press, 1961.

Gurvitch, Georges. *Traité de Sociologie.* Paris: P.U.F., 1. 1958; 2. 1960.

Husén, Torsten. "Lifelong Learning in the Educative Society". *International
Review of Applied Psychology* 17 (1969), No. 2. pp. 87 - 99.

——. *Talent, Equality and Meritocracy.* The Hague: Martinus Nijhoff, 1974.
9, Project I "Educating Man for the 21st Century".

International Labour Organization. Geneva.

Janne, Henri. *Le Système social. Essai de Théorie générale.* Brussels:
Institut.de Sociologie, 1968.

Jensen, St.; Tinbergen, J. & Hake, B. *Possible Futures of European Education.*
The Hague: Martinus Nijhoff, 1972. (Plan 2000, sponsored by the European
Cultural Foundation.)

Kardiner, A. & Preble, E. *They Studied Man.* New York: New American Library,
1966.

Lasswell, Harold D. *The Analysis of Political Behavior: An Empirical Approach.*
New York: Oxford University Press, 1949.

Lazarsfeld, Paul. *Qu'est-ce que la Sociologie?* Paris: Gallimard, 1971.
(Coll. Idées.)

Lewin, Kurt. "Group Decision and Social Science". In *Readings in Social
Psychology.* Newcomb: 1947.

——. *Resolving Social Conflicts.* New York: Harper, 1948

Lewin, Kurt. Text included in Faucheux, M. & C. (Eds.). *Psychologie et Dynamique, les Relations humaines*. (Selected texts.) Paris: P.U.F., 1959.

London, Jack. "The Relevance of the Study of Sociology to Adult Education Practice". In *Adult Education Outlines as an Emerging Field of University Study*. Chicago: 1964. Chapter 7, pp. 113 - 136.

McQuail, Denis. *Towards a Sociology of Mass Communication*. London: MacMillan, 1969.

Marcuse, Herbert. *Eros and Civilization*. Boston, Mass.: Beacon Press, 1955.

————. *One Dimensional Man*. Boston, Mass.: Beacon Press, 1955

Mead, George Herbert. *Mind, Self and Society: From the Standpointof a Social Behaviorist*. C. W. Morris (Ed:). Chicago: University of Chicago Press, 1934. A Classic.

Merton, Robert King. *Social Theory and Social Structure*. Glencoe, Ill.: Free Press, 1957. (Rev. ed.). A classic of the functional approach applied to industrialized societies.

Moreno, Jacob. *Fondements de la Sociométrie*. Paris: P.U.F., 1954.

————. *Psychothérapie des Groupes et Psychodrames*. Paris: P.U.F., 1965.

Morrish, Ivor. *The Sociology of Education: An Introduction*. Hemel Hempstead, Herts.: George Allen & Unwin Ltd., 1972. (Unwin Education Books 10.)

O.E.C.D. *The Utilisation of Highly Qualified Personnel*, Venice Conference, 1971. Paris: O.E.C.D., 1973.

Ogburn, William Fielding. *Social Change with Respect to Culture and Original Nature*. Chicago: Chicago University Press, 1922. A classic.

Parsons, Talcott. *Social Structure and Personality*. New York: The Press of Glencoe, 1964.

Perelman, Ch. & Olbrechts-Tyteca. *Traité de l'Argumentation*. Paris: P.U.F., 1958. (Coll. Logos.)

Perroux, Fr. "Foreword" to Marx, Karl. *Oeuvres. Economie I*. Paris: N.R.F. La Pléiade, 1963.

Piaget, J. *Psychologie et Pédagogie*. Paris: Denoël, 1969.

————. "Problèmes de la Psycho-Sociologie de l'Enfance". In Gurvitch, Georges (Ed.). *Traité de Sociologie*. Paris: P.U.F., 1960. 2, pp. 229 - 254.

Reuchlin, M. *L'Enseignement et l'An 2000*. Paris: P.U.F., 1973. (Study for "Plan 2000", European Cultural Foundation, Amsterdam.)

182   Henri Janne

Santomauro, Gaetano. *Civiltà ed Educazione nel Mondo contadino meridionale*. Bari: Adriatica Editrice, 1974.

Schwartz, Bertrand. *L'Education demain*. Paris: Aubier-Montaigne, 1973.

———. *Education Tomorrow*. The Hague: Martinus Nijhoff, 1975. (Project I, Plan 2000, European Cultural Foundation.)

Szalai, E. *The Use of Time*. European Coordination Centre for Research and Documentation in Social Sciences, The Hague. Paris: Mouton, 1972.

Thomas, William Issak. *The Polish Peasant in Europe and in America (1918-1920)*. New York: Dover, 1958. 2 vols., last ed. A classic.

Visalberghi, Aldo. *Education and Division of Labour*. The Hague: Martinus Nijhoff, 1973. (Plan 2000, European Cultural Foundation.)

APPENDIX

FOUR PROSPECTIVE TYPES (OR MODELS) OF SOCIAL SYSTEM

1. The following chart has been inspired by the report of a group of young researchers presented to the *York Colloquium* in 1972 as an "exercise in integration" of a first series of studies for the "Plan 2000 Education" sponsored by the *EUROPEAN FOUNDATION OF CULTURE* (Amsterdam).

2. Composition of the group
   Coordinator: Barry Hake (United Kingdom)
   Members: J. Bengtsson (Sweden), A. van den Bergh (Netherlands),
               I. Hecquet (Belgium), G. Tassinari (Italy).

3. My interpretation of these models, which I have attempted to synthesize (in a personal perspective) with the help of this chart, is to consider them as *types, epistemological tools, terms of reference* permitting a better *definition, classification* and *positioning* of the elements that appear to be the most significant for a long-term forecast of the future in social terms. They should help to detect, through the interplay of certain factors in

four global social systems, correlations that can be systematized, verified and then evaluated. These "types" are thus neither predictions nor objectives, neither probable outcomes nor normative models, nor systems offered to choice.

4. Owing to this interpretation, to the addition of certain criteria and also to the terminology used, my chart differs from the prospective sociology of the "York group". *However* - and I wish to emphasize this - it essentially retains the latter's dialectic based on the hypothesis that the models differ basically in the order of importance accorded to their constituent subsystems.

5. It should be noted that our present Western industrialized societies contain rudiments of each of the other systems. The general neocapitalist set-up (growth economy, society built on consumption) contains a rudiment of Welfare State (social security, economic rights, power of trade unions, protection of workers), a rudiment of constraining collectivism (increased economic planning and state intervention, especially to attenuate the disturbance factors of the system, to fight inflation, balance the budget and maintain full employment), a rudiment of communal libertarian socialism (tolerance of counter-cultures, "wild" industrial conflicts, sexual liberty, demands for "participation", new kinds of family relationship, trends towards a return to nature, to "doing it yourself", etc.). Social reality in present society has different degrees of influence and a different meaning in the *various national* societies: French neocapitalism, the Swedish welfare state, Soviet state collectivism, small, libertarian "hippy" communities. The "rudiments" exist everywhere, but they have different emphases. There is a certain degree of overlap among the models.

6. Finally it should be noted that still other "models" could be designed on the basis of the criteria in the chart: a "fascist model", a "technocratic model", a model or models of developing societies, etc. Moreover, additional criteria could be included: sexuality, religion, ideology, etc.

7. In this chart, attention should, of course, be focussed on the cultural subsystem of which, in all four models, education forms a very substantial part.

TABLE 4.1

FOUR PROSPECTIVE TYPES (OR MODELS) OF SOCIAL SYSTEM

Social Systems / Criteria	I Neocapitalist Society	II Welfare State	III Constraining Collectivist Regime	IV Libertarian Communal Socialism
Dominant subsystem)	Economic	Social	Political	Communal(1)
2nd subsystem (instrument of 1st))	Political	Political(2)	Economic	Cultural (*incl. education*)
More variable sequence of other subsystems	Social Cultural *incl. education* Communal	Economic Cultural (*incl. education*) Communal	Cultural (*incl. education*) Social (included in economic subsystem)	Political Social (included in cultural subsystem) Economic
Control of means of production (in decreasing order of importance)	Holdings Multinational companies Private companies State intervention	Private companies Multinational companies (smaller than in I) State intervention (more than in I)	Planned Economy State enterprises	Cooperatives Decentralization Democratic planning
Role of trade unions	Pluralist and conflictual trade unionism	Unified and progressive trade unionism	Integrative (educational) trade unionism aiming at reconciliation of interests	Trade unionism in management of companies (*very decentralized*)

educational sub-system (sector of cultural subsystem)	Trend toward vocational and utilitarian lifelong education (growing role of companies, weakly controlled)	Trend toward vocational and general lifelong education (larger role than in I of public services and private associations)	cultural and ideological lifelong education (far-reaching central control) Individual equality in selection and wide access to cultural activities	lifelong education favouring creative, free spontaneity Equality through extreme flexibility (orientation process) High degree of democratization High priority: education as an "instrument" of the system
	Limited democratization and equality of opportunity Trend toward lower priority of education (limitation of means)	Firm control of company activities More equality of opportunity and greater democratization than in I Higher priority for education than in I	*Positive discrimination* in favour of workers Development as criterion: the needs of planning High priority of education	
Equality)(3) Hierarchy) Democracy)	4 1 3	3 3 2	2 2 4	1 4 1
Individual/collective dialectic: centre of interest in social relations	Individual	Collective	Collective	Individual

(1) Based on interpersonal and communal relations
(2) Functionally closely concerted
(3) The figures indicate the importance of the criteria in each social system in *descending order from 1 to 4*; of course each system has its own forms of social hierarchy.

General remark: For a global society, model 4 is the most utopian because integration *at the global level* raises the most delicate problems. At the communal level, small decentralized societies can easily approach this type, but to what extent is it possible on a large scale, when no global organization compatible with this social model exists?

CHAPTER 5

SOME PSYCHOLOGICAL REFLECTIONS
ON LIFELONG EDUCATION

A. J. C r o p l e y

1. Structure of the Analysis

1.1 The role of psychology

Lifelong education is a concept that has received increasing attention
in recent years. Consequently, it is appropriate that it should be examined
in a systematic and organized way. Like any theory of educational organization, lifelong education has a basis in many disciplines, so that detailed description of the concept will depend on a very broad-based analysis. The contribution of the present chapter is to analyse lifelong education from the
point of view of psychology, thus providing one element in an interdisciplinary approach.

The chapter has five basic sections. The first identifies the psychological elements of contemporary life that suggest that current educational
procedures need to be changed. The second contains a criticism of existing
educational systems in the light of the psychological pressures which have
been identified. The third section contains a description of the major psychological features of lifelong education, as it is described in the relevant
literature. The fourth aspect of the analysis briefly reviews psychological
knowledge as it bears upon the major assumptions of lifelong education, and
the final section turns to more practical aspects of the psychological analysis.
Since schooling is intimately connected with learning and development, psychology may reasonably be expected to provide guidelines for classroom organization and practice. Consequently, the final section of the present chapter con-

centrates on a second role of psychology in analyzing lifelong education. The first role was that of providing a framework for interpreting and evaluating the basic philosophy and principles of lifelong education. The second is that of indicating the implications of psychological knowledge for the actual structure and organization of the educational process, within a lifelong education orientation.

2. A Challenge to Modern Education

2.1 The challenge of change

An aspect of modern society that has increasingly concerned educators recently is the rapid change taking place in almost all spheres of life (e.g., Dumazedier, 1972; Hicter, 1972; Janne, 1972). Change has been seen in the socio-cultural domain, in the form for example of enormous population increases, greatly increased social mobility, and increased public participation in political and cultural activities. One result of this socio-cultural change has been wide-spread demands for educational equality, both within societies, and between different nations of differing wealth (see Jencks, 1972 for discussion of educational equality). Change has also been seen in communications, in scientific and technological fields, in the availablity of and demand for consumer goods, and in the organization of the means of their production. Consequently, the results of change are also being seen in the vocational world, with some jobs disappearing, and new ones requiring new kinds of skills emerging (e.g., Aujaleu, 1973).

2.2 Change and the changing concept of knowledge

Because of the phenomenon of rapid change, today's schoolchildren may be preparing to enter a social and vocational world which will not exist at the time they reach adulthood. This is true of highly developed countries with relatively long traditions of schooling in the North American-European sense, and it is also true of less-developed countries, even those in which education has been almost exclusively a matter of acquiring the traditional ways of the society, for example through participation in tribal life. In both cases, it is being argued that the knowledge children are spending their childhoods acquiring will no longer be relevant to the world in which they live as adults. Consequently, educational innovators are beginning to emphasize the need for a new educational goal - education for a changing world (Kupisiewicz, 1972; Kyöstiö, 1972; Silva, 1973). In particular, an increasing need is seen for emphasis on a new kind of knowledge - "innovative knowledge" that is linked to a continuous process of further learning and re-learning in all psychological domains (Dumazedier, 1972).

2.3 Need for education to be concerned with self-actualization

A further consequence of change has been outlined by Dumazedier (1972). Rapid change threatens to overwhelm values, morals, interpersonal relations, self-image and sense of identity. In a world of excessive uncertainty, the individual will have to struggle to maintain a stable concept of who and what he is, of where he fits into society, of what he means to other people and they to him, of what rights, privileges and duties he can take for granted. If these kinds of variables become too uncertain, not only will the day-to-day matter of making sense out of the environment become a difficult and frustrating task, but people unprepared for change may develop the feeling that they can no longer control their interactions with life. A profound state of alienation may develop, alienation not only from work, but from other people, and even from oneself.

As a result, not only is emphasis moving towards a new notion of what constitutes knowledge, but it is also moving towards an increased role for school in fostering interpersonal and intrapersonal development. It is increasingly being demanded that education consciously strive to facilitate full and satisfactory personal growth and increased self-actualization. Education should help to develop people who, as part of the process of growth towards maturity, will be equipped to cope with the psychological tensions and pressures resulting from rapid change. In a world of personal and emotional instability, with consequent risk of the submergence, overwhelming or alienation of individuality, it is important that education foster patterns of intrapersonal growth that will equip people to retain their identities and to grow personally as society changes.

2.4 Educational needs of adults

A third problem confronting contemporary educational systems is that
they do not adequately provide for the needs of the largest single segment
of society - adults. Whereas children will have to cope with the changes of
the future at some later time when they become grown up, those who are already adults have no such period of grace. They are already surrounded by
change. No doubt it is correct that education should be concerned with
equipping the children of the present to cope with the changes of the
future, but today's adults are already embroiled in the momentous changes
of the present. The assumption that 10, 12 or 15 years of formal schooling
at some time in the past has equipped adults to cope with their entire lives
is finding decreasing favour in current educational thinking. Some signs of
this increasing concern with the education of adults are to be seen in, for
example, the growth of adult education in North America, and the development of organizational principles such as that of "recurrent education". In
a similar way, recently enacted legislation in France requires employers to
set aside substantial sums for the further education of their employees,
some German states have established periods of paid study leave (Bildungs-
urlaub) for all employees, while some Australian trade unions and employers
have recently agreed upon contracts providing for four days paid leave for
employees to attend educational courses. The enormous success of the Open
University in Britain, and steps to develop similar institutions in some other
countries, development of schemes like the decentralized teaching of practising social workers in the province of Saskatchewan in Canada, and similar developments, are examples of the burgeoning interest in the education of adults.
There is, then, a felt need for provision of formal educative experiences to
people beyond the conventional school years.

2.5 Education and early childhood

Yet another strand of argument concerns the importance of experience in
the earliest years of life in shaping future development. Although, in some
cases, their claims may have been based more on economic or political issues
than an analysis of the psychology of early childhood, many groups in highly-
developed countries have, in recent years, been subjecting governments to
increasing pressure to make formal provision for the education of very young

children. This has often been couched in terms of pre-school care for the
children of working mothers. In some societies (e.g., Canada) early childhood
education has also been proposed as a device for facilitating the eventual
amalgamation of children of ethnic minority groups (such as Canadian Indians)
into the dominant culture (e.g., Worth, 1972). Widespread attention has also
been paid in educational circles to projects involving early education such
as Headstart in the USA, aimed at remedying cognitive defects suffered as a
result of inadequate early stimulation. Certainly, the importance of experience in the earliest years of life is now widely recognized. One result is a
call for some degree of formal structuring of the learning experiences of pre-
school children (i.e., for schooling to be extended downwards from today's age
limits).

2.6 The search for educational equality

A separate broad line of attack on conventional educational organization arises from the changing conceptualization of educational equality that
has emerged in recent writings. Equality was initially seen as a matter of providing physical facilities of equal standard to all schoolchildren, regardless
of socio-economic status, race, and similar factors. Recent reports in the USA,
however, have suggested that equality in this sense is much closer to being
realized in that country than had previously been thought (e.g., Coleman, 1966).
Despite this, inequities in time spent at school, possession of school skills,
rates of entry to prestigeous occupations, and so on, still exist. Consequently, it is being argued that educational reforms are needed which will go far
beyond "patching up" the existing system. True educational equality will only
exist when all people in a society profit equally from educational facilities,
even if, for reasons such as lack of interest in schooling during childhood,
they do not utilize the educational opportunities available to them during conventional school years. There is, in fact, strong pressure for development of
systems of education which promote actual equality of *end result*, and not merely of *opportunity*, both between the various social strata within given societies, and also across societies of differing wealth and technological development.

Equality in this sense is not necessarily easy to define. For Jencks
(1972), the most workable approach lies in seeking to equalize incomes even-

tually earned. Equality of end result could also be conceptualized in terms of equality in the technical competences acquired, perhaps as measured by achievement tests or similar devices. Educational systems could also seek to foster equality in terms of opinions, aspirations, motivations, and so on. However, in its most profound sense, "equal" should refer to equal opportunity for each person to achieve the fullest possible degree of self-actualization. The nature of individuality may differ markedly from person to person, but true equality would consist in each individual having a sense of having had the fullest opportunity to exercise choice, and a sense of being self-actualized. Of course this is an ideal, perhaps even a dream, as the chapter on Sociological Foundations makes plain. However, at the very least, educational systems should seek to bend their efforts in the direction of this goal.

Thus, four broad criticisms can be discerned in educational thinking in recent years. The first is that schooling does not take adequate account of the fact that it is preparing children to cope with a changing world. The second is that there are inadequate educational facilities for adults. The third is that experiences prior to the age at which schooling conventionally commences are so important to the lives which people ultimately lead that they cannot be left entirely to the chance that determines that one child shall have one home environment, another a different one. Finally, it is argued that true educational equality does not yet exist. Adjusting in such a way as to cope with these criticisms is the challenge education faces.

2.7 The response - lifelong education

About ten years ago, various educational bodies began to examine systematically the implications for educational organization of the line of argument just spelled out. Their deliberations have led to the description of an educational principle which, it is now being claimed, should be accepted as the basis of the whole organization of education - the principle of lifelong education (Faure, 1972). The basic notion is that education should be formally conceptualized as a process which continues throughout an individual's life, from earliest childhood to old age. Of course, widespread, *informal* recognition already exists that education, in the sense of profiting from experience, developing one's potentials, learning about interpersonal relations, and so on,

does go on throughout life. What is advocated by proponents of lifelong education is that this knowledge should be systematized, and incorporated into
the design of schooling.

3. Defects of Present Educational Systems

Change brings threats to psychological life. At the same time, it is a
key element in growth and development. For the effects of change to be psychologically beneficial, they must be experienced to an extent, and at a speed
which is tolerable to the people concerned. An important factor in the development of a society whose members can profit from change is the extent
to which its citizens are prepared for change. Consequently, it is necessary
to examine current educational systems, and to ask whether they are functioning in a way which is appropriate to the new circumstances of life. Proponents
of lifelong education argue that schooling as it is presently organized falls
short on several counts. The following sections summarize the psychological
basis of such criticisms.

3.1 Cognitive development, knowledge, and vocational skills

A readily apparent shortcoming of conventional education is that it is
primarily concerned with the transmission of information (Coleman, 1972) which,
it is thought, will equip children with the knowledge and basic skills that
they will need throughout their entire lifetimes (Kyöstiö, 1972). Schooling is
seen as providing a "pre-packaged" parcel of skills that can be used in the
adult life to come simply by applying the contents of the parcel as the need
for them arises. The student is conceptualized as "a mere receptacle or
'stockpot' of knowledge" (Silva, 1973, p. 42). The information transmitted is
seen as a summary of the basic things a student will need to know in later life.
It is not usually expressly designed to be relevant to the immediate day-to-day
lives of students (although, of course, such immediate practical application
may occur more or less by chance). Nonetheless, the main usefulness of school
knowledge is seen as lying in the adult life to come.

Associated with this phenomenon has been acceptance of the view that cognitive development, learning and skill-acquisition are primarily confined to a

pecific age-range, usually from about 6 to about 18 (Parkyn, 1973). However,
t is now being claimed that there is no evidence that learning is really
ost efficient or desirable between those ages (Coste, 1973; Rohwer, 1971).
his means that two important stages of the process of intellectual devel-
pment have been neglected - the period of infancy and early childhood, and
he period of adulthood. As will be shown later, there is considerable evi-
ence of the importance in psychological development of the early years
Hunt, 1973) and also of continued learning far beyond the age at which school-
ng normally terminates (Tough, 1971).

A second major defect of conventional schooling which arises from its
estriction to a narrow age range and from its conceptualization as a process
uring which a student is equipped with all that he needs to know for life,
s that psychological development in the area of intellectual growth, acquis-
tion of knowledge, and development of skills, is regarded as the exclusive
omain of schools (Parkyn, 1973). This means that other major aspects of the
environment such as home, social groups, clubs and associations, and so on
ave been disregarded as factors fostering intellectual growth. In the same
way, other repositories of knowledge such as museums, knowledgeable people out-
ide the school setting, and so on have similarly been ignored or deprecated
Dave, 1973).

In brief, then, conventional educational systems do not take adequate
account of two important features of intellectual and cognitive development.
They do not utilize psychological knowledge concerning the longitudinal and
interlocking nature of development, which has shown that the whole process is a
continuing and continuous sequence with all stages highly co-ordinated to each
other (Dave, 1973, pp. 11-12). Furthermore, they make formal recognition of
only a very narrow segment of the environmental factors influencing development.

3.2 Interpersonal relationships and social roles

In a somewhat similar way, school in its traditional form is conceived of
as preparing students to play well-defined roles in an existing social structure (e.g., Ward, 1972). The likelihood that the "social relations of production" (Bowles, 1971, p. 478), as they currently exist, may alter drastically
during the lifetimes of today's schoolchildren, however, suggests that it is not
possible for schooling to train children in social roles that they will play

throughout their lives. On the contrary, a present-day child's work role as a worker, a professional man, and so on may disappear in the near future. Individuals may find that, in the course of a single lifetime, they change social roles from that of boss to worker and back again, and so on (Coles, 1972). Professions involving traditional, well-defined relationships between the participants may see a total breakdown of such patterns of relationships. For example, medicine may conceivably become a highly technological activity (e.g., Aujaleu, 1973). It is even possible that the whole system of work-related social roles may disappear completely, for example with a complete change in the role played by work in the community. Work may cease to be a means of ensuring possession of physical comforts, and become something more like a social obligation equivalent to rolling bandages for the Red Cross, a sign of altruism, an indication of social conscience, and so on.

Similarly, the role of the family in children's lives is now changing (e.g., Coleman, 1972, p. 431). A further eroding may be anticipated as a result of increasing technological growth, increasing urbanization and increasing complexity of life (Aujaleu, 1973). The result may be a "collapse of values" in which prestige, social identity, and interpersonal relationships may all become drastically different. Already, for example, the line between childhood and adulthood has become difficult to discern. In undeveloped, traditional societies this distinction has, in the past, been very clear, but this is no longer the case. Schooling can no longer hope to train individuals in certain social roles, and equip them with all the skills they will need to get along with other people. It seems, then, that education ought to contain a strong element of training in the playing of a wide variety of social roles (Coles, 1972, p. 178). Such training would make it possible for people to adapt readily to shifts in their own relationship to society, and to changes in society itself.

3.3 Intrapsychic development

Children at school today are growing up in an environment in which, as has already been shown, few things are certain. A major feature of healthy psychological development is the acquisition of a clear sense of personal identity and individuality. Such healthy intrapsychic growth is facilitated by the acquisition of a stable understanding of how one is related to the external world, what one can expect from it, what obligations one has to the rest of the environment, what rights and privileges one has, and so on. It is also facilitated by the knowledge that there are other people with whom understanding of how the world hangs together is shared. Finally, there is a sense of being able to predict or make sense out of the outcomes of one's own behaviour and that of others, and even a sense of being able to influence these outcomes.

In a world of vocational and social instability, such as that which has just been described, proponents of lifelong education argue that there is a serious danger that the process of intrapsychic growth will be inhibited to the detriment of the individuals concerned. There is a serious danger that identity, self-confidence, and individuality will be overwhelmed or swept away because of the absence of fixed and secure landmarks or props to guide and store up personal development. As Dumazedier (1972) has put it, there is a high risk of serious alienation from the self resulting from instability and uncertainty.

3.4 Emotional and motivational development

Schools have traditionally been concerned with transmission of skills and knowledge and not with education in the moral, ethical, emotional, or motivational domains (Coleman, 1972). In today's circumstances of change, however, it is doubtful that this can be allowed to continue. Traditionally, the family has been regarded as the place in which socio-affective education occurs. However, the kinds of factors outlined in the preceding three sections indicate, not only that non-school social factors have ceased to serve their traditional roles, but that emotional pressures on children, and socio-affective influences on their development are likely to be of extraordinary importance in the future. If they are to cope with the pressures of change, they will need to be extremely robust, as far as their emotional resources are concerned.

A final major area of psychological functioning which is affected by change, novelty and uncertainty is that of motivation. As will be shown in more detail in a later section, people may react to change with rigidity and avoidance. On the other hand, the presence of change and uncertainty may motivate them to seek adaptive adjustments. To a considerable extent, the *motiva-*

ting properties of uncertainty are modified by prior experience with it. Thus, it is argued by proponents of lifelong education that an educational system which provides children with opportunities to experience uncertainty and to make adaptive adjustments to it will be necessary, if students are to be prepared to live full and satisfying lives.

4. Characteristics of Lifelong Education

The response to the new psychological pressures arising from the un-precedented conditions of change in contemporary life is that of lifelong ed-ucation. The present section will outline its major characteristics from a psychological standpoint.

4.1 Continuousness of growth

Lifelong education squarely recognizes that learning occurs throughout life, although, of course, the process may not be identical at different stages of development. For example, very young children may learn primarily through actual experience with concrete objects, whereas cognitively more mature individuals may depend more heavily on symbolic processes. Nonetheless, as writers on lifelong education have emphasized, cognitive development, person-ality growth, and social, emotional and motivational development all continue throughout life. Since learning is recognized as being a lifelong phenomenon, it is argued that it should be fostered from earliest years to old age. Educ-ation is clearly seen as "a process of change leading to the development of the individual" (Silva, 1973, p. 41). As a result, it is seen as serving to facil-itate psychological development throughout life, and lifelong education is proposed as the organizing principle which will make it possible for education to function in this way.

4.2 Needs of the very young

If education is to be a lifelong process, co-ordinated to psychological growth at all ages, it will have to be concerned with very young children. Indeed, lifelong education recognizes that the early years constitute a stage of psychological development in their own right, and are not merely a waiting

period prior to later childhood and adolescence, during which schooling is
to take place. Thus, writers in the area recognize the importance of early
childhood as a crucial stage of development in intellectual development, the
capacity for attention, concentration and alertness, the capacity to interpret, analyze and organize experience, the formation of social and interpersonal relations, the understanding of self and a secure sense of identity, and so on. Lifelong education recognizes that the early years lay
down a basis on which later psychological development builds. Recent summaries of the importance of the early years are to be found in Hunt (1973)
and Hutt (1974).

A discussion of what this means for education is to be found in the
"Worth Report" (Worth, 1972), prepared under the auspices of the government
of the Canadian province of Alberta. Worth argues that education should not
be denied to the under-six, and recommends the establishment of formal
systems of early education, which he calls "Early Ed". He outlines three main
goals for Early Ed including provision of stimulation, fostering of a sense
of identity, and provision of appropriate socialization experiences (p. 50).
Of greater importance for the present purposes is that Worth specifically
rejects the notion that early education should be a downward extension of
existing systems. Its main function would not be the provision of preliminary academic training in the conventional mould. On the contrary, in advocating early education as the first stage in a system of lifelong education,
he suggests that its goal should include developing skills for dealing with
information and symbols, promoting appreciation of various modes of self-
expression, nurturing curiosity and ability to think, cultivating each child's
confidence in his ability to learn, fostering a sense of self-worth, and
finally, increasing the capacity to live with others. In lifelong education,
early psychological growth and associated educational systems are seen as
involving a complex of cognitive, motivational and socio-affective factors
which, if appropriately developed, would serve as the basis for a lifetime of
self-fulfilment.

4.3 Needs of adults

For children, most of their life lies before them. A major task of education is to provide them with the psychological basis for a lifetime of de-

velopment. However, those who are already adults also have their own needs. For example, the threat of redundancy or of obsolescence is one that already faces many workers at all levels of skill and training. According to Dubin (1974), professional engineers are already struggling with the problem of skill-obsolescence, and in the future newly-graduated engineers in the USA face the prospect of being obsolescent within five years of completing their degree programs. Overcoming obsolescence resulting from rapid change is not merely a matter of providing evening classes for adults and related physical facilities. On the contrary, psychological factors such as flexibility, willingness to switch from the role of boss to that of student, belief in one's own ability to change, confidence and hopefulness rather than fearfulness and avoidance of the new, and similar intrapersonal factors are all involved in adults' capacity to cope with change. A key factor inhibiting successful relearning, along with the associated social, vocational and personal readjustment (what might be called "psychological reorganization") is absence of a condition of psychological readiness for coping with change, absence of what Dubin called "personal initiative" (1974, p. 19). Education should be organized in such a way as to promote high levels of personal initiative for continued development if it is to meet the needs of adults.

4.4 Co-ordination of psychological domains

Psychologists have long been aware of the importance of factors other than simply intellectual power in interactions between individuals and their environment. For example, Galton acknowledged that what he called "genius", which he identified by studying persons who had been highly successful in life, was a complex of intellectual skills, appropriate levels of motivation, and favourable emotional attitudes. Lifelong education places heavy emphasis on this integration of psychological domains in the process of adjustment and self-development. The principle of horizontal integration emphasizes that personal growth results from the co-ordination of many domains of psychological functioning.

A second aspect of lifelong education's recognition of horizontal integration in psychological functioning is its emphasis on non-school sources of experience. The growth of formal schooling in the last 100 years, along with the belief that school can provide all the necessary skills needed for successful adult life, and the development of a highly specialized corps of professional educators (teachers), has led to widespread acceptance of the view that school is the only worthwhile source of information and arena for learning. By contrast, proponents of lifelong education place great emphasis on other influences in cognitive, personal and social development. For example, they emphasize the importance of museums, libraries and similar sources of knowledge. They also emphasize peers and other non-school personnel in the growth of knowledge and skills. Similarly, lifelong education stresses the role of family, playmates, workmates, spouses, children, and all other people with whom contact is made as major shapers of social and personal growth. Thus, the theory of lifelong education places heavy emphasis on the co-ordination of psychological domains and of sources of experience in the process of psychological development.

4.5 Education for personal growth

A further major feature in the psychological analysis of lifelong education is the role its proponents conceptualize it as serving in intrapersonal development. Emphasis is moving away from regarding education as primarily concerned with the provision of saleable vocational skills towards its role in fostering intrapsychic growth. One of its major tasks is seen as that of facilitating personal development throughout life (e.g., Lengrand, 1970, p. 46). This conceptualization of education as a tool for developing individuals has been found in the writings of earlier theorists such as Matthew Arnold (e.g., Johnson, 1972) and Comenius (e.g., Kryasek & Polisensky 1968). However, writers in the area of lifelong education see this need as being stronger than ever, in the light of the serious danger that the forces of change currently at work may overwhelm individuality and lead to widespread states of personal alienation (e.g., Dumazedier, 1972). Thus, a common view expressed by many writers is that a major element of education within a lifelong orientation would be emphasis on the role of values, ethics, self-awareness, individuality, self-realization, etc. In the face of massive urbanization, disintegration of the family as a major supporter of intrapersonal growth, uncertainty and even trepidation concerning the future, and highly unstable interpersonal roles, the fostering of intrapsychic growth has become a major concern to theorists in the area of lifelong education.

4.6 Education for social development

School is no longer in a position to train children in vocational
skills which can be exchanged for employment in the future, and in social
roles which fit those vocational skills and which will foster easy social
adjustment (e.g., Bowles, 1971; Kyöstiö, 1972). Consequently, the theory
of lifelong education places very heavy emphasis on education specifically
aimed at fostering flexibility in social roles, the ability to adopt changed
roles (e.g., Coles, 1972). Among other things, this involves the belief that
learning should be seen as directly related to the real, everyday, social
life of children. Lifelong education thus emphasizes the connection between
school-oriented skills and one's real life as a member of a complex of many
social groups, such as family, playmates or workmates, fellow members of
recreational groups, and so on, in all of which one plays a variety of social roles. The view expressed by proponents of lifelong education is that
such roles are likely to be subject to so much change during the lifetimes
of today's children, that education should involve experiences which will
help them to achieve the necessary changes without personal disorganization.

4.7 Education for equity

As Lengrand (1970, pp. 26-27) for example, has argued, there are powerful social forces at work today which urge that all societies and all strata
of each society should have full opportunity to realize their own potentials,
and equal access to social, economic and political advantages. Education is
recognized as an important factor in the achievement of such full opportunity
and full sharing, so that the achievement of true educational equity is a
matter of considerable importance. Conventional education systems are argued,
both in North American-European educational systems (e.g., Jencks, 1972), and
in developing countries (e.g., Parkyn, 1973), to inhibit true equality. Writers
in the area of lifelong education (e.g., Ward, 1972, pp. 179-181) argue that
school as it presently exists serves essentially to preserve the status quo and
to perpetuate inequality. Early notions of educational equality (e.g., Coleman,
1966) defined it as involving provision of educational facilities (both physical plant and personnel) of equal quality, and equally legal opportunity to

utilize such facilities. However, more recent proponents of educational
equality have argued that what is required is not merely equality of access
to educational systems, but actual equality of end result (e.g., Jencks,
1972). A much more stringent definition of educational equality has been
employed.

It is difficult, however, to see how this more recent definition of
equality could be achieved without undue coercion. For example, it does
not seem possible to force children of underprivileged groups to attend
school, and it is impossible to make them learn. What is needed is an educational organization in which all citizens have access to education at a
time when they feel the need of such access, and under circumstances in which
they find the experience congenial and stimulating. In other words, it would
be necessary to provide access to educational facilities at a time when
motivational levels were high and emotional variables were favourable. Jencks
has pointed out that this apparently requires access to education throughout
life, so that those who do not desire schooling between the conventional age
limits can still obtain an education when they are in a psychological state
favourable to benefitting from it.

A second aspect of the role of lifelong education in facilitating educational equity arises from the belief that very early experiences are of great
importance in later psychological development. If children, and especially
children from home backgrounds in which early childhood is likely to be spent
in conditions of minimal stimulation, are to develop their psychological potentials to the full, it seems to be necessary that formal provision be made
for the fostering of psychological growth in the intellectual, personal and
social domains during the crucial early years. Again, it has been suggested
(e.g., Worth, 1972) that this can best be achieved by the provision of formal
educational services in very early childhood.

5. Psychological Basis of Lifelong Education

The analysis to date has been concerned with elucidation of the psychological criticisms of conventional education in the light of rapid change, and
with a description of the main psychological features of lifelong education, as

it has been described by its proponents. The following sections review psychological evidence for the validity of the major premises of lifelong education
as they have been elucidated in earlier sections. For this purpose, five broad
psychological themes may be discerned. These are summarized as follows:

a. Rapid change poses a psychological threat, in that it has
   the potential to be disruptive and alienating.

b. Intellect functions effectively throughout life, and not
   merely during the ages of conventional schooling.

c. Psychological development during the pre-school years is
   of profound importance and requires integration into
   educational systems.

d. Learning and change pervade adult life as well as childhood
   and, again, require formal recognition in the educational
   structure.

e. Psychological functioning is co-ordinated and interrelated
   (integrated) both over time (vertically), and also across
   domains (horizontally).

The purpose of the paragraphs which follow is to provide a brief review of the
psychological evidence for the validity of these assumptions. The brief summaries of psychological findings are not intended to be exhaustive or defin-
itive. Their purpose is to indicate, in summary form, the broad outline of
psychological findings which are relevant to the present discussion only, and
not to provide an exhaustive review.

5.1 Change as a psychological "threat"

Educators are now arguing that conventional systems for the delivery of
education are inadequate, in the light of the ubiquity of change. This is not
to suggest that change is bad, or that it should be resisted. Rather, what is
needed is that education should foster skills in coping effectively with
change, in moving with it and benefitting from it. A major aspect of psychological development is the achievement of stability and permanence in a fluc-
tuating and relatively uncertain environment. In the *intellectual/cognitive
domain*, people learn that experience is systematic and organized, so that the
world ceases to be a "blooming buzzing confusion" (James, 1890, p. 488), and
becomes sensible and understandable. Causes and effects are seen to be logically connected, and techniques and strategies for understanding what is going on

"out there" are established (e.g., Bruner, 1964; Inhelder & Piaget, 1958). In the domain of *interpersonal relations and social roles*, people come to have definite roles and meaningful relationships with each other. A sense of belonging to certain groups develops, and a network of bonds with other people is built up. This web of intangible bonds of belongingness has been referred to as consisting of "sentiment relations" (Wood, 1969). An individual learns that he has certain rights and privileges in contacts with other people, and associated obligations and duties. He learns to move smoothly and easily through life as an individual with well-defined membership of a comprehensive social network, in which his work is defined by education, vocational status, personality, and similar factors (e.g., Havighurst, 1953).

In the domain of *intrapsychic development, individuality and personal identity*, a sense of self, self-worth, personal uniqueness, and so on is built up. The individual acquires values, morals and ethics. He understands that certain behaviours are repugnant to him, and others admirable. He develops an internalized value system which guides and stabilizes his behaviour, so that he becomes relatively stable for other people, and they for him. He becomes an individual person (e.g., Erikson, 1959). Finally, in the area of *emotional and motivational functioning*, the individual acquires ambitions and aspirations. He sets levels of personal expectation, strives for goals, learns to expend effort. He becomes skilled in handling success and failure, and learns to adjust his aspirations, hopes and fears on the basis of his experience with life (see Atkinson & Feather, 1966 for an extended discussion). He becomes, in the normal course of events, emotionally and motivationally stable.

In all of these areas, adaptive, effective and personally satisfying levels of adjustment are the result of a long developmental process. The infant is cognitively, socially, personally and emotionally immature and ill-equipped. However, with increasing age, development proceeds rapidly, until stable and adaptive patterns of functioning are reached. Although there are grounds for believing that some of the variation between individuals in this developmental process results from inherited sources, a major determinant is clearly that of experience during the course of psychological growth. The developing individual learns from his experiences with a stable, patterned, and systematic environment.

Of the environmental guides to psychological development, consistency and
stability are key factors. People learn from the presence of "recurring
regularities" in their lives. It is the pattern or regularity of experience which permits the individual to develop a coherent and stable
notion of how experience holds together.

However, a seeming paradox arises at this point. As Berlyne (1960) has
shown, it is uncertainty, surprisingness, unpredictability, and so on, which
energize learning. Without uncertainty, a condition of stagnation would en-
sue. In a totally predictable environment, psychological growth would stop.
Change is a normal and even desirable phenomenon. Thus, psychological development requires the simultaneous presence of stability and predictability,
but along with it uncertainty and surprisingness are needed. In other words,
change is necessary for psychological growth (and hence should not be avoided or resisted), but at the same time has the potential to disrupt and dis-
organize it. The argument advanced by proponents of lifelong education is not
that change should be impeded, but that it should be met effectively and
utilized. It is only excessive uncertainty met with total unpreparedness which
overwhelms. Those writers who have focused attention on rapid and widespread
change in modern life have, in fact, drawn attention to the fact that the rate
of change may now be becoming excessive, without special adjustment. The
stability of experience is now under unprecedented threat. It is becoming
increasingly difficult to find invariants in life - the recurring regularities
are being disrupted.

Direct evidence of the effects of excessive change is not available.
However, it is possible to study groups of people who have suffered severe dis-
location as a result of separation from the stable environment through which
they have, in the past, given meaning and purpose to their lives. This can be
done by studying, for example, immigrants who move from a known environment to
one of great unfamiliarity. They may find that their vocational skills are no
longer valid, for example as a result of rejection by the receiving society of
foreign qualifications. They may also find that values and morals are different.
Social status may be disrupted, treasured rituals may become foreign nonsense,
great events of the historical past may become minor or unknown trivialities. A
rich and proud language may be rejected as foreign gibberish. Sometimes vocational status is destroyed, values and ethics become irrelevant, sentiment re-

lations are non-existent, motives and aspirations are totally inappropriate.

The immigrant in this condition is likely to be overwhelmed by change. His life becomes unpredictable. He can no longer understand what is going on around him. He cannot control the results of his own behaviour, or predict other people's responses to him. He is everywhere uncertain. Even the simplest everyday tasks are fraught with uncertainty and at least embarrassment. He has lost control of his own life. He is, in fact, alienated. The effects on the immigrant are striking. He may, if he cannot cope with the change (as many migrants successfully can), experience social isolation, estrangement from his own children, profound unhappiness, bitterness, alcoholism, criminality, failure in mental health, and so on. (An extended discussion of the literature in this area is to be found in Kovacs and Cropley, 1975). The effects of profound change can, then, be devastating.

Extremely rapid change within a given society seems to involve conditions very similar to those experienced by immigrants. There is disruption of values, uncertainty of social roles, collapse of former vocational status, uselessness of earlier skills, and so on. The intrapersonal threat of change, then, is that it will yield alienation, through the overwhelming of individuality and identity. The challenge to education is to adjust in such a way as to meet the threat and to use change adaptively as part of a process of social and individual growth.

5.2 Intellectual functioning throughout life

There is widespread acceptance of the view that the ages during which conventional schooling takes place are the best ages for learning and, indeed, for intellectual functioning in general. For example, William James concluded that very little worthwhile is learned after the age of about 25, while Lehman (1953) argued that productive creativity is normally exhausted by the age of 40 or so. The conventional conceptualization of intellectual development is that there is rapid growth in early life, a peak at a relatively early age, a plateau period of stability, and finally a rapid decline in later adulthood. Authorities have been unable to agree on the precise ages at which the various changes in the course of development occur. However, the typical curve is that cited by Wechsler (1958). According to this graph, there is rapid growth in intellectual ability until about age 15, a plateau until about 40, a slow decline until about 60, and a period of rapid decline thereafter.

This opinion about the course of intellectual growth gains support from several influential and widely known studies conducted between the two world wars (e.g., Jones & Conrad, 1933; Yerkes, 1921), and even from more recent studies (e.g., Vincent, 1952). However, it is now clear that any decline in intellectual functioning which does occur is not general, but is specific to certain kinds of intellectual functions. For example, Tyler (1965) and Anastasi (1958) have reported that the fall-off is most marked in the kinds of abilities tapped by tests of analogies, number series tasks, and reasoning tasks. It is least marked, or even not present at all, in tests of vocabulary and arithmetic. In fact, Havighurst (1969, p. 60) concluded that there is a fall-off in performance on tasks requiring speed and high levels of perceptual skills, but there is no similar fall-off in tasks requiring experience and "know-how". What Havighurst called "competence" tends to increase rather than decrease.

This finding is supported by many well known studies. For example, Foulds and Raven (1948) showed that there was no decline in the vocabulary scores of factory workers at differing ages, although there was a decline on a reasoning test. Similarly, Fox and Birren (1950) found that elderly subjects got much better scores on some kinds of tests than on others, and supported the argument that it is incorrect to refer to a general and universal tendency for intellect to decay after adolescence. In fact, Tyler (1965, p. 280) has concluded that there is overwhelming evidence that certain kinds of intellectual functioning remain stable after adolescence or even increase up to about age 60. An important theoretical formulation that helps to conceptualize the difference between kinds of abilities that deteriorate with age and those that do not has been developed by Cattell and Horn (see Horn, 1968, for example). They distinguish between "fluid intelligence" and "crystallized intelligence". Fluid intelligence may be conceptualized in the present context as the capacity to acquire new abilities, a capacity that becomes decreasingly important and is decreasingly employed with advancing age - it may be said to decline with age. Crystallized intelligence consists of acquired abilities that have been formed (crystallized) as a result of the interaction between fluid intelligence and experience. This aspect of intelligence does not deteriorate so markedly with age. Intelligence conceptualized as the sum of the two kinds of intelligence, remains stable until age 60 or later (see Horn in Goulet & Baltes, 1970). Indeed, in a recent review,

Schaie (1974, p. 805) has concluded that the notion that the old decline intellectually is, to a substantial degree, "a myth".

Nonetheless, some skills do decline with age, and reasons why have been investigated by a number of writers. Welford (1969), for example, has concluded that ageing is accompanied by slowing down of the nervous system's capacity to deal with stimuli. Indeed, there is a body of evidence which supports the view that apparent differences in abilities of young and old human beings are largely an artefact of differences in their abilities to work at high speed (e.g., Jerome, 1962; Welford, 1969). Lorge (1936) calculated a correction factor for the effects of differing ability to work at high speed, and then re-analysed the Jones and Conrad data already referred to. He found that there were then no longer any age differences in scores. Similarly, Welford showed that where material is presented under appropriate circumstances, the elderly may achieve good levels of performance. Adults can successfully carry out intellectual tasks, given appropriate kinds of instructions, and appropriate performance conditions. While the techniques of youth may not be appropriate to middle and later life, people who mobilize their intellect and organize their abilities in appropriate ways can show high levels of intellectual ability until very late in life. This implies the need for educational systems designed to promote effective intellectual functioning throughout life.

5.3 Learning beyond conventional school age

As has been pointed out, the conventional and traditional opinion is that people quickly deteriorate intellectually beyond the age of 40 or so, and that their learning capacity is seriously impaired from about then (Comfort, 1964; Naylor & Harwood, 1970). One result of this traditional belief has been the great neglect of the adult in the study of learning and, indeed, psychological development. This state of affairs has been partially corrected in recent years by the emergence of an increased interest in the psychology of adults (e.g., Bischof, 1969; Bromley, 1971; Goulet & Baltes, 1970; Neugarten, 1964). However, these studies have tended to concentrate on the elderly. Consequently, they neglect people in what might be called the "prime of life" from about 30 to about 65 (Dubin, 1974).

One major study of adult achievement was that of Lehman (1953). He found that chemists reached their peak, generally speaking, between 26 and 30 years of age. Mathematicians peaked between 30 and 40, philosophers between 35 and 39. Authors did their best work before reaching the age of 45, while movie actors achieved their greatest popularity between 30 and 40. Of course, many people in these fields did not conform to these averages, the figures cited being generalizations describing the overall picture as it is most frequently seen. Consequently, Lehman concluded that, exceptions to the rule notwithstanding, creativity peaks in the 30s and declines slowly thereafter. In a later paper analyzing the reasons for this state of affairs, Lehman concluded that a fall-off in adult performance is not necessarily the result of mental deterioration. For example, adults may simply accept the social stereotype that they become less productive after the age of 30 or 40. Furthermore, promotion, prestige and leadership may lead away from actual involvement in creative effort and into administration, in which there may actually be advantages in reduced flexibility (Welford, 1969). Similarly, there may well be a tendency for those who achieve early success to rest on their laurels, adopting the attitude that they have done their bit, and now can reap the rewards. Hostility from the young-and-upcoming, and associated social pressure to be less active may also inhibit productivity in adults. Thus, Lehman once again emphasized that decreasing productivity in adults may reflect social pressures, values and attitudes rather than deterioration of ability.

Tough (1971) has pointed out that adults continually seek further learning, although not necessarily in conventional classroom settings. They voluntarily undertake instruction in a wide range of areas, from clinical psychology to child development, to business management and ecology. He reported that North American adults may spend up to 700 hours a year in learning projects of the kind mentioned above. Johnstone and Rivera (1965) coined the phrase "volunteers for learning" to describe the larger numbers of adults seeking further education. Studies by, for example, Thorndike (cited in McLeish, 1963), in which elderly people learned Esperanto, and Cheydlew (cited in McLeish, 1963) in which they learned French, have shown that adults are capable of school-like learning even at advanced ages. In a similar vein, Naylor and Harwood (1970) demonstrated that elderly subjects could be taught translation from German to English. One of their best students was 88! About half of the students achieved a German-to-English translation standard equivalent to University matriculation level, in only six months of instruction. In a less cerebral domain, McFarland and O'Doherty (1959) reported that airline pilots up to the age of about 60 could convert to jets from piston-engined aircraft, and so continue their working lives.

As in the example just cited, learning late in life is becoming something more than merely a hobby for large numbers of adults. Many face the possibility of job obsolescence unless they can adjust and adapt to change. Indeed, in some countries, lifelong learning is becoming compulsory. For example, in the USA the American Board of Internal Medicine now expects its members to requalify every ten years, the American Board of Family Practice every six years. Two states have enacted legislation requiring physicians to take further training every three years (Dubin, 1974).

There are, then, grounds for believing that adults are perfectly capable of learning throughout life, and there are also grounds for believing that it is increasingly important that they actually do so. This state of affairs has not gone unnoticed, and one result has been the proliferation of classes for adults, offered within a variety of organizational frameworks such as "recurrent education", "continuing education", "intermittent education", and so on. However, such programs have not met with unbroken success in all areas. One difficulty lies in the fact that some workers have been unwilling to carry out the task of acquiring new learning. They have, for example, rejected re-training as beneath their dignity as adults, experienced embarrassment or a sense of uselessness, or even rejected the idea that any change is needed. This suggests that education for adults cannot simply be grafted on at the upper end of existing systems, unless the two are co-ordinated in such a way that earlier schooling is seen logically to lead to later schooling. At the present moment, schooling is still conceptualized as something for childhood. What is needed is a system in which adult and school learning are seen as part of a continuous fabric.

5.4 Vertical and horizontal integration in cognitive functioning

The term "cognition" is used here to refer to the procedures through which people actively seek out, organize and interpret, store, and subsequently re-use information. It is thus essentially a qualitative concept referring to differences of style or pattern rather than differences in level. One phenomenon of cognitive growth involves changes in the organization of intelligence. A major theoretical concept in this area is that of "differentiation of abilities".

Briefly, it is argued that, in young children, intelligence is a global and undifferentiated phenomenon, but that, with increasing age, specific abilities are developed and co-ordinated with each other in problem solving (e.g., Burt, 1954; Garrett, 1946). However, other studies (e.g., Cropley, 1964; Dockrell, 1963) have shown that differentiation of abilities is not a universal phenomenon. In fact, as Vernon (1950) has concluded, the pattern of growth in style of intellectual functioning is largely dependent on experience.

A broader concept in the area of cognitive development is that of "cognitive styles". Cognitive processes involve a comprehensive organization of internal information-processing systems, and associated information-receiving capacities. It is possible to observe systematic and personally-idiosyncratic differences between individual people in the way in which they carry out these organizing processes. For example, when asked to recall previously-learned material, some people regularly "fill in" gaps in their recall with explicatory material (Paul, 1959). By contrast, others (Klein, 1970) simply recall the basic, factual skeleton, stripping away all superfluous details. Some people minimize variations among different elements of stimulus material, hardly noticing minor differences of detail. By contrast, others emphasize and even exaggerate such minor differences. Again, some people attend to a very broad range of environmental stimuli, and try to co-ordinate them into a broad, generalized whole. Others concentrate on a narrow substrate of a complex stimulus, and interpret it in terms of this restricted sampling.

Such differences have been described and discussed in detail by, for example, Klein (1970). Other writers have developed similar conceptualizations (e.g., Gardner, Holzman, Klein, Linton & Spence, 1959; Witkin, 1964; Cropley and Sikand (1973) have related such variables to adaptive coping with real life by showing that one major feature of differences between highly creative individuals and schizophrenics lay in the ability of the creatives to tolerate incongruity and uncertainty without excessive anxiety. Furthermore, Freeberg and Payne (1967) have shown that this aspect of cognitive development is affected by experience. Thus, the capacity to deal with one's environment in effective ways is apparently subject to a developmental process, in which training and experience play a substantial part.

In particular, the organization of the education a child receives is apparently a key factor in fostering or inhibiting differentiation of abilities. Where it stresses the unity of knowledge, cognitive functioning tends to be broad and global, with inter-relationships among domains of experience being readily perceived. By contrast, fragmentation of curriculum into a large number of relatively discrete domains fosters development of cognitive styles in which experience is treated as disjointed and separate, intellectual skills are relatively independent of each other, and transfer of skills between kinds of intellectual tasks is low. In the present terminology, the extent to which intellective and cognitive functions are co-ordinated with each other (functioning is horizontally integrated) is modified by curriculum organization. A second major implication is that different people learn in different ways. Some people learn best when information is presented in highly-structured wholes, some best grasp broad, general principles, some require large amounts of fine detail, and so on. For the classroom, this implies that there is no one, best technique for the presentation of information. On the contrary, a variety of modes of presentation and sources of information is implied.

The developmental sequence involved in cognitive growth has been most fully explicated by Piaget (e.g., Inhelder & Piaget, 1958), along with other writers, such as Vygotsky (1962), and Bruner (e.g., 1964). With the conscious omission of details and differences, all of these writers emphasize that cognitive growth is a co-ordinated, sequential process in which all stages are closely inter-related. In general, there is a fixed sequence of stages or periods which cannot be circumvented. Each stage merges into both the one preceding it and the one following it. No stage of cognitive growth can be mastered unless the preceding stage has been successfully negotiated. Thus, cognitive development is seen as a sequential whole, with earliest growth and latest phases of development intimately connected with each other.

5.5 The role of childhood in psychological development

Although early childhood has typically been conceptualized as a period of helplessness and quiescence, there is very strong evidence that an enormous amount of learning goes on in the pre-school years. For example, Bloom (1964) concluded that 50 percent of mental development occurs by the age of 4. However, since most pre-school learning involves the acquisition of skills which adults and school-age children take for granted, much of the learning goes unnoticed. Due credit for the enormous developmental task successfully negotiated by very young children is seldom given. In fact, by the age of 3-4 days, the new-born infant is already responsive to stimulation. A certain degree of skill is present from the first or second day (Kagan, Henker, Hen Tov, Levine & Lewis, 1966). Infants are much more "competent" than has previously been thought to be the case (see Stone, Murphy & Smith, 1972), for an extensive review of the evidence of the competence of infants and very young children). Of even greater importance for the present purposes is the fact that learning during early childhood serves as a basis for a great deal of future development. Early childhood is a significant stage in development and forms a crucial step in many domains. These include intellectual development (e.g., Hunt, 1973), attention, concentration and alertness (e.g., Kessen, 1967), cognitive growth (e.g., Bruner, 1964; Inhelder & Piaget, 1958), social development (e.g., Baumrind, 1967), and so on. Among the skills that are acquired at a very early age are depth perception (Walk & Gibson, 1961), discrimination of shapes and forms (Hebb, 1949), discrimination of patterns and forms (Fantz, 1963 discrimination of pitch (Leventhal & Lipsitt, 1964), discrimination of loudness (Bartoshuk, 1964), and so on.

In addition to such sensory skills, however, many elementary cognitive functions emerge, and achievements in the domain of personality are mastered. These include the achievement of object constancy (things still exist even when you cannot actually see them) (Inhelder & Piaget, 1958), the discrimination of self from environment (e.g., Flavell, 1963), the first use of symbolic behaviour (e.g., Bruner, 1964), and so on. Communication with other people is learned in the first few months, and the basic foundations of language are laid down in this period (e.g., Menyuk, 1971). Subtleties of cause and effect are acquired, along with increasing capacity to understand the abstract world of the not here and not now. The quality of experience affects the development of perceptual systems (e.g., Chow, Riesen & Newell, 1957), of alertness and interest in the external world (Dennis & Sayegh, 1965), of the ability to analyze and reflect upon the environment in abstract terms (e.g., Schubert & Cropley, 1972), and of

the basic perceptual, motor and cognitive skills which are highly correlated
with learning to read and subsequent school progress (e.g., Hunt, 1973).

Many personality traits too arise out of a basis of learning in early
childhood. The crucial beginnings of the capacity to relate to other people
are learned prior to school age (e.g., Eriksen, 1968), as are the capacities
to display appropriate mothering behaviours (e.g., Harlow & Harlow, 1966), to
express hostility and aggression in sex-appropriate ways (e.g., Maccoby, 1967),
to seek success and achievement in school (e.g., Kagan & Moss, 1959), to respond to different kinds of reward and punishment (e.g. Terrell, Durkin &
Wiesley, 1959), to be curious and inquiring or to avoid uncertainty (e.g.,
Berlyne, 1958), and so on. Finally, children acquire strategies or tactics
for analyzing their experiences with the external world during early childhood (e.g., Freeberg & Payne, 1967).

Indeed, as Jencks (1972) has strikingly shown in a recent review, by
the time a child starts school he will customarily have learned a whole complex of attitudes, feelings, values, motivations and skills. Furthermore,
these traits will largely determine the progress that the child makes in
school. The affective, motivational, attitudinal basis for learning in life
is already well-established by the commencement of school age, and is only
moderately affected by the actual process of schooling. This finding has been
confirmed by, for example, the Plowden Report.

Consequently, it may be said that psychological development in the earliest years has a double role. On the one hand, development during that period
lays down the crucial foundation for later development in many psychological
domains. On the other hand, the motives, attitudes and values learned prior
to the commencement of schooling set a pattern for the way in which the child
will deploy his intellectual and cognitive skills in later life. It is not un-
reasonable to say, then, that the events of early childhood are of the greatest
importance to psychological functioning throughout life. For this reason, as
Worth (1972) has suggested, they are too important to be ignored by the educational system and left to the vagaries of chance which determine that one child
will experience a favourable early environment, another an environment marked
by deprivation of crucial experiences.

5.6 Vertical and horizontal integration in social development

In the earliest years, the young child is dependent and relatively powerless, in terms of the society as a large group. His role is that of recipient of whatever those who control resources (food, clean clothing, etc.) let him have. He is expected to be led by adults and to train himself for the future. He is regarded as essentially helpless and in need of protection, and as basically incapable of making decisions for himself. In adolescence, the beginnings of the later adult role of wage-earner and pillar of the community begin to be laid down (e.g., Buehler & Massarik, 1968; Havighurst, 1953). At this stage, especially in modern life, a problem involving stability or in-stability of social roles may become apparent. The status of adolescence may be unclear, its members comprising a group of people who are neither adults nor children. During early adulthood, the role of parent and rising leader of society is paramount. The young adult is expected to participate vigorously in the strenuous and gainful activities of the society, and to establish him-self as one of its stable members who is capable of functioning smoothly within its particular requirements and constraints. In middle adulthood, more concern is appropriate for community works, guidance of the young, social service, and so on. In this stage of life, people may be expected to display leadership in politics, committee membership, acceptance of positions of trust in church, trade unions, and so on. As late adulthood and old age supervene, the individual is expected to become increasingly passive and dependent, to become markedly less vigorous and thrusting in his relationships with society, and to yield place to the young. To some extent, the wheel swings full circle, in that the roles assigned to the elderly are in some ways comparable with those assigned to the very young.

The sequence of events involved in social development has been described in differing ways by differing authors (e.g., Erikson, 1959; Freud, 1946; Havighurst, 1953, and so on). However, a general theme may be seen in all de-scriptions of development in this area. What is involved is a sequence of inter-connecting events during which the individual learns just how he fits into the social order. In the earliest phases, basic developments take place, including things like the distinction between self and non-self, the perception that one's life is modified by the actions and attitudes of other people, the recognition that one must behave in certain ways in order to elicit certain responses from other people, and so on. With further development, the individual learns that he is part of a complex and organized system in which he has certain rights and privileges, along with obligations and duties. He comes to understand not only the concrete "rules" on which the social world functions, but the abstract principles underlying these rules such as duty, goodness, crime, loyalty, and so on. He acquires strong convictions about how he fits in with other people, to whom he belongs, what kind of reaction he is entitled to expect from other people, and so on.

A major factor in social development involves the acquisition by the developing individual of membership in various groups. These groups form a powerful factor in mediating his social interactions with other people. The exact dynamics of group formation and cohesiveness are not completely clear. However, it is apparent that a major factor holding them together is the existence of a distinct "we" feeling. Members of a group develop horizontal bonds with others. They feel that they are part of a cohesive unit, and that there are others who are not part of their unit. As a result, a sense of "us" and "them" develops. Within the groups to which he belongs (such as his family, his neighbourhood, his school-or work-mates, his fellow countrymen, and so on) a person learns that he has certain duties and obligations, and that these are balanced by corresponding rights and privileges. He learns his role within the group (i.e., leader or follower, and so on), what authority he may expect to exercise, and similar things. This process of social learning goes on over a lifetime.

It is apparent, then, that the whole process of social development is a process of change and growth throughout life. Socializing agencies such as the home, playmates, the school, and so on, all contribute to foster and guide a lifelong developmental sequence, in which people learn what their relationship is to other people, and in which these relationships change as life progresses. Social development also co-ordinates many aspects of life. Roles are developed through interactions with many facets of society - parents, peers, adults, strangers, friends, teachers and other sources of authority, and so on.

However, it has been customary to conceptualize social development as primarily completed by early adulthood. Indeed, school often serves to function as the preserver of the social status quo, by training students to social roles which they tend to continue throughout their lives. For example, a child may

learn at school that he is to be a professional man, a leader and a pace-
setter, or that he is to be an unskilled worker, a follower and a recipient
of what life offers. Lifelong education, by contrast, recognizes the dynamic
and fluid nature of social development and argues that school should be so
organized as to promote growth and change in the social area throughout life.
Indeed, in an environment in a state of rapid social change, the capacity to
re-learn social roles outside the school setting may become a vital one.

5.7 Vertical and horizontal integration in intrapsychic development

Social development involves learning how one stands with relation to all
other people. Intrapsychic or personality development, by contrast, involves
the development of a sense of self, feelings of distinctness from other people,
a characteristic style or pattern of receiving and interpreting information,
and relatively stable ways of dealing with experience. In the very earliest
stages of life, the newborn infant is scarcely aware of his own existence as a
separate entity. By contrast, the mature adult has developed a sense of self,
and a characteristic relatively stable style of interacting with the environment and other people. It is this style of interaction that is referred to when
a person is described as "outgoing", "shy", "impulsive", "aggressive", and so
on. The process that is of interest for present purposes is the sequence of
events starting at the neonate and ending with the termination of personality
growth.

According to Buehler (e.g., Buehler & Massarik, 1968), it is possible to
discern "a regular sequence" in the process, involving three phases. The first
is a phase of expansion during childhood and early adulthood. The second is a
phase of stability in the prime of life, and the final phase is one of re-
striction in old age. This led her to talk of a "curve of life" which could be
used to summarize graphically the nature of personal development. However, in
her more recent writings, Buehler revised her earlier conceptualization of
adulthood. Initially, she had described it as a plateau period (the phase of
stability) which led into the deterioration of old age (the phase of restric-
ion). However, she now acknowledges that adulthood is a legitimate stage of life
itself, rather than a period of stability followed by decline. She has described
separate repetitions of the cycle of personal development, one as a child and

the other as an adult. Thus, she has recognized that intrapersonal development extends far beyond childhood, and that adulthood is a legitimate phase in the process, rather than merely a prolonged afternoon before the twilight of old age.

Psychoanalytic writers such as Erikson (e.g., 1968), have also made use of the concept of stages or cycles in intrapersonal development. According to Erikson, there are 8 stages of life, ranging from infancy through childhood to young adulthood, adulthood and old age. Some of the key traits of middle age and old age that can be extracted from Erikson's theory are of considerable interest to the present document. Middle age is characterized by a switch in values from emphasis on physical power to an emphasis on wisdom. Similarly, social values switch from "sexualizing" to "socializing", while emotional life is characterized by greatly increased flexibility. With old age, the transition from concern with mastery and achievement seen in young adults, concern which was already fading in the middle-aged, is complete. The self is valued above work and achievement, there is transcendence over one's body, and ultimately, transcendence over one's self. Again, as was the case in Buehler's later writings, the adult years are treated much more positively in this conceptualization. Shifts in values and emphases with increasing age are described, not as the degeneration of youthful powers, but as the achievement of new levels of transcendence.

Havighurst (e.g., 1953) describes intrapsychic development as mainly a matter of mastering "tasks" such as learning to relate to other people, mastering a sex role, and so on. The tasks are hierarchically ordered, with self-preservation tasks at the lowest level, self-fulfilment tasks at the highest. Havighurst discerned six broad stages of intrapersonal development, each stage being unified by the primacy of similar "dominant concerns" during that stage. A conceptualization somewhat similar to Havighurst's is that of Maslow (1954). He regards the major aspect of intrapersonal functioning as the seeking of what he calls "peak experience". Peak experiences are characterized by a sense of fulfilment and achievement. They are sometimes achieved in certain phases of parenthood, in experiences involving a strong feeling of oneness with nature, in moments of creative insights, or possibly in some aspects of athletic experience. According to Maslow, people experience a hierarchy of needs. The lowest level of needs involves physiological necessities for survival, such as a supply of air.

At the next level are safety needs which are concerned with access to assured supplies of food and shelter. At the third level are needs for belongingness and love. Above them is the need for esteem, and finally the need for self-actualization. Of particular relevance to the present discussion is Maslow's view that these needs are all integrated to each other in such a way that lower-level needs must be satisfied before efforts can be made to satisfy those higher in the hierarchy. For example, the necessity to expend a lot of effort in the mere physical act of survival will preclude much attention to the development of esteem and self-actualization. In the present terms, Maslow is pointing out that intrapsychic functions are *horizontally integrated*.

The kinds of theories of intrapersonal development just described all see it as orderly, sequential and longitudinally-interdependent. Intrapsychic growth is described as a process involving a continuous, reciprocal interaction with the environment. Development of a higher stage (for example, a higher level of transcendence in Erikson's terms, or a higher level of self-fulfilment in Havighurst's) depends very much upon successful negotiation of earlier stages so that the whole process is interlocking or *vertically integrated*. Consequently, psychological analyses of intrapersonal growth stress both the longitudinal or vertical integration of development in its domain and also its horizontal integration.

5.8 Integration of motives, goals and aspirations

A similar pattern of growth can be seen in motivational-affective development. In early childhood, needs and goals are short-term and concrete, and centre on such factors as food. There is minimal ability to delay gratification, and the child responds to frustration of his immediate needs with resentment and rage. With adolescence comes greater pre-occupation with social identity, establishing a sex role, developing a stable and coherent "ideology", and so on. Many goals are long-term and there is a pronounced orientation towards the future. There is much interest in self-image, and metaphysical issues assume considerable importance (e.g., questions like "Who am I?", "Why am I here?", "Where am I going?").

In early adulthood, there is great interest in child-rearing, and a vigorous attack on carving out one's place in the world, for example through

consolidation of job skills. Interest tends to switch to immediate, relatively concrete matters like the running of the family, rather than the abstract,
metaphysical problems with which the adolescent was concerned. Energy is
focussed on consolidating one's position and getting ahead. By middle adulthood, these kinds of issues tend to have been settled. Child-rearing is
probably past, some kind of job stability has been achieved, and issues involving serving society, preserving what is treasured, and similar goals begin
to dominate. Both men and women show interest in developing new careers at
this stage. For the housewife, an important factor is that the children no
longer need continual care, so that she may return to the job market, or seek
interesting activities in fields like that of social service. In late adulthood and old age, goals become increasingly short-term, with a growing sense
that the world is a difficult complex organization that is full of problems.
Metaphysical interests increase again. With old age, there is increasing social
isolation, disengagement from active struggle, concentration on passive, contemplative pursuits, and great concern for short-term concrete goals such as
food and ways to pass the time pleasantly.

Kuhlen (1963) has suggested that there are two broad meta-motives in
adult development. One involves a drive towards expansion and growth. This
motive is seen in the seeking of achievement and power, and in self-fulfilment
and self-perpetuation. This pattern of motivation is strongest in earliest
adulthood, and begins to wane after about age 50, although it may still be seen
until 60 or beyond. The other broad motive is the opposite of that just described. It involves selection of goals as a result of motivation springing from
anxiety and insecurity. This kind of motivation has several forms, including
motivation to deal with self-perceived inadequacies, unhappiness, social inadequacy, lack of identity, and physical distress. It is relatively less
prominent among young adults, although obviously still present, than the first
kind of motivation. However, it accounts for a larger proportion of motivation
with increasing age, increasing in importance as the expansion and growth
pattern of life decreases.

It is clear that both kinds of motivation are present over the entire
adult age span, so that it is not a matter of one superseding the other. However, the relative importance of the two broad kinds of motivation changes with

age, roughly approximating the loss of physical power, desirability as an
employee, sensory acuity, socially-determined beauty, and so on, which
accompany increasing age. Broadly speaking, young adults are primarly motivated by desires for mastery and personal achievement, older adults by
desires to avoid inadequacy in many domains. However, it is important to
examine the extent to which this pattern of motivation is socially-condi-
tioned. Do people learn that they become less competent and must restrict
their aspirations? If they do, could schooling foster prolonged interest
in change and development?

Early theories of motivation (see Lefrancois, 1973, pp. 114-118 for a
discussion), emphasize that the energizing factors which trigger off human
behaviour and guide towards the goals to which it moves resulted from
either built-in factors such as instincts or needs, or else resulted from
avoidance of unbalanced states in physiological systems. However, it has become increasingly clear that motives are largely conditioned by the social
environment. For example, Atkinson and Feather (1966) have summarized studies
studying the role of "need achievement" as a major human motive. Empirical
studies (see Mussen, Conger & Kagan, 1969, pp. 561-565 for a summary) have
shown that children's need for achievement is affected by parental demands
for accomplishment, close interest shown by parents in children's achievements, provision of rewards for achievement, peer influences and pressures,
and so on. Children learn, as a result of their experiences of success and
failure, to establish levels of self-expectation, and to define their behaviour as successful or unsuccessful in the light of these levels. Furthermore,
levels of expectation are affected by peer contacts, parental expectations
and similar factors. Thus, not only is motivation subject to a longitudinal
developmental process, but it is affected by social experiences and also by
non-school activities of success and failure. Other theories of motivation
stressing the role of curiosity or the need for consistency, as well as humanistic theories such as that of Maslow (1954) also emphasize that behaviour is
triggered off and guided by factors other than physiological states. Thus, it
is apparent that motives, goals and attitudes towards learning and change are
conditioned by a wide variety of experiences, many of them lying outside the
classroom as it is conventionally structured.

6. Implications for Curriculum

6.1 Can schools develop lifelong learners?

Psychological functioning is a dynamic and developing process that changes throughout life. There is also considerable evidence that it is modified by life experiences during development, and is not simply a matter of the unfolding of predetermined sequences. Human beings are limited by their biological potentials, but possess a high level of "developmental plasticity", so that they are partly fashioned by their environments (see Hunt, 1973, and Hutt, 1974). Environmental effects modify not only the acquisition of specific skills, but also affect development of language skills, social behaviour, personality, and motivation or "joy in learning" (Hutt, 1974, p. 30). These kinds of non-specific factors are now known to be important determinants of the effects of schooling, as Jencks (1972), the Plowden Report, the International Association for the Evaluation of Educational Achievement (IEA) studies and similar research have shown. Particularly in developed countries, a point has been reached at which mere provision of the physical facilities for learning in the form of schools is no longer the key determinant of whether the kinds of adaptations and personal adjustments involved in intellectual, social, personal, vocational and motivational growth will occur.

Increasingly, it is being argued that schooling, in the sense of deliberate structuring of experiences in the hope of fostering certain patterns of desirable development, will need to take greater cognizance of both the horizontal and vertical integration of psychological functioning - schools will need to be oriented towards lifelong education. Of course, lifelong education already exists, in the sense that people already develop and adjust as a result of their experiences, both throughout life and also out of school, and not merely as a result of experiences located within school buildings and during the years of formal schooling. However, the ideal envisaged by proponents of lifelong education is that educative experiences, the sum total of experiences which stimulate the development of each individual person, can be structured in some way so as to make this existing process of lifelong education more sweeping, more self-fulfilling, more valuable to society and more valuable to the individual.

This is clearly an idealized goal. In its most highly developed form it would presumably require the abolition of schooling as we currently know it in most developed countries, and as many less-developed countries are now striving to establish it. It is an ideal that cannot be fulfilled in conventional schools, as they now exist. What is needed is a new kind of educative environment that might actually be antithetical to school organizations as we presently understand them. However, advocacy of immediate abolition of schools is obviously unworkable - what would the proponents of lifelong education do if schools were suddenly closed, and the pupils turned over to them? What is needed at the present time is development of a movement in existing schools towards the goals of lifelong education; the eventual transformation of schools and of people, to the point at which the people consciously seek change and self-development (in the broadest possible sense of the term), and the schools serve to facilitate attainment of this goal.

6.2 A lifelong curriculum for schools

It seems unlikely, then, that schools will suddenly vanish. More probable, in the short term at least, is a curricular reform aimed at facilitating the emergence of people who are willing and able to adjust to a changing world, and to develop a society in which the concepts of lifelong education can truly be implemented. What will school curriculum aimed at this goal be like? The psychological principles outlined in earlier sections have indicated that such a curriculum should be organized in a way which is integrated, both vertically and horizontally. It will be heavily concerned with values, attitudes and motivations. It would strive to foster independence, self-responsibility, self-critical analysis, flexibility, and "auto-learning" (see Brock, 1972; Dave, 1973; Kupisiewicz, 1972, and so on). A broad aim of the curriculum would be the development of people who face the prospect of change with interest and enthusiasm, not fear and reluctance. If people are to face change with confidence, they will need to be skilled in playing new social roles, working in new kinds of jobs and operating within new organizational frameworks. Failure to develop the capacity to deal with change raises the threat of the over whelming of individuality by passivity and alienation (Dumazedier, 1972). Above all, a lifelong education curriculum will equip people to handle change "without being put off by the first encounter with what is new" (Dumazedier, 1972, p. 80).

This emphasis on socio-affective and motivational aspects of curriculum does not, however, imply that knowledge-oriented aspects of curriculum can be ignored. The key cognitive skill fostered in a lifelong education curriculum will involve acquiring and applying "innovatory knowledge" (Dumazedier, 1972, p. 16). The student will learn to learn through a grasp of the tactics and codes of knowledge (Hicter, 1972; Kidd, 1972). The curriculum will aim at fostering a grasp of the structure of knowledge so that past learning will function as a basis for the acquisition of new (Zhamin & Kostanian, 1972). A key cognitive element, then, will be the building of educability. Biggs (1973) has discussed this last aspect of curriculum in the school setting. He distinguished between "content" learning (learning of selected facts because they are thought to be valuable in themselves) and "process" learning (learning that changes the ability of students to deal effectively with their future lives). This latter kind of learning has several elements which Biggs has listed (1973, pp. 230-233):

1. Possessing or being able to locate information

2. Possessing highly generalizable cognitive skills

3. Possessing general strategies for problem-solving

4. Setting one's own objectives

5. Evaluating the results of one's own learning

6. Being appropriately motivated

7. Possessing an appropriate self-concept

6.3 The teacher in lifelong education

Adoption of lifelong education as the foundation of education also has implications for the role of the teacher. He himself will be living in a changing society, and hopefully, at the forefront of change, so that it will be necessary for teachers themselves to adapt and adjust continually. The teacher will become a model of lifelong learning for his students. In a sense then, teachers and pupils will become "co-learners" (Dave, 1973, p. 44). In facili-

tating self-directed learning, positive attitudes towards learning and
similar traits, lifelong education conceptualizes the teacher as an "educational consultant" (Council of Europe, 1968, p. 53), as a "specialist in
learning methods" (Frese, 1972, p. 11), as a "leader" (Hicter, 1972, p. 309),
or as a "co-ordinator of learning activities" (Dave, 1973, p. 44). The basic
role implied by all of these writers is that of guide and co-ordinator of
learning. The teacher will not simply impart knowledge in pre-digested
packages that have been selected because they contain precisely what all
students need. He will help students to diagnose their own learning needs, to
judge the adequacy of their own resources and that of solutions they propose,
and to learn in the ways best for them.

6.4 Curriculum for the very young

A basic notion in lifelong education is that it will be a process that
occurs both in and out of school. Consequently, it is possible to talk about
"curriculum", in the lifelong education sense, as not only school curriculum,
but also out-of-school curriculum. Indeed, life itself is recognized as an
important element of lifelong education, so that one can talk of a "curriculum"
for life, a "curriculum" for work, and so on. The present section is concerned
with a "curriculum" for children whose ages lie below those at which school
attendance is currently customary.

As has already been mentioned, early development greatly affects development of language skills, intellectual functioning, social behaviour,
personality and motivation (see Hutt, 1974). These kinds of skills do not require formal schooling - they can be developed as part of life itself (Biggs,
1973; Hutt, 1974). Indeed, Worth (1972) has specifically rejected the idea
that early education should simply be a downward extension of conventional
schooling. Two recent reviews of education of the very young (Eggleston, 1974;
Röman, 1974) have outlined some of the main features of curriculum for them,
within a lifelong education orientation. According to Eggleston, the key skill
to be fostered is that of language. It is language, for example, that permits
people to organize and transmit their own ideas, wishes, thoughts and feelings.
Mastery of language permits a giant step towards achievement of self-direct-
edness and consequent reduction of other-directedness. Eggleston also emphasized

the importance of early learning experiences in the acquisition of values, thus recognizing the horizontal integration of psychological functioning.

Röman too emphasized the importance of language development among the very young. Other knowledge-oriented factors he emphasized included development of readiness for mathematics and reading skills, and diagnosis and remediation of incipient learning difficulties. Röman also emphasized the development of problem-solving capacities, a necessary skill if self-directed, independent learning is to be achieved. He extended the curriculum for the very young into the social domain by stressing the need for early mastery of the capacity to communicate, and mastery of a spirit of co-operation with other people. Finally, he drew attention to the importance of the self, stressing the need for a curriculum that includes not only physical fitness, but also fostering of the capacity for self-expression through modes other than the verbal, such as art or calisthenics.

6.5 Curriculum for beyond conventional school age

Formal efforts to engage adults in further learning have often failed, especially among those with least prior formal schooling. A frequently-cited reason for this has been, in effect, that the available formal opportunities have not been organized in such a way as to foster lifelong learning among adults. A summary of some of these problems, with some guidelines for developing a lifelong education curriculum for adults, is to be found, for example, in a recent paper by Olford (1972). He suggested that such a curriculum should:

1. provide opportunity for students to *initiate* inquiry

2. provide opportunity for students to exhibit creativity and to accept personal responsibility for it

3. provide opportunity for judging of students' work according to their own individual progress

4. provide opportunity for idiosyncratic specialization

5. provide opportunity for development and recognition of a greater diversity of talent.

This outline has been extended by Schaie (1974) who has pointed out the need for a curriculum for adults that takes account of the "rustiness" they experience, or as he put it, "to reverse the cultural and technological obsolescence of the aged" (p. 805). One measure he recommends for achieving this goal is the provision of opportunities for the old and the young to interact in their learning experiences by learning together.

6.6 Curriculum for work

At one time, work was one of the obvious and most important sites of learning. However, as Suchodolski (1972) has pointed out, scientific and technological growth have made education through vocational experience impossibly inefficient and ineffective. Nowadays, a long and formal period of preparation is needed for entry into high-level jobs, while work opportunities for the completely unskilled are becoming fewer and fewer. Nonetheless, the very factors which have necessitated this lengthy formal preparation (technological and scientific change) are now rendering it obsolete at ever faster rates. What is needed in the face of this stage of affairs is a "curriculum" for the world of work that will foster the "personal initiative" (Dubin, 1974) for continued growth and development. Margulies and Raia (1967), for example, showed that this initiative for growth is fostered by supervisory behaviour that openly encourages professional upgrading and development, and by tangible rewards for updating oneself. Dubin (1974, p. 19) has stressed the importance, in a work curriculum oriented towards lifelong education, of additional factors, including:

1. provision of tools for self-assessment

2. opportunities for self-assessment

3. establishment of an organizational climate fostering creativity

4. contact with challenging work projects that promote on-the-job solutions to problems

5. peer interactions promoting the exchange of ideas and information

6.7 Curriculum for life itself

The view that education is essentially something that happens in school is of recent origin. Suchodolski (1972) has traced the rise of the notion that education requires a special environment that is quite distinct from everyday life, and that centres on schools. These schools were "good, difficult and required many years of attendance" (p. 142). Even reforms aimed at democratizing schools retained this basic idea, and concentrated merely upon provision of equal access. As a result, the idea that people can learn through life itself disappeared. Scientific and technological growth made it impossible in the work world, social complexity ruled out education through participation in the life of the society, and so on. However, the emergence of the concept of life-long education suggests that the chance has again arisen of developing a curriculum for life itself, as a result of which people will learn through "participation in social tasks and activities" (Suchodolski, 1972, p. 145), or through sharing in "the social, cultural and professional life of the age" (p. 146).

The curriculum for achieving lifelong education through life itself emphasizes that education involves more than simply intellectual knowledge - everything that promotes interest and the need to know is important. Clearer recognition of this is a major element in the theory of lifelong education. The curriculum for life involves both the idea that life itself is a major source of learning, and also the view that one can learn about life itself (largely through the process of living). Key properties have been summarized by Suchodolski (1972, p. 149), in the following list of needs for a life curriculum. It will need:

1. To teach people to apply thought to life itself

2. To teach people to want to use knowledge in life

3. To teach people how to use knowledge in life itself

4. To help people to know how to think when in contact with others

5. To help people to know how to exchange social and cultural experiences with others

6. To teach people how to think, not only in terms of the rules of science, but also in terms of the requirements of life itself

The aims of "curriculum" within a lifelong education orientation are to change the emphasis from school only, and to indicate the implications of the theory for other sources of educative experiences, such as work, out-of-school environments, and so on. A brief sketching out of some of the many educative "curricula" implied by lifelong education, and needed for its true implementation, has been carried out in this final section of the chapter.

REFERENCES

Anastasi, A. *Differential Psychology*. New York: Macmillan, 1958 (3rd edition).

Atkinson, J. W. & Feather, N. T. (Eds.). *A Theory of Achievement Motivation*. New York: Wiley, 1966.

Aujaleu, E. "Medicine of the Future". *World Health* (April 1973). pp. 23-29.

Bartoshuk, A. K. "Human Neonatal Cardiac Responses to Sound: A Power Function". *Psychonomic Science* 1 (1964). pp. 151-152.

Baumrind, D. "Child Care Practices Anteceding Three Patterns of Pre-school Behaviour". *Genetic Psychology Monographs* 75 (1967). pp. 43-88.

Berlyne, D. E. "The Influence of Complexity and Novelty in Visual Figures on Orienting Responses". *Journal of Experimental Psychology* 55 (1958). pp. 289-296.

Berlyne, D. E. *Conflict, Arousal and Curiosity*. New York: McGraw Hill, 1960.

Biggs, J. B. "Content to Process". *Australian Journal of Education* 17 (1973). pp. 225-238.

Bischof, L. J. *Adult Psychology*. New York: Harper and Row, 1969.

Bloom, B. S. *Stability and Change in Human Characteristics*. New York: Wiley, 1964.

Bowles, S. "Cuban Education and the Revolutionary Ideology". *Harvard Educational Review* 41 (1971). pp. 472-500.

Bradway, K. P. & Thompson, C. W. "Intelligence at Adulthood: A Twentyfive Year Follow Up". *Journal of Educational Psychology* 53 (1962). pp. 1-14.

Brock, A. "Blueprint for a Learning Society". *UNESCO Courier* (Nov. 1972). pp. 4-5.

Bromley, D. B. *The Psychology of Human Aging*. Baltimore: Penguin, 1971.

Bruner, J. S. "The Course of Cognitive Growth". *American Psychologist* 19 (1964). pp. 1-15.

Buehler, C. & Massarik, F. (Eds.). *The Course of Human Life: A Study of Goals in the Humanistic Perspective*. New York: Springer, 1968.

Burt, C. "The Differentiation of Intellectual Ability". *British Journal of Educational Psychology* 24 (1954). pp. 76-90.

Chow, K. L.; Riesen, A. H. & Newell, F. W. "Degeneration of Retinal Ganglion Cells in Infant Chimpanzees Reared in Darkness". *Journal of Comparative Neurology* 107 (1957). pp. 27-42.

Coleman, J. S. (with others). *Equality of Educational Opportunity*. Washington, D.C.: U.S. Government Printing Office, 1966.

———. "How Do the Young Become Adults?" *Review of Educational Research* 42 (1972). pp. 431-439.

Coles, E. K. T. "Universities and Adult Education". *International Review of Education* 18 (1972). pp. 172-182.

Comfort, A. *Aging: The Biology of Senescence*. London: Routledge & Kegan Paul, 1964. (2nd edition).

Coste, P. "Is Learning Optimal in Childhood?" *Prospects: Quarterly Review of Education* 3 (1973). pp. 46-48.

Council of Europe. "Notes of the Council of Europe on Permanent Education". *Convergence* 1 (1968), No. 4. pp. 50-53.

Cropley, A. J. "Differentiation of Abilities, Socio-Economic Status, and the WISC". *Journal of Consulting Psychology* 28 (1964). pp. 512-517.

——— & Sikand, J. S. "Creativity and Schizophrenia". *Journal of Consulting and Clinical Psychology* 40 (1973). pp. 462-468.

Dave, R. H. *Lifelong Education and School Curriculum*. Hamburg: Unesco Institute for Education, 1973. (uie monographs 1).

Dennis, W. & Sayegh, Y. "The Effect of Supplementary Experiences upon the Behavioural Development of Infants in Institutions". *Child Development* 36 (1965). pp. 81-90.

Dockrell, W. B. "Education, Social Class and the Development of Ability". Unpublished Doctoral Dissertation, University of Chicago, 1963.

Dubin, S. S. "The Psychology of Lifelong Learning. New Developments in the Professions". *International Review of Applied Psychology*. 23 (1974). pp. 17-31.

Dumazedier, J. (with others). *The School and Continuing Education*. Paris: UNESCO, 1972.

Eggleston, S. J. "Pre-school Education in Europe". *Paedagogica Europea* 9 (1974). pp. 10-16.

Erikson, E. H. "Identity and the Life Cycle". *Psychological Issues* 1 (1959). pp. 1-165.

———. *Identity, Youth and Crisis*. New York: Norton, 1968.

Fantz, R. L. "Pattern Vision in Newborn Infants". *Science* 140 (1963). pp. 296-2

Faure, E. (with others). *Learning to Be: The World of Education Today and To-morrow*. Paris and London: UNESCO and Harrap, 1972.

Flavell, J. H. *The Developmental Psychology of Jean Piaget*. New York: Van Nostrand, 1963.

Foulds, G. A. & Raven, J. C. "Normal Changes in the Mental Abilities of Adults as Age Advances". *Journal of Mental Science* 94 (1948). pp. 133-142.

Fox, C. & Birren, J. E. "The Differential Decline of Subtest Scores of the Wechsler-Bellevue Intelligence Scale in 60-69-Year-Old Individuals". *Journal of Genetic Psychology* 77 (1950). pp. 313-317.

Freeberg, N. E. & Payne, D. T. "Parental Influence on Cognitive Development in Early Childhood: A Review". *Child Development* 38 (1967). pp. 65-87.

Frese, H. H. "Permanent Education - Dream or Nightmare?" *Education and Culture* (1972), No. 19. pp. 9-13.

Freud, S. *The Ego and the Mechanisms of Defence*. (C. Baines, transl.). New York: International Universities Press, 1946.

Gardner, R. W.; Holzman, P. S.; Klein, G. S.; Linton, H. P. & Spence, D. P. "Cognitive Control: A Study of Individual Consistencies in Cognitive Be-haviour". *Psychological Issues* 1 (1959), No. 4. pp. 1-186.

Garrett, H. E. "A Developmental Theory of Intelligence". *American Psychologist* 1 (1946). pp. 372-378.

Goulet, L. R. & Baltes, P. B. (Eds.). *Lifespan Developmental Psychology*. New York: Academic Press, 1970.

Harlow, H. F. & Harlow, M. H. "Learning to Love". *American Scientist* 54 (1966), No. 3. pp. 344-372.

Havighurst, R. J. *Human Development and Education*. New York: Longmans Green, 195

———. "Adulthood and Old Age". In Ebel, R. L. (Ed.). *Encyclopedia of Educationc Research*. New York: Macmillan, 1969.

Hebb, D. O. *The Organization of Behavior*. New York: Wiley, 1949.

Hicter, M. "Education for a Changing World". *Prospects: Quarterly Review of Education* 2 (1972). pp. 298-312.

Horn, J. L. "Organization of Abilities and the Development of Intelligence". *Psychological Review* 75 (1968). pp. 242-259)

Hunt, J. McV. "Heredity, Environment, and Class or Ethnic Differences". In *Assessment in a Pluralistic Society*. Proceedings of the 1972 Invitational Conference on Testing Problems. Princeton: ETS, 1973.

Hutt, S. J. "Biological Aspects of Early Development". *Paedagogica Europea* 9 (1974). pp. 18-31.

Inhelder, B. & Piaget, J. *The Growth of Intelligence from Early Childhood to Adolescence*. New York: Basic Books, 1958.

James, W. *The Principles of Psychology*. New York: Holt, 1890.

Janne, H. "Future Policy for Education". *Education and Culture* (1972), No. 19. pp. 14-19.

Jencks, C. (with others). *Inequality: A Reassessment of the Effect of Family and Schooling in America*. New York: Basic Books, 1972.

Jerome, E. A. "Decay of Heuristic Processes in the Aged". In Tibbitts, C. & Donahue, W. (Eds.). *Aging Around the World*. Proceedings of the 5th Congress of the International Association of Gerontology. New York: Columbia University Press, 1962.

Johnson, L. "Matthew Arnold's Concept of Culture and its Significance for R. S. Peters' Analysis of Education". *Australian Journal of Education* 16 (1972). pp. 165-174.

Johnstone, J. W. C. & Rivera, R. J. *Volunteers for Learning: A Study of the Educational Pursuits of American Adults*. Chicago: Aldine, 1965.

Jones, H. E. & Conrad, H. S. "The Growth and Decline of Intelligence". *Genetic Psychology Monographs* 13 (1933). pp. 223-298.

Kagan, J.; Henker, B. A.; Hen Tov, A.; Levine, J. & Lewis, M. "Infants' Differential Reactions to Familiar and Distorted Faces." *Child Development* 37 (1966). pp. 519-532.

―――― & Moss, H. A. "Stability and Validity of Achievement Fantasy". *Journal of Abnormal and Social Psychology* 58 (1959). pp. 357-364.

Kessen, W. "Sucking and Looking: Two Organized Congenital Patterns of Behavior in the Human Newborn". In Stevenson, H. W.; Hess, E. H. & Rheingold, H. L. (Eds.). *Early Behavior: Comparative and Developmental Approaches*. New York: Wiley, 1967.

Kidd, J. R. "The Third International Conference: Tokyo". *Convergence* 5 (1972), No. 3. pp. 15-19.

Klein, G. S. *Perception, Motives, and Personality*. New York: Knopf, 1970.

Kovacs, M. L. & Cropley, A. J. *Immigrants and Society: Alienation and Assimilation.* Sydney: McGraw Hill, 1975.

Kuhlen, R. G. "Motivational Changes During the Adult Years". In Kuhlen, R. G. (Ed.). *Psychological Backgrounds of Adult Education.* Chicago: Centre for the Study of Liberal Education for Adults, 1963.

Kupisiewicz, C. "On Some Principles of Modernizing the School System as a Base for Adult Education". *Convergence* 5 (1972), No. 3. pp. 42-46.

Kyöstiö, O. K. "The Changing Role of Schooling Society". *International Review of Education* 18 (1972). pp. 339-351.

Kyrasek, J. & Polisensky, J. V. "Comenius and All-Embracing Education". *Convergence* 1 (1968), No. 4. pp. 80-86.

Lefrancois, G. R. *Of Children.* Belmont: Wadsworth, 1973.

Lehman, H. C. *Age and Achievement.* Princeton: Princeton University Press, 1953.

Lengrand, P. *An Introduction to Lifelong Education.* Paris: UNESCO, 1970.

Leventhal, A. S. & Lipsitt, L. P. "Adaptation, Pitch Discrimination and Sound Localization in the Neonate". *Child Development* 35 (1964). pp. 759-767.

Lorge, I. "The Influence of the Test Upon the Nature of Mental Decline as a Function of Age". *Journal of Educational Psychology* 27 (1936). pp. 100-110.

Maccoby, E. E. *The Development of Sex Differences.* London: Tavistock, 1967.

Margulies, N. & Raia, A. P. "Scientists, Engineers and Technological Obsolescence". *California Management Review* 10 (1967). pp. 43-48.

Maslow, A. H. *Motivation and Personality.* New York: Harper and Row, 1954.

McFarland, R. & O'Doherty, B. "Work and Occupational Skills". In Birren, J. E. (Ed.). *Handbook of Aging and the Individual.* Chicago: University of Chicago Press, 1959.

McLeish, J. *The Science of Behaviour.* London: Barrie and Rockcliff, 1963.

Menyuk, P. *The Acquisition and Development of Language.* Englewood Cliffs: Prentice Hall, 1971.

Mussen, P. H.; Conger, J. J. & Kagan, J. *Child Development and Personality.* New York: Harper and Row, 1969. (3rd edition).

Naylor, G. F. K. & Harwood, E. "Mental Exercises for Grandmother". *Education News* 12 (1970), No. 11. pp. 15-18.

Neugarten, B. L. (with others). *Personality in Middle and Late Life.* New York: Atherton Press, 1964.

Nisbett, J. D. "Contributions to Intelligence Testing and the Theory of Intelligence: IV. Intelligence and Age: Retesting with Twenty-Four Years' Interval". *British Journal of Educational Psychology* 27 (1957). pp. 190-198.

Olford, J. E. "Deschooling Further Education". *The New Era* 53 (1972). pp. 202-204.

Owens, W. A. "Age and Mental Abilities: A Longitudinal Study". *Genetic Psychology Monographs* 48 (1953). pp. 3-54.

──── & Charles, D. C. *Life History Correlates of Age Changes in Mental Abilities*. Lafayette, Indiana: Purdue University Press, 1953.

Parkyn, G. W. *Towards a Conceptual Model of Lifelong Education*. Paris: UNESCO, 1973. (Educational Studies and Documents, No. 12.)

Paul, I. H. "Studies in Remembering". *Psychological Issues*, Monograph No. 2. New York: International Universities Press, 1959.

Röman, K. "A Review of Pre-school Experiments and Research in Finland". *Paedagogica Europea* 9 (1974). pp. 163-171.

Rohwer, W. D. "Prime Time for Education: Early Childhood or Adolescence?" *Harvard Educational Review* 41 (1971). pp. 316-341.

Schaie, K. W. "Translations in Gerontology - From Lab to Life. Intellectual Functioning". *American Psychologist* 29 (1974). pp. 802-807.

Schubert, J. & Cropley, A. J. "Verbal Regulation of Behaviour and IQ in Canadian Indian and White Children". *Developmental Psychology* 7 (1972). pp. 295-301.

Silva, A. "Education for Freedom". *Prospects: Quarterly Review of Education* 3 (1973). pp. 39-45.

Stone, L. J.; Murphy, L. B. & Smith, H. T. (Eds.). *The Competent Infant: Research and Commentary*. New York: Basic Books, 1972.

Suchodolski, B. "Out of School". *Prospects: Quarterly Review of Education* 2 (1972). pp. 142-154.

Terrell, G.; Durkin, K. & Wiesley, M. "Social Class and the Nature of the Incentive in Discrimination Learning". *Journal of Abnormal and Social Psychology* 59 (1959). pp. 270-272.

Tough, A. M. *The Adult's Learning Projects*. Toronto: Ontario Institute for Studies in Education, 1971.

Tyler, L. E. *The Psychology of Human Differences*. New York: Appleton-Century-Crofts, 1965. (3rd edition).

Vernon, P. E. *The Structure of Human Abilities*. London: Methuen, 1950.

Vincent, D. F. "The Linear Relationship Between Age and Scores of Adults in Intelligence Tests". *Occupational Psychology* 26 (1952). pp. 243-249.

Vygotsky, L. S. *Thought and Language*. Cambridge, Mass.: MIT Press, 1962.

Walk, R. D. & Gibson, E. J. "A Comparative Study of Visual Depth Perception". *Psychological Monographs* 75 (1961). Whole No. 519.

Ward, C. "Anarchy and Education". *The New Era* 53 (1972). pp. 179-184.

Wechsler, D. *The Measurement and Appraisal of Adult Intelligence*. Baltimore: Williams and Wilkins, 1958. (5th edition).

Welford, A. T. "Age and Skill: Motor, Intellectual and Social". *Interdisciplinary Topics in Gerontology* 4 (1969). pp. 1-22.

Witkin, H. A. "Origins of Cognitive Style". In Scheerer, C. (Ed.). *Cognition: Theory, Research, Promise*. New York: Harper and Row, 1964.

Wood, M. *The Stranger: A Study in Social Relations*. (1934). New York: AMS Press, 1969.

Worth, W. H. (with others). *A Choice of Futures*. Edmonton: Queen's Printer for the Province of Alberta, 1972.

Yerkes, R. M. (Ed.). *Psychological Examining in the US Army*. Washington: Memoirs of the National Academy of Science, 1921. Vol 15.

Zhamin, V. & Kostanian, S. L. "Education and Soviet Economic Growth". *International Review of Education* 18 (1972). pp. 155-170.

C H A P T E R 6

ANTHROPOLOGICAL AND ECOLOGICAL FOUNDATIONS OF LIFELONG EDUCATION

C. D e ' A t h

> *"We cannot let the present ecological fad*
> *cut off the hope of material progress*
> *which most of the world needs; nor can*
> *we use the need for industrialisation to*
> *wreck the balance of the world."*
>
> Norman Pearson

> *"There will be little satisfaction in en-*
> *vironmental education that teaches us*
> *how to handle our natural environment if*
> *it does not recognize the fact that part*
> *of that natural environment is ourselves.*
> *... our drive to achieve environmental*
> *education is part of the drive to achieve*
> *adequate education for social interaction."*
>
> Michael Scriver

1. Introduction

Writing this paper induced me to a number of things:

First, it led me to see the similarities anthropology and ecology have
to lifelong education. For example, the anthropological concept of enculturation, with its dimensions of continuous informal teaching and learning throughout life, shares many of the features of lifelong education. Lifelong education
also has the notion of a learning schema embracing the whole of a person's
life. It further shares with anthropology the notion of integration. This includes how the individual integrates the whole of his life into a meaningful
pattern and how he integrates the various activities of his life with each

other and with those of his fellow men. Ecology, on the other hand, has a slightly different thrust. It emphasizes how closely man as a species is tied to, or integrated with, the natural environment. As a discipline it emphasizes not only species interdependency and interaction, but also the fragility of natural systems. Ecology also has a long term horizon when it looks at, for example, gene pools and the evolution and/or persistence of natural systems over time. Lifelong education also has long term time horizons and, for example, emphasizes interdependency through humans learning from one another and collectively contributing to and drawing on knowledge pools.

Second, it made me aware that planning or advocating lifelong education without taking into account the persistence of life systems as we know them becomes a meaningless exercise. If human life support systems cease to exist or decline in efficiency, the dreams of educational visionaries become meaningless. It is possible to have life without vision, but not a vision without life! Thus, one of the preconditions for planning in education is the need to take care of the basic biological systems on which we as humans depend and of which we are a part. Despite our advances in bio-engineering and genetic manipulation, it is unlikely in the near future that we will be able to improve significantly on the superbly integrated life and cosmic systems already in existence.

Third, I was forced to ask questions about the quality of life. How is it defined in terms of kinds of environment in which people find themselves? To do this one cannot merely ask questions about social environments, technological environments or natural environments. I had to try to think through certain syntheses which involved the man-technology interface, the man-nature interface and the technology-nature interface. Looking at the quality of human existence from these vantage points is a painful exercise. Traditional disciplines have not addressed themselves to these problems and there is a dearth of relevant material (see Figure 6.1) for a conceptualization of these kinds of interfaces.

FIGURE 6.1   Human environments — Interface areas important in their
effect on human learning.

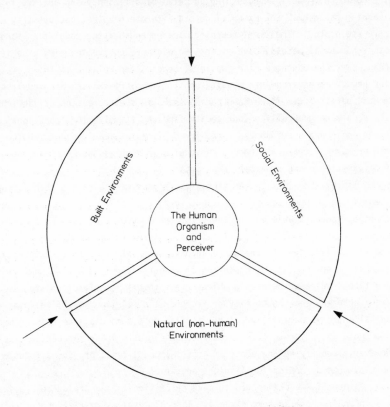

Although these interface areas are extremely important in assessing the quality
of human existence, little exists in research literature on how they might be evaluated.

Fourth, I was placed in the rather paradoxical position of asking some questions which seem very conservative, almost reactionary for an educator to ask. These questions relate to three areas. First, in our western educational system which is invading the technologically less developed areas of the world, have we lost something in terms of efficiency and quality in our learning paradigms? For example, do pre-literate peoples, because they make more use of their smelling, touching, seeing and hearing modalities, and of other humans as models, have richer, more comprehensive learning experiences than, say, the educated city-dwellers? Second, and related to the above, do our new built environments provide us with impoverished learning environments, particularly if we have had no share in their creation or fabrication? Third, are we generally encouraged to find the stimulus for educational motivation in whatever happens to be in our immediate environment, whether urban or rural, or are we induced to indulge in mindless abstractions divorced from experience and proximate environments?

Fifth, the exercise led me to take a pessimistic rather than a utopian view of the future. It became obvious to me that if I was to be concerned about enriched, viable environments for the future, I would need to take a fairly decided stand on what global issues I think are likely to cause human and global life-system stress. As an environmentalist, I quite naturally identify over-population, depletion of resources, pollution and unwise urban and technological growth as problems. This thrust immediately distances me from those who see the utility of technocratic solutions or "fixes" for every social and environmental problem. It also puts some distance between myself and those who advocate traditional economic growth on an exponential scale. However, identifying the above as issues I do, I feel, provide a focus and perhaps some direction for lifelong education.

Sixth, I was challenged to make my criticisms and prejudices against traditional school systems explicit. I shall merely summarize what I think to be their shortcomings. These criticisms, based on much travel and experience in so-called developed and less developed countries, would be:

i)   Traditional education, in schools and in time-blocks, which is
     provided at the beginning of the most formative period in human
     life, *may* be jeopardizing or inhibiting the long-term normal cog-
     nitive and affective growth patterns of *both* learners and teachers.

ii) Rapid changes - demographic, technological and environmental - are occurring outside the school but are not reflected in school curricula. Consequently, students *may* be isolated and out of touch with new global realities.

iii) In spite of the foregoing, or perhaps because of it, those in formal school systems *may* restrictively perceive the school experience as being a strategy to obtain employment and the societal approbation and leisure time with which it is linked. Because of the kinds of skill needed in specialized occupations, because of automation, cybernation, and the shrinking manpower needs of many industries, the vastly increasing use of non-human energy and the unpalatability of certain work environments, the aspirations of new employees and the expectations of employers may be very much at variance with each other. In other words, there *may* be a lack of articulation between formal educational environments and work environments, and additionally between these and leisure environments.

iv) Schooling and one of its traditional corollaries, literacy, has not, in the third world of development, had the pay-off expected. The effects of this lack of pay-off may have been accentuated where schooling has been seen *only* as an adjunct to national manpower and economic planning. On the individual human level, there has frequently been bitter resentment against a system which has appeared to offer a sure pay-off in terms of vocational participation, but which has not done so.

v) Costs, everywhere, not merely in terms of money, of maintaining large-size schools and educational systems, *may* have become prohibitive. Alternative systems *might* improve various kinds of cost-benefit ratios, both for the individual and for the state - transitory as this equation might eventually be.

vi) School personnel are failing to retool or rehabilitate themselves in terms of adopting new approaches which will de-emphasize: authoritarianism, traditional pedagogical roles in which there is cleavage between teachers and learners, and education which ensures the continuation of many kinds of unequal social *status quo* patterns.

By way of qualification I would suggest that those arguments have validity only when applied to specific, concrete settings and that there is a tremendous difference in terms of how these criticisms may be applied in so-called developed nations and in so-called less-developed nations of the third world. In the latter, survival, or "bread and butter" problems, particularly at the individual level, are much more acute. In the former, educators have the dubious privilege of being able to address themselves to very different, but no less urgent, kinds of problem, for example, the significance of the relationship of individuals to large, but potentially very vulnerable, technological systems.

2. The Approach

This paper tries to do a number of things, but not necessarily in the following sequence:

First, it attempts to identify, in a very general way, areas in which lifelong education can complement, be incorporated in, or even supplant, traditional school education. No apologies are made, for example, for being critical of traditional schools and their use of limited communication modalities.

Second, it tries to give a functional and integrative aspect to education. In other words, it labours to situate the educative process squarely in the arena of what has happened to man as a species in his evolutionary past, what is happening to him now in terms of his globalization, and what will happen to him in the future unless he attempts to come to terms with certain very real problems which have some awesome individual and collective dimensions.

Third, it attempts to get at the above by stressing the role of education in terms of:

(a) facilitating growth and development processes

(b) identifying trends, particularly in the area of technology, the effects of which might be jeopardising the biotic and social systems on which we are all so dependent.

There has been little attempt to respect traditional disciplinary boundaries, and much of what follows is drawn from a variety of disciplinary sources. By and large, I prefer to tangle with problems to which applied anthropology is relevant. I also feel that education, to the extent that it distances itself from "real" issues, becomes esoteric and its practitioners become unable to communicate or relate to problems relevant to the larger society. Hence, there is a good deal of emphasis on:

(a) What it means to be *human* without too much respect for time-space-culture constraints.

(b) *Issues* which cut across many disciplines.

(c) A juxtaposing of the education *processes* with *issues* with which education should try to come to terms.

From the vantage point of anthropology and ecology, anthropologists may be able to identify some useful universal validities, i.e. those which apply to man almost regardless of the recent global time or space in which he finds himself. Their approaches to studying and understanding people are in many ways, particularly in terms of participant observation and in having an interest in the *whole* individual in his *whole* setting over long time periods, congruent with the interests of those involved in lifelong education.

The following gives some indication of the actual interests of anthropologists. It should not be difficult for educators to see the potential for an interest and knowledge overlap:

> In the present era of increased statistical handling of data, the anthropological study of modern society is often disparaged. However, it emphasizes features increasingly neglected by other social disciplines. First, the holistic approach, which examines each phenomenon in the context of the totality, avoids (at least minimizes) the error of treating each cultural department, for example, economics, politics, religion, as if it had a separate and at best only internally consistent meaning. Closely related is the capacity for finding patterns of integrative elements in cultural systems. Third, recognition that cultural features have deep psychological involvements for the individual participants makes it possible to see the interplay between individual sentiments and cultural institutions. Fourth, the anthropologist's very naiveté makes him willing to examine aspects of life not amenable to counting and statistical manipulation and thus to utilize evidence other scholars avoid as "methodologically unsound". On the whole, what the anthropological approach brings to the study of modern society is the use of insight, introspection, close attention to detail, validation through internal consistency, and the capacity to deal at the same time with all levels of behaviour - from material artifacts to psychic life. If the results sometimes seem impressionistic, if there is a novelistic quality, nevertheless there is a closer sense of human reality than is generally provided by those social sciences traditionally concerned with modern society.[1]

Figure 6.2 gives an indication of some of the areas the study identifies and discusses.

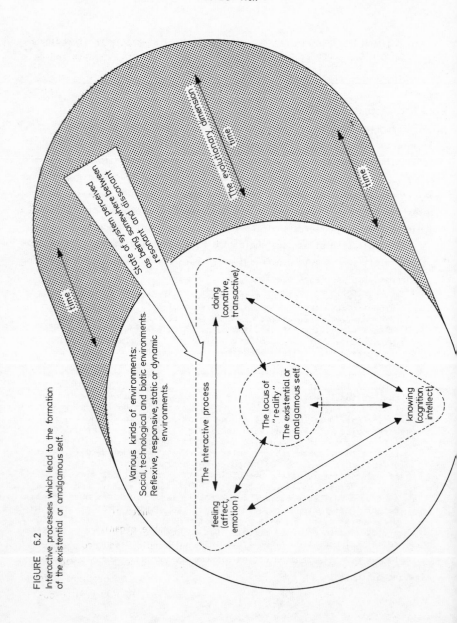

FIGURE 6.2
Interactive processes which lead to the formation
of the existential or amalgamous self.

From various perspectives, the study attempts to deal with four dimensions of man. First, a good deal of attention is given to the growth and development of the individual - the amalgamous or existential self. This growth depends on how well the individual is able to articulate his "doing, knowing and feeling" potentialities.

Second, many kinds of environment, including technological, social and biotic, are identified. The role of these environments in facilitating or inhibiting growth of individuals and collectives is discussed in some depth.

Third, man's evolutionary past is put into perspective. For example, it is suggested that there may have been some recent discontinuity in the quality of human environments as such environments have become increasingly built and technological rather than social and biological.

Fourth, some attempt is made to understand how humans, through their cultural filters, assess the states and define the attributes of the various systems and environments in which they find themselves.

This framework, it is hoped, will provide a meta - or universalistic - backdrop for the discussion of more specific or particular educational concerns. These concerns might, for example, centre on making vulnerable dependency relationships explicit. Examples of these relationships would be humans becoming over-dependent on finite resources and highly specialized technological systems.

3. Substantive Areas and Themes

This section will briefly identify a number of themes. The development of these themes in the paper should give some indication of the importance of a) the teaching of anthropology in the context of other lifelong education options and b) establishing certain principles which indicate that lifelong education is justified and indeed a desirable organizing strategy from what is known within the disciplines of anthropology and ecology.

There has been an attempt in the following to structure the paper so that a number of themes are dealt with in varying depth. The rationale for ordering and selecting the themes in the way they have been should be obvious from the following thematic summaries:

The Anthropological View of Schools and Education. To an anthropologist, education may be looked at in many ways. For example, he may see it as an acculturation, enculturation or socialization process. He may see school as just another societal institution which at any single point in time reflects the reality of the culture and society outside the school. The disclaimer, as it were, cuts schools down to size!

The Existential Self and Global Problems. This theme is an ambitious attempt to establish the interconnectedness of self with a finite universe and to effect a reconciliation of individual and global ecosystem needs.

Survival Environments. It would seem that man might be distancing himself from many of the things vital to his survival. This theme attempts to identify how this has occured.

Technology and Built Environments. What is the significance of such environments in our everyday life? Is their existence and growth beneficial or is it leading us down the road to extinction?

Growth and Life Cycles. It may well be that our built and technological environments inhibit normal human growth and development sequences. If this inhibition is occurring, where do we look for alternatives?

Primates and Foraging Societies. If we need to know about *humans* where might we look - to our closest relatives the primates, to pre-literate societies currently existing, or to the artifactual environments of pre-historic humans? In this theme the behaviour of primates is examined and some very general lessons for lifelong education are derived from the examination.

Alternative Life Styles. There is a plea in this theme for alternative life styles. There is a presumption in this section that cultural diversity maximizes individual diversity and that there is great strength in variegated biological and social systems.

Communication. This very important area is discussed in some depth. In the latter part of the theme a good deal of attention is given to the *kinds* of communication used in formal and informal education.

Commitment and Human Scale. If lack of space, large size of social collectives and the proliferation of built environments are becoming problems, how might commitment, involvement and "understanding" through education at the community level be engendered to confront such problems? This theme is presented in the form of an illustrative case study.

Acculturation and Enculturation. In the context of culture, the notions of change and lack of change are examined.

Additionally, in the following some attempt will be made to show how
each of these themes may have something to say about the individual and
about lifelong education at one level, and at another, about some of the
more pressing global crises which scholars such as Margaret Mead and Barbara
Ward write about so eloquently.[2] The liberty has been taken of very norma-
tively defining these problem areas. It is suggested that unless both lifelong education and anthropology are problem-centered and anchored fairly
firmly in what is currently happening in the world both will suffer the
same fate as traditional education, i.e. tend to become irrelevant, obsolescent and dysfunctional. In a word, fossilized. This approach is not to dis-
credit the notion that what has happened in the past is unimportant, particularly insofar as the past *is* mirrored in existing, varying cultures and
natural environments. However, it does try to shift the focus of western
education and human development into the present and toward the future and
to stress the potential role of the ordinary individual in what has become
our global "fate group", i.e. our global collective sharing in a common
sense of destiny. Hopefully, the excitement of learning about, or participating in, alternative cultural systems and relating these to one's *own*
learning potential and to possible new life styles, will revitalize a more
humane approach to education. The foregoing is in no way intended to deni-
grate existing cultures. Rather, this thrust gives recognition to global
ties which have already been established.

4. The Anthropological View of Schools and Education

It should be stated at the outset as a kind of rider or disclaimer,
that anthropologists have never assumed that education and learning have
been coterminous with schooling. Schools have been regarded as just another
institution for transmitting values and behaviours. It has always been assumed, in addition, that a person learns about others and about his environments as he progresses through his own life cycle regardless of whether
schools as they are known by Westerners exist or not. Thus, an anthropolo-

gist does not have to take the leap of divorcing learning and education from
schools as most Westerners do. This difference is important because somehow
schools have now, in the popular imagination, become inextricably linked
with a person's life chances - one's future now depends almost entirely on
whatever it is presumed one learns or will learn in school - and these pre-
sumptions are frequently in error! However, it is an individual and collective existential "fact" that schools do not have a substantial role in legitimizing individuals and in "certifying" them for a wide variety of activities. It is also highly probable that schools have a particular "style" in
the way they accent particular human communication modalities and amplify
certain cultural continuities despite the above comments about their mirror-
like qualities *vis-à-vis* the societies in which they are imbedded.

5. The Existential Self and Global Problems

Educators and religious devotees have always had the problem of reconciling the growth and development needs of the individual with the demands
and problems defined by both deities and the larger society. Now, however,
the problem has become much more acute. The greater society has become global, as have the perceived problems - those of overpopulation and crowding,
resource exhaustion, the mindless production of armaments and the defile-
ment of the natural environment. The individual is being asked to identify
with these problems and to solve them in tandem with other humans from whom
he may be acutely different in terms of ideology, culture and race. At first
blush, the problems of reconciling growth and development needs of the individual with the maintenance of a viable world would seem to be difficult.
This is because the awareness of difference and of resource scarcity is just
as likely to lead to friction and competition as to harmony and cooperation.
An elemental understanding of some of the basic assumptions made by international developers, for example, might however lead to some radically different kinds of individual and collective participation from what is expected
at present. Lifelong education might help to articulate this difference in
response and lead to individuals adopting quite different criteria for evaluating international development, i.e. moving away from narrow economic

and consumption criteria for estimating the worth of change. Lifelong education could be instrumental in not only preserving all kinds of cultural
diversity but also in placing a positive value on individual and collective
difference.

6. Survival Environments

Traditionally, anthropologists have studied small pre-literate collectives within non-western cultures. Although many of the resulting ethnographic and behavioural studies have emphasized, perhaps incorrectly, the
static nature of such collectives and the importance of cultural continuities, such studies do have value in understanding dependency relationships
in the following human activity areas:
- food gathering and production
- erection of shelter
- the making of body coverings and ornaments
- preparation and distribution of food
- the making of artifacts and the use of technology
(tools and techniques).

These areas have purposely been categorized because they are *still*
relevant to man in our modern global society. However, the key difference
now is that, because of lavish use of non-human energy, technological innovation, labour specialization, increased role differentiation and the
growth in importance of contractual rather than ascriptive human relationships, participation by the ordinary man, particularly in urban areas, in
these very basic survival activities has become very different from what
it was in the past. What is the significance of these changes? It means
that modern man has become isolated from *direct* involvement in any of the
above activities. This severance has some fairly important implications.
Man has evolved over several million years in a by no means static but
supportive bio-environment. He reached his present physical form about
150,000 years ago and started to become an urban dweller and an extensive
user of complex technology and domestic agricultural crops and animals a
mere 10,000 years ago. Thus, we see that until very recently man evolved

in a situation where:

(a) direct involvement in most if not *all* the activities previously
listed was necessary for the survival of all individuals;

(b) cause and effect relationships and feedback loops were much simpler than they are now, e.g. the effects of using a simple technology or cooperating with others were very quickly obvious to
the participants;

(c) most information received by the individual was from his bio-
environment. This included other humans using very basic but
obviously very human forms of communication; most of this information, e.g. seasonal changes, the joy and anger of other
humans, was crucial to survival;

(d) some marginal technological and social innovation was possible
so long as it did not interfere too drastically with the outcome of the survival activity. However, dissemination of such
innovation was very limited.

Now, however, the modern global dweller, particularly in the west,
spends much of his time reacting to or manipulating technological and built
environments. Much, if not most, information is *not* related *directly* to
the immediate survival needs of the individual. Skills related to basic,
survival activities have been forgotten and the individual, particularly
in urban situations, is caught up in intricate dependency relationships.
For the following reasons, he becomes extremely vulnerable:

i)   In large systems, cause and effect relationships are difficult
to comprehend, e.g. the effect on the natural environment of,
say, newspaper consumption is not readily perceptible to the
typical newspaper reader.

ii) Because of the biological and perceptional characteristics of
humans, current environmental changes cannot be readily or accurately monitored by the individual. This deficiency can be attributed to the individual not being able to discern or cope
with the gradualness of change *or* its suddenness.

iii) Most humans are now supported by large distribution systems
which are extremely vulnerable to interruptions or interfer-
ence, e.g. energy flow systems and water flow systems, and
other resource flow systems can all be brought to a halt by
terrorism, strikes, and the withdrawal of the service of specialists.

iv) Human energy is no longer required for most survival or other
activities. Lack of sufficient human energy usage/stimulus input, coupled with over-consumption of food in *some* parts of

the world, *may* for example be causing widespread bodily atrophy, distress and an increase in degenerative diseases. This can be contrasted with areas where large-scale man-managed life-support systems do not exist and malnutrition and exhausted ecosystems lead to widespread misery.

v)   Certain kinds of resources (for example energy, food supplies, water, metals etc.) seem at present, despite the optimism of technocrats, to be finite.

vi) Large-scale human organisations may make the "price" of access to life-support systems very high, particularly in terms of adaptation (behavioural modification).

vii) Because of the large size of the human gene pool and resultant tremendous human potential for variability, *standardized*, built, technological and social environments can prove very inhibiting. Humans seem to be able to adapt for short periods of time to such standardized environments but rapidly need new rejuvenating or "recharging" environments.

viii) Recently, certain man-induced, large-scale changes are having synergistic effects which are not readily "understood" by humans. There are problems of inappropriate cues, inappropriate responses and inadequate discriminations. This problem is mainly attributable to particular kinds of man-environment evolutionary pattern. For example, modern processed food with all of its new colours, smells and tastes may provide inappropriate cues for humans to discriminate as to whether it is tonic or toxic; radiation, "white sound", and gravity relaxation are other examples of phenomena difficult for the human to cope with.

ix) Individual social and technological innovations may be declining as the individual becomes more dependent. However, the innovations of a *few* can now be widely disseminated.

In the above, a deliberate but brief contrast has been made between the survival environments of pre-literate man in his small social collective and those of modern man. It is hoped that this section might stimulate a thrust in lifelong education for

i)   an understanding of the individual, existential level of different survival and information systems and what these mean in terms of creating viable environments;

ii) an appreciation for the very utilitarian energy systems and self-maintaining bio-systems of pre-literate collectives and an understanding of this strength in the context of today's global crises, including the possibility of inadequate returns from monocrop systems (which need tremendous technological and energy support systems), resource exhaustion and the like;

iii) a realization that many of these problems on the global macro-level
are directly linked to the high consumption of individuals with
certain life styles in modern societies. Pre-literate and intermediate societies, with their low consumption and simpler technologies, provide alternative models to that which has currently been
adopted in post-industrial societies.

Finally, the anthropologist may have done something in studying small-
scale collectives to point out, for example, their social and linguistic complexities. This is in sharp contrast to the popular view that people with
simple technologies have simple social systems.

7. Technology and Built Environments

About 10,000 years ago, a number of parallel but not unrelated developments occurred in the history of man. These developments were: an accelera-
tion in the domestication of animals and crops; the development of new technologies (techniques and tools); and urbanization. For the first time, man
could store food, mainly grain and pulses, over relatively long periods and
could transport it over long distances because of improved means of locomo-
tion. The growth of cities was directly related to those factors and to the
concentration there of craftsmen who produced specialized tools and artifacts.

Thus, in our very recent historical past man gained the means to master, insulate himself from, or mediate the effects of his natural environment. Or so he thought!

Since that time, through technology, he has, additionally, developed
the means to store large amounts of information in non-corporeal ways, i.e.
unlike other animals he has found a means external to himself of storing
and accessing information generated over long periods of time. This factor
has allowed him to accumulate knowledge on how to produce artifacts and
built environments. It has also been responsible for the preservation of
other cultural continua such as laws, mythology and the like - a not un-
mixed blessing because much information stored on all aspects of the past
is redundant as it were. Although the development of technology seems to
have been rapid and linear, there has not been such a rapid growth in the
understanding of its effects on social institutions and on the natural

environment. Large socio-technological systems have emerged which now have global impact. These systems may facilitate human movement, the production of large amounts of foodstuffs and be instrumental in the field of health, for example, in sustaining more and more human lives. However, the purposes for which technologies are used depend very much on the human institutions associated with such technologies, as will be shown. Each of us knows how pervasive technology is in times of even limited warfare and how, through missiles for example, it can easily distance the killer from those being killed. The involvement of most collectives in warfare is for defence and to achieve peace! The technology of war is ostensibly used for this purpose by "defence" ministries. It might be said of all technologies which are centrally controlled by technocratic elites, that they have a tremendous potential for misuse against the ordinary or global citizen.

Technology has become truly the two-edged sword. It can move people or it can immobilize them, it can heal people or it can kill them, it can help educate them or it can turn them into robots. Unfortunately, however, its long-term and unintended effects are only now beginning to be dimly understood.

It might, however, be said with some confidence that the cumulative effect of technologies has been to:

1) Create new machine-related time and space schedules for man.

2) Distance man, particularly urban man, from activities vital to his survival, i.e. food growing, shelter erection and so on.

3) Create new built environments which may or may not be coercive, depending to what degree they are standardized, non-manipulable or unresponsive.

4) Establish very pervasive but attenuated relationships, e.g. most information urban dwellers use is electronically processed and originates in loci distant to the location of the human receiver.

5) Replace human energy by non-human energy in most human-related activities.

This last point has made man extremely vulnerable. Studies such as those by Rappaport indicate that pre-literate man, for example in New Guinea, has an almost homeostatic relationship with nature.[3] Even his food and agricultural rites are functional in terms of maintaining this relation-

ship. However, modern post-industrial societies have changed this whole
equation. With copious supplies of energy, which may in the fairly short
term be finite, they have created agricultures which need extremely sophisticated technological support systems. These "artifactual" bio-techno-sys-
tems also need lots of energy in terms of fertiliser and of fuel to run the
technology, to store crops and to distribute them. Additionally pesticides
and herbicides are needed to maintain the "integrity" of monocrops. The
cities, too, need phenomenal amounts of energy for automobiles, heating and
cooling buildings and for the production of goods and services. The individual tends to take this energy availability for granted and has become
less and less involved in productive activities requiring human energy inputs. In western societies, as previously mentioned, this has led to obesi-
ty problems and to an increase in degenerative diseases amongst many others.

     Because modern man is so close to technology and is accustomed to the
new built, standardized environments, he does not understand the fragility
of the various systems on which he is dependent. Additionally, he does not
understand the "spin-offs" from technological innovation. No-one, for example, paid any attention to the noise potential of machines and electronic
equipment until quite recently. Studies now indicate that city children may
be inhibited in their learning because of their exposure to street noises
over sustained periods of time.[4] In the area of nutrition, there is some
evidence that food additives, machine processing and new kinds of coloura-
tion may have had very adverse effects on humans.[5] Large segments of modern
urban dwellers may have unsatisfactory diets and poor health, despite indicators of material affluence.

     One difference between conditions existing in pre-literate societies
and those now extant, is that the "information" received by pre-literate
man had its origin either in nature or in other humans and was, as previously suggested, all fairly closely related to survival. Information received
by modern man, however, is frequently machine or built-environment-related
and is frequently redundant to his immediate, basic survival needs. This observation has some fairly profound implications when educators talk about
making education relevant throughout an individual's life-span.

     The other area in which we should be very much interested is the im-
pact of technological development on human social interaction. For example,

in the field of communication it would seem as though such things as telephones, television and radio can have a centripetal as well as centrifugal effect; the mediation of the telephone eliminates whole dimensions of human communication - touching, seeing and the like. Additionally, such instruments as television and radio require a socially very passive stance by the recipient. There is no opportunity for meaningful reaction. No one is sure what the cumulative effects are of this kind of relationship of man to communication technology (or to other technologies). However, there is some suspicion that it may inhibit normal *affective* growth and development. This seems a reasonable supposition as one does require much human interaction to learn *how* to become socially competent and *how* to relate to other humans in emotionally satisfying ways. Continuous relationships with technology may inhibit this process, even though ostensibly it seems to bring people in large collectives closer together.

Another aspect of the man-machine interface is worth discussing. Urban man is totally dependent, for example, on technological systems over which he has very little control and about which he knows little. To gain access to the benefits and outputs of such systems he must deal with persons who emphasize contractual rather than ascriptive relationships and the similarities of users rather than their differences, *or* who tend to equate a person's worth with his ability to display *their* kind of technical competency. Because those who control a large-scale technological system, like any other human grouping, tend to build their own sub-culture, with its own jargon (language), pecking order (bureaucratic hierarchy) and artifacts (material culture), they may make access to the benefits of their technology very difficult. For the individual dependent on such a system, this may mean that a good deal of behavioural modification (compliance) is necessary for him to secure benefit. In the process he may ultimately be disadvantaged rather than advantaged. This demeaning process can happen in schools, hospitals and the military for example. If the individual is continually exposed to the predations of organisations seeking clients, *or* alternatively is excluded because organisations are socially impervious, he can readily become alienated and experience the type of anomie and malaise that outcasts experienced in pre-literate societies. In urban situations he has no option but to become an integral part of large, complex resource distribution and associated social systems.

How does the above relate to lifelong education? It means the individual in the immediate future, as he grows and develops, should be flexible enough to learn:

1) How to understand how large centrally controlled systems function, even global systems such as trade, and what the benefits and costs are of participating (or *not* participating) in such systems - particularly the social and environmental costs.

2) How dependency relationships are structured and develop and how fragile those between humans become when mediated by certain kinds of technology.

3) How fragile eco-systems are and what the unintended effect of technological innovation can be.

4) How *not* to accept all technological innovation as being potential-. ly beneficial. Examining the impact of the automobile might, in historical perspective, reveal that its overall effect or "cost" has been very negative in terms of: resource usage; creation of pollution; killing of people in auto accidents; use of space; and "brutalizing" of workers on mass production lines.

5) How to value participation and involvement in organizations that control and attempt to decentralize societal technologies, i.e. the democratization of technology. Sensitizing such organisations to the needs of ordinary citizens and encouraging them to develop a feeling of accountability to even the most disadvantaged user should be a commonly accepted citizen goal.

8. Growth and Life Cycles

Anthropological literature on rites of passage is extensive and, needless to say, much of what has been learned about rites in pre-literate societies is applicable to post-industrial societies.

However, it might be wise to examine the anthropological insights in the context of the perceptions of some other interested groups who also recognize the importance of life cycles and growth phases. For example, religious groups view the individual as progressing towards grace or disgrace. Through ritual, which is still common in most societies, religious groups explicitly recognize stages of religious and spiritual development in the life stages of an individual. These rituals give recognition to the fact that throughout life the individual has great need for public support and for reinforcement through his own public affirmations. Recognition is also given to what have been traditionally life crisis periods. For example, birth is celebrated yearly after the event by kin, and infants are still inducted through ritual into most Christian churches. Puberty is recognized by the church as being a period when a young person will accept a more significant role in the church, and the successful search for a mate culminates in a public religious marriage. Death of course is often religiously recognized as a transitional period.

Other groups also explicitly recognize progression in a person's and a group's life. Economists and businessmen see the individual as going from a state of financial penury to one of increased income and consumption culminating in more-than-adequate self-sufficiency. This is classed as "success". The demographer sees cohort groups progressing through time as bulges or troughs in his graphs. The biologist may think of humans in terms of their development as genotypes and phenotypes. The psychiatrist and psychologist look at the psychological stages of growth. Freud was very precise about what these stages should be.[6] Piaget looks at growth of the intellect.[7] The geneticist might see the individual as representing part of the gene pool and during his life passing or not passing his genes on to another generation. Many other groups have a very vested interest in the progression of a person from birth to death. These may be kinsmen who hope to inherit property or undertakers who service corpses.

In addition to the foregoing, it is appropriate to look also at the context in which these public recognitions occur. Frequently, rites of passage for the individual are, or were, linked with seasonal cycles, with biological rhythms (a new harvest), the movement of the stars and the moon and with the progression of other humans who are also undergoing changes in status. Currently they may be linked to conspicuous consumption and to surges in economic production, e.g. new season's clothing fashions in the spring.

Initiation processes, e.g. those connected with a child passing to adulthood may, through time and through an intuitive trial and error process, have become associated with physical activities which have had some fairly profound somatic and orectic implications. In other words, they may have been finely tuned to the psychological and emotional development needs of the individuals involved, particularly in the area of sexuality.

Behind all initiation rites is the implicit assumption that the individual is valuable to his collective. This was particularly so when death rates were high and life expectancies were limited. For this reason, tutors were used in pubertal rites to "educate" the inductees, the collective's charter was revealed, new rights and responsibilities were delineated, and new adult statuses were made very explicit.

Also associated with most inductions was the notion that those initiated, or novices, needed to go from a lesser status to a non-status (become "socially invisible") to a mature status and show extreme humility during the process. This non-status period was a period of self-examination and revelation, and a prelude to the acquisition of adult power and the ability to withstand the stresses and demands associated with adulthood.

What has this process to do with lifelong education? The above gives some indication that all past societies have been interested in the progression of individuals from one set of statuses and roles to another and gave explicit public recognition to these transitions. Additionally, societies themselves recognized the need for all of their members to become publicly involved in certain regenerative activities which explicitly or implicitly recognized natural cycles and certain other points along the road of their own collective evolution.

What is the current situation? Some social critics might regard educational personnel and non-kin groups as having usurped the traditional initiatory roles of those close to the novices. Educational periods in post-industrial nations may have become so attenuated that an individual's period of neo-initiation may last from almost the cradle to 80 years of age (the PhD in western societies is the ultimate rite). For the period of his formal education, the individual may initially be kept in a state of childhood, and later, in a liminal state of adolescence surrounded by peers of the same age - occasionally these may be members of only his own sex.

In addition to these school-imposed statuses, the out-of-school society may assign him other statuses, i.e., the military, the law, the taxation people, the producers of goods and services. This kind of assignation in a highly status and role-specific society can and does lead to a good deal of ambiguity. The progression which society now expects of an individual may have little to do with that individual's holistic needs, particularly in terms of his bodily exertion needs; sexual development; affiliative needs; and needs for privacy and particular kinds of space. When the individual leaves the education institution he may suffer a drastic transition as he enters employment for which he is not really prepared. There is little public recognition of the disorientation that this transition causes, nor are there any preparatory initiatory rites other than those inherent in the educative system, despite the fact that obtaining occupational status and income have become an integral part of adulthood.

The above has some lessons for lifelong educators. It suggests a number of ideas:

First, educators should sensitize themselves to the various rhythms of humans, human collectives and of the natural environment of which man is an integral part. It may well be that each individual has an optimum sleep cycle, certain times when he has a great potential for sexual adventure, and his own food consumption schedules. In a cold climate, for example, the human collective might have rhythms associated with seasonal change, particularly with spring. Other rhythms may be associated with different phases in the moon and the tides. Built and technological environments can often insulate humans from the natural environment, and even worse, from "understanding" the significance of these phenomena which occur right through an individual's life and endlessly in the natural environment.

Second, educators should be concerned about the "receiving institutions" of society. For example, when young people go from home to school for the first time or from school to employment, what kinds of discontinuity occur? What kinds of transitional support system aid individuals to adjust? Generally speaking, there is little public recognition and support given to individuals as they go from one difficult social or biological stage or phase in their life to another. These stages or phases, if they are culturally and technologically imposed, may be no respecters of the needs of the individual in terms of his own physiological growth patterns. In pre-literate society, there was always the older tutor or the mentor who was something more than an educational cypher. Additionally, there were strong supporting kinship systems.

Third, and related to the above, how can educators recognize the influence of such rhythms? This recognition may be very difficult to cope with, given the problems of identifying, in nature, cause and effect

relationships pertinent to man, especially when such relationships are culturally mediated. It is proposed, because of this, that an individual "in-
tuitively" understands what he needs to schedule activities for himself.
This suggests that he should not have rigid time schedules imposed on him
either in schools or in terms of when he proceeds from one status or activity to another in his life. Further, he should be given some understanding of the implications of natural rhythms and cycles and how these affect
him. He should also understand the potentially coercive end-effects of built
and mass-produced environments.

Fourth, somehow educators should try to work out lifelong schedules
which, as far as possible, reconcile genotypic developmental imperatives,
environmental influences and cultural demands. This might mean developing
flexible work and education schedules, preferably by individuals themselves
with the assistance of education "facilitators" rather than directors and
controllers. Much scheduling, whichever style is adopted, should be heuristic
or open-ended.

9. Primates and Foraging Societies

It is not the intention of this section to get deeply involved in
the arguments, based largely on studies of animal behaviour, regarding the
relative importance of the cultural, as opposed to the biological, imperative in primate behaviour. For the purposes of this discourse, it will be
assumed that *both* are important but that their effects are difficult to
weight.

Non-human primates, like man, are born with an "incomplete behavioural repertoire" and, like humans, they are almost a "pseudo-species" as
compared with, say, insects which, from a behavioural point of view, have
extremely well programmed life and activity schedules. Because of this behavioural "deficit", primates - and this term will be used subsequently,
unless otherwise indicated, as being exclusive of humans - must more constantly learn how to adapt and how to gain control over, manipulate or
cope with their environment.

Why should a study of primates be of interest to educators at this
point in time? First, primates are in some ways very similar to man. They

have evolved in many of the same environments as man, and have many of the
same needs as man. Second, they continue to live in "natural" environments,
and supposedly are more "integrated" with their environments than man. This
is of interest to those seeking, for example, alternatives to urban living.
And third, because of the encroachment by man and his activities on nearly
every existing terrestrial environment, primates, and the environments that
support them, may not be extant for too much longer.

Of course, the *relevance* of such studies will have to be decided on by
the individuals who care to familiarize themselves with much of the material
currently being produced by zoologists and ethologists. The leap is quite a
large one, as primates do not have speech, their brains are smaller than
those of humans and they do not have a well developed technology to mediate
their environments. Additionally, there is a good deal of behavioural variability among the different primate species. Another consideration in assessing the importance of naturalistic primate studies to education is the relationship of observed behaviour in specific kinds of environment to primal
neural structures. Man himself has these primitive neural structures over-
lain by more complex structures acquired at a later evolutionary stage. That
we ourselves are animals and have evolved very recently in very specific environments similar to those of primates seems abundantly clear. We therefore
ignore the useful "information" contained in these environments at our peril. For lifelong education, the study of primates could be particularly relevant because of the fact that it sheds some light on how, for example,
different age groups and the two sexes are integrated for special activities
and differentiated for others, how various kinds of "bonding" occur, how
the young form a common focus for adults of both sexes and are, indeed, a
kind of "currency", how age-specific roles and tasks are learned and how
hierarchical status is achieved. Obviously, it is not possible to reverse
the clock and seek to create human environments which are analogues of
primate environments. Nor is it possible for humans to totally mimic primate behaviour. However, it is possible to gain insight into such things
as infant rearing practices, social organization and how dependency relationships are played out during the life history of an individual. Additionally,
we might look closely at how social innovation occurs and is learned and
how much variability and deviance is tolerated by primates in their rela-

tively small social groups.

Like humans, infant primates have a relatively long period of dependency on adults, particularly on their mothers. Attachment to the group and identification with the species is ensured by a number of processes which begin at a very early age. One of these is imprinting.

> This process is confined to a very definite and very brief period of the individual life, and possibly to a particular set of environmental circumstances. Once accomplished the process is very stable - in some cases perhaps totally irrevocable. It is often completed long before the various specific reactions to which the imprinted pattern will ultimately become linked are established. It is supra-individual learning - a learning of the broad characteristics of the species - for if this were not so and the (animal) at this stage (as it can easily do later) learnt the individual characteristics of its companion the biological effects would be frustrated.[8]

As an example of imprinting, the infant primate and the mother, or surrogate mother, become imprinted on each other within the first six months of the infant's life, i.e. some sort of cross-fixation seems to occur. Another mechanism for securing group solidarity, group and species information, and the survival of the individual, is primary socialization. In this process the individual learns his role in: dominance-subordination equations; leader-follower patterns; sexual activities; and mutual care relationships. Although the basic patterns of behaviour within primate systems are roughly comparable in these specific areas, i.e. are partly autochthonous and genotypic, a good deal of the *detail* associated with eventual behavioural outcomes is learned, variable and allochthonous. These latter kinds of behaviour and mimetic behaviour are also characteristic of humans and have led to the evolution of a number of discrete cultures. For such primate "pseudo-species", with their at-birth incomplete lifelong behavioural repertoire, culture becomes of extreme importance.

Primates may tell us a little about what the optimum group sizes or scales are for adequate and in-depth social relations. It is very seldom, for example, that primate bands occupying a particular territory exceed more than a few score in number. Usually it is fewer. This is in line with the scale of human settlements in places like New Guinea prior to contact with westerners. However, there are a number of other factors, e.g. technological levels and ecological restricting factors such as presence or absence of food, that complicate what can be said about the optimum size

for human groupings. However, one of the things that can be said of humans
and other primates is that both find it easier to exist in groups, some of
only nuclear family size, than as individuals, and the development of socially co-operative strategies is instrumental in achieving and maintaining
group solidarity and ensuring continuity and survival. This cooperation is
particularly necessary for the working out of collective defence strategies.

Most non-human primate behaviour, except for that of gibbons, indicates that there is little sexual jealousy;the females share sexual relationships with a number of males indiscriminately. The resulting young are,
in fact, the one area of common focus for both male and female adults.
Thus, socialization turns out to be a collective task of the group as the
young grow and develop. However, the *most important* relationship, and the
most enduring of all social relationships, appears to be that which exists
between the mother and the infant.

There is an extensive literature on *defensible territory* and space.
For the purposes of this exercise, however, it is suggested almost as a
truism that primates have very specific areas for ranging as individuals,
doing things in groups and for specific functions such as eating, defecat-
ing and the like. Not a great deal is known about sequences or patterns of
behaviour associated with these activities and how these might be related
to space and its defense. However, it would be reasonable to state that
very specific settings are required for ingestive, eliminative, shelter-
seeking and investigative behaviours. This observation has very important
implications for educators in terms of allocating space for human activities.

Primates do not normally exhibit a great deal of intraspecies aggression. This lack of aggression is possibly a result of socialization in which
dominance roles are learned, sexual and age segregation occurs in certain
space-time sequences and groups are small enough for implicit codes of
"etiquette" to be well learned. However, these codes of behaviour change
when primates are confined to zoos and it is possible to speculate that the
agonistic and pathological behaviours long observed in zoos are caused by
restrictive and coercive environments. The implications of this behaviour
for educators should also be painfully obvious.

Like humans, other primates have a very complex, multi-dimensioned communication system, though unlike humans they do not have speech. It is worth pointing out, however, when comparing the communication systems of humans and other primates, that the non-linguistic signalling systems of both are fairly stable over time. This stability flies in the face of much current popular literature which suggests, usually by inference, that humans, because their technological systems have been quickly changing, have been plastic enough themselves rapidly to change their signalling patterns and communicative behaviours.

There has been much discussion recently regarding what is instinctual and what is learned behaviour among non-human primates. In a very summary form it would seem that there is some instinctual *tendency* in primates for: ranking among males (however, this is unstable among chimpanzees); the power of males to be exercised over females (again, weak among chimpanzees); male sexual continence (this is a hotly contested issue); greater subservience among females (again contested); more male bonding; and more aggressiveness among males (this aggressiveness has now been related to sexual dimorphism and the need for the larger male of certain species to defend bands which live on the ground as opposed to those which live in trees).

What have we to learn from the above? First, all primates have inherited behaviour patterns which are an amalgam and a result of genetic coding and of learning. Second, because of this coding and learning, behaviours do not occur in a random way. They are patterned. Particular kinds of environment have a role in eliciting and determining how behaviour potentials will be actualized. Third, to understand the basis for many of these kinds of relationship, it is necessary to be knowledgeable about sensory physiology, about how primates receive signals and stimuli from their environments, and about hormonal physiology which provides insights into what kinds of arousal behaviour are "appropriate" in particular social and physical settings.

In many of our educational settings we seem to have largely ignored these factors and a noted primatologist, Washburn, has made the following comment:

> A view of traditional European educational practices from the vantage point of the primatologist suggests that the school system is based on a series of traditional mistakes. ... To the student of monkey behaviour, schools seem grounded in ignorance of the kind of being they are trying to teach. The view of the human being as a particu-

lar kind of primate makes the schools seem strange and leads to the
conclusion that human customs are not necessarily efficient, necessary, or useful in the way that they are supposed to be. Educational
institutions cannot be designed effectively without regard for the
biology of human beings. ... Through a profound misunderstanding of
the nature of primate biology, the schools reduce$_9$the most intelli-
gent primate to a bored and alienated creature.

According to Herzog, a psychologist and educational anthropologist,
this statement is based on three fairly "straightforward principles and
assumptions".

1) As the result of the process of adaptation, the members of a
   species have special capabilities to learn - early, quickly, and
   easily - those behaviours which have been critical for the survival of their species during its evolution;

2) Modern man, although considerably more "open" or "plastic" than
   other animals, most efficiently learns behaviours that were earlier important to his survival as a foraging animal according
   to timetables and under conditions of acquisition specifically
   calibrated for *homo sapiens*;

3) "Man's peculiar learning characteristics evolved during a foraging mode of subsistence in which all men lived until less than
   10,000 years ago; consequently we can learn a great deal about
   the parameters of learning for modern children and youth by observing juveniles in hunting and gathering societies, as well as
   in the societies of lower primates."[10]

Herzog then proposes seven generalizations "about the learning and
development of juveniles in primate and foraging societies" which might
have relevance in persons in modern societies. These generalizations based
on research (paraphrased) are:

First, early experience has "enormous strategic significance" for
the course of later development.

Second, play has a "critical function ... as perhaps the major channel through which juveniles acquire information about their physical environment, familiarize themselves with the social structure and conven-
tions of their group and test and improve their motor skills".

Third, "in societies of both foraging humans and other primates,
the social group and the geographic niche it occupies are the juvenile's
actual learning environment".

Fourth, "the really influential socializers in primate and foraging
societies after infancy are the juvenile's peers and slightly older play-

mates.

Fifth, "the juvenile period of freedom from responsibility and of the need for self-support is unusually long in man (16 years), chimpanzees (8 years) and presumably other apes".

Sixth, "much learning in primates occurs rapidly in an all-at-once form, as a result of fortuitous or arranged intense emotional experiences. Fears in particular must be quickly learned, if the animals are to survive".

Finally, in both foraging and sub-human primate societies there is relatively little teaching (i.e. direct and deliberate tuition) of the younger members by mature individuals.

Herzog contrasts what happens in technological societies with the above and comes to the conclusion (again paraphrased) that western children are thought to be involved in only "inconsequential and uninteresting" activities until the age of five. After this point in time they are expected to "work" not play. Throughout their school life they are discouraged from exploring "the settings and activities of the adult world" by, among other things, being segregated in schools. They are taught to compete rather than collaborate and are discouraged from playing in mixed age play groups. One of the results of these strategies appears to be an attenuated but artificial period of dependency. Additionally, children are continuously taught to avoid emotion-arousing experiences and to value "safe" but controlled and repetitive environments and teaching practices. [11]

Does the foregoing have implications for lifelong education? It is suggested that it does. First, there should be a great deal of thought given to the reasons for segregating humans by age and sex at different times in their lives. For example, it might well be that environments in education which facilitate adult female-children relations and mixed age groups should be greatly expanded; spaces and resources should be made available to enhance male bonding (friendship) tendencies; and that young persons who have reached puberty should be more actively encouraged to leave the family and become independent.

Second, it may also well be that the learning of certain tasks and skills is more appropriate to one sex than to the other. The care of young children, despite the women's liberation movement, might in fact be easier for women to cope with than it is for men. However, we need to know much more about this propensity than we do at present. Children's spontaneously generated games might give us some clues as to what tasks and skills the sexes find appropriate for *themselves*. Lifelong education might provide opportunities for people to learn roles and skills which they *themselves* rather than school controllers think are appropriate to their own sex and age.

Third, "people-involvement" in non-school settings, in studies of ethology and applied animal behaviour generally, but especially in the area of sexuality, might prompt a greater awareness of the behavioural options open to humans. Sanctions embedded in many present cultures may inhibit the exercise of these options.

Finally, for both humans and non-human primates, our information about optimum environments is incomplete. However, we do know that natural environments are patterned in very complex ways and that it is naive to think of them as being less complex than, say, the coarse-grained urban built environments in which man has encapsulated himself. If the validity of this assumption is accepted it becomes a very real challenge for educators to reproduce built environments which are as stimulating as "natural" environments. It also becomes a very real challenge to create settings in which developmental sequences such as imprinting, primary socialization and the like will be adequately elicited and facilitated.

10. Alternative Life Styles

After having been to nearly every large city in the world, the writer is convinced that people in very diverse situations are beginning to adopt convergent life styles. It is possible, because of world trade systems, world information systems and, most importantly, because of extensive standardized technological and built systems, for individuals to be very imitative and draw on the creativity and talent of distant others. These transfers have decided advantages. They also have decided disadvantages. It might mean, for example, that the potential creativity of many persons is not being encouraged or is in fact being inhibited by the routinized demands of large systems which push the individual towards a certain kind of behavioural modality. There is also the question of vulnerability. Ecologists make it

very clear that diversity in plant and animal communities is vital for the
survival of all species within a community. Similarly, with humans it would
seem that unless there are many kinds of social and physical environments,
humans too will not survive. On a purely pragmatic but different level, for
example, we make ourselves extremely vulnerable by depending on meat, the
top of the food chain, the production of which depends on the yields from
very vulnerable monocrops. For these reasons, and many others, educators
should have the confidence to advocate εducational options which lead to:
the development of very different personality types; divergent life styles;
and a range of large and small scale social institutions. In agro-ecosystems
this approach would be analogous to maintaining plant and animal diversity
and to enhancing the viability of stable interspecies relationships and
systems. On a political level this thrust for diversity has some fairly profound implications. For example, it might challenge the validity of the political socialization which occurs in the schools of most nation states.

11. Communication

Traditionally, anthropologists have tended to study linguistic and lexical skills in isolation from other kinds of human communication skill. Now,
however, they are realizing that this focus is too restricted and are branch-
ing out into such exotic but vital areas as (1) kinesics and haptics (non-
linguistic body movements and touching or feeling), (2) proxemics (body space),
(3) ethology and zoosemiotics (animal behaviour with special reference to
systems of animal communication), (4) iconics (artifactual symbols), (5) epi-
meletic behaviour (signalling for care and attention), (6) pheromonics (communication through smells), and (7) trophallaxis (food exchange systems).

Anthropologists are, in fact, realizing that to fully understand man
and the life systems of which he is a part, they need to treat him as a sen-
sorium with a great number of receptor and effector modalities. Additionally,
they have realized that communication may have some very particularistic or
situational aspects. The recognition of all these dimensions has tended to
make those interested in the communicative process extremely wary of making
generalizations or stating with certainty that specific universals exist

across cultures. At best they will state in very general terms that:

1) The acquisition of natural communication skills is sequential and incremental, i.e. follows a development sequence.

2) The ability or potential to acquire communication skills seems to be inherited. However, for such skills to be actualized particular kinds of eliciting environments are needed. Culture is the most pervasive of these environments.

3) For spoken languages, the developmental sequences for all children irrespective of culture seem to be the same. Milestones in language learning are similar for *all* children. This phenomenon seems to indicate that humans are genetically or internally programmed to learn and organize linguistic sequences.

4) Inability to acquire communication skills is usually a function of inheritance and/or age.

5) Human communication systems are usually implicit. They all have order, logic, consistency and are functional in permitting the prediction of behaviour and in facilitating satisfying social interaction including cooperation to ensure survival of the species.

Although the focus above is on humans, it is sobering to remember that an exchange of information (communication) is constantly occurring in all life systems. For example, man and all other life forms are genetically coded to develop or grow in fairly specific environments. Man himself has nervous and metabolic subsystems the signals of which he ignores at his peril.

The above has some fairly profound or awesome dimensions in terms of understanding and control. However, at a much more mundane level it is worth, especially from an anthropological perspective, understanding what *control* of information means in terms of modern and pre-literate societies. Wiener describes what seems to happen in communities irrespective of culture or location. Size for him is the important variable:

> Small closely knit communities have a very considerable measure of homeostasis; and this whether they are highly literate communities ..., or (primitive) villages ... It is only in the large community, where the Lords of Things As They Are protect themselves from hunger by wealth, from public opinion by privacy and anonymity, from private criticism by laws of libel and the possession of the means of communication, that ruthlessness can reach its most sublime levels. Of all these anti-homeostatic factors in society, the control of the means of communication is the most effective and the most important.[12]

In extensive modern metropolitan cities, where business, industry and commerce are predominant, small communities cannot usually exist, and it is in this milieu that social relations have a short time scale. Individuals in such situations are, as it were, continuously on the "hop". This means that they must always learn to communicate with new people and about new things, and respond to the imperatives of new technologies. Such experiences may encourage cognitive learning but are scarcely conducive to the development of in-depth affective (emotional) relationships. Such a deficit is rather unfortunate, for it is this latter kind of interaction which engenders the most meaningful kinds of human communication. Serial human relationships and extended relationships with centralized technological systems are *not* conducive to the development of meaningful, affective social communication patterns. It is indeed ironic that global technologies and resource flow systems make people more dependent on distant others for survival. To the extent that they are caught up in this syndrome (growth of large systems and superficial human communication), they are unable to establish small-scale affective communication systems which are so vitally important to the growth and development of particular individuals. From this perspective it might be inferred that large cities come into existence because they are able to enhance *certain* kinds of communication systems but not necessarily *others* which may be more important.

Anthropologists have, as indicated, cast their nets widely to understand the significance of patternings of learned and genetically transmitted behaviours. To many anthropologists such behaviours are signals, and culture itself becomes equivalent to a construct or code which through time makes such behaviours intelligible. Extending this paradigm, social structure might then become equated with the *organization* of relationships being *expressed* in these behaviours. The anthropologist working with these kinds of assumption becomes very interested in learning how individuals and groups code themselves, how they code their environments and *how* human collectives organize themselves so as to make optimal use of interpersonal coding mechanisms and strategies. The cultural psychologist on the other hand is more interested in the *whys* of behaviour and in the intellective processes (cognition). He frequently, if not a strict behaviourist, approaches this problem by focussing on how individuals categorize, infer, discriminate, generalize and solve problems.

Non-living or built and technological environments, it is worth noting, are symbols or icons, and as such and as parts of functions, man-created systems, have signalling or coding propensities that are eminently "understandable" to man. They are representative of man and *his* thinking and abilities. Their qualities are "knowable", and the way in which their properties, including performance potential, will be internalized by persons in particular cultures is reasonably predictable. However, man does not yet fully "understand" how large-scale life systems are programmed, and which signals in these systems are really important or unimportant. As yet he cannot completely program or construct such systems or analogues of such systems himself. To the extent he cannot do this, the information he receives from extant bio-systems is incomplete and incomprehensible. At present this is one of the most enigmatic and problematic areas in communication. Once information on how life systems are coded is correctly or adequately communicated to him, he will have the awesome responsibility of deciding how he wishes or does not wish to control or manage such systems, of which he is a part.

Man, as contrasted to other species, is very flexible, although not infinitely so, in terms of the kinds of environment to which he can adapt. However, for him to be almost "niche free", he must be extremely dependent on stored information and on information from his fellow humans both living and dead. Biological factors such as: a long period in the womb; a long infancy; a slow maturation rate; and a low birth rate, also make it imperative to have adequate corporeal and extracorporeal information systems. One of the reasons for survival in the past has been the collective ability of humans to allocate special tasks and roles to different members of the species. These factors made it imperative that symbolization to facilitate communication and survival be efficient. Unreliable or unpredictable symbolization has usually led to the death or exile of deviant humans. Few traditional societies could or can afford the luxury of accumulating misinformation or discrepant information because of the presence of inadequate symbolizers. In more modern societies such persons, because they are not necessarily crucial to the survival of the collective, may be, and usually are, locked up in institutions for the insane or the lawless. It would be

interesting to speculate whether tolerance levels for discrepant symbolizers are currently increasing or decreasing. In schools, examinations and
grading quickly identify such persons.

In what follows an attempt is made to show why too much reliance on
any *one* human communication channel, e.g. the auditory-oral may be unsatisfactory for purposes of social control and species survival. Put slightly
differently, social control or organizational strategies which emphasize
only one mode of communication may have an in-built survival pathology.

Anthropologists, because of their interests in the social organization
of education, frequently become involved in assessing whether varying social
organizing strategies over time affect human learning and communicative outcomes particularly in the areas of formal and informal education. In the
following the research findings of Scribner and Cole are drawn on fairly
heavily to illustrate differences in such outcomes.[13] These two authors
suggest that if differences in the social organization of education do in
fact occur, differences in the organization of learning and thinking skills
will *also* occur and that in the past there has been an incorrect stress on
the continuity between formal and informal education. In other words,
school experiences may have promoted a kind of learning and thinking which
runs counter to or is different from that nurtured in the context of everyday, practical activities.

These authors distinguish between cognitive capacities - the ability
to "remember, generalize, form concepts, operate with abstractions and
reason logically" - and skills or functional learning systems which are
"different ways in which basic capacities are integrated and brought into
play for the purposes at hand". They suggest that different educational systems give rise to different functional learning systems and that evidence,
based on cross-cultural research in Senegal, Central Asia and elsewhere, has
indicated: 1) "unschooled populations tended to solve individual problems
singly, each as a new problem, whereas schooled populations tended to treat
them as instances of a class of problems that could be solved by a general
rule". 2) that the schooled and unschooled groups can be distinguished by
the languages they use "to describe the tasks and what they are doing with
them". Some indication is then given of how these differences are generated
by informal education in non-institutional settings on the one hand, and by

formal education in the school in different cultures on the other.

It is suggested that in informal (everyday) education the child learns basic skills and values in a particularistic way - "expectations for performance are phrased in terms of who a person is instead of rather *what* he has accomplished". Additionally, "the value of information is closely related to who imparted it". Further, education is tradition-oriented and there is a high affective charge - intellectual and affective domains are integrated. Learning content is usually inseparable from the identity of the person with a mentor status. From a number of anthroplogists the learning mechanisms associated with informal education are listed, for example, "mimesis", "identification", "cooperation", "empathy", "imitation" and "learning through looking". The emphasis in the anthropological studies referred to is on "observational learning". This kind of learning emphasizes, 1) demonstration by adult or other models rather than verbalization, 2) that meaning is intrinsic to the context, and 3) that verbalization or verbal formulations are not promoted in *either* the learner or the teacher.

Non-institutional formal education in contrast to the above is defined as any process of cultural transmission that is:

1) organized deliberately to fulfil the specific purpose of transmission,

2) extracted from the manifold of daily life, and

3) made the responsibility of the larger social group.

Such education, it is pointed out, emphasizes "values and attitudes rather than knowledge and skills". The transmittal processes in, for example, specialized language teaching, have in common with informal education the following characteristics:

1) they transmit traditional knowledge and skills with highly positive social value;

2) the learning is not depersonalized but continues to be bound up with the social status of the persons acting as teachers; and

3) it is bounded learning in the sense that it deals with a demarcated set of activities or skills with the result that the learning processes are inseparably related to the given body of material.

Formal education in schools does not seem to have a great deal of continuity with informal education. Whereas "informal education rests upon a system of person-oriented values", formal education stresses "universalistic values, criteria and standards of performance". *What* is being taught becomes, supposedly, more important than *who* is doing the teaching. Relations in formal education with the mentor become a very secondary matter for children.

What is the significance of this process? First, there may be dissonance between what the child has learned from and about his local sensate environment and what he learns in school. Second, where two cultures meet, the indigenous culture of the student may be disvalued. Third, attempts may be made to have the written curriculum pre-empt the oral traditions of the student. In short, for example, what passes for science may try to "lay common sense to rest". The authors relate a very revealing anecdote about an English speaking chemistry teacher who told his Nigerian students that in his own high school days he liked chemistry with its precise rules better than socializing with other students whose behaviour he found "confusing and unpredictable". The Nigerian students found this orientation hard to accept because they believed the natural world to be "disorderly and uncontrollable, whereas the human world can be understood and controlled".

From a brief description of the salient features of the three forms of social organization of education and their significance for learning, the authors examine how "changes in the content of education are closely connected with changes in the basic organization". They, and other researchers, suggest that functional learning systems developed in schools stress language rather than action as the principle method of acquiring information and knowledge. Additionally, teaching and learning occur "out of context". It is possible for these processes to develop because schools themselves are "removed from the context of socially relevant action". Language becomes the chief vehicle for communication at the expense of other kinds of communication and this restricts the amount of information available to the learner. Extra-linguistic skills are undeveloped or made obsolescent. Learning through observation, for example, has only a limited role in the information acquisition process. Language moves quickly away from concrete referents and the child may thus acquire many "empty verbal constructs".

The informal learner, on the other hand, has a more limited vocabulary acquired in an experiential context in which there are many "concrete exemplars". Concepts "are rich in context but often difficult to define and to incorporate in a coherent conceptual system". Emphasis in schools is on gaining control over new techniques for *processing* information rather than for *using* it. This functional learning system gives primacy to individuals being able to generalize rule-sets to a wide variety of problems. Additionally, such an approach is acquired by "deutero-learning" or learning to learn and is encouraged to occur when individuals are constantly presented with "problems of the same type".

Although much of what Scribner and Cole put forward is of a tentative or hypothetical nature, it is suggestive in terms of what kinds of alternatives or supplements lifelong education might offer to formal education as it is now socially organized in schools.

First, it might in general stress modalities of communication other than language in the learning process. Where language is to be used it should be imbedded in participatory and action-oriented learning situations.

Second, it might assist students to understand their own communication strengths better. It is probably a truism, but one frequently overlooked, that certain learners and teachers, particularly in culturally heterogeneous situations, have extra-linguistic skills of which they are not aware. This tactic would place some onus on educators to understand other than traditionally emphasized language skills.

Third, it might place some emphasis on developing studies in cross-cultural extra-linguistic and non-written communication systems and on how these are developed in the rapidly shrinking/expanding world in which educators live. It might also examine the strengths of traditional pre-literate, extra-linguistic signalling systems and activity patterns with a view to enhancing their value and seeking to preserve them.

Fourth, and most important, it might aim at reintegrating verbal and action-oriented skills. Given the usual large size of classes and the almost total orientation of schools toward language and other symbolic skills abstracted from social systems and concrete referents, it might be necessary for those developing lifelong education to examine alternative, perhaps better learning environments found in pre-literate societies. This examination could be done with a view to developing more action-oriented individuals who have a much greater sense of commitment to whatever functional learning system they are a part of, and to the human sources of information - in short to development of the "third dimension" of education: a healthy affective orientation toward mentors and their skill-transmitting abilities.

To those who espouse universalistic values, and believe that information should be validated *without* reference to the human source, the above will seem to be somewhat revisionary. However, it is suggested that by re-integrating action (as a communication skill), language, and conceptualization in meaningful social settings, much will be done to combat the present devaluation of information, which has frequently been machine-generated for its own sake, and the tendency to objectify and become alienated from the human sources of information. This schema would emphasize information on, and involvement in, skills which are directly applicable to the growth and development and survival of individuals and small groups. The two-culture approach mentioned previously, and built on the above principles, might allow individuals to develop their affective potentialities in very small or primal groups and to use the language and usual school skills in situations where "impersonal" communication is emphasized, for example in organizations concerned with the efficiency of large technological systems.

In brief, the above attempts to indicate that schools and formal education have a certain kind of social organization which stresses a particular communication modality - language skills. By restricting itself to this modality, the school places tremendous strain on one human communication channel. It, in effect, produces individuals with uni-dimensional communication abilities. Lifelong education could provide alternative models.

12. Commitment and Human Scale

Anthropologists, in common with architects, sociologists, designers, planners and geographers, are becoming more and more interested in how people use space. They are interested for a number of reasons, one of the prime being overcrowding and lack of direct access to space by urban dwellers. In the following some ways are suggested of involving and sensitizing those in built settlements to the value of space and to what kinds of interaction can occur in public spaces (which in many areas of the world are rapidly being depleted).

By way of an example, many persons might wish to know how inhabitants will use a proposed public plaza. The involved sociologist might be interested in the general socioeconomic and demographic structures of a potentially involved population. Within the context of a specific culture (or cultures, if there is more than one in a neighbourhood), this information might tell him how affluent the surrounding society is and to what kind of resources, including space, tne community already has access.

The geographer might be interested in the spatial location of other resources such as built structures, work places and where specific economic functions, such as food distribution outlets, are sited. This knowledge would give him some idea of the relation of the proposed plaza to the built morphology and functional flows of goods and services of the existing community.

The cultural anthropologist, on the other hand, might be interested in predicting how people will use the plaza. He might ask such questions as: how much of the behaviour will be cultural, e.g. shaking hands, sitting on the benches in certain ways, and how much will be situational and specific to the plaza, e.g. using a fountain in the plaza in ways for which there is no cultural precedent. He might be interested in how configuration induces certain behaviours and how far these behaviours can be attributed to the biological and primal needs of man, particularly in terms of his needs for certain kinds of space. It may well be that he needs quite extensive areas for activities equivalent to hunting, foraging and the like. The plaza might help to satisfy some of these requirements. He might be interested in how different age, sex and ethnic groups respond in terms of their use of the plaza. One could, for example, predict that if there were different ethnic groups living adjacent to it, they would use it quite differently. He might also be interested in how different income groups would use it and how those from residentially crowded areas use it as opposed to those who come from affluent, uncrowded areas. The social anthropologist might try to predict the content and quality of the social interaction. For example, he might try to predict how social hierarchies would be reflected in

different interaction patterns. He might also be interested in how acculturation and socialization would occur in the plaza. The anthropologist interested in ethology might very well interest himself in the concept of terri-
toriality - how people will define, or demarcate and defend, spaces for various activities. On a more micro-level, some attention would be given to how
individuals will define their own space - the study of proxemics.

The planner would attempt to take all the above information and integrate it with other information he had on costs, zoning and legal requirements and with his traditions which try to cope with such concepts as planning on a human scale and integrating micro-planning, such as the plaza, with
larger planning projects.

Naturally, one might ask how and why the individual as a learner should
interest and involve himself in this process. Governments and social scientists alike are realizing that citizen inputs on a continuing basis are necessary for a number of reasons. First, citizens, through involvement, receive a good deal of education about their environment and about the complexities of decision-making. Second, planners, managers, ecologists and social
scientists learn about citizen preferences and that, if a public structure
such as a plaza is built with as many inputs from as many sources as possible, it will probably be used optimally. This approach means that, as a
defined space and a built structure, the plaza will have the potential to
assist in facilitating social interaction, providing specific space for such
human activities as games, eating and the like. In other words, it will be
less likely to be a coercive setting.

From the individual perspective, involvement in the planning, the
design and even in the construction of such a public facility might assist
an urban dweller to grow and develop. Through some of the above means of
working on micro-futures, relating to the use of space and built structures,
he can understand the possibilities of creating a whole new series of social
and physical environments. He can begin to understand not only how pervasive cultural patterns are, but how in specific situations innovative behaviour, new social institutions and adaptation to new settings can occur. This
approach, involving planning, inventing and observing results, which are
seldom the same as those predicted, is potentially an exciting activity for
all age groups, particularly where such groups have a vested interest in the

project being executed.

Such an activity, with its focus on tangible and potentially meaningful community change, is something in which schools generally do not involve
themselves. This is probably because it represents a significant break with
the past. Inventing micro-futures, the "externalization" or "objectifica-
tion" of self through understanding others, comprehending the consequences
of a certain kind of human evolution and understanding environmental im-
pacts on individual groups and vice versa, are development processes which
are difficult to structure in traditional educational settings. Additionally, these approaches confront the individual with all kinds of ambiguity,
in terms of choice of what he as an individual should like and need as
opposed to what others would like and need. Such approaches also precipitate
questions relating to the uncertainty in attributing "causes" to most human
behaviours and interaction patterns. Creating new socially and physically
viable futures (ethogenesis) can commence at the community level, and eventually, by extension, have relevance in national and international settings. Lifelong education would have as its aim the involvement of individuals and groups in many projects such as the above, where some thought
is being given to multi-faceted change and in which physical structures are
only one dimension of collective social growth and development. It is suggested that unless education continuously concerns itself with problems and
issues which are *real* to the participants it will become more and more vi-
carious - an exercise in which people are taught to distance themselves
from problems rather than confront them.

13. Acculturation and Enculturation

Through cultures, men learn to relate to their physical and social environments. There have been in the past, and still are, a tremendous number
of discrete or different cultures, hence many different ways of having
one's environment filtered or mediated. It has been the "business" of social and cultural anthropologists to try to understand these cultures, their
similarities and, over time, to develop a particular thrust which is well
summarized by Goldschmidt:

The cultural viewpoint has the following features: (1) those behaviour patterns which differentiate one community from another are not
responses to differing genetically transmitted characteristics;
(2) they are, instead, a product of cultural traditions; (3) this
cultural tradition is transmitted in part unwittingly through the
human and symbolic environment in which a community nurtures its
children; and (4) modern society is not, in such matters, different from primitive societies, even though it has peculiar complexities.[14]

Because of the importance anthropologists have given to cultural continuities, there has been a tendency to stress: lack of change; the pristine
and functional nature of each culture; the irreversibility of enculturation
processes; cultural conformity and hard-core cultural personality types;
and the importance of tradition rather than environment in moulding individual and group preferences and behaviour. Because of the global integration
now occurring, many of these kinds of emphasis are no longer tenable.
Instead, the anthropologist must look at: Acculturation - what happens to
people when they find themselves at the juncture of two or more cultural
vectors? Change - what is change? What constitutes a discontinuity, particularly in the area of technological change? Dysfunctionality - do some evolving cultures facilitate better individual and group development and growth
than others? Do some emphasize such things as technological, as opposed to
other kinds of growth? And environment - which environment imperatives are
important in determining behaviour? How far can man transcend, as it were,
his historical interactive patterns with the environments in which he
evolved? What is the importance of pervasive new kinds of environment?
How might we better understand what constitutes a resonant environment, i.e.
an environment in which an individual feels there is harmony rather than
dissonance or disharmony?

Becoming aware of one's social and physical environment and asking
oneself these kinds of question on the basis of the experiences of the
unique but amalgamous *self* can be a very humbling experience. For example,
if a Westerner thinks in terms of cultural discontinuities, social change
and of creating micro-futures, he must immediately question the validity
of much that he and his ancestors have learned in the historically recent
past. By way of example, western type school systems have been in existence
for about three hundred years. Initially, their purpose was partly religious and partly custodial. Later, they became popular for politically

socializing young people and for establishing the legitimacy of rulers and of nation states. In fact, they became, and are still becoming, next to the military, the largest and foremost institution of modern states. Now, in addition to the functions of political socialization and maintaining cultural continuities, schools have assumed the role of certifying people for vocations. Other institutions could, of course, do these things. For example, there is no reason why potential employers could not evaluate the entering skills of applicants for employment. This evaluation would at one stroke obviate a very significant reason for making student evaluations "public". Additionally, political socialization and communication skills might be better acquired through the public media and small skill centres rather than in very expensive schools. Custodial functions for very young children might be better performed by cooperatives of the aged or teenagers. There would seem to be no biological imperative or support for organizing schools as they are currently organized, i.e. in standardized built environments, with children segregated into chronological age groups which relate to very few adults. Studies of pre-literate cultures and non-human primate behaviour would indicate that this does not seem to be a very wise social or organizing strategy.

If educators would step outside of their selfhoods and partly objectify themselves, as it were, by asking why certain institutions continue to persist and why they personally perpetuate them, and what the barriers actually are for changing social and built environments, they might be surprised to find how much historical and cultural baggage they were carrying around with them. What lies behind this?

First, it would seem that the human brain, aged 55,000 years in its present form, has functional limitations. It evolved at a time when man lived only in small groups. This is possibly one reason why it can only handle a limited number of communication signals, can cope only with things spatially proximate, temporally close, and few in number. Its potential for dealing with incoming signals or stimuli is thus limited. In addition to this, because of genetic heterogeneity and experiential differences, individuals process and transmit the same information differently, i.e. they are idiosyncratic. This insight helps to explain why culture is not passed on in its entirety from one generation to the next. It also helps to explain

why individuals frequently fail to observe gradual changes, such as disap-
pearance of animal and insect species or environmental degradation, or find
great difficulty in being able to handle sudden change such as being sub-
merged in a new culture - culture shock. Overlapping generations help to
prevent sudden discontinuities. However, it is doubtful whether this phenomenon can now adequately cushion the individual against the effects of
rapid technological growth or assist him to cope with large social collectives or organizations held together by such things as force and rigid
hierarchies, impersonal communication systems, specific,routine, repetitive
activity roles and rigid time scheduling. The idea is put forward, not for
the first time in this paper, that modern man at present needs two cultures. One to relate to nature and his immediate affiliates. This culture would emphasize affective in-depth relationships and would lead to the
development of a good deal of implicit communication, including that facilitated through intimate body contacts, food sharing and the like. This kind
of interaction would take care of the more primal needs. The other culture
would emphasize the impersonal acquisition of resources and man-the-exten-
sion-of-technology role. In this culture, communication and activity functions would be very explicit and unequivocal. Given man's potential to
adapt to short term stressful or non-traditional environments, the above
might suggest a workable societal model for the *immediate* future. Ultimately, however, reintegration should be a goal.

Lifelong education, grounded as it were in a somewhat standardized
world, could explicitly address itself to a kind of ethnogenesis which
would recognize some of the needs of man in terms of his developmental past.
The opportunities for experimentation are boundless if man is able to maintain access to life-supporting resources. However, as has been mentioned
elsewhere, this may be problematical. Should this experimentation occur
globally, as it now does to a limited degree in large cities, the maintenance of diversity of institutions and life styles will be ensured. This
diversity maintenance may have a number of consequences. It could satisfy
man's individual and collective desire to innovate and explore. It could
give explicit recognition to individual differences. Most importantly, it
could ensure that the diversity which gives any society strength, and
which as a principle receives strong support from ecology, is maintained

and developed.

An understanding of enculturation and acculturation assists one to understand how institutions within a society can, each with its own subculture, create adjustment problems for individuals who try to straddle them. For example, universities and churches frequently create problems for the individual who wants to participate in the activities of both. There might additionally be problems where family mores and behaviours are not congruent with those of, say, local street groups. Over time the individual may have some difficulty adapting to subcultures associated with different age groups. He may, in fact, when trying to bridge the age gap, feel analogous to a migrant in another culture. Primary socialization and enculturation institutions, such as the family, can do much to ensure that individuals are flexible and do not have major adjustment and adaptation problems as the above suggests they might have when trying to seek cultural alternatives. Some of the ways of doing this would be: to ensure that children have lots of adult, peer, and intermediate models from whom to learn; the acquisition of another culture and language(s) and frequent changes in environment through travelling and the like. Lifelong education can do much to ensure that there is strong emphasis on understanding the role of error, ambiguity, unlearning, probability and tentativeness, rather than certainty in learning. It can also be supportive of the "family" activities mentioned above.

Educators will have come far if they can learn to think of intelligence as relating not only to the ability to survive, but to the ability to grow and develop in environments which they enhance through creating *new* institutions having as their raison d'être a *respect* for the viability of all life systems rather than the *worship* of burgeoning but vulnerable technological systems.

Implicit in this ideal is the notion that educators 1) understand which aspects of diverse cultural systems *in the past* were functional in terms of ensuring human survival; and 2) which of these same aspects viewed in the context of *current* ecological imperatives and in terms of an emerging world culture may be pathological.

While this insight does not lessen the need for a respect for cultural diversity, it does increase the necessity for educators to examine innovation (or the maintenance of traditional continuities) in a much wider perspective than they have in the past. Lifelong education is a vehicle to bring about this new consciousness.

NOTES

1. Goldschmidt, Walter. "Anthropology: Study of Modern Society". In Sills, David L. (Ed.). *International Encyclopedia of the Social Sciences.* New York: Crowell, Collier McMillan, 1968. 1', p. 335.

2. Ward, Barbara. "Only One Earth". *Unesco Courier* 26 (Jan. 1973). p. 8. - Mead, Margaret. *Culture and Commitment: A Study of the Generation Gap.* Garden City, N.Y.: Natural History Press, 1970.

3. Rappaport, Roy. "The Flow of Energy in an Agricultural Society". *Scientific American* 225 (Sept. 1971), No. 3. pp. 116 - 132.

4. Glass, David C.; Cohen, S., & Singer, J. E. "Urban Din Fogs the Brain". *Psychology Today* 6 (May 1973), No. 12. pp. 94 - 99.

5. Marine, Gene, & Van Allen, Judith. *Food Pollution: The Violation of Our Inner Ecology.* New York: Holt, Rinehart & Winston, 1972.

6. Freud, Sigmund. *Three Essays on the Theory of Sexuality.* (James Strachey, Transl. and Ed.). London: Hogarth Press, 1962.

7. Piaget, Jean, & Inhelder, Barbel. *The Early Growth of Logic in the Child. Classification and Seriation.* (L. A. Lunzer & D. Papert, Transl.). New York: Harper & Row, 1964.

8. Thorpre, W. H. *Learning and Instinct in Animals.* London: Methuen, 1956. p. 116.

9. Washburn, S. L. "Primate Field Studies and Social Science". In Nader, Laura, & Maretzki, Thomas W. (Eds.). *Cultural Illness and Health: Essays in Human Adaptation.* Washington: American Anthropological Association, 1973. (Anthropological Studies, No. 9.)

10. Herzog, John D. "The Socialization of Juveniles in Primate and Foraging Societies: Implications for Contemporary Education". *Council of Anthropology and Education Quarterly* 5 (Feb. 1974), No. 1. p. 13.

11. Ibid., pp. 12 - 14.

12. Wiener, Norbert. *Cybernetics or Control and Communication in the Animal and the Machine*. New York: Wiley, 1948. p. 37.

13. Scribner, Sylvia, & Cole, Michael. "Cognitive Consequences of Formal and Informal Education". *Science* 182 (Nov. 9, 1973). pp. 553-559.

14. Goldschmidt, Walter. "Anthropology ...". See Note 1. p. 337.

ADDITIONAL SOURCES

Birdwhistle, Ray L. "Communication". In Sills, David L. (Ed.). *International Encyclopedia of the Social Sciences*. New York: Crowell, Collier MacMillan, 1968. 3, pp. 24-29.

Goffman, Erving. *The Presentation of Self in Everyday Life*. New York: Doubleday, 1959.

Gough, Kathleen. *The Origin of the Family*. Toronto: New Hogtown Press, 1973.

Guhl, A. M., & Schein, Martin W. "A Glossary of Terms Used in Animal Behavior". In *Laboratory Studies in Animal Behavior*. San Francisco: W. H. Freeman, 1968. No. 838.

Kneller, George F. *Educational Anthropology: An Introduction*. New York: Wiley, 1965.

Mead, George H. "Mind". In Morris, Charles W. (Ed.). *Self and Society from the Standpoint of a Social Behaviorist*. Chicago: Chicago University Press, 1967.

Nicholson, Clara K. *Anthropology and Education*. Columbus, Ohio: Merrill, 1968.

Roth, Heinrich. *Pädagogische Anthropologie*. 2 "Entwicklung und Erziehung". Hannover: Schroedel, 1971.

Spindler, George D. (Ed.). *Education and Anthropology*. Stanford: Stanford University Press, 1956.

———— (Ed.). *Education and Culture: Anthropological Approaches*. New York: Holt, Rinehart & Winston, 1963.

Zdarzil, Herbert. *Pädagogische Anthropologie*. Heidelberg: Quelle & Meyer, 1972.

GLOSSARY

acculturation - acquiring the cultural characteristics of another group through direct interaction

affective growth - human emotional development

agonistic behaviour - a typical behaviour, induced by abnormal environments

allochthonous - acquired from elsewhere, not indigenous

artifacts/artifactual - man-produced articles, tools, etc. - material culture

auditory-oral - hearing and speaking modalities

autochthonous - indigenous

biotic environment - an environment consisting of biota or living organisms

bonding - the special attachment relationships between members of higher species

built environments - those features of human environments which have been fabricated by man, e.g. buildings, technological features, etc.

cognitive - intellective functions

corporeal - bodily

cybernation - systems which include controls utilizing immediate feedback

ecosystem - a viable system incorporating organisms and inorganic materials

empathy - a positive feeling for other humans

enculturation - cultural or learned behaviour transmission

ethnogenesis - creating new cultural or societal forms

fate group - that group with which an individual identifies his destiny

gene pools potential supply of genes in a specific population

genotype - gene complement of an organism

homeostasis - physiological equilibrium

lexical skills - ability to manipulate language through the use of words or a wide vocabulary *liminal* - consciousness threshold

metabolic - bio-chemical processes of an organism

micro-futures - futures which will be important at the micro-level, i.e. at the level of the ordinary person

mimesis - imitation or mimicry

monocrops - crops consisting of one plant species

a niche free organism - construct which implies that an organism can survive in a diversity of environments, i.e. not bound to a specific ecological slot

orectic - desires stemming from the need for sexual satisfaction

paradigm - model

pathological - leading to death or extinction

phenotype - appearance and behavioural dimensions of an organism attributable to hereditary and learned behaviour

pseudo species - a species born without a complete behavioural repertoire

receptor and effector modalities - parts of an organism which respond to stimuli

rites of passage - culturally determined stages or phases in the lives of individuals

sexual dimorphism - physical differences between the sexes, e.g. in shape, colour, etc.

socialization - process which produces socially competent individuals for a particular society

somatic - pertaining to the body

synergistic - eliciting a powerful effect through combining two or more substances which may, in isolation, be fairly benign

CHAPTER 7

ECONOMIC ANALYSIS OF LIFELONG EDUCATION

Annie V i n o k u r

1. Introduction

According to one of the definitions most frequently given, lifelong education is "a creative process continuing throughout life which aims at integrating all kinds of learning experiences for the development of the total
human personality".[1] This formulation calls for two preliminary remarks:

First, the objective "development of the total human personality" is
vague because it is expressed in humanistic-individualistic terms without any
reference to a social context, although the purpose of education is, to quote
Emile Durkheim, "to stimulate and develop in the child a certain number of
physical, intellectual and moral conditions demanded of him by the *body poli-
tic* as a whole and by the particular social milieu for which he is destined".[2]
Yet many authors see no contradiction in this, as shown by the reference to
"almost universal agreement that lifelong education is the principle of educational organisation best suited to the individual and collective needs of
the immediate and more remote future".[3] According to these authors, lifelong
education would, on the one hand, meet the needs of development of the total
human personality and the necessity to develop in every individual creativity, initiative, a critical mind and *autonomy*; on the other, it would permit
a better *adaptation* to ever more rapid economic and social change.

Secondly, the means envisaged is a re-organization of the educational
process so that it will be (a) no longer confined to the first few years of
life, but "vertically" articulated with its successive stages; (b) no longer
limited to specific institutions, but "horizontally" integrated in all social
activities.[4]

The transformation of educational structures, which lifelong education aims at, is thus defined by reference (opposition) to the school system as it was founded and has developed in capitalist societies. The principal characteristics of education in such societies, as opposed to pre-capitalist ones, are:

- separation of the educative function from other social functions, in particular from production;
- progressive expansion to cover all children and adolescents;
- continuity of the successive levels of schooling.

These are the three characteristics that have made school an important instrument for the reproduction of such societies, i.e. for transmission of the dominant value system, training of the qualified labour force, maintenance of social hierarchies, allotment of individuals to the various positions resulting from the division of labour in the society.

Does the criticism of the school system implicit in the very idea of lifelong education mean that the social relations it helps reproduce are being questioned, or on the contrary, that school no longer satisfactorily performs its reproductive function? In either case, is the problem the same for advanced capitalist societies as it is for developing countries where, hardly ten years ago, the international organizations now propagating the idea of lifelong education launched intensive propaganda for the expansion of schooling?

As the usual definitions of lifelong education do not help to clear up these ambiguities, it is not surprising that this "rubber concept"[5] can simultaneously cover:

- "deschooling society" as well as increasing specialization and expansion of institutionalized education (recurrent education, "*pédagogisation de l'âge adulte*");
- widening the opportunities for access to knowledge as well as apportioning it selectively (e.g. certain applications of the principle of functional literacy);
- the emphasis on education for self-management as well as closer adjustment of workers to the requirements of the job as defined by others.

Recent developments show, however, that it is now no longer possible to talk of "almost universal agreement" in regard to lifelong education.[6] Among its most determined critics, denouncing it as one of the potentially

most perfect forms of subjection of the individual, are some of its erst-
while advocates who now go to the extent of suggesting that one should de-
clare war against "everlasting, total, interminable education", the "trap of
school for life".[7]

Is lifelong education an attempt to transform society, or "an ideological construct (among others) designed to maintain society as it is, if not
in terms of its present state, at least in terms of its prevailing direction?"

In view of these extreme positions it seems to us that the role of social science in this field is to suggest instruments enabling us to analyze,
first, the *ideology* of lifelong education, and second,   the *institutions* set
up in its name, *in a given society at a given moment of its development*. One
of the main difficulties of such an analysis consists precisely in the discrepancy between lifelong education as a concept - a comprehensive, organizing
concept - and the many concrete realizations claiming to have somehow been
inspired by it.

As a branch of social science, political economy studies the relations
set up between men with regard to the utilization of resources in order to ensure the material reproduction of the social structure. Its domain is thus
both "a specific field of activities concerned with the production, distribution and consumption of material goods, and at the same time, through the mechanisms of this production, distribution and consumption, a particular aspect
of all non-economic activities".[9] This definition permits a clarification of
the specific field of economics of education.

Education is primarily a non-economic activity, the carrying out of
which entails an extensive use of material resources. Hence the economist is
called upon to participate in efficient management of the resources allocated
to education in accordance with the value system of the society and its collective choices.

Therefore the economist cannot disregard education since it contributes
(a) to the development of the productive forces by producing the qualified labour force; and (b) to the transmission of value systems and the reproduction
of social hierarchies, hence to the reproduction of the relations of production.

The division of Western economists into two main schools of thought applies equally to the economics of education:

a) To the first (majority) group, economics of education is a branch of the "Economics of Human Resources", the object of which is "the study of the elements that affect the working capacity of human beings and their influence on production; that is, *the analysis of human beings as factors of production*".[10] Human beings are "factors of production" (like machinery, raw materials, etc.) when seen from the point of view of capital, the predominant social relation. The economists subscribing to this approach therefore assume that the corresponding socio-political, economic, ideological and educational structures are given (permanent). They are interested in the *quantitative aspects of education* in a society where the immediate objective of economic activity is maximization of monetary gain, i.e. where the main criterion for those who take decisions concerning production is profit.

b) The second group studies the economic aspects of societies in the process of their development. The structures of a society are therefore at the very centre of an analysis which can only be carried out in conjunction with all the other disciplines of the social science. In this, of necessity multidisciplinary, approach the economist of education is particularly interested in the role education plays in the reproduction through time and extension in space of economic structures and in the transformations of the educational structure caused by the evolution of the economic base of society, in their dialectical relations.

This study compares the theoretical contributions of both schools of thought to an economic analysis of lifelong education, limiting itself to capitalist societies.

2. Lifelong Education in the Perspective of "Human Resources" Theories

Conventional economists of education concern themselves primarily with its quantitative relationships with worker productivity (and gains) and economic growth. As a "factor of production" in a capitalist market economy, the

worker sells his labour to the employer at a certain price, his wage. The
fundamental hypothesis of the neo-classical model is that *wages tend to be
equal to the marginal productivity of labour* under conditions of perfect competition, which are fulfilled when there is a sufficiently large number of
small traders so that the contribution of each is an infinitesimal part of
the whole supply of, and demand for, a homogeneous product (here: factor of
production), and when free entry to the market, free interaction between traders, perfect mobility and perfect information are secured.

Though all economists of this school who have taken an interest in education adhere to this hypothesis, analyses of the factors determining this
productivity have recently resulted in a split into two camps: adherents of
the "human capital" theory and the "filter" theorists.

In the "human capital" theory, which up to very recent years had been
virtually the only one, productivity is (for a given structure of demand for
goods and a given state of technology) an attribute of the worker, depending
on his capacities - physical, intellectual, etc. The correlation between wage
rates and factors like age, level of school education, ethnic or social background, sex, etc. would therefore be caused by the effect that the latter
have on the productivity of the worker.

Among these factors of productivity are some that may be improved
through "investment in man": expenditures on health, education, information,
migration, etc. "It implies that not all of the economic capacities of individuals are given at birth, or at age 14 when some of them enter work, or at
some later age when some complete their schooling; but that many of these capabilities are developed through activities that have the attributes of an
investment".[11] The most important item of the investment in man being investment in formal education, the following causal sequence may be drawn up:

(1) education $\longrightarrow$ worker's characteristics $\longrightarrow$ productivity $\longrightarrow$ wage
            (training)

> Formal education, through its training process, develops superior
> abilities in the worker thereby enhancing his productivity which,
> everything else being equal, then commands a higher wage on the
> market. In this model education is an important factor of
> (a) changing the pattern of distribution ("war against poverty",
> equalization of incomes); and (b) overall economic growth.

At present a number of heterogeneous theories, assembled under the term "filter" or "screening" theories, question the first element of sequence (1). In their approach

- formal school education contributes little if anything to an increase of the worker's personal capacities;
- the worker's productivity, hence his wage, depends on the nature of his job rather than on his personal characteristics.

The role of the school (beyond compulsory education) in this model is merely to furnish employers with "objective signals" enabling them to save the costs of selection they would otherwise have to bear in order to recruit their workers and assign them to different jobs. Its function is, therefore, one of *selection* and *information* rather than of training, and the education/wage correlation would correspond to the following causal sequence:

(2) education — employment — productivity — wage
$$\underbrace{\text{education — employment}}_{\text{filter}}$$

In this scheme formal education is no longer a factor determining economic growth, nor one necessarily modifying the wage structure.

As regards educational policy-making, the human capital theory supports the development of schooling, whereas the filter theories logically imply a reduction of expenditure on schooling, since workers acquire the necessary skills principally in the course of their employment. Regarding the two components of lifelong education - extending education over the whole working life and integrating it with productive activities - their positions are thus radically different.

2.1 The "human capital" model and lifelong education

The theory of investment in human capital concerns itself with "the activities that influence future real income by imbedding resources in people".[12]

- Imbedding: there must be actual and lasting modification of the individual's capacities.
- Resources: these improvements of personal characteristics can only be obtained at a "cost": either through direct use of resources or through a sacrifice (opportunity cost).

In other words, education cannot be, for example, a cost-free by-product of another activity, such as work. As G. Becker writes: "Presumably future productivity can be improved only at a cost, for otherwise there would

be an unlimited demand for training."[13] Consequently, the allocation of resources to education, formal or informal, must follow the principles of the
neo-classical model of allocation of resources in a market economy, both at
the global and individual levels.

2.1.1 *Theory of micro-decisions on investment in education*
a) The worker's calculus

The most general formulation of this theory is that framed by G. Becker
(1962) in his analysis of the on-the-job training decision.[14] Supposing a
worker having received no education, has a constant productivity *OU* and hence
in conditions of perfect competition, a life earnings profile *UU'* throughout
his working life *ON*

FIGURE   7.1

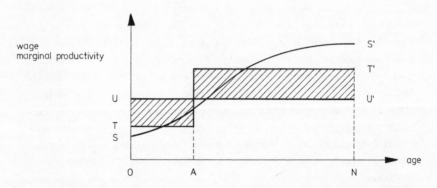

At age *O* he decides to assign resources to the improvement of his professional skills, this being the only means of increasing his subsequent marginal productivity, hence his wage. The resources concerned are a part of his
working time plus the time spent by the employer or other workers to pass on
to him their know-how, raw materials, machine time, etc. Assuming that the
total of these direct and indirect costs lowers his marginal productivity in
the firm to *OT* during his training period *OA*, the learner will during this
period receive a wage *OT*. *TU* represents his foregone earnings, or his savings
self-invested in education. On termination of the training period the worker's marginal productivity rises to *T'*, and his wage rises correspondingly,

since in conditions of perfect competition on the labour market his employer must remunerate him at the market rate paid by other employers. The shaded area above UU' represents the flow sequence of the increase in income the worker may expect from his initial investment (represented by the shaded area below UU'). The relationship between these two areas (expenditures and receipts) can be expressed by the rate of return (marginal efficiency of human capital), equating at the time of the decision the present values of expected costs and returns of the investment.[15]

The same calculation may be made for investment in school education. In that case, A becomes the age of entry into the labour market, and the foregone earnings during the period OA (fulltime studies) correspond to the wage OU, which would be equal to the marginal productivity of workers of the same age and educational level as the learner at the time he takes his decision. The same model is applicable to all forms of human investment. A "rational" individual tries to maximize the total return on his savings, i.e. equalize the marginal rates of return of all possible utilizations of these savings. This decision-making model governs:

- the distribution of his wealth among the various types of investment (human and non-human);
- as regards education, his selection from the different types, channels and forms of acquisition of this human asset;
- the optimal time schedule for education during his life.

The principle of this economic calculus in its application to education was already formulated by Adam Smith at the end of the 18th century:

When any expensive machine is erected, the extraordinary work to be performed by it before it is worn out, it must be expected, will replace the capital laid out upon it, with at least the ordinary profits. A man educated at the expense of much labour and time to any of those employments which require extraordinary dexterity and skill, may be compared to one of those expensive machines. The work which he learns to perform, it must be expected, over and above the usual wages of common labour, will replace to him the whole expense of his education, with at least the ordinary profit of an equally valuable capital. He must do this too in a reasonable time, regard being had to the very uncertain duration of human life, in the same manner as to the more certain duration of the machine.[16]

What are the implications of this model for the aspects of vertical articulation in time and horizontal integration with other social activities characterizing the idea of lifelong education?

Everything else also being equal, the benefits expected of any expenditure on education should be the greater the remoter N is, i.e., for any given life expectancy, the earlier the investment in education is made. Further, the loss of earnings tends to be the smaller the younger the individual is, and falls to zero during the period of compulsory schooling. The older a worker the less will he be inclined to engage in educational activities. Only technical progress can reverse this tendency, either by raising the rate of return on expenditure on education, or by lowering the marginal productivity of workers whose intellectual capital it makes obsolete. Whilst it is evidently impossible to amortize individual intellectual capital, expenditure on upkeep (re-cycling) can in the period of active life maintain instant efficiency at a constant level.

Adherents of the human capital theory have applied this model to individual choices between school education and training on the job. However, the model described clearly corresponds to a learning process in a craft-based economy (hence the reference by these authors to Adam Smith); but is it applicable to contemporary structures of production? The problem arose when economists of this school of thought used their model to explain the earnings structure as a function of the level of school education and of age. The lifetime earnings profiles (cross-sectional) observable in our societies actually look like those drawn in Figure 7.2.

FIGURE 7.2   Income Profiles as a Function of Age and Years of Schooling.

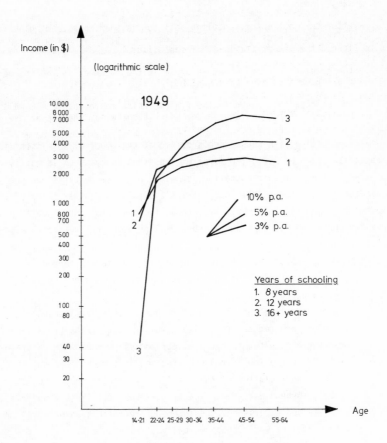

In this example the earnings include only income from work of whites in the
United States (though it is difficult entirely to eliminate other types of
income from the data used). These earnings are calculated after tax and without deduction of any direct private costs of schooling. It should also be
noted that these profiles are cross-sectional ones; the longitudinal profiles
(by cohorts) show a clear rise in the last years of working life.[17]

It will be seen that

- the hierarchy of the curves corresponds to that of the levels of schooling;

- after termination of schooling, all curves show an ascending phase, (with the rate of growth steadily decreasing), this being more prolonged the higher the level of schooling;

- the gradient of the ascending phase in these curves is the steeper the higher the level of schooling;

- the scatter (not shown in the figure, which represents the mean profiles) of incomes around the mean is the wider the higher the level of schooling and the age.

In connection with causal sequence (1) of the model of investment in human capital (see p. 290), the first of these characteristics is easily explained by the fact that education, combined with the worker's personal attributes (sex, race, social and geographic origin) and other types of investment in man (health, mobility, etc.), increases the individual's productivity and hence his earnings. A good deal of empirical research, especially in the USA, has tried to isolate the contribution of education (according to most, approx. 60%) to the income differentials observed.[18]

As to the growth phase of incomes associated with schooling, two interpretations have been advanced:

- After the completion of schooling identifiable intellectual investments are reduced to limited training activities (vocational training of adults, re-cycling, periods of promotion or re-training). Therefore the increase of incomes in time corresponds to a phase of appreciation of the intellectual capital acquired at school, through *autonomous* learning at zero cost resulting from practice and experience. The income differentials associated with schooling would thus be really attributable to it, to the extent that this phase of cost-free appreciation is *complementary* to investment in schooling. According to this hypothesis, *individuals will benefit most from maximum investment in initial schooling* (within existing educational structures, of course).

- This interpretation, however, runs counter to the theory that schooling and training on-the-job can be substitutes for each other, and also to the hypothesis that the latter cannot be free

of cost because this would lead to an unlimited demand for on-the-
job training, as mentioned earlier.

The shape of the career profiles of Figure 7.2 would thus be due to
the following facts:

- workers from all levels of schooling invest in themselves through
informal training on the job, the more so the younger they are;

- they invest most heavily in training on-the-job the higher their
schooling level, for two reasons: a) because such education is associated with personal characteristics which also determine the productivity of other human investments and so increase the propensity
to self-invest in on-the-job training; b) because schooling renders
them more capable of profiting from later training.[19]

But what cost should be attributed to this investment? The solution
to this problem has been sought in the concept of opportunity cost. Supposing that on finishing his studies a worker has the possibility of choosing
between A, a type of employment in which his immediate productivity (hence
his wage) is highest, but which, being of a repetitive, routine nature, is
not conducive to the acquisition of higher skills in the course of work and
consequently offers no prospect of advancement (the corresponding career profile - reference profile - would be comparable to profile UU' in Figure 7.1),
and B, a type of employment rich in educational activities, thus offering
good prospects of increased productivity and higher wages. If the starting
wage of employment B were equal to that of employment A, there would be a
rush of candidates for job B. The starting wage would fall below that of A
until an equilibrium was established, i.e. until the rate of return on investment in training on-the-job (constituted by the opportunity cost of foregone earnings) for those who had chosen employment type B would reach the same
level as the rate of return on other investments.

Profiles of type A, with no training and no prospects, are obviously
impossible to identify empirically for the various groups of workers classified by level of schooling. So some authors[20] infer the cost of on-the-job
training from the income differential observed between two categories of
education, using the rate of return on school education as a base, which implies assuming a single rate of return on all human investments. By thus deducing from the hypothesis of competition and rationality a specific cost
of professional experience, one can force the latter into the mould of the
formalized learning model (see curve SS' in Figure 7.1, p. 292). Moreover,

this procedure enables one to legitimate the divergences between the different career profiles, and to justify retrospectively the proposition that in existing structures individuals have a choice between two mutually substitutable forms of intellectual investment: schooling and on-the-job training. It is not surprising that this method of calculation has led to the conclusion that the volume of investment in on-the-job training is far greater than that of investment in schooling. Lifelong education (at least so far as its vocational training component is concerned) would then be a reality in present structures!

Apart from the circular reasoning by which this conclusion is reached - and the impossibility of validating it empirically -, the model presents two difficulties in our context:

- how can this prolongation in time of human investment and the large volume of investment in training on-the-job up to an advanced age be reconciled with the integration of the life expectancy of this investment into micro-economic calculation, unless it is supposed that its efficiency increases with age?

- post-school, on-the-job training in this model has no identifiable content and cannot, therefore, be the object of policy decisions. But insofar as it seems correlated with schooling, action need only be taken on the latter. Everything else being equal, both individuals and society would benefit from concentrating their educational expenditure on the initial phase of schooling before entering work.

b) The employer's calculus

Up to now the hypothesis that workers are paid at their marginal productivity implied that, being the only ones to profit from education, they should also be the only ones prepared to bear its cost. This hypothesis has, however, been partially dropped by the proponents of the human capital theory in order to enable them to explain part-financing of education by employers. An employer seeking to maximize his profit will not finance the training of his employees (i.e. pay them above their marginal productivity during the period of training) unless this investment will yield a return comparable to that of alternative investments. This requires (a) that after training the employee be paid below his (higher) marginal productivity; (b) that he remain with the firm for a sufficient length of time. These conditions can only be fulfilled if the labour market is not competitive for the quali-

fication acquired by the worker, i.e. if his training is not negotiable outside the firm that has financed it. There are several situations in which a
firm can be assured of a monopsony for the qualification concerned:

- if the qualification is "specific" to the firm (for technical reasons,
  or owing to the nature of the product or the organization) so that the
  training raises the employee's productivity only within that particular
  firm;

- if the worker's qualification is potentially negotiable in other
  firms but the lack of transparency of the market (e.g. when the
  training received is not certified by a diploma) or lack of geographical mobility of the worker ensures that the firm has a local
  monopsony;

- if the training acquired potentially increases the worker's productivity in other firms, but an employment contract (or deferred payments,
  or a policy of seniority increments) ties the trained worker to the
  firm.[21]

Only in these cases is there any incentive for the firm to invest in
training, the costs of which will theoretically be covered by the differences
between the marginal productivity of the worker who has been trained in the
firm and the wage he could obtain in the market, i.e. the wage corresponding
to his productivity before training.[22]

*All other things being equal, the firm will, therefore, finance train-
ing the more readily the less competition there is on the labour market.* Pre-
ference will also be given to the most stable categories of workers. It is
not in the firm's interest to invest in categories with a high rate of turnover, such as very young workers, women, older workers, migrants, etc. Conversely, when the demand for a firm's products is declining, it will protect
its intellectual investment by means of a policy of discriminatory dismissal
affecting those workers whose life expectancy in the firm is shortest or in
whom the firm has invested least.

It will be noted that in this model financing of training by the firm
is linked (both as cause and as effect) to the lack of worker mobility. However, if one regards - as some authors do - the early leaving of a worker
trained by a firm as an external saving, benefiting the firm that engages
him, one has an argument in favour of the internalization of these savings
by the group of firms concerned (branch of trade or industry, region, etc.)
in the form of joint financing of training specific to this group.

In this micro-economic approach *with constant structures* the collectivity can only play a complementary role, i.e. internalize, in the form of part-financing of the costs of education, the external benefits which cannot be taken into account and hence financed by individual decision-makers.[23]

As a whole, this decision-making analysis thus provides essentially a model of "rational" sharing of the expenditure on investment in education, the optimal volume of which is determined by the marginal productivity of this input into the economy at a given moment.

The aspect of education as a "durable consumer good" does not feature in this model, as the consumer's marginal calculation scheme applies to it in the same way as it does to any other commodity (i.e. equalization of marginal costs and benefits).

What are the policy implications of this human capital model at the micro-economic level? On the qualitative plane, we have already seen that it favours formal rather than informal education. On the quantitative plane, schooling becomes an instrument of income distribution policies. In this model, the distribution of income from work is explained:

- by differences in the level of education;

- within a given level of education, by differences in intellectual capacity, in the quality of teaching, etc.[24]

The income structure can thus be influenced by appropriate educational policy.

However, if the price of labour is determined by the marginal value it creates, any attempt to *equalize incomes* deviates from the economic optimum by diverting resources to less productive activities. Therefore, only a policy designed to *equalize opportunities of access* to education and to the labour market is compatible with this theoretical model. This would imply various measures aiming at making all the markets concerned competitive: the capital market to finance education, the teaching services market, the labour market. At the equilibrium, the resulting inequality of income would be both "efficient" and "equitable" insofar as it would correspond to the inequality of individuals' "natural" capacities and efforts.

Through the policy of eradicating poverty, (especially in the US), this genetic approach[25] has, however, been superseded by an environmentalist one.[26] As the measured differences in the abilities of individuals were found to be attributable not so much to purely hereditary factors as rather to socio-economic differences, compensatory educational action must be taken to create a background favourable to the development of the intelligence of children coming from underprivileged or deprived milieus. Such action is compatible with the human capital model inasmuch as its rate of social return is comparable to that of other investments. In particular it will be noted that measures of this kind are limited to intervention in schooling and do not extend to the socio-economic structures that lie at the roots of these inequalities.

To sum up: Since the human capital theory assumes that the individual's and the community's rationality are the same as that of profit maximizing firms; that markets are competitive; that firms and groups of firms can know the marginal productivity of individual workers and the effect expenditure on education will have on this productivity, it can contribute only very moderately to the analysis of micro-decisions on education and to the designing of structural policies. The very narrow structural framework it adopts reduces to nearly zero its contribution to a study of the choices concerning extension (in time) and expansion (in space) of education at this level.

2.1.2 *Macro-economic analysis: Education and economic growth*

In the neoclassical approach, the analytical framework for defining the contribution of the various inputs to the growth of the national product is an aggregate function of production, generally of the Cobb-Douglas type,[27] which establishes a general relationship between the quantity of productive services and the quantity of products obtainable *for a given state of technology*. In the fifties such a function was used, particularly by American economists,[28] to identify and measure the principal factors of economic growth in the USA in the first half of the 20th century. Capital services being represented by a stock index weighted by the earnings of these services in the year taken as base, and the inputs of labour by an index of undifferentiated man-hours also weighted by the earnings in the base year, the result found was that the quantitative increase of conventional inputs (capital and labour) accounted for less than half the growth rate observed.[29] Two interpretations have been advanced to explain so large a "residue":

a) There was a transformation of the productive function, but the conventional inputs were not changed. The residual trend is attributable to factors that are *neutral* in regard to both labour and capital (i.e., they increase the productivity of both). "Unconventional" or "invisible" factors, such as technical or organizational progress in education and knowledge, etc.,[30] account for the increase of output per unit of conventional input. Among the interpretations of this type should be mentioned the orginal one of "learning by doing" proposed by K. Arrow, which considers technical progress as an endogenous variable, a function of time and a by-product at zero cost of productive activity as a generator of "autonomous learning" at the global level.[31]

b) The conventional factors have been wrongly assessed: labour and capital have been "disembodied". It is therefore ncessary to "embody" in them the omitted improvements in quality (better educated workers, improved new capital) so as to enable the observed growth of productivity to be traced back to a *quantitative* increase of one or both of the inputs.

The two approaches can also be used simultaneously, part of the "residue" being incorporated into the conventional factors and the rest attributed to an autonomous trend or to additional variables.

The most sophisticated, and best known, attempt to assess the effects of education on the growth of the national product in the analytical framework of a macro-economic production function is the one made by B. Denison.[32]

Denison begins with a base year (1949) estimate of the income differentials by level of education for males of the same age (see Fig. 7.2, p. 295). He treats these differentials as preliminary indications of the difference which specified amounts of schooling would make to the output of randomly chosen individuals. However, as differences in schooling completed are correlated with ability, energy, and motivation, and with the parents' education and occupation, he assumes that only 60% of the observed differences are due to the differences in schooling.

He next combines the adjusted differentials for the base year with estimates of the distribution, at various past dates, of males by years of schooling completed. In this way he obtains estimates of past changes in average income

due to the rise in education measured in school years completed. He then makes
an adjustment for the rise in the number of school days per school year, on
the assumption that a greater number of days spent at school per year raises
a man's contribution to production as much as does an equal percentage increase
in the number of years spent at school.

Allowing for the weight of labour's share in the national income, the
indicated contributions of education to the growth of the US national product
during 1929-1957 would have been 0.68 percentage points, or 23% of the growth
rate of the aggregate national product and 42% of the growth rate in product
per person employed. These calculations would indicate that the *increase in
the schooling* of workers has been the most important single factor of economic
growth over the 30 year period investigated.

After adjustment of the labour factor by taking the improvements in
quality due to education and certain other factors into account, there remained a residue (increase of output per unit of input) of 0.93% from an average real growth rate of 2.93% per annum. Using the "average opinion of experts", Denison attributed this to various autonomous sources of productivity
growth, among them the "progress of knowledge of all kinds relating to production, including technology and management" (0.58%).[33]

Without going into the various criticisms that can be raised against this
method, it may be advisable to mention its principal limitations.

Concerning the analytical framework of the production function at the
macro-level:

- this macro function is a transposition of the micro-economic function reflecting the point of view of the firm (for which all inputs
  are on the same plane). This implies that the rationality of the
  firm and that of the system as a whole are identical;

- the macro function results from the aggregation of the functions of
  a large number of branches of the economy with varying production
  processes. Global policies based on this framework are, therefore,
  of limited significance;

- the structures (economic, social, political, ideological) are assumed to be given. In this conception the quantitative effects of
  education can, therefore, be assessed only within these structures.

This raises further doubts about the validity of this method for explaining the differences between the observed growth rates of, say, agriculture
and industry,[34] or between the per capita incomes of different countries, etc.,[35]

by differences in the levels of education.

Concerning the incorporation of education in the macro-economic production function:

- the method employed to quantify the qualitative improvements of
  the labour factor derives from the preceding micro-economic
  analysis and is, therefore, subject to the same criticisms
  (hypothesis of competition and remuneration of the factors at
  their marginal productivity, method of calculating the wage
  differentials attributable to school education). Above all, its
  utilization in this case is tautological, because that which is
  meant to be proved (effects of education on labour productivity)
  is taken as a starting hypothesis;

- quite apart from the entirely arbitrary nature of its evaluation,
  the "progress of knowledge" is supposed to have contributed one
  fifth of the observed growth rate of the US economy without being
  incorporated either in new capital (neutrality) or in labour.
  Where does it come from, and how does it operate?

- given the form of the function, imbedding of qualitative improvements into the labour factor implies that the level of workers'
  qualifications is not influenced by the stock capital existing
  in the economy. This excludes autonomous learning.

- on this premise, the incorporation of schooling into the labour
  factor in Denison's function implies: (a) that the internal productivity of school time in terms of output of acquired abilities
  is constant; (b) that the external social productivity of human
  capital created by a unit of this school time (one year) is constant.

Despite these limitations, this type of calculation has had considerable
policy implications:

- Denison extrapolated the results of his work to recommend that
  between 1960 and 1980 the average number of school years per pupil
  in the USA be increased by one (or a fortnight added to each school
  year), as this would raise the growth rate of the economy during
  that period by 0.07%![36]

- the international organizations have given a great deal of publicity
  to this type of study, and a large number of developing countries
  have eagerly accepted it. Investment in physical capital appeared to
  be only a minor growth factor; the principal source of economic
  growth was education, more precisely school education measured in
  quantitative terms (school years) regardless of its content, which
  implicitly postulates its qualitative adequacy.

This macro-economic approach to education in the perspective of the human
capital theory has thus contributed to the quantitative expansion of the school
systems of capitalist societies in the course of the last decade.

However, although the Denison-type approaches have served to propagate the myth of the school as the principal factor of economic growth, the majority of the educational plans of the sixties have been inspired by the so-called "manpower approach" which consists essentially in deducing schooling targets from the objectives of global and sectorial economic growth by means of "technical coefficients" of manpower.[37] This method presupposes that (a) there is a *technical* relationship between the volume of production and the structure of manpower qualifications; and (b) that for any given job there is a corresponding type and level of school education. These particularly rigid assumptions have evidently led to a homothetic growth of traditional school systems, and the failure of the educational policies based on this type of model has been one of the major factors throwing doubt on these systems and promoting the idea of lifelong education as a means of adapting workers to the requirements of the economy in a quicker and more flexible manner.

2.2 Contribution of the filter theories

Towards the end of the sixties, the human capital theory and the educational policies it had inspired came under heavy criticism because of

- the failure of the extremely costly formal education expansion programmes undertaken under the policies of economic growth and equalization of incomes;[38]

- the continually higher level of schooling employers demanded for identical jobs, and the increasing dissatisfaction of diploma-holders;

- the small part of income variance attributable to school education compared with that due to socio-professional or ethnic origin, sex, age, etc.[39]

Without basically questioning the neoclassical assumption concerning the labour market, certain members of the orthodox school[40] proposed that the relationship between education and productivity be reconsidered. In the human capital approach it is explicitly or implicitly assumed that school inculcates knowledge, develops cognitive skills, transmits know-how, etc., supposedly the main components of labour productivity. However, as the causal relationship education $\longrightarrow$ productivity is not analyzed but postulated, nothing in this model prevents those components of labour productivity that are imparted by schooling from being partly (or wholly) identical with the *attitudes* (as opposed to aptitudes) demanded of the

different categories of workers by the capitalist division of labour - namely
docility, punctuality, internalization of hierarchical relationships, motivation based on material incentives, leadership ability, etc.

In other words, the human capital model as such is not directly rejected
by the critics of the capitalist school system among the radical American economists[41] or the French sociologists[42] who focus on the way the educational
system functions as a mechanism reproducing social hierarchies and the prevailing value system; they merely deny its ability to reduce social inequalities (the myth of the democratic school). Now, if the workers' characteristics
required by the production process can only be *developed* by the school system
from "raw material" possessing qualities that are unequally distributed among
the different social strata, the optimization model is not contested so long
as there is *equality of opportunity*, i.e., if all individuals of equal capacity
have access under the same conditions to schools of equal quality. In that case,
any inequality in results (educational level reached and income) is due to the
individuals' personal characteristics, and state intervention would lead away
from the optimum.[43]

In contrast, the so-called "filter" or "screen" theories partially or
totally deny the capability of the educational system qualitatively to improve
the components of productivity (whatever these may be).

2.2.1 *The educational system as an information/selection system for employers*

Because the human capital theory implicitly postulated the ability of the
educational system to measure/certify the increase in productive capacity acquired during schooling, the limitation imposed, e.g., in the form of examinations, by the institutionalized apparatus of supply (school) on the demand of
pupils for admission never came to light. Individuals, supposedly facing a competitive educational market comparable in every way to the market for any other
commodity, could only consider the requirements of passing fron one year or cycle
to another in their decision process as a cost (financial or psychological)
varying according to their capacities. Naturally they refrained from investing in
education when this additional cost was not counterbalanced by an adequate prospective return (financial or psychological).

In the filter model, the contrary applies: the educational system's functi
of conferring grades takes precedence over its function of instruction. It dif-

ferentiates, selects and filters individuals before they enter the labour market; that is its essential function. At worst it teaches them nothing, nothing at least that would increase their productive capacities. For that reason the protagonists of the filter theory are mainly concerned with post-compulsory, non-vocational (general) education. As K. Arrow writes:

> Higher education, in this model, contributes in no way to superior economic performance; it increases neither cognition nor socialization. Instead, higher education serves as a screening device, in that it sorts out individuals of differing abilities, thereby conveying information to the purchasers of labour.[44]

The central idea is as follows: To function well, a market must be "transparent", i.e., the two sides must be perfectly informed. But on the labour market the employers have no prior information on the abilities of prospective employees. They can obtain such information by means of tests, probation periods, etc., but these methods would be very costly if they had to be applied to all candidates without any pre-selection. These "recruitment costs" are investments, the rate of return on which must be comparable to that of the firm's other investments. Hence the practice of using pre-selection "signals": age, sex, ethnic and social origin, *and diplomas*. The educational system allows employers to reduce their recruitment costs (which are the greater the higher the level of required competence, i.e., the greater the risk of loss in case of error)[45] by furnishing them free of charge with information enabling them to establish a relationship between the hierarchy of diplomas and the hierarchy of vacancies to be filled.[46] *The educational system thus provides information, not education.* On the basis of this assumption, two hypotheses emerge:

a) Post-compulsory general education is limited to *revealing* previously existing aptitudes. If it fulfils this task adequately, it contributes to making the market competitive, to permitting every individual to be employed and paid from the start in accordance with his productive capacities. This hypothesis is compatible with the model of investment in on-the-job training presented by the human capital theory.

   In this case, the educational system is socially useful because it fulfils a function of information, but the authors are concerned about the social cost this function involves: would it not be far less expensive for the community to use test systems rather than

support pupils and teachers for long years?[47] In other words,
*expenditure on education yields a private return much higher
than the social return*, and a considerable reduction of educational expenditure could legitimately be envisaged.

b) Supposing - always on the assumption that wages are equivalent
to marginal productivity - that productive capacities are
essentially acquired in the course of employment, and that
different jobs vary in the "professional stimuli" they offer
(responsibility, possibilities of change of job and promotion,
volume and technical level of the means of production employed,
contact with workers of a higher professional level, etc.), then
*training in the course of employment, being "autonomous learning",
is complementary to (linked with) the job itself*. Since jobs rich
in career prospects are rare, there will be competition for them,
and employers can make use of diplomas to (pre-) select candidates.
A diploma is then the "entrance certificate", the "education
credential" required for access to well-paid jobs, a ticket the
value of which varies according to the supply and demand situation
of such privileged positions. If, for instance, the latter remain
constant in number while the number of candidates holding the required diploma increases, employers will raise the educational
level required so as to restrict the number of candidates and consequently the recruitment costs they have to bear.

In this scheme, to which the majority of filter theory adherents sub-
scribe, the function of the school system becomes one of "keeping people with less
education out of better paid jobs[48] rather than a function of information. In
which case schooling would also have a "perverse" effect of redistributing incomes. As the barrier to entry into "good" jobs is put higher,

- the supply on this market decreases while the capacities of those
  offering their services rise; the two factors combine to produce
  an increase in their marginal productivity, hence their wages;

- on the other markets the capacities of those offering their
  services also increase, but so does their number. The two
  phenomena therefore work in opposite directions.

The consequence of setting up educational barriers to entry into certain
jobs would thus be to lower the effective marginal productivity (hence wages)

of people not holding the "entrance certificate" to a level below their potential productivity (if the market were competitive): "if education is used to
screen people, then the extra earnings a person receives from education are due
both to the skills produced by education and to the income redistribution effect
resulting from supply limitations".[49] A weakness of this analysis is that it
does not explain why, if a worker's productivity is really a *personal* characteristic, employers encountering an excessive supply of candidates should raise
the level of diplomas required for appointment rather than lower the salaries
concerned.

At first glance, this behaviour appears more rational in the model proposed by Thurow and Lucas,[50] who claim that *productivity is an attribute not
of the employee, but of the job itself.* In that case there will be competition of candidates for access to high-productivity jobs. Employers, anxious to
reduce their training costs after engagement and also the risk of error, will
base their choice of candidates on "signals" indicating ability to adapt to
the job (trainability), such as diploma, age, sex, social and ethnic origin,
experience, etc.

But in the neoclassical approach it is a heresy to say that the marginal
productivity of labour depends entirely on the job (demand). Moreover, this
theory fails to explain why excessive supply should not entail a fall in wages
(e.g., in the form that the cost of training is shared by the worker and the
firm). Taking this possibility into account would mean rejecting the hypothesis
that workers are paid at their marginal productivity, (i.e., the conventional
neo-classical model), admitting that the labour market is not competitive, and
having to explain why it is not.

2.2.2 *The demand for schooling and the "snowball" phenomenon*

We have seen that, according to the proponents of the filter theory, the
educational system as a "sorting centre" yields a poor social return. Besides,
two conditions are necessary if it is to work:

a) The private cost of obtaining a diploma must be inversely
proportional to the pupil's productivity. For, if the pupils
strive to maximize the cost/benefit ratio of their investment
in schooling (see human capital theory), and if their respective productive capacities are characteristics they begin with,

only the most productive ones should be encouraged to pursue
their studies if the diploma system is to function as a
signal for employers. If the costs were the same, all pupils
irrespective of their productivity would find it in their
interest to demand the same amount of education, and the school
system would no longer fulfil its function of differentiation.
However, as stated by M. Carnoy and M. Carter:

> if this requirement is fulfilled, then there are
> potentially an infinite number of equilibrium wage
> schedules. That is, there may be many sets of
> relative wages such that it will be worthwhile only
> for the more "able" to take a lot of schooling,
> thereby confirming the employer's initial belief
> that a high level of schooling indicates a high
> level of productivity; this possibility of multiple
> equilibria is very damaging to orthodox beliefs
> about the efficiency of competitive labour markets.[51]

b) The private rate of return on schooling must be satisfactory, i.e.,
there must be a sufficient demand for it on the part of the individuals bearing its main costs (financial and psychological). This
will be so if the individuals' efforts for monetary maximization
are deployed in a competitive education market. The adherents of
the human capital theory have shown that in this case private demand would be optimal. Some authors, however, start from the hypothesis that what individuals (or parents through their children)
seek in increased education is not so much a monetary return on
their investment as rather a *differential* advantage over others
in the form of a higher standard of living[52] or the higher social
standing conferred by the level of schooling achieved.[53] In that
case, and "under any institutional system which permits families
to choose quantities of education independently of other families
... parents are faced with a 'prisoner's dilemma'; for each parent, the optimal response or strategy is to seek ever more education",[54] if only to make their position in the social hierarchy
more secure. We thus have a model of expanding educational expenditure called "the Hobbesian snowball", meaning that the growth
rhythm of the demand for education must accelerate in step with
individuals' increasing efforts to stay where they are (as in

Alice Through the Looking Glass).

2.2.3 *Policy implications of the model*

As far as educational policies are concerned, the implications of the
filter theories are very different from those of the human capital theory,
especially with regard to the usefulness of expenditures on education and the
respective roles of schooling and post-school training on-the-job.

a) The human capital theory implies neglecting informal on-the-
   job training because, no effort having been made to identify
   and analyze it, the basic hypothesis that its rate of return
   is identical with that on other human investments does not
   affect the evaluation of the rate of return on schooling. Since
   at the macro-level the evaluation of the economic effects of
   education is based on the results of micro-economic analysis,
   the same obviously applies, and schooling will be the only object of educational policy. Besides, in this model optimum
   allocation of resources to education has the best chance of
   being achieved when individuals can freely demand the quantity
   of education they desire. Inasmuch as society offers educational
   services, some economists support the so-called "social demand"
   method of planning, which consists in satisfying, quantitatively
   and qualitatively, individuals' demand for schooling.[55] Finally,
   under this theory which postulates competition on the labour
   market, reduction of social inequality is limited to policies
   designed to reduce inequality of access to education.

b) The filter theories have the great merit of reintroducing into
   the analysis a social function of the educational system which
   had been neglected by earlier theoreticians: its function of
   selection. Schooling is not a commodity sold freely on the market;
   access to it is limited by institutional factors, such as examinations, competitions, diplomas, etc., the structure of which -
   often established at the national level - is a means of regulat-
   ing the demand for education.

However, the implications of the filter theory for the educational system
would be devastating if followed to their logical conclusions: if schooling -

at least the system of post-compulsory general education - is a "black box" with a *socially useless content*, and if its sole function is to sort out individuals according to their pre-existing characteristics, then this institution (and, obviously, especially higher education) is an enormous social waste and should be replaced by a less costly and faster grading method. Not one of the academic economists who have produced these theories goes as far as this, but the hypothesis that schooling has no influence on productivity, combined with the "snowball" hypothesis, evidently suggests that the growth rate of educational expenditure should be curbed by state intervention in the form of *more rigorous selection*, which, while retaining the pyramidal structure of diplomas, would permit reducing its height and consequently the over-investment in schooling. From the viewpoint of these theories, such intervention would benefit everybody because it would eliminate the "prisoner's dilemma" and enable each individual to choose a lower level of schooling which would provide him with the same private benefits at a lower cost.

It should also be noted that the filter theory offers an explanation of the discrimination exercised by employers in the recruitment of personnel, namely that they are inadequately informed about the real productive capacities of candidates and have, therefore, to rely on characteristics such as age, sex, race etc. to classify candidates holding diplomas of the same level. To make the labour markets function more efficiently, both from the points of view of economic efficiency and of social justice, it would thus be sufficient to oblige employers - e.g., through anti-discrimination laws - to obtain better information. On the other hand, the development of recurrent education as formal post-school education can also be considered in the perspective of the "snowball" theory, as an "addition to the educational arms race"[56] rather than as a strategy of de-escalation.

If schooling does not contribute to an increase in the productive capacities of individuals, the reason is that these capacities exist prior to it, or that the ability to profit from post-school education is a given factor. In this hypothesis *an increase in workers' competence can only result from practical experience or from training in the course of employment*, i.e., from education integrated with the job. The filter theory therefore offers considerable (though indirect) economic support for the idea of lifelong education in that it implies

development of post-school vocational training, possibly at the price of a reduction of initial general education. However, if one admits the hypotheses
that (a) possibilities of acquiring skills are linked with employment; and
(b) workers are distributed, in accordance with their initial aptitudes, between jobs "with a future" and jobs with no opportunities for learning while
working, the filter theories quite naturally lead to policies of even earlier
and closer adaptation of individuals to the existing division of labour, i.e.,
to the continuance or aggravation of social inequalities.

Although as a whole the orthodox theories we have reviewed throw some
light on certain aspects of the economic functions of school and out-of-school
education in a capitalist market economy, they evidently provide no answer to
the questions that are of major importance for designing suitable long-term
structural policies:

- What are the abilities, skills, attitudes, etc. the production
  system needs? That is, what are the components of labour "productivity"?

- What and how are these economically useful characteristics
  acquired: at school? on-the-job? and by which process?

- How do the labour markets function?

Moreover, since they assume that the structures of the social division of
labour are permanent, they can certainly not answer the questions confronting
the people responsible for educational policy in countries with economic and social
structures that differ from those of the most highly developed capitalist countries

3. Elements of an Alternative Approach to
the Economic Aspects of Lifelong Education

Conventional economics is, as we have seen, concerned with the quantitative
variations of a phenomenon within given structures. Its approach to education can,
at best, help to analyze absolute or relative changes in the *amount* of education
and in an educational system characterized by the opposition between initial
schooling and subsequent on-the-job training consumed in the framework of what is
assumed to be a market economy. This approach is necessary to us in that it reflect
the point of view of capital - man considered as a "human resource". But it is obviously inadequate to explain the economic factors of the evolution of the educa-

tional structures themselves (including the recent establishment of institutions
in the name of lifelong education), or to serve as a basis for educational
policies of a qualitative sort in developing societies.

However, the institutions that are being set up in most capitalist societies (advanced or not) generally do not correspond to the *idea* of lifelong
education as defined at the beginning of this paper. We will, therefore, try to
outline an alternative framework for analysis and will attempt, first, to propose
some hypotheses that may help to explain the progressive transformation of educational systems towards extension in time (vertical integration) and (re-) integration of on-the-job training (horizontal integration); secondly, to define
the economic conditions under which the *idea* of lifelong education could be
realized, i.e., the relations between lifelong education and the social division
of labour.

3.1 The analytical framework

The specific domain of economics is the material base of society, i.e.,
the articulated whole of its productive forces (labour force and means of production) and its social production relations (social division of labour based on
ownership and control of the means of production). Education, a non-economic
activity belonging specifically to the ideological sphere of the superstructure,
contributes to the reproduction of class societies in three ways:
- transmission of value systems
- formation of a qualified labour force
- social stratification

which are separable only for the sake of analysis. There can be no reproduction
of the knowledge (skills, abilities) needed by the labour force in the process
of production without ideological and political reproduction, that is to say
transmission of value systems ("attitudes") justifying the position of the different categories of workers in the hierarchical division of labour. Education
thus contributes to the reproduction both of the productive forces and of social
relations.

Consequently, a study of education within the social context must first define the role of the educational structure in the social whole and its relations
with the other constituent elements of this whole, in particular with the ideological sphere.

One possibility is to see these relations as hierarchically interrelated. Social development occurs through the contradiction between the developmental level of the productive forces and the relations of production within the economic structure, and through the contradiction between the economic structure and the superstructure. At a given moment in the development of a society, quantitative changes in the material base entail qualitative changes, which the superstructure inherited from the preceding period obstructs. This approach carries the risk of a *linear* view of the relations between the economic sphere and the educational system, which is regarded as "endogenous to the variations of the economic structure; man's relationship to nature, in the interplay of determined social relations".[57]

A second approach defines society as a combination of articulated "instances": economic, legal/political, ideological, etc. While this approach eliminates the risk of a linear view, it introduces another hazard: excessive autonomy of the instances and a dualistic approach. As far as we are concerned, it tends to attribute to education an autonomous way of functioning and a relationship with the economic structure which is free of contradictions. It therefore leads to theories which, though making a significant contribution to an analysis of the ideological and material mechanisms by which school as an institution participates in identical (or homothetical) reproduction of capitalist society, offer few elements helpful in an analysis of the factors and modalities of change of educational structures in their relationships with the evolving material base of society.[58]

In a third approach:

> ... the man who is at the centre of the social process of work is the same man who is involved in other social relationships, in praxis based on theory, and who has a system of values and attitudes towards life, work (as a means of self-fulfilment in society or as a means of earning a livelihood), towards women, race, etc. All this constitutes one single social process, in the midst of which the man, from his position in the specific process of social production, engages in the other aspects of social life ... Taking the mode of production as an axis, one can thus study the other aspects of a man's social activity in a given society with its class structure, like a network of reciprocal relationships interwoven with economic activity; these relations stem in various ways from the social process of work whose form is determined by the specific combination of the development level of the productive forces and the type of relations of production.[59]

Analyzed in its dialectical movement, this whole should appear as a hete-

rogeneous process comprising forms relating to different eras inherited from
the past, and germs of future ones subordinated to the dominant forms of the
present, each constituting a whole that differs qualitatively from the others.

In capitalist societies, which are governed by the cycle of capital
appreciation, the axis for our research is provided by the contradiction between the *capitalist production of commodities and the non-capitalist production of the labour force.*[60] The places where the labour force is reproduced, both private (family) and collective ones (schools, hospitals, nurseries,
etc.), belong to the non-capitalist sphere of production, but are subordinated
to (and hence transformed by) capital as the dominant social relation. This relationship is, however, not a unilateral one: these subordinated elements *condition* the functioning of the social whole, and it is in the contradiction between the two spheres - production of exchange values and production of use
values - that the explanation of the historical evolution of the forms of reproduction of capitalist social relations can partly be sought.

Before attempting to analyze in this framework the contradictions from
which the present trends towards vertical and horizontal integration of education arise, we must first characterize briefly the historical evolution of school
as an institution in capitalist societies:

a) As an "initiation of man into his social functions, which in a
class society are governed by the class to which he belongs",[61]
education takes place in all the sites of reproduction of social
relations (family, school, religious community, place of production, trade union, armed forces, etc.). Before the emergence of
the capitalist mode of production as the dominant one, education
of the labour force was carried out mostly at private sites: the
family and the place of work (both being usually combined in small-
scale businesses), and was inseparable from other activities, in
particular from production. It was, therefore, well integrated into
the time of a human lifespan and also spatially, as the division of
labour was not very pronounced. School as a specialized institution
was mainly for children from the *dominant classes*, i.e., the non-
workers.[62]

b) School as a specialized institution for reproducing the *labour
force* emerged with the initial phase of capital accumulation and

constitutes the first *collective* form of this reproduction. The
state, which controls it, "derives no inconsiderable advantage
from the instruction of the inferior ranks of people, who themselves obtain hardly any material profit from it", according to
one of the first classics. In this first phase school appears
not so much as something demanded by the workers than rather as
the ideological vector of subordination of the manual dequalified
labour force separated from intellectual work (innovation or
ganization, leadership) concentrated in capital.[63]

The main function of general (and limited) primary schooling for the proletariat is to create a class habitus favourable
to the economic and political interests of the new dominant
classes. To J. S. Mill "instruction makes the worker more circum-
spect, more willing, more honest in his daily work; it is thus an
important factor in the production of material wealth".[64] Or as
Adam Smith said: "The more the inferior ranks of people are in-
structed, the less liable they are to the delusions of enthusiasm
and superstition which, among ignorant nations, frequently occasion
the most dreadful disorders ... And they are more disposed to respect their lawful superiors, less apt to be misled into any wanton
or unnecessary opposition to the measures of government".[65]

Schooling for the dominant classes, most often linked with
administration or the armed forces, developed at the same time.
Since the needs of industry for qualified personnel could for some
time be met by highly skilled workers coming from craft-type production, it was not until the 19th century that technical schools
were set up in the most developed capitalist economies. In this
period education began to appear as one of the arenas for the
class struggle, in particular between the industrial bourgeoisie
and the declining old middle classes. Increasing attempts were
made simultaneously to promote popular education.

c) It was with the so-called "monopolist" period of capitalism that
   the different teaching institutions under state control took on
   the structure of the capitalist school in the meaning we have
   given it in the introduction, namely, a *continuous structure of*

hierarchized networks which, through inculcation of knowledge
and attitudes, and selection based on these criteria and on
financial capacity, has the main function of *reproducing* and
distributing individuals to the different positions determined
by the social and technical division of labour. In the same
period, school systems with structures copied from those of developed societies were established in colonial or newly independent countries. In the 1970s, after 15-20 years of explosive
expansion of education, these structures are being attacked
both by the pupils and by the prevailing ideology (filter theories)
as well as by revolutionary groups and, more moderately, by trade
union representatives. It is, therefore, necessary to analyze
from an economist's point of view the contradictions underlying
the "crisis" of educational systems which the institutions and
the "unifying myth" of lifelong education are trying to overcome.

3.2 Contradictions between the collective reproduction of the qualified labour force and lifelong education

1. The collectivization of educational expenditure answers the needs of
capital for *mobile* manpower.[66] From the beginning of extended primary education,
(designed to homogenize and discipline a dequalified and recently proletarianized
labour force) this part of the cost of reproduction of the labour force is not
borne by variable capital (in the form of wages), as no employer has an interest
in financing the training of workers in a highly competitive labour market. Since
that period, the contradictions inherent in education in a capitalist mode of
production have become apparent:

- first, between the necessary collectivization of these expenses,
  which thus escape the constraints imposed by the system on
  private capital, on the one hand, and on the other, the resulting
  reduction of the total surplus value. Hence the efforts to reduce
  to a minimum these "social overheads" of capital, which were a
  subject of controversy among classical economists in Britain as
  early as the 18th century;[67]

- secondly, between the necessity of this education in order to ensure the *ideological* domination of capital and the potential
  political danger accompanying any transmission of *knowledge*. Hence
  the insistence on limiting the education of the lower classes, and
  the creation of two separate categories of school.[68]

2. In its so-called monopolist phase, the accumulation of capital was accompanied by:

- a rapid development of unproductive qualified labour (services, administration, commerce, etc.);[69]
- a process of dequalification/overqualification of the productive labour force.[70]

The result was a bipolarization on the labour market, which has been studied in particular by the radical American economists in their recent theories on the *segmentation of markets*. The central hypothesis of these authors is that the trend towards homogenization (and therefore towards unification of interests) of workers has historically led to conflicts with capital concentration in its oligopolist form (strikes, revolutionary movements at the end of the last century). Freed from the restraints of short-term competition, big business seeks long-term stability through obtaining control of the markets for its products and factors of production:

- on the labour market, "historical analysis suggests that, in order to eliminate that danger, employers have actively and deliberately segmented the markets in accordance with the principle "divide and rule";[71]

- on the product market, "the efforts of the monopolists to increase their control ... have led to dichotomization of the industrial structure, which has had the - indirect and unintentional, though welcome - effect of strengthening their deliberate strategies" (on the labour market).[72]

These "ideological" determinants of the bipolarization of the labour market in conjunction with technological evolution (in itself obviously not neutral and linked with the dominant social relations in production) have resulted in two *principal* types of market:

- the *"primary" market* including most of the jobs in large bureaucratic firms and in administration. It is characterized by an intensely hierarchical division of labour and institutionalization (frequently with the collaboration of the trade unions) of recruitment criteria, career schemes, pay by seniority, etc. With relatively high wages, good working conditions, and possibilities of on-the-job training and promotion, these measures are designed to *stabilize* the labour force. This "internal" market is hardly affected by the conditions of supply and demand on the external market, except at the "entrance door" where they determine the level of the "signals" for discrimination as discovered by the filter theorists: diploma, age, sex, ethnic and social origin, etc. Some authors also note that most of the jobs of this type are characterized by the fact that productivity is closely linked with attitudes (stability, submission to the hierarchy and adherence to aims and values imposed from outside), and that the necessary skills are essentially acquired through experience in the course of employment;

- the *"secondary" market* comprises the kinds of job that require the least amount of education and experience. Wages are relatively low and working conditions bad. There are few if any chances of promotion, very little trade unionism and a high rate of turnover (most often at the wish of the firm). These jobs are the preserve of workers against whom discrimination is practised: young people, women, immigrants, etc. They are partly in large firms, but mostly in firms who hold a weak position on the external labour market and cannot compete with the big ones (small or medium-sized labour-intensive firms, sub-contractors, etc.)

The purpose of this segmentation of markets is to strengthen the domination of capital over the labour force by:

- dividing the working class in its struggles;

- justifying the internal power structure of the firm;

- limiting and channeling workers' aspirations to vertical mobility and "reducing the pressure on other social institutions, such as school and family, that reproduce the class structure".[73]

It will be noted that in this analysis only the secondary merkets can be considered competitive in the neoclassical sense. On the sheltered primary markets, it is the nature of the job that determines worker productivity (through training and experience), and the wage structure is based on elements other than market forces. In particular it is compatible with theories on the retrocession of surplus value.[74]

If one rejects the purely "technological" explanation of the capitalist division of labour,[75] one might accept the hypothesis that the necessity for capitalism in its monopolist phase to intensify and diversify the hierarchical division of labour implies the need to justify it. This would help to explain the evolution of the structure and volume of supply and demand in regard to schooling.

a) As an ideological instrument, schooling can legitimate the power structure from which it originates only by appearing autonomous and neutral in relation to capital as the dominant relation of production. It can legitimate the distribution of individuals according to the class to which they belong, within the structure of positions determined by the social division of labour, only if it appears as "one school for all" and selects candidates by a consistent process of differentiation based on class differences (which excludes practical knowledge). Insofar as the content of schooling appears to have no connection with the skills actually put to use in employment, it is this justification function which seems to make it necessary for capital to develop an educational system characterized by its separation from production, inclusion of all children and adolescents, and continuity between the successive levels, i.e. a particularly expensive educational system.

b) Since in its monopolist phase the domination of capital over labour implies a stratification of jobs, access to which is governed by certification, the pressure of demand (generally satisfied, for the reasons given under point a) above, by a Robbinsian function of supply)[76] is permanent at least for access to the different levels of the primary market. The proletarianization of the self-employed middle classes contributes considerably to this situation.

3. However, this school system provides only a temporary solution of the capital/labour antagonism. Its development is in itself contradictory. Three hypotheses could be offered to account for this:

a) Its quantitative growth: if the collectivization of that part of the reproduction of the labour force appears satisfactory from the point of view of the individual firm, since at that level it does not function as variable capital, the resulting increase in "social overheads" of capital at the global level constitutes a diversion of social surplus value which becomes increasingly unacceptable and conflicts with the global process of dequalification of the labour force.[77]

b) The internal contradictions of the capitalist schools system: it can only function as a legitimizing institution on the ideological level if it also transmits knowledge to the worker.

But in that respect it conflicts with the division, established by the capitalist production system, between knowledge and work, knowledge being a part of capital as a force of production; further, it conflicts with the capitalist structure of social relations, namely, the division between the owner class and the proletarian class based on private ownership of the means of production, in that it makes collective possession of knowledge possible, though knowledge as a force of production should be the exclusive property of the owner class. School

thus reflects the contradictions inherent in the capitalist
system: originating from it to contribute to its maintenance,
it also contributes to its destruction.[78]

c) The functioning of the capitalist school system engenders a relative over-population" of qualified workers inasmuch as the rythm of
capital accumulation does not enable the surplus of graduates to be
absorbed without dequalifying them. While this "reserve army" can be
used by capital in phases of rapid growth, it has little effect on
the wages governed by the primary market, and the political danger
it represents is obvious. This is felt particularly in developing
capitalist countries where the slow growth rate of local capital reduces the number of openings, especially in the tertiary sector. In
developed capitalist societies, where the shortage of graduates in
the years after the war led to a strengthening of measures designed
to ensure stability of qualified personnel in the firms,[79] the present abundant supply seems responsible for the formation of second-
ary-type markets parallel to primary markets: auxiliary administrative personnel on a contract basis, temporary employment, etc. On
the other hand, the influx of graduates into the secondary market -
particularly the internal secondary market of the big firms - affects the salaries in this segment, where the increasingly routine
nature and fragmentation of jobs (especially in the tertiary sector)
contribute to widening the gap between aspirations and working conditions. From the point of view of capital several solutions to
these contradictions are possible:

- Slower growth rate or reduction of educational expenditure:
  this could be achieved either by reducing the unit cost (which
  would only have a financial effect), or by increasing selection (filter theories) which would have the additional advantage of curbing the growing discrepancy between the pyramid
  of diplomas and that of jobs; but the political balance of
  forces often excludes a policy of restricted entry.

- Measures designed to discourage demand for schooling: raising
  the private cost of schooling (which would help to shift the
  financial burden), shortening the duration of cycles leading
  to a degree, compulsory prior military or other service; or
  deferment in time through facilities for recurrent education,[80]
  training schemes in the course of employment, etc.

- Policies designed to adapt the educational system closely to

the requirements of capital, i.e. to make it profitable. This
implies reducing the autonomy of the educational system,
which can be done in various ways: by greater participation
of employers' representatives in decisions concerning school;
by agreements between educators and users of the qualified
labour force; by direct financing of part of the educational
expenses by employers and development of the private sector
of education. In these developments the conflicts of interest
among employers play an important part.[81]

Making expenditure on education profitable also means giving priority in
allocation to the reproduction of that section of the labour force that is directly productive for capital, e.g. in developing countries, applications of
the principle of functional literacy,

the selective and intensive nature of which indicates that the priority
aim is to make labour more productive in those sectors and projects where
it is necessary and possible, i.e. in the modern sector of agriculture
and in the technically relatively advanced industries, as against the
other productive activities existing in the country.[82]

In developed capitalist economies, "permanent training" on the job enables the labour force to be closely and rapidly adapted to technical and organizational changes. If it is collectively financed, wholly or partially, this
enables the firm to transfer a cost it would previously have had to bear (in
particular if, in order to benefit from governmental financial participation,
the firm "formalizes" previously informal training).

Institutions of lifelong education also meet the conflicting requirements
of big firms (regarding *stability/mobility* of manpower) for collective management of the surplus labour force at the level of the external market,[83] and for
internal management of primary market jobs, as an aid to policies designed to
render this market more competitive in periods of capital concentration and
"excess" supply of graduates (by, for example, reducing the advantages linked
with seniority, incentives to geographical mobility, etc.).

Insofar as capital questions the school's function of ideological reproduction, lifelong education activities on-the-job enable the *site of this re-*
production to be shifted: the association of education with work, i.e. the
"integration" of educational activities with work, especially for the labour
force employed in the secondary market, is conducive to the acquisition of the
desired attitudes and behaviour.

It is also often used as a reward/punishment system on the internal primary market of the firm.[84] Lifelong education in the firms tends to aggravate

the inequalities between the different categories of workers. Experience in France, for instance, shows that the principal beneficiaries are the workers of the primary market (skilled workers, technicians, supervisors, foremen, managers) at the expense of the young, women, immigrant workers, and other employees stuck in secondary markets. It accentuates the division of wage earners and reinforces the hierarchical power in the firm, which it helps to justify by:

- turning on-the-job learning into "schooling" (development of a body of specialized "instructors" in the firms);

- using the higher grades in the hierarchy to train the lower ones;

- enhancing the prestige and power of the "specialist", i.e. the monopoly of the school as a "distributor/justifier" of individuals in the social division of labour, for the entire length of their working lives.[85]

Institutionalization of lifelong education also makes it possible to absorb popular education movements and put them under state control. Finally, it may be mentioned that the development of a parallel, competing and decentralized education system could provide a considerable outlet for the industries producing what Theodore Roszak, in a light vein, calls the "electronized-individualized-computerized-audiovisual-multi-instructional consoles".[86]

The present *institutionalized forms* of lifelong education could thus be criticized in many points by the most fervent advocates of the *idea* of lifelong education, particularly in respect of their ideological aspects. However, such criticism often takes the form of total rejection:

Permanent education will reinforce the established social order, controlling and manipulating the destiny of whole populations.[87]

Being merely schooling in another guise, a policy of lifelong education can never be anything but a trap for attempts at deschooling society.[88]

It's bad enough to promote technocratic control via media in the false name of equal chances for one nation. What is even worse is to propose it for the whole world. That is what stands out as the message of the report of UNESCO's International Commission on the Development of Education called *Learning to Be*.[89]

Hence this conclusion by A. Gorz, at the colloquium on lifelong education held at Cuernavaca in June 1974:

Recurrent education must therefore either go along with the radical transformation of the work process and the social relations of production or else be nothing more than a stratagem by which the firm, or society as such, seeks to attain a more effective adjustment of workers[90] to pre-established goals, work situations and processes.

What these authors forget is that on-the-job training integrated with productive activity cannot get away from the contradictory manner in which education functions in a system of capitalist production.

It permits collective acquisition of knowledge by the workers, in the sphere of production where class antagonism is most transparent. And it is most often through the introduction of educational activities in the firm that the nature of the educational system and the role it plays in the reproduction of the relations of production become clear to the workers.

It works the better for capital if it is not attested by a diploma and does not entitle to promotion, whereas workers demand it mainly for the sake of better wages and working conditions.

It occasions conflicts between trade unions and employers, but frequently also between the personal interests of workers (individual promotion) and trade union policy (social promotion and collective action). It may, therefore, become a new arena for social struggles.

3.3 Lifelong education and the social division of labour

In the broad definition we have quoted at the beginning of this paper, lifelong education is an ideal which political economy can only approach through studying its relationship with the social division of labour.

First of all, we have to eliminate the all too frequent references made by the proponents of lifelong education to nostalgic views of the pre-capitalist division of labour, i.e. to authors such as Diderot: "The combination of wisdom and skill was readily to be found in the workshops where apprentices were trained"[91], or Goethe to whom the best type of education was

the one of the hydriotes. As islanders and seafarers they take their boys along with them on their ships and let them work their way up. If they are successful they participate in profit, and this wakens their interest in commerce, bartering and booty, and it forms expert[92] sailors, the smartest merchants and the most daring pirates.

We find the same idea in the works of Adam Smith, who notes, when comparing the education of farmers' sons behind their fathers' ploughs with the apprenticeship systems of craftsmen, that the proofs of mastery which they were required to provide (crowned by the presentation of their chef-d'oeuvre) served not so much to teach them their craft as rather to restrict access to the mastercraftsman grade in the guilds.

To us these references are of twofold interest as they contain two
themes frequently recurring in the literature on lifelong education:

a) The belief that integration of education with work is an essential
   means of producing complete human beings. This is also to be found
   in Marx: "In the future, the education of every child above a certain age will combine productive work with teaching and physical
   training, not only to permit growth of social production, but because this is the only way to produce fully developed human beings".

b) Rejection of selection by the school, which does not, however, eliminate other kinds of selection (through birth or through abilities
   shown in working life).

They apply exclusively to a division of labour *by trades* (in a system
of simple craftsman production), which is obviously considered the one allowing fullest development of human beings in contrast to alienating, fragmented work.

As a project for a future society, lifelong education aims at "total development of the human personality" by means of integrating education with
the entirety of an individual's activities at all stages of his life. There
are two ambiguities here: (a) in that education is considered to be both an
individual and a social undertaking ("autonomy" and "adaptation"); and
(b) in the position given to education in relation to other individual activities and experiences.

From this point of view two principal approaches can be distinguished
in current socialist thinking:

a) The first emphasizes the role the ideological superstructure plays
   in the transformation of the material base of society. In capitalist societies, this finds expression either in a reformist attitude (the raising of the cultural level of the masses by post-school
   educational activities linked with their working experience could
   foster a fairer social structure in which manual labour would be respected), or in revolutionary projects exploiting the internal contradictions of the capitalist school. A. Visalberghi, for example,
   considers the possible results of the contradictiion between the
   pressure of demand for education and the necessity for capital to

exclude from access to "equality of opportunity" the growing part
of the population that is engaged in dequalified, fragmented jobs
as follows:

Either, the educational system must "rationalize" the class
structure, "in other words, the educational system - including
lifelong education - will have to predetermine the entire vocational, cultural, and socio-economic life of the individual by
placing him on the appropriate level of the employment hierarchy".
But such "perfect meritocracy" would be a "nightmare" bound to
fail because it would mean that children of the upper classes
could be relegated to the bottom of the hierarchy. Or, an "imper-
fect meritocracy" maintaining the privileges of the middle and
upper classes by a school selection based on class criteria may
subsist, but then "it is obvious that such a solution would require authoritarian support from political circles, either open
or disguised; in such a situation the fictional nature of
selection and guidance procedures in the educational system
would be too evident not to arouse violent reaction from the less
favoured classes".[93]

Consequently, there could be no intermediate, moderate
solutions. The only possible one would be "a new classless society". This kind of analysis attributes to the educational
system a disproportionately large role in the reproduction of the
social relations of production.

b) The second approach considers transformation of the social division of labour to be the necessary prerequisite for true lifelong
education. But then lifelong education is no longer an educational venture but a societal one, since it is not a matter of
basing educational activities on experience but of ensuring that
experience consists exclusively of "educational situations", i.e., of

> situations in which, individually and collectively,
> (men) can shape their way of living and working,
> their environment and their tools as they best see
> fit in their community's interest; in such situations,
> the separation between working and learning becomes
> impossible; you keep learning because of what you
> want to do and you keep doing new things because of
> what you learn.[94]

It is not merely a matter of arranging ("enriching" or "expanding") work, but a process of self-government.[95]

Other projects of transforming the social division of labour have been proposed to meet the needs expressed in the demand for lifelong education, such as vertical and horizontal rotation of jobs in time,[96] which - while preventing that a section of the labour force be condemned to an entire lifetime of hard, fragmented and dequalified labour - would enable every individual (since the whole of the population would be sufficiently qualified) to combine in his entire working life manual and intellectual work, execution and conception, etc.

The difficulty, however, is to differentiate between utopian discourse (whether bourgeois, reformist or revolutionary in intent) and projects firmly based on an analysis of the complex reality.

NOTES

1. *Lifelong Education*. Report of the meeting of experts, August 1970, in New Delhi. New Delhi: Asian Institute of Educational Planning and Administration, 1970. p. 18.

2. Durkheim, E. *Sociologie de l'Education*. Paris: Presses Universitaires de France, 1961.

3. Carelli, M. D. "Foreword". In Dave, R. H. *Lifelong Education and School Curriculum*. Hamburg: Unesco Institute for Education, 1973. (UIE monographs 1).

4. See in particular Hartung, H. *Pour une Education permanente*. Paris: Fayard, 1966. - Illich, I. *Deschooling Society*. New York: Harper & Row, 1970. - Schwartz, B. *Réflexions sur le Développement de l'Education permanente*. Paris: Presses Universitaires de France, 1967. (Perspective 14). - Dave, R. H. *Lifelong Education and School Curriculum*. See Note 3.

5. "Concept-caoutchouc", a term used by R. Pucheu in "La Formation permanente: Idée neuve, Idée fausse". *Revue Esprit* 10 (Oct. 1974).

6. e.g. the communications (yet unpublished) made by Gorz, A., Guigou, J.; Ohliger, J.; Verne, E.; Ginisty, B.; Dohmen, G. to the symposium on life-long education held by the Centro Intercultural de Documentación of Cuernavaca, Mexico, in June 1974. - See also *Revue Esprit* 10 (Oct. 1974).

7. Interview of I. Illich by Varin, O. in *France Culture* (10 Sep. 1974), and Illich, I. & Verne, E. "Le Piège de l'Ecole à Vie". *Le Monde de l'Education* (Jan. 1975).

8. Tardy, M. *Le Champ sémantique de l'Expression "Education permanente"*. Strasbourg: Council of Europe, 1970. p. 13.

9. Godelier, M. *Nationalité et Irrationalité en Economie*. Paris: Maspero, 1968. p. 28.

10. Correa, H. *Economics of Human Resources*. Amsterdam: North Holland Publishing Company, 1963. p. 13.

11. Schultz, T. W. "Reflections on Investment in Man". *Journal of Political Economy* LXX (Oct. 1962). No. 5. Part 2. Supplement. p. 1.

12. Becker, G. S. "Investment in Human Capital: A Theoretical Analysis". *Journal of Political Economy* LXX (Oct. 1962), No. 5. Part 2. Supplement. p. 9.

13. Ibid. p. 11.

14. Ibid.

15. The following formula will yield the rate of return r by balancing the present value of the cost and income returns of the envisaged education at the year t = o of decision:

$$\sum_{t=o}^{N} R_t \, (1 + r)^{-t} \quad = \quad \sum_{t=o}^{N} C_t \, (1 + r)^{-t}$$

where N is the expected lifetime of the investment in education,
R_t is the increase in net income at year t attributable to the envisaged education
C_t is the cost (direct cost and foregone earnings) of the education to be borne by the individual.

16. Smith, Adam. *The Wealth of Nations*. London: University of London Press, 1961. Book I, Chapter X, Part 1. p. 113.

17. See also Manoury, J. L. *Economie du Savoir*. Paris: Armand Colin, 1972.

18. As examples of the method used, see Morgan, J. & David, M. "Education and Income". *Quarterly Journal of Economics* 77 (Aug. 1963), No. 3. pp. 423 - 437; and Hirsch, W. Z. & Segelhorst, A. W. "Incremental Income Benefits

of Public Education". *Review of Economics and Statistics* 68 (Nov. 1965), No. 4.

19. Rosen, S. "Learning and Experience in the Labour Market". *Journal of Human Resources* 7 (Summer 1972).

20. See Mincer, J. "On-the-job Training: Costs, Returns and Implications". *Journal of Political Economy* LXX (Oct. 1962), No. 5. Part 2. pp. 50 - 73.

21. This is how A. Okita explains that in view of the shortage of qualified workers and engineers in the heavy engineering and chemical industries in Japan, "private firms were obliged to undertake specialized training of their personnel themselves. This necessity gave rise to the system of 'employment for life' and pay by seniority, which still characterizes the employment market in Japan". "Manpower Policy in Japan". *Revue internationale du Travail* (July 1964).

22. It may, however, be necessary to use material incentives to motivate workers to undergo training. In that case, the increase in the worker's wages after training enters into the firm's profitability calculation of human investment. This investment is optimal for the employer when the total actualized cost of the worker's additional training is equal to the total actualized increase of returns. That is to say:

$$\sum_{t=0}^{T} (\Delta M_t - \Delta W_t)(1 + r)^{-t} = K$$

where T = duration of anticipated employment of the worker in the firm,
ΔM_t = increase in the worker's marginal productivity in the firm at time t attributable to the investment in education,
ΔW_t = increase in the trained worker's wage at time t (or variable cost of the investment in training),
K = fixed cost of the investment in training (direct cost and wage paid to the worker during training),
r = rate of return.

23. The equilibrium of collective intellectual investment can be stated as follows:

$$C_0 = \sum_{t=0}^{n} (Y_t - y_t) \, M_t \cdot P_t \, (1 + i)^{-t}$$

where C_0 = part of the cost of an additional unit of education borne by the community,
Y_t = social return on this unit in time t
y_t = private return on this unit in time t
M_t = probability of the beneficiary's surviving in time t,
P_t = probability of his residing in the community in time t,
i = rate of interest chosen to represent the community's rate of depreciation.

24. See in particular, Becker, G. "Human Capital and the Personal Distribution of Income". *Woytinski Lecture* No. 1. Ann Arbor: University of Michigan, 1967.

25. See, for example, Jensen, A. R. "How Much Can We Boost I.Q. and Scholastic Achievement?" *Harvard Educational Review* 39 (Winter 1969), No. 2.

26. See Coleman, J.S. *Equality of Educational Opportunity*. Washington, D.C.: U.S. Office of Education, 1966, and "Equal Schools or Equal Students". *The Public Interest* 1 (Summer 1966).

27. i.e. first degree homogeneity:

$$P = b \ L^k \ K^{1-k}$$

where P = global production
L and K = labour and capital inputs
b = a coefficient of dimension depending on the measuring units used
k and 1-k = the partial elasticity of production in relation to the factors labour and capital.
This function being homogeneous, P is equal to the sum of the respective parts of labour and capital remunerated at their marginal productivity; k and 1-k are therefore respectively the parts of wages and capital earnings in the national product.

28. See Kendrick, J. *Productivity Trends in the USA*. New York: National Bureau of Economic Research, 1961.

29. See Denison, E. *The Source of Growth and the Alternatives Before Us*. New York: Committee for Economic Development, 1962. Supplementary paper, No. 13.

30. See, for example. Aukrust, O., who names the "third factor: 'organization'". "It is an assembly of diverse elements: the technical and commercial knowledge of directors, employers and workers, their drive, their will and ability to work, the whole of the social conditions and the international situation in which production intervenes". "Investment and Economic Expansion". *Revue de la Mesure de la Productivité*. (OECD) (Feb. 1959), No. 16. p. 48.

31. Arrow, K. "The Economic Implications of Learning by Doing". *Review of Economic Studies* 29 (1962). pp. 155 - 173.

32. Denison, E. "The Sources of Economic Growth in the USA". - "The Contribution of Schooling (and of the Residual Factor) to Economic Growth". In: *The Residual Factor and Economic Growth*. Paris: OECD, 1964.

33. Denison, E. "The Contribution of Schooling ..." Ibid.

34. See Page, A. *Economie de l'Education*. Paris: Presses Universitaires de France, 1971. p. 83.

35. Psacharopoulos, G. *Rates of Return to Education*. Amsterdam: Elsevier, 1973.

36. Denison, E. "How to Raise the High Employment Growth Rate by the Percent-
    age Point". *American Economic Review.* 52 (May 1962), No. 2. Papers and
    Proceedings. p. 67 ff.

37. For example, *Economic Models of Education*. Paris: OECD, 1965. - *Mathema-
    tical Models in Educational Planning*. Paris: OECD, 1967.

38. For example, *Enseignement et Distribution du Revenu*. Conférence sur les
    Politiques d'Expansion de l'Enseignement. Paris: OECD, 1970. - Khoi,
    Le Than. "L'Education, Facteur ou Frein au Développement". *Options
    méditerranéennes* (1974), No. 20.

39. See Jencks, C. *Inequality. A Reassessment of the Effects of Family and
    Schooling in America*. New York: Harper & Row, 1973. - Boudon, R.
    *L'Inégalité des Chances: la Mobilité sociale dans les Sociétés indus-
    trielles*. Paris: Armand Colin, 1973.

40. Among the principal proponents of the "filter" or "screen" theory are:
    Arrow, K. J. "Higher Education as a Filter". *Journal of Public Econo-
    mics* (1973), No. 2. pp. 193 - 216. - Taubmann, P. J. & Wales, T. J.
    "Higher Education, Mental Ability and Screening". *Journal of Political
    Economy* 81 (Jan. - Feb. 1973), No. 1. p. 28. - Wiles, P. J. "The
    Correlation between Education and Earnings: the External-Test-Not-
    Content Hypothesis". *Higher Education* 3 (Feb. 1974), No. 1. - Thurow, L.
    & Lucas, R. *The American Distribution: A Structural Problem*. Washington,
    D.C.: U.S. Government Printing Office, March 1972. - Spence, M. "Job
    Market Signalling". *Quarterly Journal of Economics* 87 (Aug. 1973).

41. For example, Jencks C. See Note 39. - Bowles, S. & Gintis, H. "I.Q. in the
    U.S. Class Structure". *Social Policy* (Jan. - Feb. 1973). - Bowles, S.
    "Schooling and Inequality from Generation to Generation". *Journal of
    Political Economy* 80 (May - June 1972), No. 3, Part II.

42. Bourdieu, P. & Passeron, J. C. *Les Héritiers*. Paris: Editions de Minuit,
    1964. - Bourdieu, P. & Passeron, J. C. *La Reproduction*. Paris: Editions
    de Minuit, 1969. - Baudelot, C. & Establet, R. *L'Ecole capitaliste en
    France*. Paris: Maspero, 1971.

43. See Ribich, T. "The Case for Equal Educational Opportunity". In: *Schooling
    in a Corporate Society. The Political Economy of Education in America*.
    M. Carnoy (Ed.). New York: David McKay, 1972.
    This approach is implied in the methods of calculating the "ability re-
    serves" of the population: the "raw material" of the school system is
    classified by its "content" in aptitudes capable of being "transformed"
    by schooling to yield a good return, measured by the probability of
    success of children from different social backgrounds. See Halsey, A. H.
    (Ed.). *Ability and Educational Opportunity*. Paris: OECD, 1962. - Correa,
    H. *Economics of Human Resources*. See Note 10.

44. Arrow, K. J. "Higher Education as a Filter". See Note 40. p. 194.

45. To give an example: a large American firm, which stated in 1951 that it spent 5.4% of the total of salaries and wages on recruitment and training expenses, spent five times as much on the recruitment of a higher-level employee than on an unskilled worker. For the latter, training costs were equal to recruitment costs, for the higher-level employee they were 100 times higher. - See Oi, W. "Labour as a Quasi-Fixed Factor". *Journal of Political Economy* LXX (Dec. 1962). No. 6.

46. Vance Packard quoted in 1962 an executive saying: "We desperately need a means of screening. Education is one quick means of preliminary screening without having to think too much about it." But he also noted that college costs had been rising faster than family income and that "two thirds of the brightest young people in the land - those with IQs of higher than 117 - had not had the benefit of a college diploma". *The Pyramid Climbers*. New York: Crest Books, 1962. p. 37.

47. Spence, M. "Job Market Signalling". See Note 40. - Wiles, P. J. "The Correlation between Education and Earnings ...". See Note 40: "... in all non-vocational cases, a good one-day test of docility, perseverance and ability costing about £ 20 instead of £ 3,000, would do as well (to reveal employability)".

48. Taubmann, P. J. & Wales, T. J. "Higher Education ...". See Note 40. p. 29.

49. Ibid. p. 43.

50. Thurow, L. & Lucas, R. *The American Distribution ...*". See Note 40.

51. Carnoy, M. & Carter, M. "Theories of Labor Markets, Education and Income Distribution". Contribution to the colloquium on "Is Education a Profitable Investment?", University of Mons, November 1974. p. 19. (Mimeographed).

52. For example, Stubblebine, W. M. "Institutional Elements in the Financing of Education". *The Southern Economic Journal* 32 (July 1965), No. 1, Part 2. Supplement. pp. 15 - 34.

53. For example, Wiles, P. J. "The Correlation ...". See Note 40. p. 51.

54. Stubblebine, W. M. "Institutional Elements ...". See Note 52. p. 23.

55. The method used especially in Britain and France.

56. Gannicott, K. *The Economics of Education: A Review of Recent Work*. Paris: OECD, Oct. 1973. (Mimeographed).

57. Delaunay, J. C. *Essai marxiste sur la Comptabilité nationale*. Paris: Editions Sociales, 1971. p. 230.

58. See Althusser, L. "Idéologie et Appareils idéologiques d'Etat". *La Pensée* (May-June 1970). - Bourdieu, P. & Passeron, J. C. *La Reproduction*. See Note 42. Baudelot, C. & Establet, R. *L'Ecole capitaliste ...*". See Note 42.

59. Dowidar, M. *L'Economie politique, une Science sociale*. Paris: Maspéro, 1974. p. 249.

60. "In order that capitalist production reproduce itself, the labour force must in every production cycle appear as constant, and not as the result of production. Since capitalist surplus value originates from extra work, i.e. the difference between the work necessary to reproduce the labour force and the work actually done, no surplus value will be produced unless the labour force is sold at a price determined on the basis of this necessary work, that is on the basis of the value of the goods coming from the sphere of exchange and consumed by the worker. If the production of the labour force were a capitalist production, and if consequently this production would yield a profit, the necessary work would no longer correspond to the price of the labour force, and there would be no basis for determining the production of surplus value." Therefore "progress in knowledge of the reproduction of social relations, which is also the condition for progress in knowledge of the production process itself --- lies outside the field of political economy; more precisely, it requires an analysis not only of the exchange value cycle but of another cycle, that of use values. Once sold, the goods disappear as exchange values but continue to circulate as use values, are transformed, consumed, and finally provide the basis for the production of an ultimate use value, that of the labour force, which acquires an exchange value on the market". From Lautier, B. *La Reproduction de la Force de Travail*. Thèse pour le doctorat d'Etat de Sciences économiques, Grenoble, 1974. (Mimeographed).

61. Hoernle, E. *Das proletarische Kind*, 1928, quoted in Lindenberg, D. *L'Internationale communiste et l'Ecole de Classe*. Paris: Maspéro, 1972. p. 231.

62. Except for the clergy who were frequently recruited from the lower classes.

63. "The intellectual powers of production develop only on one side because they disappear from all others. What the workers in fragmented jobs lose is concentrated in their antithesis, capital. The division of labour inherent in industrialized production sets the intellectual powers of production against them as somebody else's property and as a power dominating them." Marx, Karl. *Capital*. Paris: Editions Sociales, 1960. 2, p. 50.

64. Mill, J. S. *Principles of Political Economy*. 50. 1, chapter 7, paragraph 5.

65. Smith, Adam. *The Wealth of Nations*. See Note 16. 2, p. 309.

66. (even to philanthropic economists) "education really means one thing: making every worker learn to carry out as many activities as possible, so that, if he has to get out of one branch because of new machinery or a new division of labour, he can without difficulty enter another one". Marx, Karl. "Wages". In *Oeuvres*. Paris: Editions de la Pleiade, 1958. 2, p. 158. First published 1847.

67. Regarding this controversy between Adam Smith and Malthus on one side and J. S. Mill on the other, see West, J. "Private versus Public Education:

A Classical Dispute". *Journal of Political Economy* 72 (Oct. 1964), No. 5. pp. 465 - 475.

68. When the *Collèges d'Enseignement secondaire* were set up in France, Victor Cousin declared in 1831, "it is not advisable to throw them open without discretion to the lower classes. ... Those young people pursue mediocre studies there which are of no use to them and do not correspond to their future trade, and they acquire habits and tastes which make it difficult, almost impossible, for them to go back to their fathers' humble jobs. The result will be a race of restive men, dissatisfied with their position ... ready to launch themselves into every avenue of servility or revolt." Quoted by Poignant, R. "Démocratie, Expansion économique et Réforme de l'Enseignement". *Avenirs* (1957), No. 88.

69. As a means of checking the falling tendency of the profit rate.

70. The incorporation of technical progress into the means of production implies a growing need for engineers, technicians etc., and the lowering of the skill levels (and hence of the cost of the labour force) needed by workers using these means of production.

71. Reich, M; Gordon, D. & Edwards, R. "A Theory of Labour Market Segmentation". *American Economic Review* 63 (May 1973), papers and proceedings. p. 361.

72. Ibid.

73. Ibid. p. 364.

74. For example, Baudelot C.; Establet, R. & Malemort, J. *La petite Bourgeoisie en France*. Paris: Maspéro, 1974.

75. On the controversy between the "technical" and "ideological" explanations of the capitalist division of labour, see Gorz, A. (Ed.). *Critique de la Division du Travail*. Paris: Editions du Seuil, 1973.

76. That is, by the so-called "social demand" planning method, which consists in creating the number of places necessary to meet the projected demand for enrolment in schools.

77. "The state must accept that the growth of its working expenses be stopped. I cannot request you urgently enough to draw the attention of the authorities to this point, in particular in two fields: health and national education. Whatever the needs and the justifications put forward on this subject, there can be no sensible budget if these expenses are allowed to rise from year to year. Morally it is, of course, very difficult to stop this trend; but it must be done - otherwise we will kill the goose that lays the golden eggs." Extract from a speech by President Georges Pompidou to the French Chambers of Commerce in February 1969, quoted in Launay, J. "Elements pour une Economie politique de l'Education". *Economie et Politique* (Nov. 1969), No. 184.

78. Petit, V. "Les Contradictions de 'la Reproduction'". *La Pensée* (April 1973), No. 168. p. 11.

79. In particular, different payments, loans, housing, children's education, etc.

80. (they) "provide a safety valve for the educational system by controlling and channelling the quantity explosion". Visalberghi. A. *Education and the Division of Labour*. The Hague: Martinus Nijhoff, 1973.

81. e.g. in the application of the 1971 law on further education: A uniform tax on wages paid disadvantages the labour-intensive firms; besides, the domination of the big companies makes itself felt in their control of the organizations managing the collected funds, and workers in dominated firms who have received training according to the provisions of the 1971 law and and who have few possibilities of promotion, enlarge the external market of the dominating firms on the labour market. See Groupe de Recherche sur l'Education (G.R.E.) "La Demande de Formation professionnelle continue: Analyse du Comportement des Directions d'Entreprise". *Education permanente* (March/April 1974). pp. 39 - 53.

82. Papayannakis, M. "Alphabétisation fonctionelle et Développement économique". *Options mediteranneennes* (1973), No. 21. p. 63.

83. This applies both to developed economies (training and retraining of unemployed, by methods differing from one country to another) and to developing ones (as pointed out by I. Illich, Peru provides lifelong education for fishermen deprived of their working tools).

84. Ginisty, B., commenting on the 1971 legislation on continuing education in France, writes that it "seems like a new form of social security, which allows not only the training programmes to be cut down to the contingencies of the historical development of neo-capitalism", but also "to induce a notion of consumption of training analogous to medical consumption, and fulfilling a similar function: to reduce deviation from societal norms". *Les Ambiguités de l'Education permanente: quelques Propositions*. Colloque CIDOC, June 1974. Cuernavaca, Mexico: CIDOC, 1974. (Mimeographed).

85. This function is fulfilled all the better as access to lifelong education appears to be more open but is in reality more difficult. The Chancellor of the British Open University stated in 1973 that this institution "offers probably one of the most difficult ways of getting a degree yet devised by the wit of man". Quoted in Ohliger, J. *Is Lifelong Education a Guarantee of Permanent Inadequacy?* Colloque CIDOC, June 1974. Cuernavaca, Mexico: CIDOC, 1974. (Mimeographed).

86. Ibid.

87. Professor H. Frese, University of Leiden, Holland, quoted in Ohliger, J. *Is Lifelong Education a Guarantee* ... See Note 85.

88. Illich, I. & Verne, E. "Le Piège ...". See Note 7.

89. Ohliger, J. *Is Lifelong Education a Guarantee* ... See Note 85.

90. Gorz, A. *The Hidden Curriculum of Adult Education*. Colloque CIDOC, June 1974. Cuernavaca, Mexico: CIDOC, 1974. (Mimeographed).

91. Diderot, D. Prospectus de l'*Encyclopédie*.

92. Goethe, J. W. "Maximen und Reflexionen 347". In *Goethes Werke*. Sonderausgabe Europäischer Buchclub, Aus Kunst und Altertum. Vol. 3. p. 697.

93. Visalberghi, A. *Education* ... See Note 80.

94. Gorz, A. *The Hidden Curriculum* ... See Note 90.

95. Some small-scale community projects based on this idea have been attempted. For details see, for example, Bugnicourt, L. *Action Training*. Dakar: United Nations, I.D.E.P., 1972.

96. Visalberghi, A. *Education* ... See Note 80.

CHAPTER 8

ILLUSTRATIVE CONTENT ANALYSIS AND SYNTHESIS

R. H. D a v e

1. General Purposes of the Chapter

This chapter attempts illustrative analyses and syntheses of the ideas presented separately in the preceding chapters based on selected disciplines. It extends the methodological discussions contained in chapter 1, and describes a procedure both for content analysis of the specific discipline-based foundations and for the formulation of an interdisciplinary synthesis of the various foundations.

2. Analysis and Synthesis of the Foundation Content

2.1 Purpose of the content analysis

The separate foundation studies by disciplines have elucidated various aspects of lifelong education, each in its own characteristic way. However, in order to derive operational guidelines from these studies it was necessary to identify and isolate specific ideas and to present these in an organized and consistent manner, unified within a conceptual framework. As a first step this necessitated a content analysis of each discipline-based foundation.

It was also necessary to ascertain the total contribution of all foundations, taken as a group, to the various content categories (see Table 8.1) used in the initial content analysis. Whereas the first step concentrated on the contribution of each individual foundation to all of the selected content categories, the second was concerned with the total contribution of all foundations to each particular content category. This called for a synthesis of the relevant ideas from the different foundations, to yield a broader understanding of each of the content categories. Using this two-pronged procedure, it was possible to identify and highlight a number of examples providing general perspectives and guidelines for operational decision-making and other similar purposes. A more exhaustive application of this approach should prove helpful in identifying and organizing many more guiding principles regarding all major aspects of lifelong education.

2.2 Procedure

2.2.1 *Nature of the content analysis*

The content analysis, both in its analytic and in its synthetic phases, was qualitative and not quantitative in nature. The purpose of the analysis was to identify certain ideas and inter-relate them, not to test formal hypotheses or to carry out frequency counts of the occurrence of particular ideas. As stated before, the analysis was illustrative, and by no means exhaustive. This is particularly true of the separate analyses of the various discipline-based foundations. In this instance, one or two key ideas were simply identified from each foundation and reported in order to demonstrate the feasibility and use of the methodology as well as to give some idea of the general "flavour" of the foundation.

2.2.2 *Content categories and recording units*

The criteria for selection of the particular content categories, such as goals, precautions and preconditions, structures, and so on, have been explained in Chapter 1. The categories finally employed are listed in Table 8.1.

TABLE 8.1

CONTENT CATEGORIES

---

1. *Goals*

         - general
         - specific

2. *Content*

         - general
         - specific examples of areas of study

3. *Learning Processes and Strategies*

         - processes
         - situations
         - general strategies

4. *Policy, Structure and Organization*

         - general policy
         - intra-educational structures
         - relation with extra-educational structures
         - organization and administration

5. *Cost Factor*

         - resources
         - economic returns

6. *Precautions and Preconditions*

         - obstacles
         - preconditions for success
         - prediction of consequences

7. *General Perspective*

         - need, scope, significance
         - supporting and limiting factors
         - elucidation of specific terms and concepts

The sub-categories were worked out for the purpose of clarification only. The analysis was made in terms of categories, but the sub-categories were specified in certain cases, particularly for categories 4, 6 and 7.

The basic units of analysis selected for isolating ideas pertaining to each of these categories and to record them (the recording units), were single, largely self-contained ideas, ordinarily contained in one or two sentences. Longer units had occasionally to be extracted in order to make an idea self-contained and to see that the statement was still meaningful when read in isolation. Some recording units, of course, belonged to more than one category. A total of 424 units were identified and recorded on cards.

2.2.3 *Major steps*

The first step involved a careful reading of each individual foundation document and the selection and marking of recording units. These were then checked over, and transferred to separate file cards, one card containing one unit. A coding system for identifying units once they had been recorded was developed. This system identified particular foundations involved, using the following labels for each foundation:

Anthropological and Ecological Foundations	AEF
Economic Foundations	EF
Historical Foundations	HF
Philosophical Foundations	PhF
Psychological Foundations	PsyF
Sociological Foundations	SF

The cards were also identified according to the content category of the idea contained in the recorded unit, the serial number of each unit within its particular discipline and content category, and finally, the page number in the final draft of the foundation on which the idea had been stated.

Cards were arranged or sorted in two ways, to facilitate the content analyses. Initially they were arranged according to the different content categories, within a given foundation (e.g., PhF or AEF). Subsequently, during the interdisciplinary phase, they were arranged under a particular content category across disciplines (e.g., all goals from the various disciplines, or all statements of obstacles and preconditions, and so on).

2.2.4 *Use of the materials*

Illustrations for the intradisciplinary analysis were constructed chiefly on the basis of these cards. However, remaining material in the various foundations was not neglected. For example, it was used for reviewing the context of a particular idea, while unrecorded materials were also used to flesh out the various examples constructed. Much of the interdisciplinary synthesis was also carried out on the basis of these cards, again fleshed out through the use of non-recorded material.

2.3 Some observations about the method

The cards, the coding system and the entire procedure were found to be very helpful, and the system worked without serious problems or major flaws. The recorded units proved very useful in identifying specific points relevant to one or more aspects of lifelong education, and greatly facilitated co-ordination and synthesis of ideas for developing guidelines.

It became apparent during the content analysis that different disciplines had not contributed equally to all content categories. For example, PhF contributed heavily to goals and precautions, while AEF contributed heavily to preconditions and processes. The relationship of different disciplines within a particular content category turned out to be sometimes common, sometimes complementary, sometimes of an antecedent-consequent nature, and sometimes even conflicting. These and other observations emerged in the process of analysis and interlinking. All in all, the methodology of the present study was found to be simple and effective, and readily capable of being adopted or adapted by other workers in the area.

3. Intradisciplinary Analysis

The main purpose of the content analysis of separate disciplines was to select one or two major themes developed in each particular foundation and to develop these in terms of the content criteria already listed in Table 8.1. This procedure was intended to illustrate the kind of outcome that emerges from the application of this method to the individual foundations. It is not suggested that the summaries in any way exhaust the ideas contained in each foundation. On the contrary, the material given here is highly selective and merely scratches the surface. However, the section does demonstrate that the content criteria selected and the method described for content analysis could be used to give a highl

organized analysis of each foundation in terms of perspectives and guiding
principles of lifelong education

Because of the fact that this section is based on separate analyses of
the various foundations, it was felt desirable to capture some of the essential
"flavour" of each individual author's ideas. For this reason, extensive use is
made of direct quotations from the various chapters. This is done either by the
incorporation into the text of key words and phrases from a particular foundation, identifying them with quotation marks, or by the listing of selected
passages at the end of discussion of a particular point.

3.1 Philosophical foundations

3.1.1 *General perspectives - the transformation of life in its totality*

As explicated in the philosophical foundations, lifelong education
involves "an entire philosophical system centred upon man and his creative development". It is concerned with the sweeping necessity for mankind "to master
that great social and technological reality which he (man) has created and which
he is still creating". Thus, lifelong education embraces the whole way of life
in its totality. It would involve a transformation of both man and society. As a
result, its significance is too great for it to be left to professional educators
and politicians alone.

> These reflections show that the problems connected with the
> realization of lifelong education considerably exceed the
> range of thought of education-oriented politicians. ... It
> also exceeds the horizon of educationalists in general. (p. 77).

3.1.2 *Obstacles and preconditions - the "education-centred" society*

However, the philosophical foundations identify certain obstacles and preconditions for lifelong education that are found in some societies today, because
they are dominated by "the fetishism of material values". These are the "consumption-centred" societies, in which people achieve a sense of worth from material
possessions and conspicuous consumption. Production and consumption foster each
other in a cycle, into which people are locked by conventional education. Such
systems provide for the material well-being of people, but lead to rivalry,
aggression and alienation that act as major obstacles to genuine lifelong education.

- In some countries the economic system focuses human attention on material values, it lays the foundations of rivalry
  and aggression and encourages exaggerated consumption, it
  makes man a slave of ambition and status symbols. Such an
  economic system cannot guarantee the full realization of
  the idea of lifelong education. (p. 69).

- While raising their material living standards, it leaves
  them alone in a "spiritual desert", it does not point to
  any values which would make life worth living ... (pp. 81/82).

By contrast, lifelong education foresees a different kind of society -
the "education-centred" society, in which "the possession of things is no
longer an indication of the 'position' a person has reached". Such a society
would rest upon humanistic values. It would be concerned with "the spirit of
humanity", and would seek to establish a truly "humane" civilization. Lifelong education is the precondition for such a society.

- The need to find a way out of the labyrinth of the production
  and consumption society is one of the justifications for advocating a "learning society" ... But a society of this kind
  is an ideal which can only be realized if lifelong education
  is available to all ... the "learning society" depends on
  lifelong education, and not vice versa. (p. 83).

- The ideals of producing and consuming which have formed the
  contemporary mode of everyday life are counterbalanced by
  ideals which are ... manifested in an "education-centred
  society", based on the idea that the continuous development
  of man forms an integral part of his existence. (p. 65).

- The future development of lifelong education depends on
  whether man will be successful in his efforts to render
  civilization more humane and to base his happiness on a
  way of life which really deserves the epithet "human". (p. 89).

3.1.3 *Communication of values through art - a major content of education*

Whilst the educational content needed to achieve the goals just outlined
shares some features with existing systems, education in and through art
("aesthetic education") would assume greater importance. Art can serve two
novel purposes, according to the philosophical foundations, in addition to
sharpening "aesthetic sensibility". It can be a vehicle for experiencing and
expressing values, and it can also help people to "renew, extend and deepen"
their contacts with each other. Consequently, not only in art but also in other
areas of curriculum, lifelong education, as delineated in the philosophical

foundations, would emphasize *values* on the one hand, and *communication* on the other.

- Art initiates, moulds, and develops a feeling for social values. Whether it creates an imagined world of human situations and events or appeals to us only by sounds. colours, and form - in either case it is an important sphere for social contacts and human interrelations. Aesthetic education - or, using a more common term, education through art - is not limited to developing aesthetic sensibility for its own sake. It can make this sensibility a factor in the process of extending and enriching human interrelations, human cooperation and mutual understanding. (p. 86).

- ... great emphasis must be placed on creative artistic work. It should be intelligible to all social classes; it should express ideas and feelings in a form that corresponds to the language and experience of all social classes ... What we need are valuable, comprehensive, and at the same time directly intelligible creations in all fields of cultural life, from the sciences to the fine arts. (p. 76).

3.2 Historical foundations

3.2.1 *Transcendence to a new humanism - a perspective of lifelong education*

According to the historical foundations, lifelong education is vast and comprehensive in scope. It involves "transcendence from the confused and troubled state of contemporary man" to a new humanism. Its subject matter is thus the meaning of life itself. In perspective it transcends the geographical and historical present, seeking to find a single, human unity in "the diversity of culture" on the one hand, and in the relationship of past and present with "throbs and glimmers of the future", on the other. It also transcends material values, turning away from "the measure of GNP as an indicator of development", and substituting as a goal for education the achievement of peace and harmony, through the establishment of a new global order based on humanistic principles.

- The urgent need for a renewal and resurgence of the spirit of man calls for a revolutionary transformation of education ... Lifelong education arises from a growing crisis of contemporary civilization; lifelong education is required to fulfil the need ... for a new quality of life and for a meaningful quest of more appropriate values of the spirit. (p. 98).

- The American, the French and the Russian revolutions were
  conspicuous highlights of an historic process of the liberation of the mind of man and of the fabric of social
  organization ... all the stabilizing elements of a social
  order rooted in the past began to be questioned and the
  spirit of scepticism developed alongside the economic and
  political changes arising from the Industrial Revolution,
  the advent of democracy and the rise of that new form of
  Western dominance which is popularly labelled as modernization. Western societies were often in the vanguard of
  progress towards democratization, but the movement has
  become truly worldwide. (p. 102).

- The relevance of history to lifelong education is perennial and inexhaustible ... Only in the knowledge and
  awareness of the past and the throbs and glimmers of the
  future ... can we escape the narrow temporal prison of the
  present, and enter the experiences and aspirations of our
  fellow beings in all ages. (p. 125).

3.2.2 *A new quality of life – the goal of lifelong education*

In keeping with this vast scope of lifelong education, its general goal
is also far-reaching; that of effecting "a great renewal of the spirit of man",
and achieving a new "quality of life" derived from "the roots of the past". This
will necessitate a global civilization in which there is genuine democracy and
achievement of full human rights. More specific goals include "the foundation
of peace in the minds and hearts of men", establishment of "a non-violent social order", "democratization" of society, and "world-mindedness". These broad
goals will be possible when education succeeds in its more specific goals of
freeing humanity from "self-centredness", "intolerance", "absence of imagination",
"overriding concern with the present", "lack of balance of mind", and "obsession
with one's own preoccupations and needs".

- Each society must seek its own quality of life from the roots
  of the past, the strivings of the present and the vision of
  the future; but there are certain humanistic values which
  should be sought and shared by all. The concept of quality of
  life is in essence the vindication of the human spirit which
  was weakened by the worship of mammon and machine. (p. 106).

- The implementation of human rights calls for the means and
  modalities of lifelong education, and the principle of democratization has to be applied to education and culture as
  well as the working of the political systems and the economy. (p. 102).

- ... the necessity for a global order ensuring peace and

gradually undertaking planetary tasks and responsibilities is now beyond question. Education for peace and world-mindedness must permeate the life-span and employ all possible modalities ... Education for a non-violent social order is a viable form of lifelong education and essential to the building of the foundation of peace in the minds and hearts of men. (p. 106).

3.3 Sociological foundations

3.3.1 *The goal of lifelong education - people who make responsible choices*

In view of the ubiquity of change, the fundamental goal of lifelong education is people who can adapt. This requires an education that, even in times of rapid change, permits them to organize knowledge, to choose values, to communicate with others, and through their vocations to contribute to society and assume its various roles. These requirements make lifelong education necessary so that people can become capable of developing their individual personalities to the full - of *'making'* themselves rather than being made. In this way educability will be greatly enhanced, through people's ability to make responsible choices in a process of self-directed learning. Specifically, in the sociological perspective, the goals of lifelong education include "full self-awareness", "a sense of responsibility", "respect of other people's identity", "capacity for self-evaluation", and "ability to co-operate in groups for common ends". These "action values" will permit achievement of further progress towards the central goals of democracy, humanism and total development of the self.

- In this view the principle of lifelong education ... will be interpreted *functionally* as an adaptation to the rapid changes in technology and scientific knowledge and to the increased cultural needs due to the growth of leisure and the facilities offered by the intensification of mass communications. The problems arising from this great change ... are therefore, essentially problems of adaptation. (p. 141).

- It is, therefore, necessary to master not so much knowledge as all-round 'know-how' (approaches, methods, logics, 'languages') representing intellectual tools for the solution of certain types of problem. (p. 173).

- Since the moral and cultural values of the society are also in dispute, uncertain and in a crisis, education must enable everyone to make a critical choice of values rather than internalize 'prevailing' ones. (p. 153).

348   R. H. Dave

- Altogether these developments demand a revision of the
  fundamental concepts of education. Education of the young
  should cease trying to turn out a *finished* person and
  adopt instead the model of an adult who *develops* and has
  been *rendered capable of doing so*. (p. 162).

3.3.2 *The structure of lifelong education - reintegration and flexibility*

Learning and living, which have drifted apart, stand in need of "reintegration". The educational structures required to achieve this goal will
involve learning not only throughout life but also in all aspects of life (i.e.,
integrated learning structures). Consequently, within schools the classroom
system will be replaced by "a flexible system of options", in which the learner
can "'locate' himself according to his personal characteristics and his present
position in society". All sources of knowledge will be integrated, both with
each other and with life itself, so that "society itself becomes educative".
This will include integration of school and place of work, and of learning and
doing. According to the sociological foundations, such a structure means that
education will necessarily become highly decentralized into "units of limited
size enjoying functional autonomy". Otherwise, initiative and change will be
stifled by the inertia of large, bureaucratic structures. However, elements of
centralized 'quality control' will remain. For teachers this new structure, with
education covering all ages, no rigid grade structure, and local autonomy, means
changed roles; the teacher will become a co-learner rather than a director of
other people's learning. Furthermore, persons who possess relevant information
but never knew they were teachers ("non-professionals") will consciously contribute to other people's and their own lifelong learning, as will other "qualified
personnel (guidance experts, counsellors, animators, communication experts, etc.)".

- The very function of the teacher will change radically:
  instead of being 'responsible' for a homogeneous age
  group to whom he furnishes explanations or demonstrations, he will become an individual within a heterogeneous age group, an orientator, animator, a counsellor.
  (p. 172).

3.4 Psychological foundations

3.4.1 *"Immigrants" in our own societies - the need for lifelong education*

According to the psychological foundations, the need for lifelong education is established by the risk of "submergence, overwhelming or alienation of individuality", as a result of the pervasiveness of change in modern life. The resulting uncertainty in such aspects of life as family relationships, group memberships, or the meaning of work threatens achievement of a clear sense of identity: we are all in a sense becoming "newly arrived immigrants" in our own societies. Uncertainty in life has established the precondition requiring life-long education, while the capacity of people to learn and adapt throughout life (provided that they are "psychologically ready" to do so) has established the precondition permitting it. However, it will have to be truly lifelong in scope, not merely involving people beyond the conventional school age but also stretch-ing downwards to the earliest years, because the foundations for lifelong learning are laid in early childhood.

- Rapid change threatens to overwhelm values, morals, interpersonal relations, self-image and sense of identity. In
  a world of excessive uncertainty, the individual will have
  to struggle to maintain a stable concept of who and what
  he is, of where he fits into society, of what he means to
  other people and they to him, of what rights, privileges
  and duties he can take for granted. (p. 188).

- ... it is now clear that any decline in intellectual
  functioning (with advancing age) ... is not general, but
  is specific to certain kinds of intellectual functions ...
  there is a fall-off in performance on tasks requiring speed
  and high levels of perceptual skills, but there is no similar
  fall-off in tasks requiring experience and 'know-how'. (p. 206).

- ... two important stages of the process of intellectual development have been neglected - the period of infancy and
  early childhood, and the period of adulthood ... there is
  considerable evidence of the importance in psychological
  development of the early years ... (p. 193).

3.4.2 *Profiting from uncertainty - the process of lifelong education*

A major goal of lifelong education is that of developing "readiness for coping with change", through acquisition of "skills for coping effectively" with it. For those who are equipped in this way, change and resulting uncertainty will serve to energize learning, not to hinder it. This would require people who are able to learn continually whenever their lives offer novel experiences. In other words, it requires people who are highly "educable". Educability would be en-hanced through development of understanding of "the unity of knowledge", and

capacity to make use of "a variety of modes of presentation and sources of
information", as a result of possession of generalized learning and thinking
skills. Learners of different ages and stages would also be allowed to learn
side by side, so that special kinds of inter-learning between generations
would occur. Learning processes would also emphasize self-learning and learning
to change, for example as a result of "self-assessment", as well as non-formal
learning, for example through "contact with challenging work projects". An
important process would be inter-learning, achieved through "peer interactions
promoting the exchange of ideas and information", or through experience in "how
to exchange social and cultural experiences with others". Finally, there would
be heavy emphasis on learning "in life itself", and to think "not only in terms
of the rules of science, but also in terms of the requirements of life".

- Education should help to develop people who ... will be
  equipped to cope with the psychological tensions and
  pressures resulting from rapid change. In a world of
  personal and emotional instability ... it is important
  that education foster patterns of intra-personal growth
  that will equip people to retain their identities and
  to grow personally as society changes. (p. 188).

- Lifelong education ... involves both the idea that life
  itself is a major source of learning, and also the
  view that one can learn about life itself largely through
  the process of living. (p. 227).

3.5 Anthropological and ecological foundations

3.5.1 *Understanding global systems - a factor in lifelong education*

From the ecological point of view, an important need in lifelong education is development of wider understanding that human life is only one element
in a large, highly integrated, global eco-system. This system is no longer changing
so slowly as to be nearly static in terms of human time perspectives. Furthermore,
human beings now have the potential to destroy the ecology (the physical basis of
survival), while their social systems are also impairing the quality of emotional
life (the subjective basis of survival). What is needed, then, is understanding
of "how large centrally controlled systems function", and of recognizing "the
social and environmental costs" of such systems. Otherwise mankind will experience
"survival pathology".

- First, educators should sensitize themselves to the various rhythms of humans, human collectives and of the natural environment of which man is an integral part. (p. 257).

- ... educators should have the confidence to advocate educational options which lead to: the development of very different personality types; divergent life styles; and a range of large and small scale social institutions. In agro-ecosystems this approach would be analogous to maintaining plant and animal diversity and to enhancing the viability of stable interspecies relationships and systems. (p. 266).

- (Lifelong education must ask) ... how to value participation and involvement in organizations that control and attempt to decentralize societal technologies, i.e., the democratization of technology. Sensitizing such organizations to the needs of ordinary citizens and encouraging them to develop a feeling of accountability to even the most disadvantaged user should be a commonly accepted citizen goal. (254).

3.5.2 *Communication - processes, content and structures of lifelong education*

According to the anthropological and ecological foundations, a major process of lifelong education is that of communication. In particular, there is need for recognition of a variety of communication modes, including "extra-linguistic" communication. Currently, alternative modes of communication are neglected in favour of "traditionally emphasized language skills", so that learning is formal and abstract. There would also be great emphasis on non-formal learning that is "participatory and action-oriented", and on self-directed learning in which people "learn roles and skills they themselves ... think are appropriate". This would ultimately involve "using" information and not just "processing" it. To facilitate these processes, an educational structure is envisaged that is "heuristic or open-ended", and that is organized partly in terms of "natural rhythms and cycles". It would not involve "segregating humans by age and sex" but would permit interactions between males and females, between old and young. In content, it would involve a great deal of similar interaction, through "learning about, or participating in, alternative cultural systems" of different societies.

- (Lifelong education) ... might assist students to understand their own communication strengths better. ... certain learners and teachers ... have extra-linguistic skills of which they

are not aware. This tactic would place some onus on educators
to understand other than traditionally emphasized language
skills. (p. 273).

- This might mean developing flexible work and education
  schedules, preferably by individuals themselves with the
  assistance of education 'facilitators' rather than directors
  and controllers. (p. 258).

- Much scheduling, whichever style is adopted, should be
  heuristic or open-ended. (p. 258).

3.6 Economic foundations

3.6.1 *General perspectives - formal analysis of lifelong education*

Discussions of lifelong education are sometimes internally inconsistent.
To be really effective, analyses of the concept need to be systematically concerned with its ideology and with the institutions it would create. In particular,
an economic analysis needs to study lifelong education from the point of view of
its implications for the production and distribution of resources. However, this
cannot be done in a context-free way - attention needs to be paid to the prospects of lifelong education in particular societies at particular times. For
example, its role or even its desirability in developing countries may be quite
different from that in advanced, capitalist societies, where existing educational economic structures reflect extensive experience with an industrialized
economy. If the role of lifelong education is merely to function as a device for
bolstering up the social and economic status quo in the face of pressures for
fundamental reform, then it is a principle that is fraught with the danger of becoming an instrument for the subjugation of human beings.

- ... it seems to us that the role of social science in this
  field is to suggest instruments enabling us to analyze,
  first, the *ideology* of lifelong education, and second, the
  institutions set up in its name, *in a given society at a
  given moment of its development*. One of the main difficulties
  of such an analysis consists precisely in the discrepancy
  between lifelong education as a concept - a comprehensive,
  organizing concept - and the many concrete realizations
  claiming to have somehow been inspired by it. (p. 288).

3.6.2 *Transforming the economic structure of society*

For lifelong education to work, it would have to become "no longer an educational venture, but a societal one". It would involve horizontal integration of education and life, not simply as a result of finding educative experience in everyday life, but through "ensuring that experience consists continually of 'educational situations'". This would require "transformation of the social division of labour". It is not merely a matter of arranging ('enriching' or 'expanding') work, but a project of self-management". One possible way of making people's working life continually provide opportunities for learning would be by rotating jobs among the entire population at regular intervals.

- *... transformation of the social division of labour* (is) ... the prerequisite for true lifelong education. But then lifelong education is no longer an educational venture but a societal one, since it is not a matter of basing educational activities on experience but of ensuring that experience consists exclusively of 'educational situations'. (p. 327).

- Other projects of transforming the social division of labour have been proposed to meet the needs expressed in the demand for lifelong education, such as vertical and horizontal rotation of jobs in time, which - while preventing that a section of the labour force be condemned to an entire lifetime of hard, fragmented and dequalified labour - would enable every individual (since the whole of the population would be sufficiently qualified) to combine in his entire working life manual and intellectual work, execution and conception, etc. (p. 328).

4. Interdisciplinary Synthesis

The individual foundations have examined lifelong education largely from the point of view of particular disciplines. When these foundations are viewed together, it becomes amply clear that many valuable ideas and findings that they provide are either common, complementary or supplementary in nature. It is, therefore, possible to synthesize this material around several important aspects of lifelong education. Such a synthesis should not only clarify a number of operational guidelines and principles that emerge from these foundations, but also combine the material of the individual disciplines into a new and broader whole.

The following aspects and issues were chosen as "binding threads" for constructing a fairly extensive illustration of interdisciplinary synthesis.

4.1 Need, Scope and Significance of Lifelong Education

4.2 The Practicability of Lifelong Education

4.3 Obstacles and Preconditions

4.4 The Goals of Lifelong Education

4.5 Guidelines for the Content

4.6 Learning Processes, Materials, Media and Strategies

4.7 Structures and Organization

It may be noted that these are based on the content categories outlined in Chapter 1, and further explicated in Section 2 of the present chapter (See Table 8.1). Furthermore, they are quite closely related to the operational tasks concerning lifelong education, and thus act as a bridge between theory and practice. Some of the guidelines and perspectives stated under each of the above categories were explicitly mentioned in two or more foundations, while others were derived from fusion of two or more complementary or supplementary ideas presented in different foundations. The resulting guidelines are presented in the form of a unified and continuous discussion organized around the content categories already referred to.

Wherever possible the particular foundation or foundations from which a given point arises or in which it is most cogently discussed are identified. This is done in three main ways. The first involves citation of a foundation identified by its coded abbreviation (as on p. 341) in brackets after a particular statement has been made. The second employs direct quotation of words or phrases from a foundation, and again identifies it by giving in brackets after the quotation the abbreviation of the particular foundation involved. In the third method, passages from one or more foundations are directly quoted but, because of their length, they appear as brief passages set off separately in the text, again identified by their discipline code. In this section less use is made of direct quotation than in section 3 in order to save space.

4.1 Need, scope and significance of lifelong education

Although lifelong education is an old concept having its origin in the distant past, there is now a new need for it because of a number of perceived problems in contemporary life and the apparent inability of existing educational systems to cope with them. In this context, different foundations have emphasized a number of important factors explaining the need, scope and significance of lifelong education. These factors provide a broader perspective of this concept, as illustrated below.

4.1.1 *Change and the problem of its effects*

Unpredictability. In the past people have been shielded from the shock of contact with change, because of its slowness relative to the brevity of a human lifetime (SF). However, in contemporary society change is occurring at a speed so great that drastic alterations may occur during an individual life (AEF). This means that the social environment has become "alien" (PhF) or unpredictable to many people. They can no longer rely on social roles, values, attitudes and the usefulness of vocational skills to persist throughout life, and hence to render their interactions with the environment stable and predictable.

Internal Uncertainty. The result of this external state of unpredictability is that people are experiencing an internal state of uncertainty (HF; SF). Uncertainty is experienced in the areas of self-image and sense of personal worth (PsyF) and also in the areas of vocational skills, social relationships, values and ethics (HF; SF).

The Threat of Change and Uncertainty. The state of uncertainty just described can be frightening and disorganizing, especially when it strikes at existential questions like those of identity and self (PsyF). The danger is that individual personality will be overwhelmed and creativity and flexibility lost, as a result of a sense of being a "stranger" even in one's own society (PsyF).

4.1.2 *The changing relationship of man, social organizations and technology*

A further aspect of change involves the structures through which people relate to each other (work, family, friendship groups, and so on). These are rapidly being transformed by the effects of technology.

Technology and Work. For example, the idea of what work means for an individual person is rapidly changing with advancing technology (AEF; PsyF; SF). In many developed countries, the small hand-worked farm is disappearing, as is the small tradesman working raw materials with his hands and simple tools. This transformation has also begun in many developing countries. The workman is becoming more and more remote from the final product of labour, and work no longer serves as a source of personal identity. Indeed, in some societies economic security is ensured even if there are periods without employment.

Urbanization and the Disintegration of the Family. The growth of
technology has also resulted in the development of large urban conglomerates,
with a serious reduction in the quality of interpersonal contacts (AEF). The
family, for example, is breaking down as a primary source of both interpersonal
contacts and of ethical and cultural values (AEF; PsyF).

Dissociation of Cognitive and Affective Functioning. The effect of urbanization and technology are not, however, confined to social relationships. One
important effect has been an increased emphasis on the cognitive functions suitable for interactions with a complex technology, and a greatly decreased emphasis on the emotional processes appropriate for personal interactions with other
people (AEF). This may be forcing people to adopt two distinct modes of inter-
acting with experience, thus causing a dissociation between cognitive and affective life and inhibiting emotional development (AEF), with a consequent increased
risk of mental illness (PsyF).

Dysfunctionality, Fragility and Vulnerability. As a result of the factors
outlined above, people are coming to live more and more in environments that
are drastically different from those in which the species evolved - in artificial
or "built" environments (AEF). Such environments are increasingly fragile and
vulnerable. They depend, for example, on the smooth running of machines for their
continuance, require very complex systems of supply, consume enormous quantities
of non-renewable resources, and poison the environment with their waste products.
Thus they generate high levels of "survival pathology" (AEF).

4.1.3 *The crisis of contemporary civilization*

The Threat of Alienation. Contemporary man thus finds himself in a situation
in which his way of life is less and less capable of satisfying many of his
essential needs (AEF). Socially he is cut off from his family and friends, and
from familiar sights and places, as a result of his great mobility and his increasing tendency to live in large cities (AEF; PsyF; SF). Culturally, values and
ethics are fluid and inconstant, while he has lost contact with the wisdom of the
past which used to be transmitted through family and elders (AEF; HF). Emotionally, he has few opportunities of expressing himself or of entering into relationships deriving from an affective base. All of these deprivations lead to growing
states of alienation; alienation from other people, alienation from society and
culture and, indeed, alienation from himself, so that "man feels the social sit-

uation to be hostile and alien to him" (PhF).

The "Spiritual Desert". The explosion of knowledge in recent years, massive social and ethical change, the technological and intellectual revolution in contemporary life, huge population growth, the threat of global annihilation through destruction of the environment, and the alienation that stems from them have all combined to produce a society that tends to become a "spiritual desert" (PhF). This is the crisis that is faced by contemporary civilization.

Lack of Balance. If the crisis of contemporary life is to be remedied and social and physical annihilation avoided, and yet an advanced and efficient society is to be achieved, there is a profound need for a new and different state of balance between the three major forces in human civilization - the natural environment, the spirit of man, and the social structures including technological structures (AEF; HF). It appears that such a balance does not exist at present.

Overemphasis on Production and Consumption. Technologically advanced societies in the modern world are dominated by materialistic values, in which the possession and consumption of goods has come to be a major measure of who and what people are (PhF). In this "consumption-oriented" society, alienation has become a major problem. What is needed is a society in which spiritual values have greater emphasis, permitting a "renewal and resurgence of the spirit of man" (HF) as a result of achieving transcendence over "mammon" (HF). Such a society is the "education-centred" society, in which humanistic values would predominate to yield a truly "humane" civilization (PhF).

Increasing Inequalities. A major problem standing in the way of the education-centred society arises from the inequities that presently exist, both between societies and between different elements of the same society.

> (An) ... obstacle ... is the division of society into classes,
> stabilized by the school system. There have been many attempts
> to put an end to the function of the school system as a factor
> of social selection, but they meet with persistent opposition ...
> (PhF, p. 70).

However, remedying inequities between nations may not require repetition of the historical sequence of educational development that has been seen in developed countries. For developing societies lifelong education may be of particular relevance because they already possess rich and extensive systems of informal ed-

ucation. In the absence of all-pervasive and strongly established educational
bureaucracies, such societies may be in an excellent position to implement
certain features of lifelong education, with prospects of possible reductions
in cost.

4.1.4 *Lifelong education as a response*

Inadequacy of Existing Systems. Existing educational systems are not fully
adequate to cope with the crises of contemporary life that have been outlined (SF),
and will become progressively more inadequate. Lifelong education has been viewed
as an essential element of response to the new needs and challenges. It holds
promise of coping effectively with the needs now being felt more acutely than
ever before.

Extending Purposeful Learning Throughout Life. At present, deliberate and
conscious learning is largely confined to the school years, although there is no
evidence that these are the only or even the best years in which to learn (PsyF).
As a matter of fact, informal lifelong learning is already the norm in many societies (AEF; HF). The special feature of lifelong education is that it would
involve purposeful learning throughout life, with the conscious understanding
of the learner and with his willing consent. Where such structures already exist,
as for example in developing societies where they are especially visible, the
task of lifelong education is to *identify, understand, recognize* and *improve* them.

Reintegration of Learning and Life. Clearly, this lifelong extension of
purposeful learning could not be purely school-based, as formal education is at
present. Lifelong education would be integrated with life itself. This would mean
a reintegration of learning and work, with the place of work functioning as a
place of learning also, and vice-versa (EF; SF). In a similar manner, lifelong
education would involve reintegration of culture and education, with the lore and
wisdom of the culture acting as a source of educative experiences (HF; PsyF; SF).

Education and Human Fulfilment. A major aspect of such a transformation of
education is that it would cease to function as a means to the end of later prosperity, once education had ended and life begun. Instead of being only a tool for
preparing people to play their part in the vocational and productive life of the
society, education would become a goal in itself (PhF). It would serve, in fact,
as an instrument for human fulfilment (HF).

Education and Humanistic Values. The values of lifelong education are thus humanistic, involving concepts like renewal of the spirit of man, human happiness, peace and freedom, and equality and democracy. However, they also recognize the need for "efficiency" (PhF). What is required is a humanizing of the forces of science and technology, so that they enrich human life rather than govern or threaten it (AEF).

4.2 The practicability of lifelong education

Two basic issues arise in connection with the practicability of lifelong education: (1) the ability of people to learn throughout life, and (2) the availability of the physical means of providing lifelong education. Different foundations provide some insights in this connection.

4.2.1 *Personal growth throughout life*

Plasticity. Human beings are not fully 'pre-programmed' at birth as, say, insects come close to being (AEF). On the contrary, they are capable of adapting to the environments in which they live, because they possess "developmental plasticity" (PsyF). They are not, however, infinitely capable of adjusting since they are limited by their biological structures (AEF). The process of adjustment is lifelong, continuing into old age. Indeed, as has already been pointed out, in some developing societies lifelong learning is a normal, natural and well-known process (AEF; HF). People not only *can*, but *do* adapt throughout their life-times (PsyF). From the point of view of educators, then, the question is one of quality, motivation and conscious effort rather than that of people's ability to learn.

Intellectual Growth. Traditionally, intellect has been regarded as something that develops early in life, reaches a peak in adolescence, and then, after a plateau period of slow decline throughout early and middle adulthood, falls off sharply in later years (PsyF). However, more recent knowledge suggests that the growth of intellect throughout life is better understood in *qualitative than in quantitative* terms. Some abilities do reach an early peak, but others continue to develop. The *pattern* of special intellectual strengths and weaknesses changes with increasing age, but there is not necessarily a generalized decline. "Competence" to deal effectively with the daily problems of life, for example, may

continue to increase until very late in life (PsyF); similarly, many highly
creative people have reached their peaks of productivity at advanced ages (PsyF).

Implications for Education. Intellectual functioning changes throughout
life, with certain kinds of skill predominating in the young, others in the
older (PsyF). This pattern of growth and decline is strongly affected by schooling; for example, extended schooling slows down the decline in some kinds of
abilities (PsyF). These findings suggest that lifelong education is not only
feasible, in that intellectual capacity persists throughout life, but that educational systems need to be co-ordinated to this rhythm of development and
change in intellectual functioning (AEF). Furthermore, they suggest that continued education would be one of the best devices for fostering sustained intellectual power (PsyF).

4.2.2 *The means of lifelong education - communications and mass media*

The Need for Communication Systems. Lifelong education would require decentralization and dispersion of educative experiences, so that they were freed
from physical confinement to specific locations usually called "schools". It
would also require the means for integrating information from many different
sources, such as work, cultural activities, leisure and school. Some of this
information would be stored in the form of things like relics of the past, works
of art, and so on (HF; PhF), so that lifelong education would have to be freed
from the temporal confines of the present, and also from the confines of the
concrete here and now. Finally, lifelong education would involve great emphasis
on transfer of information from person to person. As a result, it would only be
practicable in the presence of appropriate devices and techniques for the very
extensive communication network that would be involved.

The Role of Language. In order to render information abstract and symbolic,
and thus to release it from the physical events out of which it arises, efficient
systems of symbols are needed (AEF; PsyF). Of these, language is the most dominant (AEF; PsyF): indeed the human disposition to form linguistic structures
may have a genetic base (AEF). If lifelong education is to be practicable, it is
essential that communication systems be highly efficient. Consequently, not only
linguistic, but also "extra-linguistic" modes of communication need to be employed (AEF).

The Role of the Mass Media. Lifelong education requires techniques for transmitting information in addition to the face-to-face contact of the traditional classroom. Consequently, the mass media assume great importance. They permit widespread distribution of information and obviate the need for all students to be in formal classrooms as we currently know them. They also permit communication through alternative modes, such as vision. Through the mass media information can be presented in a highly abstract form to widely diffused audiences, but can still be linked to everyday life (in the workplace or at home, for example). Mass media make it possible to utilize informal learning processes and sources of information that are not physically attainable, for example by selecting and emphasizing certain educative aspects of a society's everyday life, or by depicting the past or the future of the society. Finally, the media permit contact with sources of learning that are geographically remote, such as other societies, or temporally remote, such as the scientific or cultural past of one's own society. They are thus a major cornerstone of the practicability of lifelong education. They should, however, be used wisely. Spreading only superfluous information of transitory value would be a disservice to genuine lifelong education.

4.3 Obstacles and preconditions for lifelong education

4.3.1 *Changed conceptualization of education*

New Meaning of Education. Education is conventionally seen as something that goes on in schools under the direction of teachers, and during certain specified age periods when it is considered to be especially appropriate (PsyF). By contrast, lifelong education is conceptualized as something that occurs at all ages. Furthermore, it encompasses many kinds of structures, formal, non-formal and informal. Lifelong education also makes use of many different processes and patterns of learning other than the formal, structured, teacher-directed learning of the conventional classroom. This permits learning experiences to be highly integrated with each other and, more importantly, with the normal processes of life itself, thus expanding the concept of education to encompass life in its entirety through the development of the "education-centred" (HF; PhF; SF) or "learning" society (HF; PhF). Acceptance of this conceptualization is a fundamental precondition.

Narrow Conceptualization of Lifelong Education. However, even when it is accepted that education need not be confined to childhood and to schools, life-long education is sometimes narrowly conceptualized as being essentially an extension of the idea of retraining, vocational upgrading or adult education without taking into account humanizing qualities of individual and collective life (HF; PhF). It is important to go beyond this narrow view if the genuine meaning of the concept is to be understood (PhF).

Heterogeneity and Diffusion in Lifelong Education. In fact, conventional conceptualizations of education regard it as a standardized, homogenized and centralized process. If lifelong education is to be achieved, it is important to understand that it is a widely diffused and

> ... a heterogeneous organization not tied to age (except perhaps in youth to make allowance for the different psycho-physiological phases of growth) and liberated from space ('school') ... (SF, p. 173).

4.3.2 *Obstacles in the structure of society*

The Political Will. Lifelong education requires considerable change in society. Part of this societal change will be political in nature, with a continuing movement not only towards democratization of education (HF), but also towards the democratization of society (AEF). In some ways, the implementation of lifelong education would be a political event of similar significance to the French, American and Russian revolutions, and become one of the

> ... highlights of an historic process of the liberation of the mind of man and of the fabric of social organization. (HF, p. 102).

As a result, one can only implement lifelong education where there is the will to implement it and to accept the social and political consequences.

The Effects of Social and Cultural Factors. Some social systems cannot support lifelong education (PhF; SF). For example, when a society seeks mainly material goals, it establishes a social system based on "rivalry and aggression", making man "a slave of ambition and status symbols" (PhF). Hence, culture can be a source of lifelong education, or an obstacle to it. What is needed for the achievement of lifelong education is a change in value systems (PhF), so that hedonism ceases to be a major value and education and self-development are again recognized as normal, natural and everyday processes of life (AEF; HF).

The Effects of Technology. In recent years, the rate of growth of technology has been very rapid (AEF). However, there has not been a similarly rapid growth in the understanding of its effects on social institutions and on the natural environment (AEF). Technology may also inhibit emotional development in favour of cognitive growth (AEF). In fact, it is "a double-edged sword" (AEF) which can both benefit and plague humankind. An understanding of the effects of technology is one of the conditions supporting lifelong education, while failure to appreciate its effects constitutes an important obstacle.

Economic Factors. The most widely accepted economic/educational models in capitalist societies offer no real role for lifelong education. For example, the "human resources" model implies that education should occur early in life, that it should be formal in organization, and that it should be scarce and costly (EF). The "filter model" contains a limited role for lifelong education in the form of on-the-job learning (EF). However, both models accept the existence of inequities in educational outcomes (despite lip service to the contrary view), and aim ameliorative measures only at improving the training aspects of education. Even if lifelong education became a reality, the main beneficiaries in the present economic organization of society would be workers in the "primary market" (EF). For workers in the "secondary market" the effect of lifelong education would be mainly to increase job dissatisfaction (EF). Furthermore, there is a serious danger that some aspects of lifelong education would serve primarily to make education "profitable" to capital, or to stifle educational dissent. For example, it could serve as a device for rapidly adapting the labour force to the changing needs of industry, or for keeping surplus labour docile and under control. If "collectively" financed, it could shift the burden of the cost of upgrading and retraining off the shoulders of industry, while providing a ready-made market for the products of the education. It could also offer a way of absorbing and controlling popular education movements by incorporating them into the lifelong education apparatus (EF). Consequently, the existing "social relations of production" provide a major obstacle to the true realization of lifelong education. Indeed, lifelong education will become "a new arena for social struggle" (EF), because it will require "a classless society" (EF).

4.3.3 *The problem of inertia in large systems*

The Rigidity of Educational Personnel. A very large corps of educators already exists in the person of teachers, administrators and other educational workers. These people are well-entrenched in society and are extensively trained and practised in many of the values and customs that have already been described as obstacles. Consequently, lifelong education may be accepted in principle among educators "as a factor of radical change of society" (SF), but may be blocked in practice by the inflexibility of the group.

The Extensiveness of the Educational Apparatus. A second related problem arises out of the sheer size and complexity of existing structures for providing education. Large systems have an inertia of their own so that

> ... owing to the huge apparatus it has to penetrate, any really profound change in the educational system takes considerable time to progress from conceptualization to practical application. Changes in education proceed more slowly than technological changes. (SF, p. 171).

This reality has to be taken into account in planning and policy-making.

4.3.4 *The need to develop the inclination to learn*

For lifelong education to become a reality, it will be necessary for people to want to learn (PsyF). This raises several issues.

The Importance of Motivation.

> The principle of lifelong education is based on a fundamental premise: the adult must be *motivated* to pursue educational activities (studies) continually ... (SF, p. 163).

However, the social system can easily reduce or destroy motivation (PhF; PsyF).

The Importance of Self-Image and Attitudes. In many societies, learning has come to be regarded as something that goes on exclusively in schools and during the years of childhood (PsyF; SF). Many people define themselves as non-learners, and see learning as something separate from and unrelated to their lives - they develop negative attitudes to learning and a negative self-image in the area of learning.

> ... some workers have been unwilling to carry out the task of acquiring new learning. They have, for example, rejected retraining as beneath their dignity as adults, experienced embarrassment or a sense of uselessness, or even rejected the idea that any change is needed. (PsyF, p. 209).

The Importance of Childhood. The capacity for sustained learning requires not only positive motivation for continued learning but also self-definition as a learner. These psychological traits are modified by experiences, so that education is capable of fostering them and thus of establishing a major precondition for lifelong learning. However, their foundations are laid in early childhood (PsyF). As a result, the period now regarded as the "pre-school" years assumes profound importance in establishing the conditions in which lifelong education will be possible. This emphasizes that lifelong education should be truly lifelong, rather than just added on at the end of the conventional school years (PsyF).

4.3.5 *Education as a prerequisite for itself*

The Avalanche Effect. As has been shown in earlier sections, lifelong education would necessitate a changed conceptualization of what education is, a great deal of restructuring of society, the overcoming of inertia in existing educational systems, and finally, the development of the inclination to learn in the members of society. All of these factors, however, play a dual role. They are not only preconditions for the establishment of lifelong education, but also outcomes that will be realized if lifelong education is established. In other words, the conditions necessary for lifelong education will themselves be fostered by lifelong education: the more the principles of lifelong education are established, the fewer obstacles will stand in its way, and the more the necessary preconditions will exist. As a result, the implementation of lifelong education is likely to follow an accelerating growth curve, with each gain serving as the basis for a new and larger gain.

> So one can take the view, even if it may sound paradoxical, that one indispensable condition for the realization of a continuous and generally available education is education itself. Changes in the motivations and needs for education can be compared to an avalanche. (PhF, pp. 74/75) .

4.4 The goals of lifelong education

4.4.1 *Conventional goals*
The goals of lifelong education may be thought of as falling into four

groups. The first contains goals that are already well known and widely stated, whether in the context of lifelong education or not. These include acquiring basic social skills, literacy, numeracy, and rudiments of health and hygiene, as well as elementary practical skills (PhF; SF). Goals of this type do not require any explanation here because of their very familiarity, and because of the fact that, while important, well worth emphasizing, and not neglected in lifelong education, they have only a general significance for it.

4.4.2 *Goals that need renewed emphasis*

In the second group are goals which, while still well known and widely recognized and stated, have a particular significance for lifelong education and, in any case, need repeated and renewed emphasis. In the present foundations, these goals have mainly been stated in the form of ideals for the development of society. They include development of:

    (1) a society that has achieved "peace" and "democracy" (HF; SF)

    (2) a society that offers its citizens "freedom" (PhF) and
        "happiness" (HF)

    (3) a society which functions with "efficiency" (PhF), but
        without suppressing the "spirit of man" to the point of
        alienation (HF; PhF; PsyF; SF).

4.4.3 *Goals of central importance*

The third group contains goals which are of central importance to lifelong education. In the ultimate analysis, lifelong education seeks a "new quality of life" (PhF). The achievement of this new quality in personal and collective life would require the acquisition of a number of characteristics.

Intrapsychic Stability. Change is a major aspect of modern life (PsyF; SF). What is needed is people who have a strong and stable sense of personal identity that permits them to withstand the possible harmful effects of change. The greater the threat of external change, the greater is the need for internal stability. Stable personalities possess a mental 'healthiness' that can be likened to physical health.

Emotional Robustness. Many of the special conditions of modern life foster cognitive or intellectual growth, but provide few possibilities for the expression of emotions. As a result, there is a tendency for cognitive and affective functioning to become separated or detached from each other (AEF). Lifelong education would help to develop people emotionally robust enough to withstand this state of affairs (PsyF), and even to achieve eventual "reintegration" of the two kinds of functioning (AEF).

Inward Youthfulness. Lifelong education implies continuous growth and development, flexibility, curiosity and creative development (HF; PhF). This would require a continuing exuberance in the face of the new, the unknown and the untested instead of being "put off by the first contact with the new" (PsyF) - it requires a state of "inward youthfulness" (PhF).

Capacity for Responsible Choice. What this means is that people will have to be able to cope with competing or conflicting alternatives, and to take responsibility for making decisions by making "responsible choices" (SF). Skill in making choices about their own development will help people to "build" themselves, rather than being built by other people's structuring of their environments, as is very often the case at present (SF).

Social Commitment. Lifelong education links learning with the everyday processes of social and vocational life (PhF; SF). As a result, it requires a high level of interaction between education and the life of the society. This implies that lifelong education would require a "profound commitment to social tasks" (PhF), for its full realization.

Exceeding One's Own Achievement - A Personal Commitment. One of the major commitments that every individual should make is to keep on improving himself unceasingly by adopting his own previous attainment as a criterion for comparison and further progress. One should continuously exceed one's own accomplishments through the processes of lifelong learning (HF; PhF) in all spheres of life. Such a development is possible (PsyF), and hence one of the central goals of lifelong education is for every individual to make a personal commitment to strive for continuous progress towards a higher and better quality of life.

Acquisition and Renewal of Knowledge. In cognitive terms, the goal of lifelong education is continuous acquisition and renewal of knowledge. This goal requires development of general knowledge and of basic life skills, along with professional, technical and vocational know-how. However, lifelong education also requires the capacity continually to update, renew and expand knowledge, and linked with this, the ability to integrate all aspects of knowledge. In this way, it seeks to achieve enlightenment and wisdom, rather than mere accumulation of information.

4.4.4 *"Instrumental goals" of lifelong education*

Finally come goals which are both the processes and the outcomes of lifelong education. In order to achieve the broader goals as they have been outlined
above, it will be necessary to accomplish several of these interconnected instrumental goals. These are, therefore, goals of great importance.

Learning to Learn. Lifelong education emphasizes the importance of acquiring general thinking skills based on a grasp of the structure of knowledge
and familiarity with its languages and logics (HF; SF), rather than on acquisition of specific units of information. This process is usually referred to
as "learning to learn" (SF). The goal is to build skills in self-learning as a
result of learning to learn.

> Moreover, rather than applying themselves to learning, people
> must 'learn to learn' (to use a phrase that is getting a little
> worn but remains nevertheless valuable). (SF, p. 153).

Inter-learning. However, lifelong education does not suppose that individual people will learn only in isolation. On the contrary, a major goal of
lifelong education is enhancement of the ability to learn with and through other
people, whether it be in school or in the family, at work or in recreational
groups, clubs and societies (PsyF; SF). This is the process of "inter-learning".
This process of sharing knowledge and experience is of great importance for establishing a learning society, rather than an elitist society of learned persons
(PhF). In the area of evaluation, inter-learning implies a process of "inter-
evaluation" involving participatory, co-operative or group evaluation.

Enhancement of Educability. No doubt the skills of learning to learn and
learning to share knowledge with others are essential for lifelong education
(PhF; SF). However, two other clusters of skills that are of equal significance
and complement the former are learning to evaluate and learning to change and
improve (PsyF). These four sets of skills constitute what may be called "educability". It is important to enhance the capacity of every individual to profit
from educative experiences wherever and whenever they occur. This, therefore, is
a major instrumental goal and should be stressed right from early childhood and
initial stages of formal learning (PsyF; SF).

Self-Directed Learning. Educational initiative on the part of the individual
is an important requirement for lifelong education. Learning is not to be limited
to schooling or to direction by other individuals and agencies. It will increasingly depend on the choice and responsibility of each individual learner (HF; PhF;

SF). He should consciously identify learning needs, set learning goals and pursue them, whether through individual learning or group learning. He should have a commitment to himself for progress in life (PhF; PsyF; SF). In order to fulfil this commitment he should make full use of his educability which, in a sense, becomes the skill for self-directed learning.

4.5 Guidelines for the content of lifelong education

4.5.1 *Nature of the content of lifelong education*

Integration of Knowledge. A major concept in lifelong education is that knowledge is a continuous fabric (PsyF; SF). Hence its content should stress the unity of knowledge, in a number of ways. Within particular disciplines broad principles and general implications should be emphasized. Across disciplines, there should be a horizontal integration of arts and science (PhF), so that boundaries between disciplines will tend to disappear (HF). At the same time,

> lifelong education will not be limited to the present formal
> division of knowledge into a number of disciplines. It will
> rely more and more on the solution of real problems, the
> understanding of complex and changing situations and the
> creation of new ideas and relationships... (HF, p. 124).

Linking of Knowledge, Motivation and Affect. Integration will occur in yet another way, with the placing of emphasis on the role of present learning as the basis of future learning (PsyF). This means that the affective and motivational aspects of the content will be taken into account, with the purpose of exciting interest and arousing motivation for further learning.

4.5.2 *Scope of the content of lifelong education*

Extension Beyond Schooling. The content of lifelong education is not limited to the kinds of things involved in formal, school-based curricula. On the contrary, there is valuable educative content in family life, in community activities, and in activities at a national or even international level. Life itself is educative (PsyF). The mass media, for example, offer enormous quantities of valuable learning material which often goes untapped (PhF; SF). Contemporary problems as well as those that arise at different stages of life point to the nature and scope of the content of learning and application during the school stage and beyond.

Learning through Social and Cultural Activities. The socialization process plays an important role in lifelong education. The very process of socialization yields a large variety of information which is transmitted in many ways, most of them being informal and 'natural' rather than formal and structured, as in schooling. The materials involved in cultural learning may be in the form of writings from the past, verbally transmitted traditions and even riddles, proverbs, traditional games, folklore, and the like (AEF; HF). Much of this cultural content consists of information about how to get along in the world, so that it may be said to involve a process of enculturation. Some of the content provided by mass media and institutions of formal education results in a process of acculturation as well, especially in many developing societies.

> Learners in lifelong systems of education will need to understand the complexities of human nature and the working of human institutions in order to adapt themselves to rapid changes in the human and social environments. (HF, p. 122).

Relationship between School-Derived Content and Cultural Content. Sometimes the contents of the everyday 'cultural' education and those of the formal school-based curriculum may be identical. On other occasions the one serves to flesh out the other, so that the two play a complementary role. There may also be occasions when the two conflict. Finally, the content learned in the home or friendship group may actually provide a basis for formal learning, in such a way that learning at home acts as an antecedent factor that controls and conditions school learning (PsyF).

4.5.3 *The content of formal learning*

There will be a considerable change in the nature of the content of formal education imparted by schools and similar institutions (HF; PhF; PsyF). Consequently, it is necessary to provide guidelines on the contents of school-based learning within a lifelong education perspective.

Not Knowledge but 'Know-How'. In lifelong education a substantial change in the treatment of knowledge seems likely. The dialectic relationship between knowledge and 'know-how' should be sufficiently emphasized in the process of formal learning. In particular, instead of concentrating on bodies of facts, it will involve learning to see problems and difficulties, and to use knowledge for the solution of problems.

> Lifelong education can do much to ensure that there is strong emphasis on understanding the role of error, ambiguity, unlearning, probability and tentativeness, rather than certainty in learning. (AEF, p. 281).

"Logics" and "Languages". A second aspect of the content of school
curriculum in a lifelong education framework involves emphasis on knowledge as
a way of organizing experience and a way of analyzing, transforming and storing
it. This means that, for example

> ... history becomes more a mode of thought to guide action and
> life-experience than a well-defined and limited discipline of
> knowledge. It is in this way that it will be best used in life-
> long education. (HF, p. 124).

In a similar way, lifelong education will involve

> ... wide and versatile but in-depth education in the mastery of
> certain types of 'logic' and languages constituting a suffi-
> ciently homogeneous epistemological approach to a given *field*.
> (SF, p. 152).

Content Relevant to Personal, Social and Vocational Efficiency. Emphasis on
orientation towards the teaching of "know-how" and "logics" and "languages"
rather than bodies of facts does not mean that lifelong education will abandon
concern for content relevant to personal skills, such as looking after one's
health, social skills, such as getting along with other people, or skills relevant to vocational/professional efficiency. Several of the foundations emphasize
that education will always have a major role in these areas (e.g., EF; PhF;
SF). What is needed is a broadening of content and a re-setting of priorities.

4.5.4 *Guidelines for selected content areas*

The foundations have provided guidelines for formal, non-formal and informal learning for a number of specific content areas. The following have been
included as examples which are indicative of further work necessary in this
direction.

Communication Skills. Accurate symbolization of experience and communication of information is important in any society (AEF). In lifelong education this
is more important than ever. For example, the increasing impersonalization of
technologically-advanced societies requires that every opportunity for interpersonal communication be taken. Furthermore, mastery of language is needed for
symbolic learning, for inter-learning, and for self-directed learning (PsyF), as
well as for sharing in the culture of one's society both in the present (PhF; SF)
and in the past (HF). This suggests that linguistic skills will need to be highly developed, for example through the study of more than one language (AEF). However, it is also important that extra-linguistic skills be capitalized upon in

communications (AEF), and also that verbal and "action-oriented" skills be reintegrated (AEF).

Art and Science Education. From the perspective of lifelong education, art education is considerably more than a matter of cultivating "aesthetic appreciation". Art becomes a fundamental mode of communication with other people, as well as a means of communicating with the past of one's society through works of art (PhF). Through art, for example, it would be possible to learn about alternative cultural systems and hence to strengthen understanding of one's own. Science education, too, would be integrated with life and work, and with social education, through the humanization of science and technology (HF; PhF).

Work Education. Work education receives different emphases in developed and developing countries. In the developed countries, it is largely a matter of "re-cycling of the labour force" (SF), whilst in developing ones it is a matter of acquiring basic skills, modernizing tools and techniques, and raising productivity to increase national wealth (SF). Lifelong education places great emphasis on initial as well as recurrent work education.

> Old trades and specialities are disappearing while new specialized jobs have to be filled. This means that training must become a fundamental factor of work organization and study a recurrent activity of a large number of workers. (SF, p. 152).

In fact, conventional systems either allow no role for work education, or else stress only its vocational training aspects (EF), whereas lifelong education emphasizes the unity between work education and general education, for example through the harmonization of education at the place of work with personal and social development (SF). This should happen in both modern and traditional sectors of production.

4.6 Learning processes, materials, media and strategies

4.6.1 *Learning modes and skills*

Besides guided learning as it currently exists in conventional education, lifelong education requires certain special learning processes. They include self-learning, inter-learning, self-evaluation, co-operative evaluation and enhanced educability. These skills, coupled with corresponding attitudes, would make the lifelong learner proficient in self-directed education. These basic

learning modes and skills will not be described here, as they have already been
discussed in greater detail in Section 4.3.3 of this chapter.

4.6.2 *Learning situations and their integration*

Broad-Based Learning. The learning processes just described do not occur
only in school. Inter-learning, for example, can involve a wide range of "adult,
peer and intermediate models from whom to learn" (AEF), including the family
(AEF; SF), the community, the culture both of the past and the present (HF;
PhF), the place of work (EF; PhF; SF), places of recreation and leisure (PhF;
SF), and so on - "life itself is a major source of learning" (PsyF).

Horizontally and Vertically Integrated Learning. Learning processes will
be inter-connected and closely integrated, despite their broad base. For instance,
education may be arranged so that it can take advantage of the learning opportunities in everyday life (HF; PhF; SF), or society itself may become a series
of "educational experiences" (EF) in a process of "horizontal integration". Learning will also be "vertically integrated", for example through co-ordination of
learning experiences at different ages with the rhythms of life (AEF; SF), with
the sequences of cognitive development (PsyF), or with the changing social roles
of learners during the course of their lives (PsyF). A special example of the
integration of learning would occur through

> ... the provision of opportunities for the old and the young
> to interact in their learning experiences by learning to-
> gether. (PsyF, p. 226).

4.6.3 *Flexibility in learning*

Varieties of Learning Styles.

> ... different people learn in different ways. Some people learn
> best when information is presented in highly-structured wholes,
> some best grasp broad, general principles, some require large
> amounts of fine detail, and so on. (PsyF, p. 211).

Recognition of these differences in personal learning styles also requires, in
lifelong education, acceptance and utilization of a wide variety of techniques,
materials and modes of information presentation and intake.

Varied Patterns and Forms of Learning. In a similar manner, lifelong education would capitalize on many different arrangements for learning, from the
highly structured and formal learning that now predominates, to peer and adult

interactions (AEF) of an informal or unstructured kind, and even learning experiences such as

> Listening to the radio, watching television, visiting museums
> and monuments of art ... (PhF, p. 62).

Many informal arrangements for learning already exist, both in developed and
developing societies (AEF; HF), but they are often under-valued in conventional education systems. Informal learning processes of this kind may well be
important for lifelong education, especially if they can be improved upon and
systematically applied (AEF; HF).

4.6.4 *Learning strategies and educational technology*

New Media for Learning. The mass media offer many opportunities for new
and varied learning processes in lifelong education (AEF; PhF; SF). For instance, they make it possible for a special kind of learning to take place
through study of the past of one's own culture (HF). They also free learning
from the physical confines of the classroom and from the temporal confines of
the present, since people can learn from events they are not actually witnessing, and which are not occurring at the present moment in time. This freedom
means that education would be much more widely available to people of many ages
and in many social settings.

Educational Technology. The new educational technology can contribute sub-
stantially to the flexibility of educational processes, for example through
highly individualized and self-evaluated learning programmes, greatly increased
capacities for self-learning, and at the same time greatly increased opportunities
for inter-learning. Technology also provides multiple learning opportunities,
through a variety of modes and in a variety of places at a variety of times (SF).
This diffusion of education offers hope of reduced costs in the long run, especially important for developing countries whose national economies cannot
support formal systems, but whose cultures already contain well-established
systems of non-formal and informal learning.

> By far the most important modalities of action are provided by
> the mass media. The recent advances in educational technology,
> such as radio, film, television and computers ... will surely
> make powerful contributions to the spread of lifelong educ-
> ation in all societies. (HF, pp. 103/104).

Communication Processes. Conventional education is presently dominated by
emphasis on abstract verbal communication (AEF). As a result, not only are the

processes of the classroom remote from the "action-oriented" (AEF) behaviours of the real world, but they fail to use (or even suppress) emotional and other forms of communication. By contrast, lifelong education stresses the use of a variety of modes of communication, including extra-linguistic modes (AEF), as discussed earlier.

4.6.5 *Motivation – an indispensible prerequisite for learning throughout life*

Energizing Learning. It has already been pointed out that lifelong education requires the will to learn (see 4.5.1). An important aspect of the processes of education, then, is their capacity to arouse motivation to learn and to continue learning. This is the problem of "energizing" learning (PsyF). Of key importance are

> ... factors such as flexibility ... belief in one's own ability
> to change, confidence and hopefulness rather than fearfulness
> and avoidance of the new ... (PsyF, p. 198).

Among the factors contributing to the process of energizing learning are social pressure for learning (SF), and a personal and societal commitment to "social tasks" (PhF).

4.7 Structures and organization

4.7.1 *Structure of school-based education*

Lifelong education seems to suggest that rigid types of school as we know them will cease to exist (PsyF; SF). It will be necessary to introduce a number of major changes in the existing structure of schools.

Deformalization. One probable organizational change is that the monolithic structure of the school and classroom will be broken, with the goal of projecting "the principle of self-education for adults into school education" (SF), in the hope of laying the foundations of self-directed learning. For example, institutionalized education structured according to lifelong education would recognize the legitimacy of many different kinds of qualification for entry. Alternative structures to the conventional classroom would be developed, including more flexible systems that could be varied for different students or different purposes (AEF; PhF; SF). Qualification for progression through classes would also become less formal and less standardized, in a general process of deformalization.

Decentralization. The administrative and decision-making apparatus of
lifelong education would be largely decentralized, because

> Decentralization of the greatest possible number of decisions
> is indispensable in a system founded on responsible choice,
> on individualization and education defined as 'learning'
> rather than 'teaching'. (SF, p. 170).

goals such as democracy, equality, or global-mindedness might require a
strong regional, national or even international element, while central supervision would be needed to maintain quality of teaching, equality of facilities,
and similar factors (SF). However, lifelong education would involve decision-
making by the smallest feasible units, such as teams of local teachers, parents
and youth, as well as local unions, associations and other groups in the
community.

Classroom Management.

> There should be a great deal of thought given to the reasons
> for segregating humans by age and sex at different times in
> their lives. (AEF, p. 264).

The principles of self-learning, flexibility and individualization of learning
processes all suggest that lifelong education will not be carried on only in
classrooms involving groups of students selected by age and achievement level,
and all required to study the same curriculum (SF). A system in which students
evaluate themselves and then make responsible choices implies "a flexible system
of options" (SF) more loosely organized than the classroom as we presently know
it (AEF; SF). However, self-evaluation and subsequent responsible decision-
making would require provision of extensive counselling and guidance systems,
with the result that such systems would assume greater importance in classroom
management. Finally, the role of the teacher would change greatly, permitting
him to function as "an orientator, an animator and a counsellor" (SF).

4.7.2 *Special formal structures of learning*

Diffusion of Education. However, lifelong education would leave the confines of the classroom wherever this was possible, becoming an integral part of
all activities of the society.

> ... if education is to constitute an aspect of every phase of
> life it must necessarily enter into *all* human activities *where-*
> *ever they may take place* ... Education will no longer be con-
> fined in time and place to youth and school: it will be 'diffus-
> ed'. (SF, p. 129).

This implies that lifelong education would make use of a wide variety of non-school structures, with varying degrees of formal organization. Examples would be the open university, community learning centres, teaching by radio to students in their own homes, and similar expedients.

4.7.3 *Informal structures of learning*

Integration of Learning Sources. There are many aspects of life that offer opportunities for learning but are not part of the formal, institutionalized educational structure (PsyF). These include cultural features of society, such as museums and historical monuments, theatres, art galleries, and so on (PhF). They also include societal structures that have an educational element (of which they may or may not be explicitly aware), such as governmental agencies, public societies, special interest clubs, recreational associations and the like. Finally, work itself offers many opportunities for educative experiences, and indeed, may be one of the most important sources of learning in life (EF). The deformalized, diffused organization of lifelong education would make it possible to integrate all of these sources into a unified learning structure.

The "Educative Society". Conventional educational structures

... may have promoted a kind of learning and thinking which
runs counter to or is different from that nurtured in the
context of everyday, practical activities. (AEF, p. 270).

By contrast, the structures of lifelong education would have a close relationship with societal and vocational structures. In fact, the true implementation of lifelong education requires not merely that education be restructured, but that society itself become a source of learning experiences - the whole societal structure will become a learning structure (HF; PhF; SF). This is what is meant by the "educative" society.

5. Suggestions for Further Analysis

The content analysis contained in sections 3 and 4 provides a set of analytic, and subsequently synthetic, procedures for conceptual clarification and practical application. It is important that some such technique be employed if *optimum use* is to be made of the content of the foundations.

A more thorough and comprehensive analysis of the separate foundations by disciplines would require analysis of each discipline in terms of all of the content categories (goals, preconditions, structures, etc.), or, of course, analysis in terms of separate or additional categories (such as, say, the role of the teacher, or the place of a particular curriculum area). Such extended analyses would bring out all of the important elements of a particular foundation, or at least all of those important to *a particular user*, and would thus provide a fuller view of each foundation's contribution to understanding and applying the concept of lifelong education.

Similarly, a more detailed and more complete synthesis at the inter-disciplinary level is possible, and indeed necessary. The synthesis reported here is fairly extensive in coverage, in that it utilizes all of the content categories selected for the present study, but it is not exhaustively intensive. It would therefore be possible, and useful for some purposes, to carry out a more intensive cross-disciplinary study pertaining to one or more particular content categories such as, for example, preconditions for the implementation of lifelong education, or indeed to develop additional categories and carry out the synthesis in terms of them. In fact, it would be possible for researchers, planners, curriculum workers, teacher educators and others, to treat the various foundations presented in this report as essentially *"data"*. They could then carry out their own analyses and syntheses, both within and between disciplines, in a variety of ways designed to meet their specific needs.

6. Suggestions for the Use of the Findings

The findings of this study include: (i) the ideas presented as foundations by disciplines in chapters 2 to 7, (ii) the guidelines and perspectives high-lighted and reorganized through content analysis as in sections 3 and 4 of this chapter, and (iii) the methodological explanations described in chapters 1 and 8. It is obvious that these ideas, observations and guiding principles, which have multiple connections with the needs and interests of many professionals, can be of use to them in various ways.

For example, both intra- and interdisciplinary findings should prove helpful in the *initial* decision-making regarding the acceptance of lifelong education as a major guiding principle for reforming an education system in a country, community or an individual institution, as is being done in Indonesia, Hungary, Japan and the Canadian States of Alberta and Ontario. In some cases, such as Peru and Tanzania, a socio-political decision of far-reaching consequences may have to be taken for considering educational reform as an integral part of the larger social reform for both urban and rural development. For instance, the ideas about the learning society, the threat of alienation, and dissociation of cognitive and affective functioning are of great relevance. Furthermore, when such a decision is made, it becomes necessary to develop more specific educational policies and plans; reorganize existing educational structures or evolve new ones, and harmonize them with the social and economic structures; and utilize more effectively the non-formal and informal patterns of community learning besides the formal one. For all these important tasks, the perspectives and guidelines of lifelong education would be necessary.

The findings can also be profitably used for curriculum development. They provide many ideas pertaining to educational objectives, content, learning processes and evaluation which constitute the major components of a systematic curriculum. However, the guidelines concerning goals, content and processes are not confined to basic and higher formal education alone; they are equally applicable to the non-formal and informal systems of learning. A number of examples pin-pointing the use of the foundations content in curriculum planning for varying modes of education are available in different chapters.

Works on educational foundations have always found a favourable place in teachers colleges. This particular study, which has been focussed on a wider meaning of education, is likely to be of use to teachers, teacher educators and research scholars from the standpoints of content and methodology. It may be useful to mention that some of the initial draft material was used with profit by a few training colleges for experimental work on lifelong education.

For the levels of continuing, recurrent and adult education, this study provides some material for thought and application, particularly in connection with *change* and its effects, over-emphasis on production and consumption, intellectual functioning in adulthood, and so forth. Those responsible for workers' education - general as well as professional - will also find the ideas, especially those discussed in the philosophical, sociological and economic foundations, useful in several respects.

Since the study has covered a much broader canvas than usual because of the comprehensive character of lifelong education, its findings have applicability to those areas of activity which are not generally included under the education sector. These include radio, TV and other media of mass communication, cultural programmes and institutions for leisure activities, and other social programmes of high educational significance. For the purpose of making a variety of important decisions and for optimizing their genuine educational values, the multiple perspectives of lifelong education developed by this study would be useful.

7. Some Implications for Further Studies

The field of lifelong education is very rich in ideas for research and reflection. A large number of such challenging ideas and problems are implicit in the content presented in the preceding chapters. Limitations on space will not allow the making of a long catalogue of these problems. However, a few studies that have a direct bearing on the present inquiry are suggested below:

(i)   The present study was chiefly exploratory both in content and method. It will therfore be useful to carry out a more intensive study by developing the discipline-based foundations further, and synthesizing them along the lines indicated.

(ii) The content developed in the present study itself can be further analyzed as stated in the preceding sections. This may be done by using the content categories given in Table 8.1 or selecting other categories according to the specific purpose of a particular investigation. Again this may be done within one discipline or between two or more disciplines. For example, it would be interesting to analyze the sociological foundations to obtain guidelines for remodelling educational structures. Similarly, the anthropological, philosophical and psychological foundations could be analyzed and interlinked to formulate a set of specific guiding principles for developing a policy on communications in a particular country or community.

(iii) Although certain relevant fields, like biology or human physiology, technology, culture and others, have been indirectly covered in this study, more direct and in-depth studies in such additional fields need to be conducted. The methodology evolved in the process of the present study may be of some help in mounting similar studies in additional disciplines.

(iv)   Further explorations are also necessary in the methodological
       domain. Not much methodological work has been done so far for
       the *systematic* development of educational foundations. There
       are several critical issues involved in such a task which
       should be thrashed out. For example, the foundation studies
       and other similar inquiries, especially on a broad concept
       like lifelong education, anticipate an interdisciplinary
       approach. This, in turn, implies team research on a common
       problem. Content analysis and co-ordination of findings is
       another important issue. These procedures require a variety
       of "working tools" to facilitate team work and interdisciplin-
       arity. All these demand greater attention to the methodolog-
       ical elements involved in the construction of educational
       foundations.

(v)   Studies on the foundations of lifelong education should be
       carried out at the national or sub-national level so that
       they could be made more cohesive compared to the inter-
       national studies. In this context, the present international
       study provides a starting point for similar studies at the
       national level. Moreover, these studies should be made re-
       current if the findings are to be continually used by policy
       makers, planners, curriculum workers and others concerned. If
       these studies are repeated periodically, it becomes possible
       to take advantage of new developments in the relevant dis-
       ciplines. For this purpose, it is desirable that a national
       research institute or a similar agency undertakes the re-
       sponsibility of conducting such a fundamental study on a
       recurring basis.

(vi)   This study has generated many hypotheses and raised many
       researchable issues in the areas of goals, content, processes,
       policy making and so forth. For instance, one of the goals of
       lifelong education is to strengthen intra-psychic stability
       in order to meet the threat of external change and un-
       predictability. It is now necessary to carry out research on
       how to accomplish this goal, what knowledge already exists in
       this area, what further experimentation is needed etc. Many
       such issues call for a variety of experimental and develop-
       mental studies.

8. In Conclusion

Ever since the concept of lifelong education, in its new perspective, came
to be recognized as a major guiding principle for educational regeneration, a
need was felt to examine the concept in greater depth and thus construct its

foundations with the help of several relevant disciplines. This was considered significant, first, to grasp the multiple perspectives of lifelong education, and second, to move further towards its practical implementation in a sound manner. The present study has made a modest attempt in this direction. In doing this both intra- and interdisciplinary approaches have been tried, and some methodological issues tackled.

It is now necessary to carry out further work in this direction at the national and local levels. More research is certainly necessary. However, it is also important to take the next step of actual implementation, of course with an experimental attitude. If we wish to hasten progress towards the establishment of a comprehensive, unified, flexible and democratic system of education for attaining a higher and better quality of life, it is essential now to initiate the processes of implementation of promising ideas, and thus develop both theory and practice concurrently rather than sequentially. This is a formidable task ahead.